T0176712

KNOWLEDGE AND DISCOURSE MATTERS

KNOWLEDGE AND DISCOURSE MATTERS

Relocating Knowledge Management's
Sphere of Interest onto Language

LESLEY CRANE, PhD MA BSc Hons

Published by John Wiley & Sons, Inc., Hoboken, New Jersey
Published simultaneously in Canada

For general information on our other products and services or for technical support, please contact our Customer Care Department within the United States at (800) 762-2974, outside the United States at (317) 572-3993 or fax (317) 572-4002.

Wiley also publishes its books in a variety of electronic formats. Some content that appears in print may not be available in electronic formats. For more information about Wiley products, visit our web site at www.wiley.com.

Library of Congress Cataloging-in-Publication Data:

Crane, Lesley (Lesley Margaret), 1960–
   Knowledge and discourse matters : relocating knowledge management's sphere of interest onto language / Lesley Crane.
      pages   cm
   Includes bibliographical references and index.
   ISBN 978-1-118-93185-1 (cloth)
1. Knowledge management.   2. Discourse analysis.   I. Title.
   HD30.2.C7225 2016
   658.4′038–dc23
                                                                    2015020798

Cover image courtesy of VLADGRIN/Getty

Set in 10/12pt Times by SPi Global, Pondicherry, India

Printed in the United States of America

10 9 8 7 6 5 4 3 2 1

1   2016

For Phil, who put up with a lot. My love as ever.

And for Anne Whyte, my friend, who asked the troubling question 'so what?'

CONTENTS

    14.1 Knowledge Sharing Accomplished from a Subject Position, 219
    14.2 Context, Participants, and Expectations, 221
    14.3 Problems, Complexities, and Appeals to Common Sense, 221
           14.3.1 Invoking Positions of Authority, 223
           14.3.2 Formulating a Script for the Client, 226
           14.3.3 Influencing Effects of "the Script", 228
    14.4 "Seasoned Exhibitionists" and Bombshells, 229
           14.4.1 Shifting the Position of Authority, 230
           14.4.2 Issuing a Bombshell and Working to Save Face, 231
    14.5 Preliminary Reflections, 233
    Further Reading, 234

15   Building Identities as Expert in an Online Forum   **235**

    15.1 Introduction, 235
    15.2 Data, 235
    15.3 The Trigger: More than a Request for Advice, 236
    15.4 Constructing "In-Groups" as Markers of Expert Status, 237
    15.5 Positioning and Group Membership, 239
    15.6 In-Group Rivalry, 240
    15.7 Consensus Patterns, 242
    15.8 Claims to Privileged Knowledge, 243
           15.8.1 Listing, 244
           15.8.2 Metaphors, 244
    15.9 Preliminary Reflections, 245
    Further Reading, 246

16   On Matters of Context   **247**

    16.1 The Importance of Contextual Particulars, 247
    16.2 Data, 249
    16.3 Shared Understanding, 249
           16.3.1 Displaying Knowing What's on Others' Minds, 250
           16.3.2 Gisting and Elaboration, 252
    16.4 Stance-Taking, 255
           16.4.1 Invoking the Context of Courtroom, 255
           16.4.2 Doing "them and us", 258
    16.5 Doing Historicity, 260
    16.6 Preliminary Reflections, 263
    Postscript, 264
    Further Reading, 264

17   Finding Meaning, Implications, and Future Directions   **265**

    17.1 A Management Practice in Search of an Object, 265
    17.2 Finding Meaning, 267
           17.2.1 Constructing Live Issues and Concerns, 267
           17.2.2 Influencing Knowledge Sharing, 271

LIST OF FIGURES AND TABLES

FOREWORD

Many years ago, the company I worked for had just been bought by IBM as one of the basic elements of what was to become IBM Global Services. I had been a part of it for well over a decade, rising from a developer working on decision support systems through to general management and to a leading role in strategy. The GENUS program I put together combined Rapid Application Methods, Legacy System Management, and Object Orientation in a synthesis that had sufficient novelty to win marketing awards against Microsoft's latest release of Windows and was also credited with being a significant part of the turnaround of the company that made us attractive to IBM in the first place. Freed by the acquisition into a free-floating *do whatever interests you* role with some important top cover, I had a chance to go back to my origins in decision support and pick up the reins again with the emerging disciplines of Knowledge Management. That led to my joining Larry Prusak in the Institute of Knowledge Management, working on counterterrorism before and after the tragic events of 9/11 and eventually into complexity theory and the newly formed Centre for Applied Complexity at Bangor University in my native North Wales.

Now, I tell that story, not just to set a context for what follows, but also because it tells some of the story of knowledge management over the years, a story that continues in fits and starts, but continues nevertheless. Lesley's book, to which I am honored to write the foreword (and flattered to be referenced therein), is a significant contribution to the development of the field, but as importantly to an understanding of its journey. My goal here is not to summarize her argument but to compliment it. I do not agree with the idea that Discourse Analysis is the solution—in fact, that is not what Lesley is suggesting—but rather, as she notes, it is a valuable and neglected aspect of the field that could extend the directions of current thinking. I also think that she has made a significant contribution simply by pointing out the absence of coherent theories of language from most thinkers and practitioners in the domain. Her work and analysis would be important for that insight alone, but she also goes on to expand the theory and practice of one approach to rectify that omission.

So what do we know about knowledge in organizations? There is little dispute that it is a critical aspect of service provision, competitive advantage, strategic development, and so on. Hence, the value is rarely disputed; however, the practice of knowledge management is controversial in theory, practice, and adoption. The reality is that most knowledge management initiatives rarely survive in the long term, or at best become a subsection of Information Management within the IT function. A variation in professional services companies sees it manifested as the modern version of what used to be a library or registry. But it is no longer strategic as a function, despite being strategic as a practice. In the early days, we had Directors of Knowledge; now, they are few and far between. Not only that, companies seem to go through multiple adoption and abandonment cycles. In one industry that will remain nameless to protect the naively innocent, I have seen three knowledge management teams arise and two fall over similar time scales. The team, having established a reputation on the conference circuit, then went on to form a consultancy unit that sold recipe-type approaches based on their self-reported successes. I confidently expect the third team to follow in due course. The various institutes rose and died in their turn. But despite this, people keep coming back; the trouble is that by the time they come back, they have forgotten (the supreme irony for knowledge management) what went wrong last time. Thus, they are doomed to repeat the same follies with the same inevitable result.

Lesley correctly points to a failure of definition in the field as a reason for this, or more specifically the brutal fact that the dominant paradigm is to treat knowledge as an object, with tacit knowledge an inconvenience of little value that *walks out of the door each night* until it is codified in digital form, at which point it becomes an *asset*. That paradigm traces back to *The Knowledge Creating Company* and Nonaka's SECI model, now rebranded as BA. There are two facts about that book that people tend to neglect:

1. The book was never intended to start a movement; it was an attempt to document the process of knowledge creating in product-based manufacturing. In that context, the process of observing and understanding a skill (such as the much quoted baker) and transferring that insight into an explicit form that will allow a product to be manufactured makes a lot of sense.
2. The publication coincided with the height of the Business Process Reengineering movement and the directly related rise of Enterprise Wide Resource Planning systems and the parallel growth of Management Consultancy from a small craft skill to a manufacturing process in its own right. The assumption was that knowledge management would follow a similar vector, with a focus on consultancy-led standardization enforced by technology-based augmentation (or more frequently replacement) of human agency.

The net result was that knowledge management as a discipline started in the wrong place. The problem was made worse by the obsession with case-based approaches in management science. That meant academics, who had knowledge that might have prevented the lapse to objectivization of intangibles, were not engaged. A very, very few of us, with a background in Philosophy, realized at the start that the paradigm being adopted was deeply limited, but we were *voices crying in the wilderness*.

One early method I created in an attempt to stem the flow toward codification was a simple form of mapping together with a perspective question to force people to think about the issue from a more diverse set of lens. The process involved self-ethnography, reporting of decisions, and associated information flows by employees. The results were then clustered, like-with-like, and we consolidated the information flows. The result was rather like a spider's web in the early morning after a light rain. You could see a coherent pattern, but it was messy. We then went to each decision cluster and asked three questions of each decision:

1. What artifacts were used?
2. What skills were needed?
3. What heuristics or rules of thumb came into play?
4. What experience is critical?
5. What natural talent exists that simply makes some people better at this than others?

Known as the ASHEN model, it continues in use (often in modified form) to this day. The goal of the ASHEN question was to look at knowledge from multiple perspectives, but in such a way that people would realize that some things simply could not be codified and in consequence employee retention was more effective than codification. We also compared the process map with the decision map to show gaps between actual practice and formal process and then matched the knowledge objects (any grouping of ASHEN aspects coherent enough to be managed) against core business goals. From the dependency maps that resulted, we ended up with portfolios of pragmatic knowledge projects. A knowledge management program thus became a portfolio of knowledge projects that emerged from day-to-day practice, informed by strategic needs. That method is still in play to this day, and if anything is growing in use.

The process of engaging in ethnography around decisions also produced an accidental effect. We found that decisions were best revealed in stories, so we went hunting for those. Not the grand stories of workshops or interviews, but the day-to-day stories of practice that inform and instruct. From those, we could extract the decisions. As a group, we came to the story from the perspective of discovery, not communication, and that produced one of the genuinely novel approaches of the last two decades, namely, scalable or distributed ethnography, now manifested in the SenseMaker® product. With the benefit of hindsight, it was inevitable that narrative forms of knowledge retention, capture, and distribution would emerge. We all come from cultures in which oral history dominated for ages. In work with Boisot, we identified that knowledge acts as a transitionary device between the purely tacit knowledge of the person and the explicit knowledge of the database. Since then, that approach has extended to Development Sector evaluation, Patient Journeys, pre-radicalization monitoring, and understanding of entrepreneurial culture. That is, to name a limited number of what are now myriad applications, some of which might have been labeled knowledge programs in the past, but these days stand on their own.

While narrative is a form of language, I accepted Deacon's (The Symbolic Species) and others' refutation of Chomsky's idea of grammar being genetic. We realized that narrative carries with it essential ambiguity and constant change. That can be interpreted by Discourse Analysis but not in real time. So we moved to self-created and high-abstraction metadata to allow novel capture, interpretation, and advocacy-based solutions. That means we could allow field engineers to capture narratives on the go, rather than write reports or be forced into a community of practice. The self-signification meant that recall of fragmented knowledge across silos became easy without the formal structures of taxonomies and Communities of Practice. We started to move to peer-to-peer knowledge flow, allowing conceptual blending of diverse fragmented memories and observations to come together in the context of a need to create a real and novel solution.

Also the fragmented, loosely coupled aspect of micronarratives (as they became known) required new theories of systems and an encounter with the literature of Complex Adaptive Systems Theory. Known as the science of uncertainty, complexity deals with systems that have no linear causality, and this cannot be engineered to goals. Instead, they are dispositional and need to evolve; the management of evolution is a very different process from that envisaged by most engineers. That led to the Cynefin framework, which appears in two award winning articles: *Complex Acts of Knowing* and *A Leader's Guide to Decision Making*. Lesley references the framework later in this book and kindly shows its capacity to embrace conflicting theories in a single framework by recognizing different states or types of causality that permit and disallow different approaches to both understanding and management, not just of knowledge but also more widely.

I have recounted this as a narrative of accidental discovery, as that is what happened. But the discoveries were informed by reading, reaching, and discussing with experts from many fields. At a seminar at Mussolini's former palace on Lake Garda, now the conference center for the University of Milan, I found that process had a name, namely, exaptation. The contrast with adaptation is deliberate. A dinosaur's feathers evolve over time for warmth or sexual display. That is a linear adaptation; then, we get a nonlinear exaptation for flight. It would not have evolved on its own; it required something to develop for another purpose first. In the same way, the cerebellum adapted over time to do fine-grained manipulation of muscles to allow seeds to be picked for seed pods, but then that capability exapts to allow the sophistication of grammar in language. Art also precedes language in human evolution, allowing limited neuron clusters to handle abstract concepts rather than simply naming things. Human language is a glorious accident, a key knowledge component, but one that delights in ambiguity and meaning change.

So at its best, knowledge management has created a new form of generalists in a world of increasing specialization. That capability goes beyond the simplistic tacit to explicit codification of knowledge that dominates too much practice. But to embrace that capability, we have to develop a capacity to manage inherent, irreducible uncertainty and complexity. That requires a new simplicity and humility of the glories of human evolution, knowledge that can be articulated and communicated, but which allows and enables chance discovery, adductive not inductive reasoning, and the ability to fall into discovery by accident. Mary Midgley, one of the great British philosophers, wrote a wonderful book *Science and Poetry*, in which she says more about knowledge management and the role of aesthetics in effective knowledge creation than many a dedicated textbook. Then, as to management, well maybe we need to go back to the original meaning of the word. I quote from an article I wrote with Kurtz some years ago:

> the English verb "to manage" was originally derived from the Italian maneggiare, meaning to handle and train horses. ...the emphasis is on learning with, abiding with, adapting to, respecting, and working with another complex entity: the horse and rider as co-evolving brambles in a wider thicket of social traditions surrounding beauty and form. Around the early 18th century, this original meaning merged with the French term menage, or household, making it easier to adapt the meaning of the combined term manage to the metaphor of the obedient machine, to the corridors of power, and to the actions of controlling and directing.

Thinking of knowledge management as riding a horse is a useful metaphor. Continuing to develop transdisciplinary approaches to the field is vital. Lesley has made a significant contribution to that, and I commend the book and am privileged to have been allowed to write the foreword.

Professor DAVID SNOWDEN

Founder and Chief Scientific Officer
of Cognitive Edge

Director of the Centre for Applied Complexity
at the Bangor University

ACKNOWLEDGMENTS

The author would like to thank the editors and publishers of the *Journal of Knowledge Management Practice* and the *Journal of Knowledge Management* for permission to include in this book some of the material that has appeared in articles written by the author (or as lead author, in one instance). This is specific to:

Crane, L. (2013). A new taxonomy of knowledge management theory and the turn to knowledge as constituted in social action. *Journal of Knowledge Management Practice*, 14, (1): http://www.tlainc.com/articl332.htm (accessed June 11, 2015).

Crane, L. (2012b). Trust me, I'm an expert: identity construction and knowledge sharing. *Journal of Knowledge Management*, 16, (3): 448–460.

Crane, L. and Bontis, N. (2014). Trouble with tacit: developing a new perspective and approach. *Journal of Knowledge Management*, 18, (6): 1127–1140.

The author would also like to thank Dr David Longbottom and Richard Self, both of the University of Derby, England, for their encouragement and critical assessment of the source thesis work on which this book is based. Finally, the author thanks Professors David Snowden and Nick Bontis for their support and encouragement over the years in the making of this book.

INTRODUCTION

KNOWLEDGE IS IMPORTANT

"Speech is the best show that man puts on."
(Benjamin Whorf, Language, Mind and Reality, 1942: 171)

It may seem a little odd to start a book about knowledge management with a statement about speech made by the American linguist Benjamin Whorf more than seven decades ago. It will, in the course of the following chapters, come to be seen as a very appropriate starting point for any discussion on this subject.

This book is located within the academic discipline and professional practice of knowledge management (KM). "Knowledge" is a term that can refer to several different, often related concepts. From the KM and organizational perspective, knowledge is generally thought of as an important and valuable commodity, essential to economic success and innovation. It would be hard to argue with this. Similarly, it would seem unreasonable to argue with the idea that knowledge, certainly from the point of view of the organization and most likely from many other points of view, is an accomplishment of people's interactions with one another. Meetings, for instance, and research activities, presentations at conferences, training sessions, performance appraisal reviews, job interviews, reports, proposals, and just about anything else that you can think of all share a common goal: to do something with knowledge.

KM is concerned with understanding what knowledge is, how to manage it, and how to develop strategies that will successfully leverage the knowledge that resides within any given organization. All sorts of ideas and theories have been developed and tried over the years. And most of these do, it has to be said, emphasize the important role of

Knowledge and Discourse Matters: Relocating Knowledge Management's Sphere of Interest onto Language,
First Edition. Lesley Crane.

communications and social interaction in the accomplishment of "knowledge work." However, relatively few go as far as conceptualizing social interaction as the site of interest in its own right. That is precisely what this book does. In locating organizational knowledge work in social interaction, putting what is referred to as "discourse"—talk and text—front and center as the phenomenon of interest and the object of research, the ultimate aim of this book is not to tell the reader about knowledge work, but to show *how* knowledge works in real life.

It was stated at the start that the concept of "knowledge" can raise different connotations for different people. Philosophers, for example, have been interested in and debating knowledge for thousands of years. Interestingly, the definition of knowledge as "true, justified belief" that comes down to us from the Greek philosopher and mathematician Plato (427–347 B.C.) can be found in one of KM's most influential theories. As it turns out, the nature of knowledge is one of the longest and most pervasive debates within the academic field of KM. Largely centered on the question of whether knowledge is a commodity or an object or whether it is a far more complex phenomenon, these debates are not only to be expected in a field that is concerned with its management, but they also underwrite most if not all of the other issues that KM engages with.

KM'S CHALLENGES

The field of KM is immense, contested, complicated, and endlessly evolving. There can be few subjects of practice and academic inquiry that attract such a breadth and scope of theory and points of debate. Moreover, KM theory more often than not draws on other domains such as the science of complexity, social psychology, cognitive psychology, organizational theory, and philosophy, as we noted earlier. It is by any stretch of the imagination something of a mongrel with schizophrenic tendencies in the perception of the equally immense gulf separating KM as a professional practice and KM as a topic for academic research.

Organizations today face challenges from at least three directions. First, they need to adapt to an increasing pace of change and technological development. They operate in demanding, highly competitive, and complex environments and are themselves viewed as complex systems: a recent study of chief executive officers, for instance, identifies as the greatest challenge the gap between organizational readiness and the growth in complexity of the business environment. Second, there are growing concerns over the now ongoing retirement of the "baby boomer" generation, representing a mass exodus from the workplace with all of the knowledge that this generation possesses. Third, they face an explosion in information. As reported in Forbes in 2012, "(S)scientists have worked out exactly how much data is sent to a typical person in the course of a year—the equivalent of every person in the world reading 174 newspapers every single day."[1] Worse, not all of this information can be trusted: IBM predicts that around 80% of corporate data will be "untrustworthy" by 2015. It is not difficult, then, to imagine how important the management of knowledge has become in the organizational world. But these are not the only challenges—KM has challenges that are very specific to its field.

KM's distinctive challenges come from many directions. In addition to those associated with the nature of knowledge, there are definitional difficulties surrounding the

[1] Derbyshire, 2011; as cited in Quast, 2012: http://www.forbes.com Why Knowledge Management is important to the success of your company [Online]. Accessed October 21, 2012.

constitution of KM itself. This is seen by some as a major issue with KM described as an ill-defined field that nonetheless makes substantial claims. This is perhaps indicative of its diverse origins and tendency to dip into other disciplines for ideas and perhaps even substance. (As a small aside, the latter comment is not meant as a criticism because, as subsequent chapters will show, I do exactly the same myself!) Some go so far as to question how such a "poorly executed" field, with alleged low rates of reported success, can survive in the modern corporate world.

In fact, the challenges and debates on KM's alleged high failure rates remain very topical indeed despite what is described as KM's thriving literature of practice, research, and theory. This latter, theory, is itself held up as an issue. For instance, there are too many theories in KM according to one perspective, while another sees the absence of a unifying theory on the near horizon as one of the greatest challenges for KM, its theorists, scholars, and practitioners. In terms of challenges, this is the merest tip of the iceberg. As a small preview of what is to come, other challenges center around the role of technology in KM, the effects of cultural differences, the question over ethics, as well as those around how to foster effective knowledge creating and sharing. These are just some of the topics covered in the following chapters. Nonetheless, it is these characteristics that make the field of KM a fascinating topic of study that never fails to surprise.

ONE THEORY DOMINATES

The spotlight on KM theory reveals, at first sight, a somewhat chaotic landscape. To bring some order, a substantial sampling of KM theory is organized on two bisecting continua: those with a focus on the organization versus those concerned with personal knowledge and those that reify knowledge as an object versus those that perceive knowledge as or embedded within social action. This "taxonomy" of KM theory is introduced later in the book, and it is hoped this will be seen as a useful roadmap to what is otherwise a complicated and tangled enterprise.

Undoubtedly, the theory that has had the greatest impact and influence is Professor Ikujiro Nonaka's theory of the knowledge-creating firm and its various evolutions since its first publication in the early 1990s. This conceptualizes knowledge as consisting of two types—tacit and explicit—and describes the organizational transactions by which one can be converted to the other as the prerequisite to the generation of new knowledge. The promotion of the benefits of converting knowledge from one type to the other raises a minefield of debate and challenge all on its own. Yet despite coming in for considerable criticism, as will be shown in subsequent chapters, this framework remains the most influential, contentious, and most unproblematically adopted.

The "competition" to this influential theory comes in the shape of those theories that are classified as approaching knowledge as or embedded in social action, and which include the "knowing how–knowing that" formulation promoted by, among others, Paul Duguid. This particular perspective approaches knowledge as comprising two principle elements which are fundamentally prerequisite one to the other: "knowing how" (equivalent to tacit knowledge) makes "knowing that" (equated to explicit knowledge) actionable. This proves to have particular significance and salience for the ideas investigated and developed in this book.

In spite of all these debates, there is one aspect of KM about which most if not all practitioners, theorists, and researchers agree on, and that is that knowledge is a prime—if not *the* prime—resource of the modern organization.

A VIEW OF KNOWLEDGE

Clearly, any view of the nature of knowledge has profound consequence for KM theory and its practice, research methods, and so on. Nonaka is credited as being the first to introduce the dualist concept of tacit–explicit knowledge to KM in the 1990s, and the trace of this can be seen in the majority of its theories. Beyond the field of KM, however, the tacit–explicit formulation of knowledge appears much earlier. In social psychology, for example, the role of tacit knowledge in intellectual competence makes an appearance in the mid-1980s. The tacit–explicit distinction is reputed to have been initially introduced to the management literature in the early 1980s. Tacit knowledge, as the product of implicit learning, appears even earlier in the cognitive psychology field, starting in the mid-1960s.

Nonaka specifically draws these terms from the work of the philosopher and scientist Michael Polanyi who was working from the 1950s onward. This would turn out to be one of the most significant moves in the developing field of KM because, for whatever reason, the result was that almost every writer (the present one not excepted) and theorist and probably many practitioners too started to not only refer to Nonaka's work but also to that of Polanyi. The interpretation of Polanyi's work, in particular, has become something of a subtopic in KM, as evidenced in a growing literature devoted solely to this purpose. For these reasons, the reader will notice that when referring to Polanyi's work here, his own words are frequently quoted.

A competing view of knowledge to that promoted by Nonaka is also very much in evidence in the field as noted earlier, although because it is highly fragmented in terms of its source and variation on its theme, it does not appear to be a coherent perspective on first inspection. This view approaches knowledge as a phenomenon (practice, accomplishment, action, behavior, and so on) either as embedded in or as constituting social interaction. This view particularly emphasizes the importance of language and communications in doing knowledge work. This is the view of knowledge that is developed throughout this book, aligning with a constructionist theory of knowledge as action constructed and accomplished in discourse—hence the relevance of Whorf's statement at the outset of these discussions.

What this brief survey indicates is that knowledge is important to organizational well-being, development, and success. It logically follows, then, that harnessing this phenomenon by controlling, leveraging, and applying it will enhance an organization's opportunities to achieve its objectives. But while one can argue that the management of organizational knowledge is more than a passing fad, there is a question over the extent to which knowledge can be harnessed to any degree of predictable effect when the phenomenon is neither well understood nor comprehensively specified.

THE CASE FOR AN APPROACH THAT FOCUSES ON DISCOURSE

As we touched on earlier, many KM theorists, researchers, and practitioners agree that knowledge work is largely accomplished in social interaction, but few if any have located theory, research, or practice in discourse itself. The work reported here concludes that discursive psychology can provide both the theoretical framework and research methodology for an approach to organizational knowledge work. This effectively extends the directions that many in the KM field are already indicating and have been since the early 1990s.

From the perspective of discursive psychology, knowledge is not an object to be captured, codified, stored, and passed around. Rather, knowledge is an accomplishment of social interaction with others: knowledge is constructed and shared in talk and text in interaction. A research focus drawing on this particular paradigm directs the inquiry to *how* knowledge work is done in talk interaction and with *what* consequences. To make such a proposition relevant and of pragmatic use to the field of KM and its practice, the present research reaches into the academic field of implicit learning (cognitive psychology) for an explanation of tacit knowledge, reasoning that tacit knowing ("knowing how") in action is precisely what this type of research analysis reveals. An important distinction to draw concerns the dualist version of knowledge mentioned earlier and the view of knowledge expressed here. In referring to "tacit knowing" and "knowing how," and all other versions thereof, it should not be inferred that we are erecting a line of demarcation between these and explicit knowledge. Knowledge is approached here as a holistic concept comprising both tacit (know how) and explicit (know that) fragments, with the sum of both constituting knowledge.

The research and analysis reported here focus on organizational knowledge sharing actions in the context of everyday interactions. Knowledge sharing is arguably one of the most fundamental, complex, and problematic topics on KM's agenda. Drawing on KM research and theory, four thematic categories of knowledge sharing are identified, which form the target of our analysis: identity, trust, risk, and context. What the findings show is that not only are these four themes present in the data, as linguistically constructed by speakers and (discussion forum) contributors, they are also corelational and influencing on the scope and directions of knowledge sharing actions. A key conclusion is that trust, risk, and identity are themselves contextual phenomena invoked in knowledge sharing actions. This is shown to be corroborated when the analytic focus investigates what contexts per se speakers invoke in their knowledge sharing discourse, finding these three principal contextual phenomena are shown to be present. In short, a principal argument made is that the present investigations and their findings provide empirical support for those who support the "knowing how–knowing that" formulation in the practice of KM, in particular the influential properties of knowing how on the actions of sharing knowledge.

CONTENT STRUCTURE

The book is divided into two parts: Part One reports a comprehensive and critical review of the field of KM and two other fields that are shown to be relevant: discourse analysis, with the emphasis on discursive psychology, and implicit learning drawing on the field of cognitive psychology. Part Two presents the analysis and findings from the primary research drawing on discursive psychology.

Part One

The first chapter investigates the nature of knowledge as described and debated in the KM and other relevant literatures, which sets the groundwork for what follows. Chapter 2 turns the attention onto KM itself and its origins and multiple perspectives with the implication of limitless boundaries. In particular, we consider the influence of technology as a key "push factor" in the interest, development, and take-up of KM. Other relevant questions such as whether knowledge should be managed at all from an ethical perspective are also addressed. Chapter 3 investigates other leading and current themes and debates in the KM literature such as determining KM's success or failure and the problem of measurement, arguing that these are largely rooted in the troubles over the definition of knowledge. Special attention is given to the topic of knowledge sharing, finding a number of factors proposed in the KM literature to be significant and influential in these types of organizational activities. In the following chapter, the taxonomy of KM theory reveals a sharply divided field, but one that is dominated by one single paradigm.

Proceeding from there, Chapter 5 introduces an alternative way of approaching knowledge from the perspective of social constructionism. Developing on these themes and ideas, Chapter 6 explores discourse analysis as a research methodology, with a very particular perspective on the traditional scientific method. The focus is on discursive psychology and how this and other discourse analysis paradigms have made significant contributions to our understanding in a number of topics. Three of these—identity, gender, and computer-mediated communications—are singled out for detailed reviews of research and their findings.

Chapters 7 and 8 move the investigations into the field of cognitive psychology and implicit learning theory in pursuit of a more robust understanding of tacit knowledge. A comparison between perspectives finds considerable correspondence between those of KM and those drawn from implicit learning. What we gain is a clearer notion of the "tacit" and empirical evidence for tacit knowing as an influencing factor in human action. This is followed by a more detailed consideration of what have been identified as the four thematic categories of knowledge sharing. A brief summary and set of conclusions round off Part One.

Part Two

The first major chapter in Part Two is a detailed and thorough discussion of research methodology, giving particular attention to the methodology adopted in the present research. The subsequent five chapters each report in detail the analysis and findings of original research topicalized on each of the four knowledge sharing thematic categories ("identity" is split across two chapters). The final chapter brings all of these findings together in a detailed discussion framed around the research questions, subsequently linking these findings to the debates and issues in KM raised in the earlier parts of the book.

Does this change anything? What is to be hoped is that the discussion, arguments, and evidence in the following chapters lead to a firmly grasped recognition of the advantages and insights to be gained in understanding the organization as a "knowledge system" in which the real action takes place at a far deeper and more fundamental level—discourse. From the outset, it is made clear that what we are about is simply extending directions in which many in the KM field are already indicating—and that is a view worth seeing.

PART ONE

1

THE NATURE OF KNOWLEDGE

1.1 KNOWLEDGE: THE MOST PRECIOUS ASSET AND THE GREATEST CHALLENGE

> Knowledge represents the "…highest value, the most human contribution, the greatest relevance to decisions and actions, and the greatest dependence on a specific situation or context." (Grover and Davenport, 2001: 6)

At the turn of the millennium, Varun Grover and Thomas Davenport reflected the opinions of many involved or interested in the organizational practice of knowledge management (KM) when they cast knowledge in the role of the organization's top prize. It is also one of the most challenging and complex topics on the organizational agenda.

The value of knowledge to the organization is in fact one of the few areas of consensus in a field otherwise defined by its many debates, controversies, and disagreements. With the modern organization operating in an increasingly complex world marked by change and uncertainty, that value can only intensify. Consequently, knowledge has come to be seen as a firm's most precious asset, the key to new product and service development, essential to understanding customers and market trends, and the principle ingredient to innovation, to name just some of its stellar attributes. It is also the asset that most easily walks out of the door.

Yet, as it turns out, the nature of knowledge is one of the greatest challenges facing organizations and the field of KM, according to the economist and business consultant Robert M. Grant and many others. This one word stirs up more of a storm of controversy than any other issue. As Grant points out, the search for a *definition* of knowledge is far

Knowledge and Discourse Matters: Relocating Knowledge Management's Sphere of Interest onto Language,
First Edition. Lesley Crane.
© 2016 John Wiley & Sons, Inc. Published 2016 by John Wiley & Sons, Inc.

from resolved, although some in the academic domain of philosophy might well dispute that.

This chapter has two main objectives. Firstly, it attempts to convince on the salience and importance of engaging with the question over the nature of knowledge. Secondly, it offers an overview of the shape of the debate in KM: what does it look like, and how does the perception of the knowledge phenomenon impact on its practice? The shape of the debate is itself something of a challenge: it does not conform to a dialogic debate in which one opinion can be seen as building on another, but rather is pulled this way and that, splintering off in this or that tangent. The question of the nature of knowledge is so broad that it is very easy to succumb to the superlative or to lose sight of the objective in a tangle of deep thought inspired by philosophical accounts. To be clear, we are interested in a conceptualization of knowledge from the perspective of the organization, and the practice of KM, and not that (or those) conceptualization(s) discussed within philosophy.

So, beginning with an overview of why this question is important, the discussions open up a critical review of the various ways in which knowledge is described with particular interest in what is arguably the most widespread and popular, yet most contested, of these: the tacit–explicit duality. This is contrasted with alternative ways of understanding knowledge, which are shown, in subsequent chapters, to be consistent at least in part with a perspective with considerable empirical support. This leads to a view of knowledge that is developed throughout this book as the central tenet of a way of thinking about knowledge and its management that extends some directions that many in the field have been indicating for the last two decades or more.

1.2   WHY AN UNDERSTANDING OF THE NATURE OF KNOWLEDGE IS CRUCIAL

Given the eons of debate around the nature of knowledge, it is hardly surprising that a consensus eludes the field of KM. For instance, Peter Heisig, a researcher at the University of Cambridge's Engineering Design Centre, trawled through 160 different KM theories, concluding that a "uniform understanding" of knowledge is simply not available. Instead, there is a melting pot of confusion, ambiguity, and contradiction over its nature, constitution, and even its location (see the end of the chapter for a list of suggested further reading).

Of course, the irony in all of this is that while on the one hand knowledge and its management is understood as a vital part of organizational strategy, as the metaphorical key to organizational success and growth, there is on the other the absence of anything resembling a "uniformly" accepted definition. Now allowing for the fact that large disparate groups rarely agree on definitional matters (political parties, for instance, and the question of what constitutes economic success), this state of affairs inevitably casts a shadow of doubt over both theory and practice. Quite simply, if a product cannot be specified, how can it be the subject of theory? If it cannot be grasped, how can it be managed, measured, or otherwise leveraged? How can the manager claim success in managing knowledge, if there is disagreement over what it is? Ask any group of people within an organization to describe what they mean by knowledge, and it is virtually guaranteed to result in as many variations. Michael Polanyi, undoubtedly one of the most influential voices in the field—albeit indirectly—proposed that definition rises from "formalization" of meaning. From this perspective, a definition of knowledge would represent a generally accepted and unambiguous meaning shared by the majority. And in this case, "majority" refers to those within the KM field.

The bottom line is this: if it is the role of KM to improve the handling of knowledge, then it is important to arrive at an understanding of what knowledge is—that is, an understanding that is relevant to the organization and its activities, goals, and so forth, which can be subscribed to by the majority.

Developing this line of thought, Polanyi proposes that a word's meaning takes shape in its repeated usage. More specifically, Professor and psychologist Kenneth Gergen suggests that the definition of knowledge is no more or less than as expressed in the language conventions favored by certain groups at certain times—that is, "meaning" as truth exists in shared consensus. Or, put another way, it is whatever is fashionable with a majority at any given time.

These viewpoints can be interpreted as diffusing any sense of urgency for definition and even as establishing a rationale for seeing a definition of knowledge as whatever is fashionable. But this raises a question: fashionable for whom, and shared and used by which groups? Is one group's viewpoint more important than another's? Or more right? Also, while the "fashionable perspective" offers the prospect of an escape route from a troublesome debate, it does not help in addressing other questions: Is knowledge objective, subjective, or both? Can knowledge only ever be personal, rooted to the individual's experiences, beliefs, attitudes, and so forth, or can it exist as a communally shared phenomenon? Can knowledge ever be seen as a true representation of the world, or is it entirely socially constructed, influenced, and molded by human action? Is it an object or a commodity—is it a practice, or can it be either? And so on, and so forth. This is the proverbial tin of worms—and this is what KM sets out to manage.

These are complex questions, with profound consequences for the practice of KM. If knowledge is seen as one particular color, with energies and strategies geared around that, then there is a risk of ignoring knowledge of another color. Haridimos Tsoukas of the Athens Laboratory of Business Administration and Efi Vladimirou of Planet Ernst and Young, in their essay on the relationship between organizational and personal knowledge, take an even more pragmatic approach: criticizing those who claim there to be no need for a "concrete definition of knowledge," they reason that where there is theoretical confusion, it should not be a case of simply abandoning theory, but rather it should promote the search for clarity and cohesion.

Arguably, it is this lack of a definition of knowledge that underpins many of the issues and debates, which characterize the field. For example, researchers and authors France Bouthillier and Kathleen Shearer, writing in 2002, point to 18 different definitions of KM practice in their investigations of methodologies adopted by various organizations in published case studies. Almost a decade later, Patrick Lambe, principal consultant at Straits Knowledge in Singapore, also draws attention to this issue, remarking that throughout most of the 1990s, the same names were being applied to quite different concepts by different people in the KM field. The question over what constitutes the practice of KM is taken up in more depth in the following chapter.

The point should be adequately made by now. This is murky territory. So murky, in fact, that many scholars, researchers, and practitioners simply avoid any reference to the nature of what they focus on. For instance, a study of KM practice's impact on firms' innovation capabilities investigates the human barriers associated with knowledge generation, codifying, sharing, and application, but does not define the subject of the research. Another research study investigates how processes such as knowledge creation and between-firm knowledge sharing impact on innovation in firms in three different countries but also neglects to define what is meant by "knowledge." Even Thomas Davenport, one of the most respected scholars and authors in the field, and who was named one of the top 25 consultants in the world in 2003,[1] is not immune. In his illustration of how technologies can be successfully deployed in firms for the management of knowledge, he seems to step aside from any definition of the subject of his investigations, although offering detailed and thorough discussions around, for instance, types of knowledge companies and attributes of the knowledge manager. He is, however, a prolific and widely respected author and authority and is likely to have tackled this issue elsewhere. Nonetheless, it is perhaps revealing that, in the context of a book aimed at business managers, this particular text avoids the question. Is it simply that no one is interested?

Here is another reason why the nature of knowledge *should* be of interest to the organization's leaders and practitioners: if there is a mountain of viewpoints on what constitutes knowledge, then, as noted earlier, this unavoidably has an impact on the definition of KM itself. And that has consequences for *what* is practiced.

Lambe's reference to the "1990s" suggests phases of development. David Snowden, founder of Cognitive Edge based in England, offers a concise and useful developmental context against which to pin the knowledge definition debates. He proposes three ages or "generations" of development. The first, before 1995, is very much dominated by technology and process reengineering, with its focus on managing the flow of knowledge to decision-makers. This was the age of "human replacement"—if a machine could do the job of the worker, then the worker had to go. The second generation, beginning in the mid-1990s, is ignited by the publication of Ikujiro Nonaka and Hirotaka Takeuchi's groundbreaking and influential book, *The Knowledge-Creating Company*, and its introduction of what would become the most famous—for some, infamous—perspective on knowledge: the tacit–explicit duality. The start of the new millennium ushers in a third generation, mobilized by Snowden himself with his formulation of knowledge as paradoxically both a "thing" and a "flow." As the following discussions illustrate, both notions of knowledge are very much part of the polarized dialogue.

So, if theoretical confusion over the nature of knowledge is the case, the solution is not to avoid the issue—however tempting that might seem—but rather to evolve more and better theory, as argued by Tsoukas and his coworker. So how is "knowledge" defined by those brave enough to take a stand?

1.3 WAYS OF DEFINING KNOWLEDGE AND THE RISE OF A SINGLE PERSPECTIVE

It has been suggested here that the labels applied to knowledge—the *ways* in which it is defined—have a significant impact on its management, both from the perspective of a practice and a subject of research. What we find is that groups of opinions are ranged like troops on a battle field: no matter which opinion looks strong and well equipped, there is

---

[1] Consulting Magazine.

always an opposing force. Such matters are important because the stakes are high. Writing about knowledge and competitive advantage in 2007, scholars Laurence Prusak and Leigh Weiss point to a report that estimates that an organization employing 1000 knowledge workers could waste as much as US$6 million a year on time spent searching for nonexistent knowledge or duplicating knowledge that already exists. One could, however, question what it was that "employees" are looking for or duplicating—knowledge or information? A more recent study by Dublin Institute of Technology researchers Mohamed Ragab and Amr Arisha equates the loss of one experienced manager from a Fortune 500 company to around US$1 million worth of lost knowledge. An organization's knowledge needs to be managed, but manage what? There are three underlying connected themes at issue: knowledge as an object versus knowledge connected to social action, knowledge as objective or subjective, and personal versus organizational knowledge.

1.3.1 Knowledge: "Thing" or "Action"?

The lines can generally be drawn up into those who—explicitly or otherwise—reify knowledge as an object, and those who view it as social action. On the latter, "social action" refers to the notion of knowledge as action accomplished in interaction with others. This latter understanding requires a little explanation. Taken to its extreme, the idea of knowledge as action accomplished socially might suggest that it is only in social interaction with other people that knowledge comes into existence. But this interpretation causes problems for the idea of individual capability to experience a "light-bulb" moment in solitude, for instance. Alternatively, it could be interpreted as "knowledge as a psychological phenomenon experienced in social interaction with others, or through the individual's interaction with their environment." Where knowledge is approached as constituting social interaction or as its product, this does not necessarily imply that knowledge is always spontaneous to that interaction. In other words, the germ of knowledge new to the recipient may be seeded in social interaction with others, but may not emerge as such until some later point, perhaps triggered by some unconnected event in the environment. It is to this latter understanding that we refer throughout this book.

Those who offer a reified account of knowledge, although they may well resist such a classification, include Professor Ikujiro Nonaka of the Graduate School of International Corporate Strategy, Hitotsubashi University; Dorothy Leonard of the Harvard Business School; Varun Grover, distinguished professor at Clemson University; and Thomas Davenport. On the other side, advocates of knowledge connected to social action include professor of anthropology and director of the Institute for European Studies at Cornell University Davydd Greenwood, Professor Morten Levin of the Norwegian University of Science and Technology, and Professor Frank Blackler of the University of Lancaster. A prestigious line up by anyone's standards, but can they all be right? Recall David Snowden's paradoxical perspective of knowledge as both an object and a flow. According to this, they can. This is a debate in which no perspective can be said to be "right" or "wrong" for that matter.

The substance of debate is this: there is a world of difference between a strategy geared toward managing and leveraging knowledge as an object, lying out there to be found, a commodity to be codified, counted, stored, and even sold, and the view of knowledge as a socially constructed and distributed phenomenon. The two respective sides are fairly entrenched with, for instance, Greenwood and Levin describing the commodity view as "petty." All of this, of course, suggests an either/or case, which according to Snowden is old thinking. But this is an incredibly complex issue. It is so complex that it is a theme to which these discussions return to throughout most chapters of this book. It is, for instance, fundamental to theories in KM, to which an entire chapter is devoted. In among all of this complexity, it is nonetheless clear that whichever agenda is adopted, it will have major ramifications on any business strategy designed to manage knowledge and on precisely what is managed.

But what of the traditional hierarchical model: data—information—knowledge? Max Boisot of the School of Administration in Barcelona suggests that data is out there in the world, knowledge is in people's heads, and information is the element that mediates between them. Can this not offer a concise understanding of the nature of knowledge, as defined in relation to data and information? Unfortunately not, but a clearer understanding of this particular model can be gained following a discussion of the issues and competing formulations of knowledge.

So far, a landscape has been imagined in which the ranks of "knowledge as object" are pitched on one side, with those of "knowledge as social action" on the other. To put these polarized viewpoints into perspective, two further questions are briefly considered: the subjective versus objective view of knowledge and the debates around organizational versus personal knowledge.

1.3.2 The Subjective versus Objective

The subjective/objective debate, which can be equated to the debate over knowledge as a "thing" versus knowledge as "action," has a lengthy tradition in the philosophical and scientific domains, with a recent trend seeing a shift away from a strict distinction between the two. A simple way of looking at this is to see the subjective as personal, open to bias and opinion, evaluation, attitude, and belief. By contrast, the objective relates to undisputable facts, divorced from bias, experience, or influence.

As background to the subjective versus objective question, consider two cases of "objective accounting" drawn from psychology: witness accounts and scientific reporting. Witness testimony is idealized as "objective," an unbiased account of what happened, and in fact, many witnesses will go to extreme lengths to frame their accounts as such. Social psychologists Abigail Locke and Derek Edwards, for example, studied President Clinton's testimony before the US Grand Jury concerning his relationship with Monica Lewinsky. According to their fascinating analysis, Clinton portrays himself as determined to focus solely on the facts of the matter—the objective, knowable account of events— and thus is able to sidestep awkward questions by appealing to his faulty memory.

Witness accounts are not just confined to courts of law: in everyday conversation, for instance, we routinely frame our reports, accounts, and descriptions of events as valid and authentic as firsthand experience. In his study of "witness accounts" by callers to a radio station, Ian Hutchby of Brunel University finds that narrators of firsthand eyewitness accounts show themselves as in possession both of the rights to recount the experience and also how it emotionally affected them, whereas the person listening to the story usually does not. If the recipient were to retell the account and couch it in their own emotional response, this would seem odd. Moreover, as Elizabeth Loftus, professor of psychology and law at the University of Washington, has shown in her empirical studies of eyewitness accounting, memory is remarkably faulty and seriously open to influence. How unbiased is that?

According to folk wisdom, scientific reporting would stand as the paragon of unbiased, objective accounting. But it is also undeniably bound to human perception. Consider an account often related in psychology texts to underline the concept of "individual differences." In 1795, Nevil Maskelyne (1732–1811), England's royal astronomer, sacked his assistant, David Kinnebrook. According to the account given by psychologists Duane and Sydney Schultz, Maskelyne noticed variances between his assistant's observations and his own of the same phenomena. He concluded that his assistant's work was inaccurate, and thus Kinnebrook became victim to one of the earliest records of human individual differences. Twenty years later, the German astronomer Friedrich Bessel (1784–1846) proved that it had indeed been a case of individual differences—the innate, unavoidable disposition of the individual to uniquely perceive the world—sufficient to result in small observational differences.

The question then is to what extent can anything ever be objective or wholly subjective for that matter? Alan Chalmers, professor of the History and Philosophy of Science at the University of Sydney, questions whether science and its knowledge can ever be considered objective. He is not alone. Michael Polanyi, referring to knowledge, argues that complete objectivity is not only a delusion, but a false ideal, claiming that "...the act of knowing includes an appraisal, and this personal coefficient, which shapes all factual knowledge, bridges in doing so the disjunction between objectivity and subjectivity" (1962: 17). What he means is that all "factual knowledge" comes drenched in personal, individual evaluation—experience and context—which renders even the most factual of knowledge as an inevitable mix of the subjective and the objective. Kenneth Gergen is even more critical of the idea that truth and knowledge are somehow lying "out there" to be discovered, citing human "individual differences" as the rug that pulls the feet from under objectivity. Everything—or mostly everything—is therefore subjective—or mostly subjective.

The objective/subjective question of the nature of knowledge takes on strategic importance in the context of knowledge as an organizational asset to be managed and leveraged. Those, for instance, who adopt a "systems approach" (i.e., with an emphasis on information technology (IT) as the primary means of managing knowledge) tend to apply an "object" label to the commodity they manage. This touches on yet another schism in KM: for some, its practice is mainly concerned with technologies and how they are used in managing knowledge, taking its roots from information management. So we see a proliferation of "knowledge repositories," "yellow pages," knowledge discussion forums, and a ramped-up increase in interest in the use of social media. The concerns of the systems approach center on effective content categorization strategies: the ability to find documented knowledge at the point of use and the people who possess the knowledge that is needed, for instance. Such technologies are valuable through their communicative potential, but can their contents really be called "knowledge"?

As might be expected, there are equally strong opposing views to the central role that some give technologies. For instance, in their analysis of case studies of information and communications technology-focused knowledge initiatives, Kenneth Grant and Umair Qureshi of Ryerson University in Toronto found high failure rates, which they correlate to initiatives' emphasis on technology. In mitigation, IT projects are notoriously prone to risk and failure but, as Grant and his colleague conclude, knowledge IT projects come with an additional set of complicating parameters and must account for the personal nature of knowledge and the importance of communities.

An early conclusion to be drawn is that the either/or approach to knowledge as object or social action, as objective or subjective, has significant consequences for what is managed or studied and their outcomes. Grant and his coworker's reference to personal knowledge leads into the next theme.

1.3.3 Organizational versus Personal Knowledge

This concerns the question of whether knowledge can only ever be personal or whether it can exist collectively, typically referred to as "organizational knowledge." Once again, polarized sides are encountered. Scholars including Michael Polanyi, and Robert Grant writing in 2002 support a personal knowledge agenda. The latter, for instance, suggests that the more productive perspective is to view collective (viz., organizational) knowledge as an aggregation of the knowledge in individuals' heads. It is precisely the relationship between the two that Grant calls into question, arguing that an emphasis on organizational knowledge simply clouds the relationship between collective and individual knowledge. This is a question considered in some depth by Haridimos Tsoukas and his colleague. In an admittedly confusing definition, they suggest that personal knowledge is the ability of the individual to operate effectively within a collective drawing on their understanding of its context and all things associated with this including its "theory," which they contrast with organizational knowledge described as a set of organizational rules that people are able to draw and act upon. What they conclude is that these are two distinct types of knowledge, implying a requirement for two equally distinctive types of management.

What these many sides of the debate tell us is that KM, in its practice, research, and theory, targets a disparate—often incompatible—array of artifacts and phenomena. Is there any commonality at all to be found? In fact, there is and it is to this that we now turn.

1.4   THE TACIT–EXPLICIT CONUNDRUM

There may be no common *definition* of the nature of knowledge in KM's literature and evidence, but there is one *structural* framework that is beyond doubt the most popular version (but short of a majority) of affairs: the tacit–explicit duality. According to the essence of the dualist perspective, explicit knowledge can be easily articulated, specified, codified, captured, stored, and generally treated as one would a sheet of paper, a computer file, a book, or a report. This sort of view of knowledge is very much behind what we have seen David Snowden describe as the first two generations of KM with their emphasis on technologies.

Tacit knowledge, by contrast, is difficult to articulate and costly to share. It is also, according to Dorothy Leonard, "sticky" in the sense of being hard to extract from its host. The implication of Leonard's viewpoint is that it is the personal, individual context that the "host" attaches to their tacit knowledge, which gives it its meaning, and further that if tacit knowledge is divorced from its context, it would lose that meaning. (Although glossed over here, the subject of context and knowledge becomes a recurring theme and particularly comes to the fore in Part Two.)

This leads into what is, arguably, the most contentious issue in KM: the conversion question. Professor Ikujiro Nonaka and his colleagues, in their formulation of the "knowledge-creating company," perhaps unwittingly threw down the gauntlet with their theory that tacit knowledge can be accessed and leveraged through *converting* it to explicit knowledge, given the right circumstances and environment. (This particular theory is considered in detail in subsequent chapters, but, for now, the concern is with models and definitions of knowledge.) The upshot is a field of organizational practice that is broadly split between those who adopt the tacit–explicit duality, with or without embellishing elements, and those who take a different approach. There is no other single competing construct of knowledge with anywhere near the same level of influence as the knowledge duality model and its project of conversion. But where does this construct come from, and how has it achieved what Stephen Gourlay, a scholar at the UK's Kingston University, describes as such paradigmatic status, albeit not a "universal" one?

Nonaka is widely credited with introducing the tacit–explicit dualist structure of knowledge to the KM field in the early 1990s, drawing on the work of Michael Polanyi. However, it would not gain traction until the publication of a subsequent version, the *Theory of the Knowledge-Creating Firm*, in 1995 along with coworker, Hirotaka Takeuchi. Interestingly, David Snowden suggests that the reason for the delay in excitement over the new theory is explained by the then commitment to process reengineering, which was in "full flow" in the earlier part of the decade. Whatever, with the 1995 publication, the KM machine was given a fresh momentum. Perhaps it was seen as a palliative to what Snowden describes as a growing organizational disillusion with the earlier reengineering fashion and perhaps the realization that in replacing man with machine, the baby had been quite literally thrown out with the bathwater. In this and subsequent works, the theory of the knowledge-creating firm became inextricably bound to Polanyi's philosophies, which are largely focused on the nature of personal knowledge in the context of the exact sciences.

As a result of Nonaka's (and colleagues') work, which locates the tacit–explicit model as a central component, Polanyi's ideas have become among the most widely referenced in the KM field, second only to Nonaka himself. His ideas have also become what could be described as the most misrepresented and misunderstood, as will be discussed presently. In short, the fact that Nonaka bound his influential theory to this particular knowledge structure has proved significant, and in particular his emphasis on the importance of the tacit component has impacted the directions of the field—both in practice and academia. In that sense, tacit knowledge has become something of a chalice cup.

Predictably, the whole idea of a tacit–explicit structure of knowledge, especially the idea that tacit and explicit knowledge can be converted from one to the other, and then shared, has come in for a barrage of criticism. It has been pointed out, for instance, that to hold up tacit knowledge as the most valuable form on the one hand while on the other to insist that it needs to be converted to make it explicit poses something of a contradiction. Logic suggests that if it is no longer "tacit," then it is no longer of value. Researchers Ulrike Schultze and Charles Stabell, who adopt this line of reasoning, also point out that once converted tacit knowledge can be copied resulting in a risk to competitive edge. However, this is perhaps a circular argument as it first assumes that tacit as a distinctive structure of knowledge exists and second that it can be converted to explicit. Neither of these two assumptions should be taken for granted in the absence of supporting scientific evidence. But this reasoning does suggest that Nonaka's model is flawed.

A further critical theme, and one more widely reported, is the suggestion that Professor Nonaka and his colleagues, while drawing quite openly on Michael Polanyi's hypothesis for their construction of knowledge, have in fact misinterpreted and even misrepresented the Polanyi's claims in respect of knowledge, particularly of the tacit dimension. If this proves to be the case, does it not crumble the foundations of the theory of the knowledge-creating firm? A question, though: Nonaka and his colleagues' work may be frequently criticized for "misrepresenting" Polanyi's ideas with consequences for the validity for their model, but that criticism assumes that Polanyi—in any accurate understanding—is right.

1.4.1   What Did Polanyi Really Say?

It may seem "off message" to slip so easily into a discussion of the works of a scientist and philosopher who was not even specifically addressing the concerns of KM. But, as noted earlier, KM refers to his work so frequently as to suggest that he was in fact writing with a management theme in mind, which, of course, he definitely was not. Polanyi's concern is to dispense with the objective, impersonal ideals of scientific detachment in favor of recognizing "knowing" as an art in which the skill of the knower is a fundamental part of scientific understanding. What he is proposing here, according to this interpretation, is that it is the scientist's *participation* in both discovery and validation of knowledge, which is itself a part of that knowledge and of the science. Consequently, science and its facts—knowledge—can never be entirely objective, because they will always include a personal *subjective* component.

Think of it like this. A market researcher canvasses opinions about a new product, which she does using semistructured questionnaires. She herself conducts the interviews, transcribes the results, and interprets the findings. At all of the following points of the exercise, the researcher could be shown to have, perhaps unknowingly and unwittingly, introduced her own personal interpretation of events based on past experience, beliefs, and attitudes:

- The selection of the research topic
- The selection of the interview candidates
- The selection and presentation of the questions
- Her own involvement in the interview
- The transcription of the interviews
- Interpretation and reporting of the findings

At any of these points, bias can slide in. The same could be argued about any research involving questionnaires, interviews, and even political polls, for instance. Why? For the simple reason that humans by their nature are designed to operate in a (un)conscious state of constant "sensemaking." Everything you know, everything you think you know, everything you can do, or think you can has arrived with you via your sensemaking filter—your perceptual senses. This notion of "sensemaking" is returned to in more depth in later chapters. For the present, and with this point made, what does Polanyi have to say on the subject of the "tacit"?

In the course of fashioning his claims over the nature of subjectivity and objectivity, he particularly focuses on tacit knowledge. He variously describes this as personal, practical, ineffable, indefinable (sic.), instrumental, and residing in subsidiary awareness. It is, in sum, unspecifiable. Thus, in his own words, "(A)an art which cannot be specified in detail cannot be transmitted by prescription, since no prescription exists" (1962: 53).

If that is Polanyi's brand of tacit knowledge, what of its relationship with the other kind, explicit? Recall Nonaka and colleagues' tacit–explicit model and the imperative to convert one to the other, a *distinction* that is widely subscribed to. A substantial number of those who disagree with this model, including Paul Duguid of the University of California, Berkeley, have interpreted Polanyi's claims as denying any divorce between the two phenomena: accordingly, all knowledge contains both tacit and explicit elements. In his railing against economists' reductive treatment of knowledge to the level of "widgets," Duguid persuasively reasons that the tacit cannot be reduced to the explicit. Moreover, the tacit is essential to engaging an understanding of the explicit. This he describes as evidenced in a long list of philosophical thought reaching back to the ancient Greeks several thousand years ago, and which understands what we call tacit knowledge as the underpinning cognitive dimension that mediates—"tells us how to use"—what we refer to as codified or explicit knowledge. The tacit, in this interpretation, is the key to unlocking the explicit.

Unfortunately, Polanyi does not offer an explicit, "cards on the table" explanation of the tacit–explicit relationship in a way that would have relevance and resonance for KM. Instead, a scenario that he uses to talk *around* the subject might shed some light. Imagine you learn to play the piano: at first, you concentrate on your fingers on the keys and their movement from one key to the next. Eventually, after much practice, you can play the piece without looking at your hands or even thinking about tapping keys. What began as the acquisition and application of what might be called explicit knowing—knowing that is necessarily in full focal awareness because you must concentrate on what you do and consciously apply the task's rules—has become tacit knowing. That is, knowing that has become subsidiary to conscious awareness to the extent that if you switched your full conscious attention onto your playing, you would probably lose your ability to play. ("Focal" and "subsidiary" awareness are Polanyi's terms.) So, from this scenario, it would appear that the explicit can become tacit through practice and experience, but the minute you attempt to "convert" that to explicit, you risk a reduction or loss in ability. However, I would suggest that the subtlety here is that both tacit and explicit knowing are implicated from the outset of the task: what changes is your awareness.

There is whichever way you approach it a lot of confusion over what Michael Polanyi actually meant. What is clear is that the majority of scholars and practitioners in the field approach knowledge as comprising two or more types, of which tacit and explicit are the primary classes. The main point of debate is over the nature of tacit knowledge, and whether this can be harvested and converted to the explicit, as many suggest. Or, as others claim, such attempts at "managing" the tacit are wholly inappropriate and a wasteful undertaking. The tacit question is returned to in a later chapter, where the discussions turn to a different scientific discipline for a more evidence-based understanding of the phenomenon. Now however consideration is given to some of the alternative accounts to the tacit–explicit duality.

1.4.2   The Importance of Context: What Context and Whose Context?

There is an argument that places "context" in the role of the most important aspect in any definition or understanding of knowledge. Cambridge University scholar Mark Thompson and his colleague, for instance, propose context to be an embedded knowledge element, and that this is what Michael Polanyi meant when he described the structure of knowledge as containing a "personal coefficient." According to this formula, knowledge, or knowing, is meaningless without its context, and that context is specific and unique to the individual. But where does this context come from, and how does it emerge?

For some, context is personal, while others, for instance, Charles Despres, Daniele Chauvel, and Ganesh Bhatt, seem to be positioning context as a referent to environment or culture. From the standpoint of context as personal, which position Polanyi arguably adopts, for knowledge to have meaning, it must be filtered through the mesh of the individual's beliefs, experiences, expectations, and so forth. These may be organizationally shared meanings, or they may be unique to the individual. For instance, Mark Thompson and his colleague understand context from an organizational perspective, seeing it as comprising the shared meanings and experiences of organization members, implying an "organizational cultural context." Similarly, Davydd Greenwood and his colleague define knowledge as inherently collective ("knowing"), socially constructed, and distributed, embedded in the individual's understanding of how to act in the world, all of which can be interpreted as representing "context." Based on these accounts, it is clear that the notion of "context" is used in a broad and sometimes ambiguous sense. As something of a tangential indulgence, an interesting perspective on "context" can be drawn from psychological studies of memory.

The topic of memory has one of the longest traditions in psychology, and Alan Baddeley has made it his particular field of expertise. In his book *Essentials of Human Memory*, based on decades of research, Baddeley hypothesizes that we store our knowledge in a mental structure known as "semantic memory," and much of this is not capable of expression in words. This rings considerable bells with Michael Polanyi's perspective on tacit knowledge. For Baddeley, context is not so much the influence of the external environment, but rather our interpretation of it using the tools of our stored knowledge. For instance, referring to our interpretation of words, knowledge of the world that exceeds in most cases the boundaries of words' meaning is essential to understanding. This has correspondence with Paul Duguid's formulation of an uncodifiable substrate, which tells us how to use the "code."

Taking an example of context at work, Baddeley reports on a number of studies by Endel Tulving, whom he describes as one of the most significant contributors to our understanding of memory retrieval. In one of these, participants were presented with a word to be remembered (the target word), simultaneously associated with a "cue word," which had a loose association with the former: for example, if "city" was the word to be remembered, it might be associated with "dirty" or "village." In retrieval tests, the findings persuasively demonstrate that participants given the cue word were far more able to accurately retrieve the target words than those who were not. In this sense, the cue word acts as a kind of context. In the broader sense, context informs and influences meaning—our understanding and interpretation of our knowledge of the world. In other words, sensemaking is context driven.

In a more elaborate experiment of context-dependent memory recall, Baddeley and his colleague, D.R. Godden, got divers to learn word lists in one of two environments: underwater or on dry land. Their findings show that words were more accurately recalled when divers were in the environment in which the original learning took place and worse in the opposite environment. It was not the physical environment that was doing the influencing, but rather the participants' interpretation of it. Remove the context, and you remove the "sense." To quote a story recounted by Baddeley and his coworker, a man is found to be an expert dancer in a small room containing a trunk, around which he must negotiate his moves. With the trunk removed, his performance became compromised.

The intention of including these couple of examples from psychology is to point to these topics of research and investigation as a source of relevance and interest for the present discussions.

So what has all this to do with a KM perspective on context? According to Kenneth Gergen, "(S)seeing is a theory-laden undertaking" (1991: 92). This understanding of context (here conceptualized as the context of observation), both in terms of cueing access to stored knowledge and as binding knowledge to experiential, cultural, environmental, and social factors, renders it unique to the individual. People may well share common knowledge within an organization, for instance, and they may even coconstruct knowledge. However, no two people will ever possess identical knowledge, but shared *elements of context* enable a platform for shared meaning. As an idea, this is not so very far apart from many of the formulations around knowledge discussed in KM.

It is worth noting that Nonaka and his colleagues feature the importance of context in their theory of the knowledge-creating firm in various guises. In 1994, Nonaka proposes a cycle of knowledge in the form of a continuous spiral in which the tacit becomes the explicit, and vice versa, which is performed on the stage of social practice. In a later work, along with coworker Noboru Konno, this idea is developed through the introduction of "Ba"—a uniquely Japanese concept of social space that can be physical, mental, or virtual—drawing on the ideas of a Japanese philosopher. The point is that in this monumentally influential theory, "social practice" can be equated to what others would call "context," but this aspect of the theory tends to be overlooked. We now turn to social action in more detail.

1.4.3 A Preference for "Knowing" as Action

Writing in the mid-1990s, the start of Snowden's second generation of KM, Professor Frank Blackler proposed a rather radical departure from the "traditional rational-cognitive" formulations of knowledge. What he argued for was that it would be more appropriate to approach knowledge as action that people do rather than something that they possess—thus "knowing" rather than knowledge, action rather than commodity. Central to this argument is the idea that if "knowing how" is located in action, then a direct link is created between action and knowledge.

Blackler argues that the traditional conception of knowledge as abstract, disembodied, and formal is unrealistic. Instead, he proposes five "images" or types of knowledge, building on work by H. Collins published 2 years earlier: embrained, embodied, encultured, embedded, and encoded. Note that Blackler's interpretation of encultured knowledge as socially constructed and open to negotiation, which is consequently heavily dependent on language, introduces a "discursive" aspect. The difficulty with Blackler's arguments stems from an apparent contradiction between suggesting a move toward viewing knowledge as action and his primary observation of a shift away from embodied and embedded knowledge toward the other knowledge "images." It is not clear whether Blackler is arguing for a reversal of this shift or not. The original work by Collins is worth a visit in its description of two types of human action—regular and behavior-specific acts: he argues that the former underlies tacit knowledge and is centered around "rule following" and "rule establishing," which are hard to describe and transfer, whereas the latter are decontextualizable. He also implies the action orientation of discourse. This idea is increasingly developed as the present work progresses and represents the "main event" in Part Two.

As we saw earlier, a preference for "knowing" as opposed to "knowledge" finds support elsewhere, notably in the works of Davydd Greenwood and his colleague and Paul Duguid. These scholars particularly link the idea of "knowing" to tacit knowledge, which, similarly to Collins work, underlines its action orientation. Such a conceptualization of knowing has obvious implications for KM's project.

Not unexpectedly, the relationship between "know how" and tacit knowledge—if indeed there is one—has attracted its share of debate and contradiction. On one side of the debate, "know how" is explicitly mapped to tacit knowledge: they are one and the same. The opposite side denies such a relationship: for instance, Stephen Gourlay, in his criticism of Nonaka and his colleagues' conceptualization of knowledge and their knowledge creating model, proposes that "know how" and "know that," rather than equating to tacit/explicit, represent two different types of behavior—everyday and reflective. In contrast, John Seely Brown and Paul Duguid, for instance, map "know how" to tacit knowledge, ascribing it with the same properties (not easily transferable, a product of experience). Interestingly, they also note that "know how" is embedded in practice. Such a perspective is not surprising given the importance and emphasis that Brown and Duguid place on communities of practice in the development of new knowledge. The reader's attention is drawn to Gourlay, Brown, and Duguid's use of the terms "know how" and "know that," compared with, for instance, Greenwood and his colleague and Duguid's (writing several years later) preference for the term "knowing." Practically and arguably, the only difference between these lies in the inference of action in "knowing," and the potential for reification in consideration of "know how" for instance.

What we have seen thus far is a multifarious, often confusing, display of perspectives on the structure of knowledge, so much so that it is little wonder if the majority of those interested in KM adopt the, by comparison, simple and clear-cut tacit–explicit dualism. There are two more principle themes to consider in the present discussion of the nature of knowledge, before we might attempt to draw some conclusions—semantic frameworks for knowledge and the hierarchy of knowledge—mentioned earlier in this chapter.

1.5 FRAMEWORKS OF MEANING

Research suggests that most definitions of knowledge in the field of KM tend to be—to a larger or lesser extent—structural in nature. A significant number hang their clothes on a dualist model. But what of semantic definitions? Beginning with the most influential account, how do Nonaka and his colleagues semantically define knowledge?

Adopting what he describes as an essentially Western view of knowledge, Nonaka defines it as the dynamic process of justifying personal beliefs on the road to seeking truth. Thus, in his knowledge-creating model, knowledge is "justified, true belief," which was in fact originally proposed by Plato (427–347 B.C.), the Greek philosopher. However, in a departure from the traditional perspective that gives primacy to "truth" according to Nonaka, he chooses to emphasize the components of "belief" and "justified." Gourlay, a critic of Nonaka's theory as noted earlier, points out that justification can be based on false premises, in which case "justified belief" can be wrong. So, to suggest that justified beliefs are true, and always true, when they are fallible conjures a meaningless state of affairs. Note that Nonaka, Umemoto, and Senoo subsequently criticize the "Western" definition of knowledge for being deficient, reformulating it as meaningful information that consists of a true, justified belief and/or an embodied technical skill.

Does Nonaka's definition of knowledge as "justified true belief not sound rather personal? Does it not conjure a sense of knowledge as some private, inner mental construct, hidden from casual view? If KM and knowledge managers are concerned with identifying, leveraging, storing, and applying "justified true beliefs" for the economic and competitive benefit of the firm, does it not begin to feel awkward?

More complex semantic definitions of knowledge frame it as a mix of truths, beliefs, perspectives, concepts, judgments, expectations, methodologies, and know how. Haridimos Tsoukas and his colleague, Efi Vladimirou, in their discussion of the relationship between personal and organizational knowledge, point to one definition in particular, which describes knowledge as a mix of "framed experiences," spiced with values, information from context and expert insight, and which springs from people's minds, but is often embedded in the paraphernalia of organizations—practices and routines, document, repositories, and so forth. This, they suggest, packs far too many things into a definition of knowledge, risking a specification of the phenomenon that is so wide-ranging that it renders it useless. Neither of these definitions arguably leads to a comfortable, commonsense, and *usable* perspective on knowledge. Will a consideration of hierarchy lead to a more acceptable perspective?

1.6   A HIERARCHY OF KNOWLEDGE

The hierarchical perspective of knowledge considers its relationship with and differences from data and information. Again, we find two polarized ends of a spectrum with, at one end, Stephen Gourlay, for instance, warning against any formula for knowledge that includes a reference to information. At the other, Nonaka sees no problematic distinction between information and knowledge: information is imaged as a flow of messages, whereas knowledge is created and organized by this flow, which is grounded in the commitment and beliefs of the individual. Recall David's Snowden's third-generation conceptualization of knowledge as a "thing" and a "flow."

The traditional hierarchical model has data in the lower tier, with knowledge occupying the top, and an implied flow from bottom to top. Much of the debate in this area centers on the relationship between the tiers. One question we might ask is this: can this flow ever take the reverse direction? Can knowledge transform into data? This would seem illogical, but, in theory, and by rights of this hierarchical model, one could take a chunk of knowledge and reduce it to its data elements.

The attraction of the model lies in its simplicity, and it is consistent with what might be described as a content management—or systems—approach to KM. This leads to the suggestion that the hierarchical model of knowledge, coupled with Nonaka's influential proposition of the dualist tacit–explicit structure of knowledge and the imperative to convert one to the other, is behind the perceived dominance of the technology-centric view of KM, particularly in practice. Perhaps fortunately, and as implied in the transition through three generations of KM, there has been a notable change in emphasis in recent years to a more people-centric focus.

A more sophisticated view is offered by Vincent Barabba of the General Motors Corporation and his colleagues. First off, they propose a hierarchy that includes "understanding" and "wisdom" in addition to the conventional line up, and they warn against the "huge mistake" of ignoring the distinction in meanings between them. Their claims favor a view of the organization as a system that cannot be reduced to its parts and that it is the interaction between the parts, like an activating network, that defines the organization. In their book, data must be processed into information in order to be of any use; information is contained within descriptions (who, where, when, what, how many); knowledge is contained in instructions (how) and awareness (I know who I am); understanding is contained in explanations (answers to "why" questions); and wisdom is concerned with "effectiveness," that is, the value of the outcome of behaviors. In essence, they wrap KM into organizational learning. This is a commonsense approach, one that has a great deal of synergy with the theory and perspective that is developed across the span of the present book.

1.7   SUMMARY AND CONCLUSIONS

At this point, one could be forgiven for wishing to quietly close the door on the nature of knowledge, ignoring the complexities and difficulties in the debate. Whatever it is, as argued by the psychologist Stephen Suddendorf in his account of the "gap" between humans and nonhuman species, it is in our nature to be in a continuous state of learning new knowledge and, through sensemaking, transforming that knowledge uniquely into our own. Human culture throughout known recorded history is thematically watermarked with the urge to share what we know with others. Yet its nature has been the source of debate for just as long, and with no immediate consensus—certainly within the field of KM—remotely on the horizon. It has been shown that the academic field and practice of KM is not immune to these issues. Some of the core questions center around the notion of knowledge as commodity contrasted with knowledge as an accomplishment in social interaction, its objective versus subjective nature, and whether it can be both organizational and personal.

There is, however, one structural formulation of knowledge that has attracted pervasive popularity—the tacit–explicit dualist model—originally introduced by Professor Nonaka and his colleagues. This draws on the earlier work of the philosopher-scientist, Michael Polanyi, yet many have criticized this structural formulation—and the theoretical model of knowledge creation that it underpins—for misrepresenting Polanyi's ideas. Alternative perspectives on knowledge emphasize the importance of context and a preference for "knowing how" as a form of social action. What has also been sewn is the seed of an idea of knowledge connected to discourse as action. This marks the beginning of what will emerge and develop across the following chapters.

As with the tacit–explicit dualist model, Nonaka and colleagues' semantic explanation of knowledge as "justified true belief is also widely popularized, although more complex descriptions of knowledge are also proposed. Perhaps the latter should not be so easily dismissed as being overly complex: they, at least, give consideration to the pervasiveness of knowledge—particularly the view of knowing as action—in all aspects of everyday life. To what extent are "knowing action" and "knowledge" requisite facets of every cognitive and physical action that humans do?

So what can be concluded from all of this? It is, perhaps, too early on in the investigation to arrive at any sensible, evidence-based, evaluation of the nature of knowledge, and one relevant to the organizational practice of KM. But one conclusion that can be drawn is that "knowledge," whatever it is, is important to the modern organization as it attempts to make its fortunes in what Nick Bontis describes as a sea of change and turbulent times. That being the case, an understanding of the constitution of knowledge takes on a paramount urgency. In the next two chapters, some of the other key issues and debates that infuse KM are explored, beginning with a consideration of what constitutes KM itself, finding mixed perspectives.

FURTHER READING

Collins, H. (1993). The structure of knowledge. *Social Research*, 60, (1): 95–116.

Duguid, P. (2005). The art of knowing: social and tacit dimensions of knowledge and the limits of the Community of Practice. *The Information Society*, 21: 109–118.

Nonaka, I. and Takeuchi, H. (1995). *The Knowledge-Creating Company*. New York: Oxford University Press.

Polanyi, M. (1962). *Personal Knowledge: Towards a Post-Critical Philosophy*. Chicago: The University of Chicago Press.

Tsoukas, E. and Vladimirou, E. (2001). What is organizational knowledge? *Journal of Management Studies*, 38, (7): 973–993.

2

THE CONSTITUTION OF KNOWLEDGE MANAGEMENT

2.1 ADDRESSING SOME KEY QUESTIONS

The following two chapters consider some of the other big questions in knowledge management (KM). What we find, like those around the nature of knowledge, is that the principle issues have changed little over the last two decades. One in particular concerns the question over what KM is all about. This might seem a little surprising considering how long KM has been active in organizational management and research. But this remains a live issue as we will find in the following discussions, and in Part Two in the analysis of a public online knowledge manager's discussion forum which is themed on this precise question (the topic of computer-mediated communication in general is reviewed in Chapter 6). The roots of the issue can be clearly traced back to the debate over the nature of knowledge itself and the influence of the systems approach.

The present chapter focuses on the constitution of KM, beginning with an investigation of its origins revealing a variety of often competing opinions and viewpoints. The discussions then move onto KM itself, finding multiple perspectives and near limitless boundaries. Particular consideration is given to the question of whether KM is merely a passing management fad. The role of technology as both a defining and push factor in the drive to take up KM reveals interesting perspectives with the suggestion of a further schism in the field: those who consider the nature of knowledge as the KM defining factor and those who approach technology as the single most important factor in its constitution. Inevitably, all of these issues and debates lead to the question of whether knowledge should be managed, with the implication of an ethical issue that is largely unresolved.

Knowledge and Discourse Matters: Relocating Knowledge Management's Sphere of Interest onto Language,
First Edition. Lesley Crane.
© 2016 John Wiley & Sons, Inc. Published 2016 by John Wiley & Sons, Inc.

2.2 THE ORIGINS OF KNOWLEDGE MANAGEMENT

KM is variously described as having its roots in the 1960s and 1970s, in the 1980s and the early 1990s, and even in the seventeenth-century scientific revolution. Then, there is what David Snowden terms "the three generations of KM," which we touched on in Chapter 1. Taking a practical line, Karl Wiig proposes that in reality humans have been explicitly or otherwise managing knowledge since the earliest agrarian settlements. One could safely conjecture, following psychologist Thomas Suddendorf's reasoning, that humans have been managing knowledge for a lot longer than this, implying that sharing and creating knowledge is a basic human behavior. But it has only emerged as a business practice in the latter half of the twentieth century. By far, the majority of commentators locate the beginnings of organizational KM in the mid-1990s marked by the publication of one book. Supportively or otherwise, many credit Ikujiro Nonaka and Hirotaka Takeuchi as the progenitors of modern organizational KM with their book *The Knowledge-Creating Company*.

Nonaka and Takeuchi's book presents a detailed account of the theory of the knowledge-creating firm, which arguably stands as one of the most significant KM theories so far developed and which continues to evolve. An earlier account, published in the *Harvard Business Review* in 1991, resulted in Nonaka being described as "Mr. Knowledge" by *The Economist* magazine and, elsewhere, as the author of KM. Beyond doubt, the publication of this book and its subsequent rise to fame have had a paradigmatic impact on the shape, direction, values, and validity of KM in almost every sense.

An important feature of Nonaka and his colleague's theory is that it draws significantly on the philosophical and scientific domains, particularly on the work of Polanyi as we have already seen in the previous chapter. Consequently, Polanyi's work has become the second most cited after Nonaka's in the KM literature. This is shown to have consequences for an understanding of the nature of knowledge (see Chapter 1), with implications for KM success or failure (see Chapter 3) and practice in general. Nonaka's work and its many derivatives may well set their roots in philosophy and science, but they are roundly criticized in many quarters for misrepresenting, ignoring, or even misinterpreting what these disciplines have to say on the subject of knowledge. In fact, similarly to a labeling of the tacit–explicit distinction as close to achieving the status of banality, criticism of *The Knowledge-Creating Company* has reached equally mundane status.

A recent alternative to this "received" view of KM's origins comes from Patrick Lambe who argues that KM is more properly and accurately located in the disciplines of economics and sociology and more specifically organizational learning, intellectual capital, and data and information management. Referring to KM's "collective amnesia," he claims that the "five golden years" of KM during the 1990s, which saw the publication of the popular KM classics, effectively erased all traces of its antecedents, thus setting a new agenda for decades to come. As Lambe states: "…a better understanding of prior thinking … can perhaps clarify some of the confusions and inconsistencies that beset knowledge management practitioners, [and] bring focus to some of the muddy thinking and silly doctrines that still abound in knowledge management …" (2011: 178). His central argument is that KM's direct origins lie in the works of Arrow, Machlup, and Rogers published in the 1960s. These, Lambe insists, laid the foundations of social and economic theory for the next five decades. Moreover, these and similar works debate and address precisely the issues that KM wrestles with today. It is this "carelessness" in ignoring its parentage that is at the heart of KM's dichotomies, according to Lambe.

However, it is not strictly true that *all* KM has totally ignored Lambe's interpretation of "parentage": for instance, both Nonaka's *Dynamic Theory of Organizational Knowledge Creation* and Robert Grant's *Knowledge-Based View of the Firm* make reference to works by Machlup and Arrow. Nonetheless, from Lambe's perspective, there is a hint that KM has run before it can walk.

2.3 MULTIPLE PERSPECTIVES AND LIMITLESS BOUNDARIES

It seems a simple enough question—what is KM? But like the nature of knowledge this question opens the proverbial tin of worms. From one perspective, an organizational manager could argue that the management of knowledge is defined and scoped in accordance with what the organization practices. From another, it would make sense to suggest that variations between organizations, industries, cultures, and so on make the need for any kind of common definition of the field somewhat irrelevant. Furthermore, J.C. Spender of the Kozminski University Business School claims at the outset of KM's "third generation" (see Snowden's generational account of KM in Section 1.2) that the "vast bulk" of managerial interest lies in a perception of knowledge as an object and a concern with how organizational knowledge is different from the management of other resources. This, he concludes, leads to the conflation of knowledge, information and data, and an approach to KM centered on gathering all of an organization's "knowledge" into some database.

Writing in the same timeframe as Spender, researchers Bouthillier and Shearer use a framework of six "dimensions" of KM initiative (goals and objectives, the nature of the knowledge under management, the sources and users of knowledge, knowledge processes and methodologies, and technologies used) to investigate publicly available organizational KM case studies. They report eight "distinct KM methodologies" ranging from an emphasis on communication to one on action. What is particularly intriguing about this study is the suggestion of the prime organizational focus on "tacit knowledge," which they criticize as ill-defined. However, on a cautionary note, Bouthillier and her colleague's interpretive study is based on an investigation of published case studies and could consequently be questioned on the grounds of selectivity. The researchers do nonetheless raise the valid question of whether KM is just a "faddy" new name for information management, suggesting that the differences between the two disciplines are not well expressed. Such a conclusion would certainly be consistent with that drawn by Spender. However, it could also be interpreted as simply the result of a combination of concern with best practice and organizational differences.

But that being the case, how is the field to evolve and develop, to improve and become more effective if its boundaries cannot be seen? Can there ever be boundaries to the practice of managing knowledge? Interestingly, in the first public outings of his theory, published in 1991 and 1994, Nonaka does not actually define KM. And why should he? His work is concerned with promoting the concept of the knowledge-creating organization at the expense of the traditional "input–process–output" or "learning" conceptualizations of the organization. We do not have to look far to find definitions and accounts elsewhere. The following brief discussions address thematic issues that all arguably stem from the multiplicity of perspective and near boundless constitution of what is referred to as "KM."

2.3.1 The Organization as a Body of Knowledge

In the late 1990s, consultant and author Karl Wiig clarifies KM as a defined process by which all things related to knowledge such as policies and programs are managed with the aim of building and deploying intellectual capital effectively for the purposes of gain. This perspective can almost be seen as the antithesis to the ideas of, for instance, Frank Blackler discussed in Chapter 1. But it does endorse a view of the organization as a "body of knowledge." Taking a wider approach, Nick Bontis claims that KM should focus on the two related phenomena of organizational learning flows and intellectual capital stocks: they are related on the principle that the more readily an organization can acquire knowledge, the greater its tendency to use it. It is a principle that makes rational sense but, taking the side of the devil's advocate, just because an entity assimilates knowledge does not necessarily mean that the same entity is equally proficient at applying it. Bontis' strategy is to emphasize paying attention to how knowledge moves and changes within organizations. On one level, his emphasis on "learning flows" and "capital stocks" is reminiscent of Snowden's take on knowledge (a thing and a flow; see Chapter 1). But contrastingly, Bontis is not talking about definitions of knowledge but instead a conceptualization of the organization as a living organism akin to Wigg's inference of the body of knowledge. Writing slightly earlier, Spender also notes the trend toward viewing the firm as a body of knowledge.

In this way, the conceptualization of the organization can be seen as the driving force behind a conceptualization of KM itself. That is, how an organization views itself determines how it strategically and pragmatically manages what is widely described as its most important asset. It thus also suggests a gulf between actual KM practice and academic theorizing and research, something that Grover and Davenport draw attention to in their *General Perspectives on Knowledge Management*.

2.3.2 Gulf between Practice and Academia

Developing this theme, in one research study, I compared and contrasted the findings from an analysis of discourse in a knowledge manager's online forum with issues and debates in the literature. A key finding is that while forum participants axiomatically treat knowledge as object, the reification of knowledge remains the topic of considerable debate in theory and research and is a topic returned to in the following chapter. Bouthillier and Shearer's analysis of case studies finds that while organizations appear to be applying Nonaka's model of the knowledge-creating firm, they find somewhat bizarrely that the acquisition of knowledge, the creation of new knowledge, and identification of knowledge needs are—in all cases—not on firms' agendas, though knowledge sharing is.

2.3.3 Knowledge Management from the Perspective of the Learning Organization

Following on from this, are organizations not simply doing what they are being urged to do? The scholar Michael Zack, for instance, promotes the idea of knowledge as most important strategic resource that an organization can possess, with the ability to manage and leverage this effectively representing the most important capability in achieving and maintaining a competitive advantage. He further reasons that firms need to identify what they do and do not know and address the gaps as part of an overall organizational strategy linked to economic value and competitive advantage. In other words, most of us are familiar with the "training needs analysis," but this implies a "knowledge needs analysis": is there any difference? Based on Bouthillier and her colleague's case studies and my own study around a knowledge manager's forum, we can see evidence of Zack's first imperative, but perhaps not the latter.

The idea of addressing knowledge gaps, and its implication of training, connects to the notion of the "learning organization." However, Nonaka claims that learning is a limited and static concept. Accordingly, it seems that another marker of the variation in approaches to KM can be seen in two contrasting perspectives of the knowledge organization: in one, learning is a subset or subsidiary, perhaps even separate, activity to KM while the other sees the "knowledge organization" as inherently a learning organization.

2.3.4 The Systemic Approach and Connections to Social Interaction

Developing this latter perspective, Vincent Barabba and coworkers essentially wrap KM into "organizational learning," criticizing "most purveyors of KM" as anchored to the industrial way of thinking, which they argue is responsible for KM failure. They emphasize organizations conceptualized as fully interconnected systems with an equally holistic view of organizational learning. In their systemic approach (not be confused with the "systems approach" with its focus on information technology (IT)), success derives from understanding that performance of the whole is not concerned with the sum of its parts, but rather with their interactions. They contrast this with KM's conventional "inventorying" approach, which attempts to assign values to individual parts.

The "systemic" or "systems thinking" approach invokes a hint of social interaction. Accordingly, a further theme positions knowledge as a social phenomenon, accomplished in social interaction. We considered this idea in the previous chapter. In her proposal for a new framework for knowledge creation to replace that proposed by Nonaka, Maria Jakubik of the University of Applied Sciences in Helsinki calls for a better understanding of knowledge as embedded in human action and interaction. This has correspondence with the emphasis on human factors (culture, people, and leadership) as key success factors in KM. Leading scholars Robert Grant and JC Spender both implicate a social view of organizational knowledge raising a question over how it might or should be managed. This question is taken up directly later in Section 2.6.

2.4   IS IT A PASSING MANAGEMENT FAD?

A valid question touched on earlier in this chapter concerns whether KM is a "trendy" name for information management. A related question, which has troubled many, concerns whether KM is merely a passing management fad. Laurence Prusak of IBM's Institute for Knowledge Management insists that KM "…is not just a consultants' invention but a practitioner-based, substantive response to real social and economic trends" (2001: 1002). However, he does acknowledge that there is some credibility to the "skeptic" perception of KM as a consultant's new economic gravy train to replace declining revenues from the practice of "reengineering." Echoing this perspective, Katsuhiro Umemoto of Japan's Graduate School of Knowledge Science points out that KM has become "a lucrative" industry in its own right. Hardly surprising when as consultant Steve Denning reports in 2012, the World Bank, to quote just one example, spends US\$4 billion *a year* on knowledge services.

Others by contrast express incredulity that KM has even survived as a corporate practice when, according to published research, it has a fairly poor and often negative reputation with, as we have already seen, comparatively high "rates of failure." Drawing on another example from Denning's report, a large consulting firm motivated its staff to record "knowledge objects" in an IT repository. Within a few years, around 1.6 million "objects" were stored in the system. One measure might suggest that this was a successful implementation in terms of "outputs," but from the perspective of *outcomes*, it was a failure because no one was using it *as a knowledge resource*. Rather than representing a professional response and toolset for evolving market needs, corporate trends, and pull factors, as Prusak suggests, is KM no more than a manufactured doctrine with a practice designed to generate funds for its practitioners and inventors? Or does it have real substance and a justifiable foundation?

It is suggested here that KM is more than a passing fad. Why? For three pragmatic reasons: Firstly, as researcher Donald Hisplop concludes, the sheer number of journals, books, and conferences devoted to KM, which appears to be increasing, is a testament to the topic's enduring attraction. Secondly, billions are spent on its practice. Thirdly, perhaps more fundamentally, it is highly unlikely that organizational leaders are going to turn aside from the attempts to leverage that which is generally acknowledged to be their most precious asset. One can also conclude that it takes its origins from multiple directions, which surely make it a far-reaching organizational endeavor, perhaps one with limitless boundaries at that.

2.5   TECHNOLOGY AS A DEFINING "PUSH FACTOR"

Technology, in particular the rapid developments in Information and Communications Technologies (ICT) and Web 2.0, is implicated by many scholars and authors as an influential driver for the development and uptake of KM. For instance, Bouthillier and her colleague note a reliance on IT in their analysis of KM case studies, consistent with the perceived emphasis on knowledge sharing. If organizations are only intent on knowledge sharing supported by IT as concluded by Spender (see Section 2.3)—and by default, coding, recording, and storing—is it not the case that the object of their intent is not, in fact, knowledge, but rather information? It would seem that in practice KM is at least in part defined by technology and technology practices.

Taking the "technocentric" approach, a recent study by Sirous Panahi and his colleagues at Queensland University of Technology, for instance, emphasizes the role of Web 2.0 and social media and their affordances for sharing tacit knowledge. Specifically, they claim that social media supports tacit knowledge sharing through triggering social and information communications, facilitating collaboration and brainstorming, making personal knowledge accessible, and reducing the time and effort needed to share such knowledge. However, they do admit to a dearth of empirical support for such a thesis. Writing some 16 years earlier, Wiig also notes the lack of academic and management research to support KM in general, so not much has changed. The influence of technology is something of a double-edged sword. Over the years, there has been considerable criticism of KM theories and practice for placing too much emphasis on a systems (IT) approach to the point of risking a loss of distinction from information management, an issue raised at the start of Section 2.3.

Critics of the systems approach include, somewhat ironically given his role in IBM, Prusak who argues that the focus on technology has reductively defined KM as nothing more than "moving data and documents around." This, and again the irony is inescapable, he blames on the IT vendors. In a similar vein, Charles Despres and his colleague condemn the rush to take up technology solutions and the brushing aside of accumulated wisdom of cognitive sciences, philosophy, and other disciplines. Perhaps then, the "rush to adopt technology" is an explaining factor in Lambe's problem with "ignored parentage." Researchers Ragab and Arisha point to evidence that implies that many organizations' KM initiatives that took a 100% IT-based approach have in fact failed, blaming this state of affairs on the belief in "exaggerated predictions." The implication is that it was the vendors of IT solutions who were making the predictions—and probably still are.

In Section 3.3, we will encounter the revealing case study reported by Ashley Braganza and his colleague Gerald Möllenkramer. Their forensic investigation of US giant PharmaCorp's failed KM initiative recounts how, despite having the highest priority, with strong top management support, adequate funding, and dedicated teams of experts, the initiative had no connection with people's everyday jobs and eventually the KM team was closed down. Braganza and his coworker draw useful "lessons learned" and suggestions for the avoidance of similar pitfalls. What they do not do is draw close attention to the inability of the IT teams to deliver the IT systems in what was essentially a 100% IT-driven strategy, and that this could be construed as a major contributor to failure. Without the intended tools, even if they had turned out to be irrelevant to people's everyday jobs, the KM initiative could not be implemented as strategically designed. There is no mention of the IT teams being held accountable. Many have pointed to IT-based approaches as the cause for failure. In how many instances was it more a case of IT not fulfilling on its part of the deal, rather than the KM strategy per se failing?

The adherence to technology has softened somewhat, and none but the most dedicated IT purist would consider that technology is the start and end solution to any organizational activity. As John Seely Brown and his coworker argue, problems cannot be solved through the use of information technologies alone, and that to try to do so is to make the error of conflating knowledge and information. Nonetheless, any casual online search for jobs in KM today quickly reveals that IT continues to be the defining hallmark. A recently advertised lectureship at a university, for instance, explicitly linked "KM" to "information systems" in the role's title. Despite the debates around it, technology, as a specifiable, tangible resource, is perhaps an easier prescription to apply than some of what we will encounter in Chapter 4 on theory.

We have already noted how recent years have seen a marked shift toward a more ecological approach to KM with a more people-centric perspective. Haridimos Tsoukas, for instance, reasons that treating personal knowledge as a definable "thing" that can be withdrawn from the head of its owner and converted into explicit knowledge risks diluting the former's values. In part, this change in emphasis could be explained by the Web 2.0 phenomenon and its impetus for sharing, broadcasting, and socializing. But, in contrast to Panahi and his colleagues' perspective on Web 2.0 and tacit knowledge, it is perhaps more a case of web developments ushering in a new era of social networking tools that enable people to become push participants as opposed to passive pull voyeurs.

With KM's apparent obsession with technology from its earliest days, it is a compelling notion to consider that it is technology in the shape of social networks and media services that are again shaping KM's theory and practice. But, as ever, there are two sides to the coin. For instance, a research study into the causes of "wikifailure" in a research institution cautions strongly against making the assumption that Web 2.0 tools are the all-in-one solution in overcoming issues with knowledge sharing. Contrastingly, Prusak and Weiss' emphasis on social networks and new search technologies in facilitating effective KM sounds like support for a Web 2.0-based solution. They do, however, point out that one of the factors underlying "early wave" KM failures was the primacy given to technology. Note though that while their arguments and viewpoints are based on the somewhat slim evidence of anecdotes and references to other literature, the "wikifailure" study, albeit small scale, draws on original empirical evidence. On the point of the usefulness of evolving web technologies, "wikifailure" researchers Garcia-Perez and Ayres conclude that there is still much to understand about Web 2.0 technologies. If this is the case, then what chance for KM and "big data analytics," with the latter recently identified as constituting both a threat and an opportunity? (see Crane and Self, 2014, for a discussion).

In the alleged rush to take up new technologies and exciting applications, there is evidence that a schism is emerging in the KM field, between those who approach technology as the defining factor in KM and those who prefer a definition based on the conceptualization of its product—and the firm's most valuable asset—knowledge. Further, technologies continue to be an influential driver, but this paradoxically places KM in a position of risk: What will happen to KM as technologies continue to develop and evolve, opening radically new ways of leveraging their capabilities and contents? But from any perspective, should knowledge be managed at all?

2.6   SHOULD KNOWLEDGE BE MANAGED?

If knowledge is quintessentially social, as many have claimed, should it be managed? In particular, should it be managed, controlled, and ordered in the way that KM seems to suggest? These questions suggest a potential ethical issue. In his review of KM frameworks, researcher Peter Heisig finds that the most frequently discussed KM activities are knowledge transfer, generation, use, storage, management (e.g., organizing and classifying), and acquisition. These can all be understood as "control activities." (Note that this report, published in 2009 is based on data acquired in 2003 and is drawn from frameworks that include anything from an academic theoretical piece to a firm's published organizational strategy.)

Evidence of "control" is also found in a study by Sally Burford and her colleagues at the University of Canberra. They divide the literature into two discordant theoretical themes: the traditional approach contrasted with the practice-based approach. The traditional view emphasizes high-level organizational strategy, with work directed and knowledge controlled at every stage from production to use, and the role of manager as central to knowledge work. In contrast, the practice-based view has learning and knowing as embedded in everyday practices and experiences, from which knowledge emerges. In their opinion, it is the latter that is the more successful and practical approach. In other words, traditional KM is about decisions made by managers, and in this paradigm, knowledge simply slips through the organizational net. Connecting back to the question of interest, this view of the practice-based approach has some consistency with the findings of an interesting ethnomethodological study of how representatives of an alliance of organizations evolve into a distinctive and unified social entity through their everyday practices and sharing of experiences: they become a practice in their own right, *and there is no suggestion of any attempt to manage the group's knowledge.*

Stephen Gourlay raises the key point made here. In referring to the social nature of knowledge, he suggests that collective knowledge can also be viewed as behavior. In this sense, then, "(T)the issue of consciously influencing others' unconscious behaviors also raises important ethical questions" (2006: 1429). Among the few researchers who tackle the subject of ethics head on, Isabel Rechberg and her colleague at the Kent Business School, University of Kent in England, focus on the issue of ownership. They claim that this raises a conflict in that while employees have knowledge inside their heads (which they own), their employers require that they share it. Their reasoning suggests that this creates a tension in knowledge processes and potential ethical concerns in the organizational conduct toward those individuals. Their solution is a moral contract between employees and employers, suggesting that such a contract would lead to improved KM practices. That is however speculation, but at least they question the ethics of the assumption that organizations have rights to the contents of employees' heads.

The whole issue of the appropriateness of managing what some view as a social phenomenon, or as "sticky" to the individual, is sparsely covered in the literature and remains open to debate.

2.7 SUMMARY AND CONCLUSIONS

What can be concluded from these discussions on the constitution of KM is that commentators largely agree on the primary aims of KM, albeit often using differing terminologies, but disagree on where its primary emphases should lie and how KM should be practiced. This is in part explained by the difference of opinion in where KM finds its origins with Lambe, for instance, claiming that KM has ignored its real "parentage," with its connotations of a case of running before walking.

The multiple perspectives on KM's constitution raise a question over how the field can develop if its boundaries are so blurred—and changeable. However, it could be inferred from all of these perspectives that how an organization conceptualizes itself is a significant factor—perhaps an obvious one—in how it manages its most prized asset. We can see this in two ways: first in the apparent delineation between those who view learning as a subset of knowledge and those "knowledge organizations" that are inherently learning organizations. Second, we can see it the technology marker: the notion of whether the practice of KM is defined by technology or whether it is the conceptualization of knowledge that defines the practice. As a further marker for KM, the systemic/systems thinking approach, with its conceptualization of knowledge as a social phenomenon, accomplished in social interaction, which is a theme introduced in Chapter 1 and which recurs in successive chapters, raises clear implications for the management of knowledge.

All of these questions and debates indicate an apparent gulf between the academic field of KM and that of practice, which surely cannot help but add to the sense of a "disunified" field. This, in turn, raises the question of what scholars and theorists can offer to KM leaders and practitioners who, it seems, may not see the relevance of such avenues of debate—the issue of ethics, for instance, which is largely unresolved.

Perhaps the core lesson is that there is more to managing knowledge than digitization and ICT/IT and that an emphasis on these directions, like Barabba and colleagues' criticism of KM for an "inventorying approach," is largely responsible for KM failures. There is perhaps some substance to concerns that KM is too poorly distinguished from IT. But is KM just a passing management fad? The widely held belief in the values of knowledge, the billions spent on its management, and the growing numbers of publications and conferences would suggest that, despite what Vincent Barabba and his colleagues describe as the increasingly negative attitude toward KM, there is no terminal point on the near horizon.

FURTHER READING

Barabba, V., Pourdehnad, J. and Ackoff, R. (2002). Above and beyond knowledge management. In Choo, C. and Bontis, N. (Eds). *The Strategic Management of Intellectual Capital and Organizational Knowledge*. Oxford: Oxford University Press.

Hislop, D. (2010). Knowledge management as an ephemeral management fashion? *Journal of Knowledge Management*, 14, (6): 779–790.

Lambe, P. (2011). The unacknowledged parentage of knowledge management. *Journal of Knowledge Management*, 15, (2): 175–197.

Prusak, L. (2001). Where did knowledge management come from? *IBM Systems Journal*, 40, (4): 1002–1007.

Spender, J. (2002). Knowledge Management, uncertainty, and an emergent theory of the firm. In Choo, C. and Bontis, N. (Eds). *The Strategic Management of Intellectual Capital and Organizational Knowledge*. Oxford: Oxford University Press.

3

KEY ISSUES AND DEBATES

3.1 INTRODUCTION

This chapter continues the investigation of some of the key issues and debates in knowledge management (KM), which, it is claimed, have an absolute impact on what is managed and measured, what is researched, and what is theorized. Key points drawn in the previous chapter suggest that how an organization defines itself, or conceptualizes itself to use a broader term of reference, influences how it approaches the management of its knowledge. It is also concluded that, while many continue to emphasize the role of technology, now cast as a defining marker, too much emphasis in these directions is implicated in KM failure. This is an issue that is particularly highlighted in the following discussions. On a positive note, there is a pragmatic case to be made for KM being more than just a passing management fad.

The chapter begins with a consideration of the "commodification and reification" issue. This leads into issues around KM's reported high rates of failure. As it turns out, the difficulty in the measurement of KM failure or success is itself identified as a failure factor. With a brief pause to consider the role of culture themed around the question of whether "one size fits all," the discussions move onto a discussion of two of the most significant debates in KM, namely, creating and sharing knowledge. Again, as we have already seen elsewhere, what we find is a multiplicity of perspective and approach. The subject of "knowledge sharing" (KS) is of particular interest given that it represents a more practical focus of study as opposed to, for instance, new knowledge creating. Consequently, we highlight some of the key factors reported in the literature as influencing, in some way, KS practices. These factors collectively establish some early and novel directions for the research which forms the central topic of Part Two.

Knowledge and Discourse Matters: Relocating Knowledge Management's Sphere of Interest onto Language,
First Edition. Lesley Crane.
© 2016 John Wiley & Sons, Inc. Published 2016 by John Wiley & Sons, Inc.

3.2 THE COMMODIFICATION AND REIFICATION OF KNOWLEDGE

A significant feature of the traditional perspectives on KM is the commodification and reification of knowledge. The field is largely split on its views on this issue with some claiming that it leads to poor practice, while others see it as a business opportunity. For instance, Professor Linda Smith of the University of Auckland, in her paper on research-ing ethnic minorities, concludes somewhat pessimistically that far from being inspired by the pursuit of knowledge, the knowledge economy has the goal of turning knowledge into a commodity, which is perhaps inappropriately referred to as "knowledge creating." As if to evidence her point, Kazuo Ichijo of Hitotsubashi University, a colleague of Nonaka's, defines KM as the process of sharing, creating, protecting, and discarding knowledge: this arguably constructs it as an object of value to be traded and leveraged. But where does this notion come from?

An early clue is found in writer, professor, and management consultant Peter Drucker's visionary paper on the nature of future organizations. He predicts that an organization of 20 years hence would have fewer tiers of management, relying instead on "knowledge workers" who would be seen as specialists. It is difficult to work out which year Drucker had in mind, as while the paper was originally published in 1988, this version is taken from a 1998 publication, and there is no evidence to support any variation, or not, bet-ween versions. He was either, then, referring to 2008 or 2018. The reader may be the judge of whether his prediction finds an echo in the modern organization's environment. On this note, from a modern perspective, Drucker rather quaintly draws positive synergies between this future organization and the workings of the Indian Raj and UK's National Health Service. The latter is frequently painted by the UK media as being on the verge of total collapse.[1] As well as being among the first to introduce the notion of the "knowledge worker," Drucker also gives a radical definition of knowledge:

> Information is data endowed with relevance and purpose. Converting data into information thus requires knowledge. And knowledge, by definition, is specialized. (1998a: 5)

It is the latter statement coupled with the notion of specialist knowledge workers that per-haps unintentionally set the commodification of knowledge in motion. In Drucker's vision, workers are the ones who will do the majority of work, and they will do this because they are specialist. Moreover, specialists are needed by the transformation that technology—principally IT—is bringing to the workplace. One interpretation of Drucker's vision suggests that it is the knowledge specialists who are the "commodity" rather than the knowledge that they possess. A "devil's advocate" might argue, however, that it was Sir Francis Bacon (1561–1626) who laid the foundation stone for the commod-ification of knowledge when he allegedly described it as "power."

By the mid-1990s, the commodification of knowledge had become deeply entrenched, which is consistent with the chronology of development referenced in Chapter 1. Knowledge had become labeled as the essential feature of the successful company, linked to innovation abilities and capabilities, competitive edge, and indeed just about any other positive attribute of an organization that one can think of. As Spender and Grant

---

[1] See, for instance, the BBC's report on "collapsing hospitals": http://www.bbc.co.uk/news/health-19577489 [Online]. Accessed March 26, 2014.

summarize, knowledge had become acknowledged as the main source of "economic rent," and its management had become a major force in business thinking.

If a product can be a commodity with a value, does it necessarily follow that it must be seen as an object? Not necessarily: it is more tied to how the product is treated. In their study of the role and importance of context to knowledge, Mark Thompson and his colleague are particularly critical of Nonaka's approach to knowledge, which, in their opinion, reifies it as an object. This is arguably a point of interpretation as Nonaka does not make a direct reference to the reification of knowledge. The implication of "reification" mainly emerges because of the knowledge conversion process that lies at the heart of his SECI model. This is explored in greater detail in Chapter 4.

Another way in which knowledge has been commodified and reified is through the emphasis on technology. There are countless critics of the brand of KM which lays too much before the altar of ICT and IT. As noted elsewhere, there has been a recent shift of emphasis toward a "softer" view of KM, mainly stemming from the turn to knowledge as social action. But it would be redundant to insist that technology plays no part in KM. Indeed not only do many credit technologies as major drivers behind KM (as seen in Chapter 2), but technology is today a ubiquitous, vital, and embedded part of most organizations.

Ironically, alongside these ideas and arguments over the commodification and reification of knowledge, against a backdrop of general agreement over its importance to organizational success, there are ongoing questions over KM's future. Have Grover and Davenport been proven correct when they predicted that KM, if it realizes its full potential, should eventually become so embedded in the organization that it is all but invisible. Invisible or simply not there? This leads to a review of successes and failures.

3.3   DETERMINING SUCCESS OR FAILURE

In their review of the historical and contemporary developments in KM, Laurence Prusak and his colleague conclude that around 50% of the initial KM implementations in organizations failed for a variety of reasons: too much emphasis on technology, a failure to link KM initiatives to organizational strategy, a one-size-fits-all approach, and, of particular interest here, a lack of focus on the social aspects of trust and relationships. This finding, while drawing on no more than anecdotes and references to other literature, is consistent with the period in which knowledge is predominantly seen as a commodity. Their final point will also be shown to have some gravitas based on the research reported in Part Two. Incidentally, Prusak and Weiss do not specify *how* they define "failure." Building on Prusak and his colleague's initial point, researcher Rosina Weber notes 15 failure factors in her literature review focusing on repository-based KM approaches: she concludes that attempts to build a "monolithic organizational memory" are doomed. Based on her analysis, she cautions against approaching technology as the "silver bullet."

A particularly fascinating case study of "KM failure" is reported by Ashley Braganza of the UK's Cranfield School of Management and his colleague, featuring US pharmaceutical giant PharmaCorp. This case study was touched on in the previous chapter in the discussions around technology as a "defining push factor." In the mid-1990s, the company's top executives took the decision to implement a KM initiative in the face of what were seen as growing problems with order handling operations. The initiative was given the highest priority, full funding, direct reporting access to the board, and a high profile within the organization. Yet within a couple of years, the project was deemed to have failed, and the KM team shut down. Why?

Braganza and his coworker draw out a number of lessons (which should be mandatory reading for any KM initiative leader), but perhaps the most interesting center around a failure to link the initiative to the everyday jobs that people do, the poor and unmaintained nature of "knowledge" stored in IT repositories, the transition from an "informal" KM project team to a formal "business line," as well as the "turf wars" that broke out between the KM team and the IT teams. But perhaps most significant of all is that this KM initiative was entirely dependent on the introduction of new seamless IT throughout the business: this was never delivered. From a simplistic perspective, that is the responsibility of the IT department. Without its plank, the KM initiative, as strategically envisioned, could not work. Yet it was the KM team that took the "wrap."

The lesson learned here is that when KM failure is reportedly blamed on an overreliance on IT, it is worth reflecting on whether that is because it was strategically misdirected or whether its tactical foundation failed to materialize. This conclusion finds support in other studies, particularly where KM initiatives are solely focused on ICT projects. Another example is a research project that investigated the use of a custom-built "Wiki" as a KS environment for academic researchers. Despite the academics' involvement in its design, and stated intentions to use it, the Wiki failed over time through lack of use. The researchers unpick the reasons, finding that lack of time and inertia are key factors resulting in low contributor rates and visit duration. Elsewhere, researchers investigate how Chinese culture affects KM practices, finding that a company website established as a formal KS platform attracted little use. In fact, most of the contributors to their study were not even aware of its existence. Note, though, that both of these studies use participant interviews as part of their research data and these, as noted in Chapter 1, are potentially susceptible to researcher bias.

Harvard Business School Professor David Garvin, in his critical focus on learning and knowledge-creating organizations, offers a rather unique perspective on failure. Claiming that there have been more failed programs than successes, which is largely consistent with other findings, Garvin suggests that it is the scholars with their "near mystical terminology" who are largely to blame for this failure. They have been too quick to jump on "…the bandwagon, beating the drum for 'learning organizations' and knowledge-creating companies" (1998: 49). (Interestingly, in the same collection of edited papers, another contributor pins the blame on consultants who, the authors imply, will sell your secrets to other firms!) Too much emphasis has been placed on knowledge creation, Garvin claims, and not enough on its application. More recently, research has shown a KM failure rate of up to 70%. Ilkka Virtanen of the University of Tampere in Finland bluntly ascribes KM failure as due to popular theories of KM being simply wrong. This suggests that in the near two decades since Garvin pinned the blame on scholars, little has changed.

A further explanation for KM failure is arguably due to traditional thinking. In their review of the field, Angela Burford and colleagues find that organizations ingrained in traditional thinking (or as Vincent Barabba and his coworkers describe it, industrial-age thinking) have a tendency to objectify knowledge (in one organization, the "knowledge repository" became known as the "information junkyard") and to force the establishment of communities of practice rather than allowing these to emerge ecologically. Interestingly,

Nonaka refers to the informal community as the location of emergent knowledge and new ideas, but then proposes that, because these are so important, they should be related to the formal hierarchical structure of an organization. This should surely lead to a formalization of these communities, which is precisely what Burford and her colleagues suggest leads to failure.

To round off the catalogue of failure factors, other studies have concluded that the lack of a KM culture, limited top management commitment and lack of supportive leadership, resistance to change, lack of worker involvement, and poor usability of KM systems are all implicated. With direct reference to the popular *Theory of the Knowledge-Creating Firm*, a report by Kenneth Grant and his coworker concludes that initiatives designed to convert tacit to explicit knowledge are equally likely to fail.

All of this paints a fairly depressing picture of KM and the jobs of KM practitioners. However, there is an important mitigating factor. This evidence is drawn from a wide range of studies, many of which can be criticized in, for instance, their use of secondhand data (e.g., case studies drawn from the literature). This raises the implication of interpreting someone else's interpretation, with who knows how many layers of interpretation underlying the latter. Additionally, case studies are often presented without dates raising the possibility that the researchers' conclusions are based on old data. The upshot is that for each reported failure, one could probably produce a success story. It is also worth raising the issue of motivation to report success or failure: typically one would expect scholars in particular to be more likely to report success rather than failure, but there is a suggestion here that the opposite is the case. The field could consequently be skewed.

Despite these points, a broad conclusion that can be drawn is that early KM initiatives were not entirely successful perhaps largely because organizations latched onto the tangible, digestible, measurable features of KM such as the introduction of new ICT. But what of measurement: the apparent inability to show measurable benefits is itself indicated as a failure factor, something that I picked up in a previous study of a KM managers' discussion forum in which practitioners' concerns are contrasted with key questions in the KM academic field.

3.4 MEASURING KNOWLEDGE MANAGEMENT OUTCOMES

Very little exists, certainly in the academic literature, in terms of robust and tested methods for measuring the success or failure of KM initiatives. This is not surprising given the difficulties over definition: if the subject of measurement is not well specified, how can it be measured?

This is further compounded when one considers the multiplicity of perspective on what exactly constitutes KM. An intriguing exception is offered by Jenny Darroch of the University of Otago in New Zealand: she claims to be the first to develop a scale for measuring KM behaviors and practices. This, she suggests, will help in the development of a theory of KM. The scale is specifically developed to measure behaviors in knowledge acquisition, dissemination, and responsiveness (use), and has allegedly been subject to rigorous development and validity testing. In the apparent absence of any other similar scale, this particular work stands out uniquely as a scientifically based, psychologically orientated empirical work. A point to note though is that while she makes much of the definition of KM, she does not discuss or define its product.

Taking a different approach, another exception involves measuring five organizational factors—strategy, people/HRM, IT, quality, and marketing—deemed to be critical to effective KM. In a review of the literature, the report finds that motivation and reward have notable impacts on KM and that an environment that facilitates trust is essential. This study by Pieris Chourides and colleagues at the University of Derby, England, uses surveys and interviews limited to private sector firms, finding little hard evidence to back the *perception* that KM leads to improved performance, claiming that performance measures are not well developed. Additionally, they emphasize the need to be able to demonstrate unambiguous links between KM and the "bottom line." The idea of KM leading to improved performance as being little more than a perception finds support in a more recent study by Ragab and his colleague. Their review of work in the field concludes that while a causal link between KM and performance is widely proposed, there is little research that would evidence this. Secondly, they speculate that the impetus for KM measurement emanates from the "billions" spent on its activities, and thirdly, based on their analysis of some 350 published works, they conclude that there is as yet no convincing method of measuring performance, echoing the conclusion of Chourides and his colleagues.

This difficulty in measuring KM impacts and outcomes is a point of ongoing debate, arguably underlined by the problems with knowledge and KM definition, but is also suggestive of an apparently enormous amount of belief in a business practice with limited evidence of its ability to deliver.

3.5 KNOWLEDGE MANAGEMENT AND CULTURE

The theme of culture is discussed in more detail in subsequent chapters, so here the sides of the debate are positioned in overview. The principal question concerns whether "one size can fit all." Can a framework or theory and its associated practice that is allegedly shown to work in, for instance, a Japanese culture, transmit, translate, and operate effectively in other cultures? However, the question is further complicated in that it is not just concerned with national culture but also organizational culture, even culture at the level of group. Thus, the notion of "culture" can be understood to refer to societal culture in its wider meaning of "context" (see also Section 1.4). A number of research studies provide some interesting and illuminating findings relevant to the "one size" question.

A recent empirical study that focuses on how Chinese national cultural factors influence KM practice in high-tech firms concludes that factors such as fear of losing face, hierarchy consciousness, and preference for face-to-face communications result in a general tendency to keep knowledge implicit but with a willingness to share informally. Arguably, one would find the same outcomes in Western firms but for different reasons. A study of Korean organizations similarly finds that cultural factors influence KM outcomes—in this case, intentions to share knowledge.

Others have investigated organizational factors on KM practice and outcomes. A study of 111 Spanish firms finds that organizational culture, leadership, and human resource practices affect KM practices on innovation outcomes. In his theoretical piece, Rajnish Kumar Rai of the Indian Institute of Management argues that organizational culture is critical in building and reinforcing new knowledge but admits that little is known about how this works. In their fascinating and revealing comparison of the effects of US and Korean culture on a single multinational, Yoo and Torrey perhaps unsurprisingly find major differences in KS behaviors between the two: Koreans tend to share knowledge in informal settings, while their American counterparts perceive their (formal) KM IT system as their primary vehicle for KS.

The results of these and other studies suggest that a one-size-fits-all approach will simply not work. Organizations vary considerably in structure, scope, culture—not forgetting language—and many other aspects such that a standardized approach will not deliver the desired KM outcomes. William Starbuck of Stern School of Business, New York University, makes a very good point when he reasons that organizations are not going to achieve the outstanding success and competitive edge that they seek by adopting a "one size" approach in attempting to copy the "properties" of others. Developing this perspective, innovative organizations are, by default, unique systems that emerge, evolve, and metamorphose as a consequence of their people, their products, their suppliers and partners, their markets, their temporal and geographic qualities, and so forth.

Culture understood in the wider sense of "context" influences KM and its outcomes on at least three interrelated levels: group, organizational, and national. From a psychological perspective, there is a fourth even more complex layer to this based on the theory of individual differences and social relationships, an idea touched on in a previous chapter (Section 1.3). In social psychology, mainstream research in the study of personality places considerable emphasis on measuring individual differences (e.g., variation in anxiety levels in response to tests) and the relationships between these. JC Spender hints at such differences when, drawing on Kant, he claims that knowledge is formed from individual sensory impression, implying its uniqueness to the individual rather than constituting some universally shared truth about the world out there. It is the subject of creating new knowledge that is turned to next.

3.6   CREATING NEW KNOWLEDGE

According to Peter Drucker, new knowledge is the superstar of entrepreneurship, a concept that would be difficult to challenge. In fact, the importance of new knowledge and its role in achieving and maintaining organizational competitive edge and in leveraging innovation—even allowing for the debates over its definition and substance—are generally accepted. The ongoing debate in the KM literature concerns the "how" based on an interpretation of the "what." Chapter 1 has already discussed issues around knowledge from a definitional standpoint and will, in subsequent chapters, go on to consider it from a theoretical one. Here, the concept of new knowledge creation is considered from a learning perspective.

Two assumptions can be drawn out from the KM literature (albeit themselves the subjects of debate). First, that new knowledge is generally created in social interaction between people with "social interaction" understood in the broadest sense. Second, the creation of new knowledge involves a learning process although the learning aspect of new knowledge in particular is underrated in the field of KM according to Max Boisot and others. For instance, John Seely Brown and his colleague, while emphasizing the role and importance of organizational communities of practice and the social nature of knowledge, make no reference to the learning process. It is also on these grounds that some scholars criticize Nonaka's theory of the knowledge-creating firm. More specifically, Frank Blackler draws attention to Nonaka's distinction between knowledge and learning that he considers a mistake. Similarly, by implication, David Garvin distinguishes between learning organizations and knowledge-creating companies, claiming that too much emphasis is placed on knowledge creating at the expense of knowledge application (with the inference that this application refers to learning). By contrast, one of the few empirical studies to focus specifically on organizational learning culture, involving 120 firms, finds that a learning culture positively affects knowledge process capabilities (defined as the capability to acquire knowledge, convert it, apply, and protect it).

Harvard scholar Dorothy Leonard, in her discussion on knowledge transfer, emphasizes the role of active learning through guided practice, observation, and problem solving. Her fundamental argument is that when knowledge is transferred from one person to another, it rarely remains identical to its original as the knowledge becomes mapped to the recipient's preexisting internal store of knowledge, experience, categories, and concepts. Thus, transferred knowledge effectively becomes new—and unique—knowledge to the recipient. It also implies that *any* transferred knowledge is in effect new knowledge to the recipient—even if the recipient "thinks he/she already knows it." People interpret data in different ways (data also being understood as "stimulus" and again invoking the notion of "individual differences"), according to Max Boisot. From this perspective, he claims that knowledge creation can be likened to problem solving through hypothesis testing and that this is fundamentally a learning process.

As a comparison, the learning process can be considered from the psychological perspective. Learning is structured as a subset of human memory that has been the subject of scientific study for more than a century. According to the psychologist Endel Tulving, memory is the ability to acquire, store, and use knowledge or information. Although memory is closely related to learning, Tulving differentiates between the two cognitive functions on the assumption that learning deals only with the first stage of memory—acquisition. One could argue that the differentiation is more complex than this: learning could be associated with retention and use of knowledge. Tulving, however, is referring to the cognitive process of learning as the stage of acquisition in what is otherwise formulated as a highly complex mental mechanism and process. As it stands, the process by which new knowledge (concepts) is learned is poorly understood. Nonetheless, considerable research in this field suggests that it is an individual's personal store of knowledge about the world, coupled with the predictability of language that is essential to making sense of the environment, that fuels the process of generating new knowledge. This is an important conjunction of concepts, which is returned to in Chapters 5 and 6.

Further insight can be drawn from a consideration of Bloom's Taxonomy first published in 1956 and subsequently revised by David Krathwohl, one of its originators, in 2001. Its original purpose was to create a kind of universal, hierarchical psychologically based matrix against which all learning objectives could be mapped and measured. It consisted of six elements, listed in terms of their relative and incremental complexity: evaluation, synthesis, analysis, application, comprehension, and knowledge. The revised version comprises two dimensions—knowledge and cognitive process. The knowledge dimension's substructures are "factual," "conceptual," "procedural," and "metacognitive." Those of the cognitive process comprise "remember," "understand," "apply," "analyze," "evaluate," and "create." This is a widely adopted framework within education and beyond (for instance, anecdotal evidence suggests the Taxonomy is often referred to in organizational learning strategy and design implementations) yet receives little attention in the KM field. What this framework represents is a description of the goals of education and their interrelationships.

A comparison of Bloom's Taxonomy (revised) with ideas about knowledge creation within the traditional approaches to KM suggests that the latter are overly simplistic. According to Bloom's Taxonomy, the creation of new knowledge is the pinnacle of a hierarchical, multitiered, corelational, and incremental cognitive process that recognizes four types of knowledge. Furthermore, these knowledge types are defined clearly within the Taxonomy—no mention of the tacit–explicit construct here. From the Bloom's Taxonomy perspective, knowledge is *a part* of the learning process, and new knowledge creation is *one outcome* of the process. Importantly, the significant implication of Bloom's Taxonomy is that knowledge *can* be managed, but from the learning process perspective. This turns us in the direction of KS, another major area of debate in KM.

3.7 SHARING KNOWLEDGE

One of the strongest organizational imperatives associated with KM is that of KS. Many scholars consider KS as key to improving organizational performance. From a common-sense perspective, the prospect of an organization in which its members do not share their knowledge either in conversation or in text would seem inconceivable. More specifically, KS is connected to competitive advantage, increased productivity; it is key to creating value, critical to innovation; KS supports response to change and quality improvements and contributes to new knowledge creation. The organizational practice of sharing knowledge is also linked to cost reduction. Based on all of these attributes, it would seem reasonable to propose that KM's success is reliant on KS as a focal and fundamental organizational activity.

One critic of this conventional view of the underpinning importance of KS is Max Boisot who claims that it is not knowledge that is shared but rather it is information. From a pragmatic perspective, his argument is somewhat weakened by the title of his work—*The Creating and Sharing of Knowledge*—and the impression that he uses the terms "knowledge" and "information" interchangeably. For instance, having argued that "…it is never knowledge as such that flows between agents, but rather data from which information has to be extracted and internalized" (2002: 72), he subsequently reasons that in order to share knowledge, there needs to be at least some degree of articulation of that knowledge. Setting this confusion to one side, he does offer an interesting and entirely plausible explanation for KS as signifying a "degree of resonance" between the "repertoires"—the expectations and behaviors—of two or more people. Boisot is one of the few who describe KS in terms of a process that is arguably indicative of the myriad issues associated with the definition of knowledge itself (see Chapter 1).

Evidence in support of KS as an advantageous organizational practice can perhaps more readily be seen in the battery of barriers, critical factors, and enablers thrown in its direction. Before taking up some of these issues, it is worth noting a compelling perspective offered by Thomas Suddendorf who we encountered in both of the previous chapters. Suddendorf claims that the instinct in humans to share knowledge is innate, irrepressible, and a significant underpinning feature and factor in human evolution—"… by linking our minds to those of others we have enormously increased our predictive capacities and powers of control" (2013: 158)—and that humans by their nature give preference to situations more likely to result in new information and understanding. From these perspectives, humans are born with the motivation to share their knowledge with others. Contrary to this view, a study of Korean organizations finds that extensive KS in organizations is the exception. What is going on? Youngjin Yoo of Case Western Reserve University and Ben Torrey of Accenture Inc. astutely identify the key question: "(I)if knowledge sharing is so universal an aspect of the human experience and critical to relationships, then why is there an issue when it comes to the organizational context?" (424)

One explanation is offered by M. Max Evans of McGill University in Canada, whose study focuses on the human social and cognitive factors affecting KS practices in a Canadian law firm. He reasons that because KS involves highly complex social interactions, influenced by trust and other sociocognitive factors, it is by its nature difficult. The point that he makes is that knowledge is not a commodity, and as such it cannot be "shared out" in the normal understanding of the action to share—in the sense of, say, a book or a DVD. He particularly focuses on the factors of trust, homophily (the tendency to associate and connect to others perceived as similar to oneself), shared language and vision, tie strength, and relationship length: the findings show that trust is the single most important influencing factor, followed by a "willingness to share" and shared vision. Interestingly, length of relationship is shown to have no effect, while tie strength and homophily have a minimal impact on KS. Signaling a word of caution, however, note that these findings are based on a study of a single Canadian firm, using self-reporting survey questionnaires, methods that we have elsewhere called into question. Despite any potential reservations regarding research methodology, this study offers some interesting and relevant insights. In particular, the importance of trust in KS activities is supported elsewhere in the KM literature, along with a mixed bag of other factors and features.

Any glance at the KM literature on the topic of KS reveals innumerable barriers and issues including what is described as the natural desire to store and hoard one's knowledge, costs associated with KS, and the threat of reputational damage. Some point to the lack of incentives to share, but contrastingly other scholars find that extrinsic rewards can work as a hindrance to KS. A study of Wiki use by Alexeis Garcia-Perez and Robert Ayres of Cranfield University in the United Kingdom finds that issues concerning time and a lack of critical mass are implicated in online community contexts. Others warn that low values placed on mentoring can particularly impede the sharing of tacit knowledge. In fact, there are so many barriers reported that one wonders if knowledge can ever be shared. Fortunately, a review of the critical and enabling factors reveals a more discernible pattern.

Technology is frequently connected to KS, distinguished by two contrasting perspectives. Garcia-Perez and his colleague, for instance, study KS behavior in the context of a research group's (failed) Wikipedia. They conclude that technology does not constitute the "silver bullet," a perspective shared by many others. In contrast, Michael Earl, professor of information management at the London Business School, claims that strategic KM success relies on recognizing the importance of communications networks implying the mediating effects of technology. Web 2.0/Enterprise tools are also claimed to be key enabling factors, although one proponent, perhaps controversially, suggests that their use must be controlled. Clearly, technology in some form has a role in KS—as it does in almost every aspect of the modern organization's operations. But technology is a tool of which the perceptive value is dependent on many factors. Consequently, the present discussions will not pursue this topic beyond these few points drawn from the literature, principally noting the debate's focus on the extent or otherwise of technology's role in delivering and mediating KS activities.

Culture (understood as "context": see Section 3.5) is also a frequently visited theme in debates specifically around KS. Earl's communications networks, mentioned earlier, imply a culture of mutual support as a critical factor to successful KS. Mutual support also suggests trust (a topic that starts to take on increasing importance as the ideas develop throughout this book). Others more explicitly implicate a culture based on trust: in their literature review and case study examining the effects of culture in KM practices in general, Yoo and Torrey draw an explicit relationship between KS, trust, integrity, and status. The importance of a trusting and mutually supportive culture can be seen as the explaining factor in some of the barriers noted earlier. For instance, without a trusting culture, one might very well be disposed to "protect" one's knowledge and guard against reputational damage.

Extending from there, we find a strong theme of the social world in accounts of what enables KS. Person-to-person communications in the form of regular meetings, physical proximity, and shared narratives are promoted as key—and commonsense—enablers. These have synergies with an emphasis on the social group, networking, and the idea of "density." A study of Spanish firms' sharing of best practices finds that coaching and leadership are important. There are of course many other factors mentioned in the KM literature: knowledge "stickiness," for instance, and "knowledge gaps," with the former relating to difficulties in sharing knowledge as a result of problems in separating it from its source (host) and the latter referring to differences in the knowledge of transmitter and receiver. What can be drawn from all of these perspectives is that barriers and enablers (collectively referred to hereafter as "KS factors") are rooted in fundamental organizational practices, suggesting both the contextual (see Section 1.4 for a discussion around the importance of context) and foundational nature of KS behavior.

A closer analysis of these factors suggests that these can be related to one or more of four thematic categories: trust, risk, context, and identity. The first two, as we have seen in the previous discussions, are explicitly referred to in the KM literature on KS. The third, context, can be applied to those factors that refer to the action environment and its associated social norms such as those relating to "culture." The final category, identity, while not specifically referenced in the accounts of KS, is embedded to factors such as leadership, the urge to store and hoard personal knowledge, and the threat of reputational damage, for instance. Table 1 makes this mapping explicit.

These mapping categories are positioned as psychological phenomena. All that has been done here is to organize this lengthy list of claimed influencing factors in KS into a pattern of subjective psychological phenomena. This mapping is itself admittedly subjective and interpretive in that the factors are drawn from multiple different authors, each of which has their own aims and agenda. The general heuristic adopted has been to regard each factor as emanating from perceptual experience and to ask, in the case of "shared narratives," for instance, given that it is one's perception that leads one to understand this as an experience of shared narratives, what are the psychological phenomena that might give rise to this. In the case of shared narratives, context, identity, and trust are conjectured to be the phenomena that are intrinsic to an understanding of the activity of "shared narratives."

TABLE 1 Knowledge Sharing Factors Mapped to Thematic Categories of Context, Identity, Risk, and Trust

KS Factor	Mapped Category
Naturally store and hoard knowledge	C I RT
Lack of incentives to share	C
Extrinsic rewards act as a hindrance	C
Trust, integrity, and status as key to KS	I T
Culture of mutual support	C I T
Trusting culture/climate	C T
Reputational risk	C I R T
Coaching	C I T
Leadership	C I T
Values placed on mentoring	C R T
Associated costs of KS	C R
Threat of reputational damage	C I R T
Time-diverting work time away from real work	C R
Lack of personal recognition	C I R T
Lack of critical mass	C R
Regular person-to-person communications	C I T
Physical proximity	C
Shared narratives	C I T
Emphasis on social groups (networking, density)	C I T

C, context; I, identity; R, risk; T, trust.

3.8 SUMMARY AND CONCLUSIONS

The discussions over the "commodification and reification" issue unsurprisingly reveal polarized views. This raises an interesting question: if how the organization is conceptualized influences how it approaches the practice of KM, as suggested in the previous chapter, is a reified account of knowledge the variable outcome of "conceptualization–influence"? That is, how an organization views itself as a determinant of how it approaches the management of its knowledge will also determine *what* it manages. Or is a reified perspective of knowledge the starting point? Which comes first, the chicken or the egg? In other words, if the starting point is a view of knowledge as object, with KM strategy sensibly organized around this concept, is there any point at which this is mapped to the conceptualization of the organization itself? Could it be that misalignments in this particular organizational narrative are an underlying cause of KM failure? That can only be considered as speculation.

Leading on from this speculation, the debates and questions around KM success or failure are interesting if for no other reason than that little account is given for what such success or failure actually looks like. There is also the potential that "blame" for failure is apportioned in the wrong direction. Nonetheless, according to the various case studies and reviews featured here, there is a theme of high rates of failure with reasons variously ascribed to organizational strategy (e.g., too much emphasis on technology, lack of supportive leadership and disassociation from central organizational strategy, a reliance on "traditional thinking"), economic impact (e.g., lack of measureable benefits and an impact on working time), and sociopsychological factors (e.g., a lack of focus on the social aspects of knowledge work such as trust and relationships and resistance to change). We have however raised a question over where this evidence comes from and how it has been interpreted: is there a tendency to prioritize the reporting of "bad news" rather than success stories?

The issue over difficulty in the application of a robust measurement to KM activities is not only categorized as a failure factor in its own right, but also results in a lack of supporting evidence for KM as an advantageous organizational practice. The assumption of the connections between KM and increased performance is, for instance, claimed to be based on no more than a perception. That is arguably a theme that could be applied to all of the foregoing. Also indicated as a failure factor, the "one size fits all," seen from the cultural perspective, is claimed to be ineffective due to the complexities and variation in national cultures. It is further suggested that this variation persists at the organizational, group, and individual levels, as understood from the wider viewpoint of "context." On a more positive note, what can be inferred from these claims and debates is that "context" influences KM. That being the case, then it stands to reason that a "check box approach" lacks credibility. KM as a practice, in this sense, cannot be treated as an "off-the-peg, ready-to-wear" suit.

The discussions around new knowledge creation and sharing knowledge generally reprise similar issues to those raised elsewhere. It is interesting to note that while the literature considered here spans a period from the late 1980s to the present, the same issues are shown to recur. With reference to knowledge creation, an important conjunction of four human factors is identified: the idea that a person's individual store of knowledge, mediated by the predictability of language, is what enables sensemaking in the social world, and this results in the generation of new knowledge (to the individual).

This has some synergy, albeit loosely, with the factors shown to be implicated in KS, which are themselves mapped to the four thematic categories of trust, risk, context, and identity. In most cases, each factor maps to more than one KS category, and this suggests a potential for corelation. For instance, "leadership," "shared narratives," and "trusting climate" map to the same categories, which open a question of whether these categories are corelational in KS actions. Arguably, the same set of categories could be applied to factors claimed to be implicated in KM failure. From a pragmatic perspective and for the purposes of the research presented in Part Two, the practice of KS—rather than KM failure, for instance—represents a more viable and accessible focus. Thus, these thematic categories become a focal point of investigation.

This chapter has critically reviewed and discussed some of the most significant and influencing debates and questions in KM and in particular has identified a set of thematic categories of particular interest. The following chapter engages with the KM theory. To bring some constructive order to what is found to be a substantial field, theories are organized onto two bisecting continua relating to "knowledge as object versus knowledge as social action" and "personal knowledge versus organizational knowledge." Support is found for some of the social themes already uncovered in this and the preceding two chapters. The discussions around theory particularly look for indications of the KS thematic categories.

FURTHER READING

General

Braganza, A. and Mollenkramer, G. (2002). Anatomy of a failed knowledge management initiative: lessons from PharmaCorp's experiences. *Knowledge and Process Management*, 9, (1): 23–33.

Darroch, J. (2003). Developing a measure of knowledge management behaviours and practices. *Journal of Knowledge Management*, 7, (5): 41–54.

Garcia-Perez, A. and Ayres, R. (2010). Wikifailure: the limitations of technology for knowledge sharing. *Electronic Journal of Knowledge Management*, 8, (1): 43–52.

Krathwohl, D. (2002). A revision of Bloom's taxonomy: an overview. *Theory into Practice*, 41, (4): 212–218.

Examples of KM literature that support the thematic categories identified with knowledge sharing.

Identity

Akhavan, P. and Pezeshkan, A. (2013). Knowledge management critical failure factors: a multi-case study. *VINE*, 44, (1): 22–41.

Bock, G., Zmud, R., Kim, Y. and Lee, J. (2005). Behavioural intention formation in knowledge sharing: examining the roles of extrinsic motivators, social-psychological forces, and organisational climate. *MIS Quarterly*, 29, (1): 87–111 (also Trust, Risk and Context).

Rechberg, I. and Syed, J. (2013). Ethical issues in knowledge management: conflict of knowledge ownership. *Journal of Knowledge Management*, 17, (6): 828–847 (also Risk).

Venkitachalam, K. and Busch, P. (2012). Tacit knowledge: review and possible research directions. *Journal of Knowledge Management*, 16, (2): 356–371.

Trust

Earl, M. (2001). Knowledge management strategies: toward a taxonomy. *Journal of Management Information Systems*, 18, (1): 215–233 (also Context).

Evans, M. (2013). Is trust the most important human factor influencing knowledge sharing in organizations? *Journal of Information & Knowledge Management*, 12, (4): 1350038 (17 pages).

Leonard, D. (2007). Knowledge transfer within organisations. In Ichijo, K. and Nonaka, I. (Eds). *Knowledge Creation and Management: New Challenges for Managers*. Oxford: Oxford University Press (also Context).

Lin, T. and Huang, C. (2010). Withholding effort in knowledge contribution: the role of social exchange and social cognitive on project teams. *Information & Management*, 47: 188–196 (also Context).

Prusak, L. and Weiss, L. (2007). Knowledge in organizational settings: how organizations generate, disseminate, and use knowledge for their competitive advantage. In Ichijo, K. and Nonaka, I. (Eds). *Knowledge Creation and Management: New Challenges for Managers*. Oxford: Oxford University Press (also Context).

Yoo, Y. and Torrey, B. (2002). National culture and knowledge management in a global learning organization. In Choo, C. and Bontis, N. (Eds). *The Strategic Management of Intellectual Capital and Organizational Knowledge*. Oxford: Oxford University Press (also Context).

Plus see above listings.

Risk

Alguezaui, S. and Filieri, R. (2010). Investigating the role of social capital in innovation: sparse versus dense networks. *Journal of Knowledge Management*, 14, (6): 891–909.

Leonard, D. and Sensiper, S. (2002). The role of tacit knowledge in group innovation. In Choo, C. and Bontis, N. (Eds). *The Strategic Management of Intellectual Capital and Organisational Knowledge*. Oxford: Oxford University Press.

Plus see above listings.

Context

See above listings.

4

KNOWLEDGE MANAGEMENT'S THEORIES*

4.1 FINDING SOME NEW DIRECTIONS

What has been uncovered so far is a highly complex landscape, not least in the diversity of opinion over the nature of knowledge itself. This single issue is shown to impact on most if not all of the other debates in knowledge management (KM): for instance, the definition of KM, ethical issues associated with the management of knowledge, the commodification and reification of knowledge, reportedly high failure rates, the question of how to measure knowledge outcomes, whether knowledge is personal or organizational, or both, and cultural specificity. In considering two of the most prominent themes in KM besides that over the definition of knowledge—knowledge creating and sharing—we find that the diversity of perspective on the former lies behind the variety of claims in respect of influencing and impacting factors in both of these themes. All of these issues, it has been suggested, have potential consequences for research and practice. If the definition of knowledge is the subject of such considerable debate, what of KM's theories?

It seems that KM finds its origins in many different disciplines, which might imply a broad theoretical spectrum. We can see early evidence of this in an ambitious survey of 160 KM frameworks by the researcher Peter Heisig (see also Sections 1.2 and 2.6). He uses a statistical content analysis method to identify how these frameworks approach three issues: how knowledge is understood, knowledge management activities, and identification of critical success factors in KM. Of particular interest, top success factors

* Elements of this chapter are published: Crane, L. (2013). A new taxonomy of knowledge management theory and the turn to knowledge as constituted in social action. *Journal of Knowledge Management Practice*, 14, (1).

Knowledge and Discourse Matters: Relocating Knowledge Management's Sphere of Interest onto Language, First Edition. Lesley Crane.

are categorized as "human orientated" (e.g., culture, people, and leadership), "organization," and "technology," which has resonance with mainstream thinking. References to context, environment, and learning are found to be absent. This absence, as the directions of this and subsequent chapters illuminate, is significant. Still, the finding of a broad consensus on the importance of human factors in KM success is encouraging, if a little obvious. Knowledge would not "exist" without people nor would organizations for that matter. This is nonetheless one of the few studies that attempts to rationalize the theoretical landscape.

Writing in 2001, Thomas Grover and his colleague predicted that KM would melt into the fabric of the organization becoming part of the daily operations and strategies. Do KM's theories steer its practice along this course? This chapter investigates some of the most influential and popular theories (and some which should have been), showing how one in particular has dominated for more than two decades despite its alleged flaws and misrepresentations. Theories are classified according to a novel taxonomy of theory to better enable the comparing and contrasting of various paradigms: classification criteria are "knowledge as social action" versus "knowledge as object" and a focus on the "organizational level of analysis" versus a focus on the "personal level". It draws on a critical review of almost 50 theories and frameworks. In particular, the taxonomy illuminates what could be seen as a growing trend toward a view of knowledge as accomplished in social action and bound to context. "Context" has been identified in the previous chapter as one of the four categories of knowledge sharing (KS).

The practical aims and objectives of the following discussions are (i) to provide managers and organizational leaders in particular with a "ready-reckoner" to assist in the identification of theories of interest and compatibility with their own organizational strategies and (ii) to offer a compass of theory to rationalize both navigation and analysis. The overall ambition is to investigate and analyze KM theory with the aim of identifying trends, themes, and gaps, which can, in turn, be used to determine potential new directions for the field of KM.

The discussions begin with a brief discussion around what constitutes a theory to set some preparatory groundwork. The main investigations and discussions are initiated with an introduction and explanation of the taxonomy of KM theory. Using this as a framework, we are able to compare and contrast theories classified at various points on the taxonomy's axes, highlighting those of particular interest and relevance. An entire section is devoted to what is described as the most influential and popular of all KM theories, *The Dynamic Theory of Organizational Knowledge Creation* and its various developments. In particular, the investigations address the principle ways in which this theory is criticized.

This chapter's penultimate section briefly discusses what is meant by inductionism, explaining how, from these perspectives, the most influential KM theory, and indeed many others, may be questioned on matters of validity, for instance. The chapter concludes with four primary conclusions based on the foregoing analysis. First, that there is a significant trend toward a view of knowledge as social action (a theme that has been highlighted in previous chapters), and which is rooted to context, and that "social action" can be understood as discourse (talk and text) in social interaction. Second, it is claimed that those theories classified as approaching "knowledge as social action" implicate in some way the KS thematic categories of identity, trust, risk, and context, while those which approach "knowledge as object" are more ambiguous. Third, although many theorists emphasize the central role of language and communication as the site of knowledge work, discourse itself is largely ignored as a serious location for research. Fourth, a theory of language is found to be all but absent from the KM field. This leads to the overall conclusion that focusing on research and analysis on organizational discourse, informed by a theory of language, holds the potential for a different approach to KM.

4.2 WHAT CONSTITUTES A THEORY?

Any investigator of the KM theoretical literature quickly becomes aware that there is relatively little use of the word "theory." Instead, many use terms such as "framework." Why the reticence? Patrick Lambe (private correspondence) suggests that it is the incommensurate, discipline-specific languages that underpin KM together with the lack of a single body of integrated theory, which leads to this unusual absence. The conventional scientific understanding of the meaning of "theory" is that it is an explanation and prediction about a state of affairs given a certain set of circumstances and that such predictions can be empirically tested and shown to be statistically probable or not. If this understanding of theory is adopted, then arguably quite a lot of what is loosely grouped together as KM "theory" would be considered problematical. So, a "looser" agenda is needed, opening the possibility of accepting as theory any work that describes itself as such or as a framework. However, the absence of the category "theory" is not the only absence.

A further observation of the KM theoretical literature is the reliance—as evidence—on what others have reported rather than the evidence of first-hand empirical research data. For instance, Tsoukas, in his robust arguments for a phenomenological framework of tacit knowledge, bases his principle largely on an exposition and interpretation of what Michael Polanyi wrote on the subject with no obvious reference to empirical research. Maria Jakubik, of the University of Applied Sciences in Finland, offers a new framework based around the notion of "becoming to know," as a replacement *in part* of Nonaka and Takeuchi's theory of the knowledge-creating firm. The evidence in support of her proposal is drawn from what others have theorized rather than empirical research findings. Where frameworks or theories do draw on evidence from field research, this tends to be of relatively limited scope in terms of, for instance, sample sizes or in their reliance on secondhand or anecdotal data.

There is in fact little evidence of empirical testing of KM theory. A recent review of 2175 journal articles published in the KM field reports the somewhat "shocking statistic" that only 0.33% of research actually involves field studies (see Further Reading). One notable exception is a study by Nonaka and coworkers, which investigates the hypothesis at the heart of Nonaka's theory of organizational knowledge-creating. The study is based on an opportunity sample of 105 Japanese businessmen attending a seminar, and uses self-reporting questionnaires. The findings, it is claimed, provide strong support for the theory: "(T)tacit knowledge is thus mobilized through a dynamic 'entangling' of the different modes of knowledge conversion in a process which will be referred to as a 'spiral' model of knowledge creation" (1994: 342). It is not made clear how this conclusion can be drawn from returned questionnaires using Likert-like scales, nor whether there are any alternative viable explanations for the findings. Is this an indication that for decades knowledge practitioners may have been pursuing strategies based on limited evidence?

4.3   AN APPROACH TO KNOWLEDGE MANAGEMENT'S THEORIES: A NOVEL TAXONOMY

An earlier review of the theoretical literature by Despres and Chauvel counts 72 different KM theories: they report that while there is little universal agreement over the nature of knowledge, similar to Heisig's findings (see Section 1.2), there is a broad consensus across most theories that people are the cornerstone of KM (again, consistent with Heisig's conclusions, as mentioned earlier). According to Despres and his colleague, the majority of KM theories approach knowledge as a social construct, and this raises the notion of knowledge as action-orientated. Following this finding, but with the proviso of not being in agreement with all of their conclusions (e.g., that organizational knowledge does not exist), it is proposed here that KM theory can be organized into the bisecting continua of "organizational knowledge versus personal knowledge" and "knowledge as object versus knowledge as social action" (see Figure 1). This is based on a critical review of almost 50 KM theories. Interestingly, Spender offers a similar formula, splitting the KM field into two "radically distinct domains," one that unproblematically construes knowledge as object versus the other that not only rejects the whole idea of knowledge reification but also denies any transformation properties.

These continua are reflective of two of the most contentious debates in the theoretical literature: the question of whether knowledge should be approached from the perspective of it being personal or organizational, and whether it should be managed as an object, or approached as the product of social action. The former of these questions is the subject of some confusion, so will be returned to subsequently.

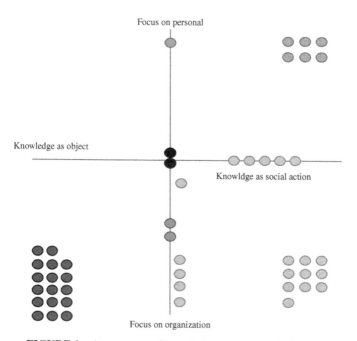

FIGURE 1   A taxonomy of knowledge management's theories.

The sampling of KM theory (48 in total) on which this taxonomy is based is certainly not exhaustive. Each point on the axes in Figure 1 represents a theory or framework. (Note that this categorization was originally published in 2013, based on 36 theories and frameworks: the version here is considerably revised and extended.) As can be seen, a clear majority of theories are located along the "knowledge as social action" axis (26, two of which are credited to Frank Blackler, and five of which are considered to be "border-line"). This is consistent with, for instance, Charles Despres and his colleague's findings in their review of KM theory. However, when one factors in that these are split based on their primary focus on personal or organizational knowledge, an inconsistency is revealed with the latter's finding that theory, in the main, disputes the existence of organizational knowledge. This taps that issue mentioned earlier—the confusion over organization versus personal knowledge.

Those theories located on the axis line itself are interpreted as bilateral—their focus is both on knowledge as personal/organizational or knowledge as object/social action. By contrast, the group of theories occupying the knowledge as object space (17, five of which are credited to work by Professor Ikujiro Nonaka and colleagues) are all committed to a focus on organizational knowledge—which is logical. If a theory reifies knowledge as an object, it seems reasonable to conclude that knowledge is approached as an object (asset) of the *organization*.

Table 2 shows the detail of the source for Figure 1, with all theories shown chrono-logically to allow for the analysis of developing trends. According to this sampling, it is obvious that since the early 1990s the focus of theory has been overwhelmingly on organizational knowledge. Almost hidden is a steady "trickle" of perspectives, which advocate a focus on personal knowledge. What can also be seen are two clearly demarked camps—those who posit knowledge accomplished in social action and those who take a reductive approach. So while the KM that is accredited to Nonaka and his colleagues has, beyond doubt, proved the most influential and best known, there has been—working alongside—a persistent voice offering a radically different perspective. But why has this perspective not been adopted in practice with at least equal enthusiasm to the other? Perhaps the reason for this is very simple: despite a majority of theories locating knowledge in social action, this is often the only thing they have in common. Consequently, the alternative viewpoint to that advocated by Nonaka, his colleagues and supporters, is a fragmented one.

Of course, this categorization of theory is entirely subjective in nature. It is not the case—unfortunately—that each author raises the rhetorical flag to mark their theory as treating knowledge as this or that, or that their focus is on organizational as opposed to personal knowledge. Such classifications are arrived at through an interpretive reading of the texts. As Paul Duguid succinctly points out in his treatise on the theory of Communities of Practice, no text is able to determine the rules of its own interpretation. In this view, no writer can precisely proscribe how the reader will interpret and understand their words, as this is in the minds of the readers. And that applies to all texts—whatever their nature.

The object/social action classification is based on how authors treat the subject of their theories: in some cases, notably Frank Blackler and Stephen Gourlay, the author expressly describes or implicates knowledge as social action, while with others it is more an inter-pretive choice based on the theorist's descriptive and action language used to describe knowledge and how it is managed. On the organization/personal classification, the inter-pretation is more straightforward: is the theory/framework more focused on one or the

TABLE 2 Specifies the Source for Figure 1

Authors (Year)	Main Focus	Focus on Organization	Focus on Personal	Objectifying	Social Action
Gaines (1989)	Knowledge acquisition		X		X
Nonaka (1991, 1994)[a]	The knowledge-creating company	X		X	
Blackler (1993)	Organizations as activity systems	X			X
Collins (1993)	The structure of knowledge	X	X		X
Blackler (1995)	Activity theory and "knowing"	X			X
Nonaka and Takeuchi (1995)	The knowledge-creating company	X		X	
Nonaka et al. (1996)	Technology in support of the knowledge-creating company	X		X	
Quinn et al. (1996)	Managing professional intellect	X		X	
Spender (1996)	Knowledge as the basis of a dynamic theory of the firm	X	X		X
Grant (1996)	Knowledge-based theory of the firm	X	X		X
Leonard and Straus (1997)	Creative abrasion	X (B)			X (B)
Drucker (1998a)	The coming of the new organization		X		X
Kleiner and Roth (1998)	Learning histories	X			X (B)
Nonaka and Konno (1998)	The concept of "Ba" as the foundation for knowledge creation	X		X	
Brown and Duguid (1999)	Architecture for organizational knowledge	X			X
Cook and Brown (1999)	Generative dance between organizational knowledge and organizational knowing	X			X
Wenger (2000)	Communities of practice and social learning systems	X			X
Markus (2001)	Theory of knowledge reuse	X		X	
Tsoukas and Vladimirou (2001)	Organizational knowledge	X	X		X
Earl (2001)	"Schools" of knowledge management	X		X	
Bhatt (2001)	Knowledge management as an interaction between technologies, techniques and people.	X		X	
Barabba et al. (2002)	The organization as a system	X			X
Choo (2002)	Organizational knowing	X		X	
Boisot (2002)	"I-Space": creating and sharing knowledge	X	X		X
Grant (2002)	Knowledge-based view of the firm		X	X (B)	X (B)
Leonard and Sensiper (2002)	Tacit knowledge and innovation: the "innovation funnel" theory	X	X		X (B)

Snowden (2002)	Complex acts of knowing: "Cynefin"	X		X	X
Jimes and Lucardie (2003)	Reconsidering the tacit-explicit Distinction: the functional view theory of tacit knowledge	X		X	X (B)
Schultze and Stabell (2004)	Theory-based framework of assumptions about knowledge and its management	X	X	X	X
Thompson and Walsham (2004)	Context as an inseparable art of knowing	X			X
Duguid (2005)	"The art of knowing": Communities of practice	X			X
Gourlay (2006)	Knowing how and knowing that	X			X
Lytras and Pouloudi (2006)	Framework for knowledge management from the learning perspective	X		X	X
Leonard (2007)	Transferring tacit knowledge within organizations	X		X	X
Prusak and Weiss (2007)	Importance of social groups	X			X (B)
Lee and Lan (2007)	Conversational collaboration and pillars of collaborative intelligence	X			X (B)
Ichijo (2007)	Knowledge enablers	X		X	
Buchel (2007)	Creation and transfer of tacit knowledge within organizations	X		X	
Nonaka and Toyama (2007)	Theory of the knowledge-creating firm	X		X	
Weber (2007)	A new framework to address failure factors in repository-based knowledge management initiatives.	X		X	
Ehin (2008)	Unmanaging knowledge workers	X		X	
Guzman (2009)	Practical knowledge—a framework		X		X
Burford et al. (2011)	The practice-based theory of knowledge	X			X
Jakubik (2011)	Framework for knowledge creation: Becoming to know	X	X		X
Rai (2011)	Integrative framework for organizational knowledge management and organizational culture	X		X	
Tsoukas (2011)	Phenomenological framework for tacit knowledge		X		X
Quintane et al. (2011)	Innovation as a knowledge based outcome: a new framework and definition	X	X	X	
Crane and Bontis (2014)	A new approach to tacit knowledge	X	X	X	

The "B" in brackets indicates that the selected classification is borderline.

"Nonaka's 1991 and 1994 papers are included as one because they are more or less the same work.

other, or is it focused on both? Admittedly, a different analyst may arrive at a different interpretation.

The debate around the "personal versus organizational knowledge" question is the subject of some confusion in the literature and consequently merits a brief discussion.

4.4 THE PERSONAL VERSUS ORGANIZATIONAL KNOWLEDGE QUESTION

Many have asked whether knowledge can only ever be personal, or can it be organizational. This is possibly something of a red herring question. It is in the nature of things that each individual has knowledge that is personal to them and, equally obviously, an organization consists of individuals. So what of organizational knowledge? In fact, some scholars are critical of the emphasis on "knowing organizations." Robert Grant, for one, suggests that such a conceptualization sidesteps the question on how individuals link their sets of knowledge to create this knowledge collective. Humans do not (yet) possess the ability to routinely connect their brains one directly to the other. So when some scientists talk about "linking our minds to others," they are not talking about extrasensory perception. Rather, what is being described is the essential human propensity for collaboration and cooperation. So what is meant by "organizational knowledge"?

Professor Haridimos Tsoukas and his coworker address this very question (we touched on this work in Chapter 1). In their theoretical piece, which uses a single case study to illustrate their theory in practice, they investigate the links between personal and organizational knowledge, and human action in organizational contexts. They suggest that the lack of a theory of organizational knowledge, not least of knowledge itself, is responsible for definitional difficulties. They also note that the work of Michael Polanyi, on which much of the KM theorizing is based as we have seen in previous chapters, has not been well engaged with. Tsoukas and his colleague's definition of personal knowledge is interpreted as the ability of the individual to apply their own understanding of context—consciously or not—and which ability mediates that individual's actions in a given context: for instance, the formulation of a judgment, the solving of a problem, and so forth. This is slightly difficult to digest, but becomes clearer when we consider Tsoukas and his colleague's formulation of organizational knowledge and their inferred distinction between this and personal knowledge.

Tsoukas and his coworker propose that organizational knowledge is the *process* by which people draw upon and act on a corpus of generalizations—generic rules produced by the organization, about which communities have shared meanings and based on which people formulate judgments. People understand these rules only by connecting them to their own informal judgmental capabilities, or personal knowledge. In this theory and interpretation, personal knowledge facilitates meaning for organizational knowledge, and which is inherently action-orientated. Recall Paul Duguid's formulation of "knowing how" and "knowing that" introduced in Chapter 1 with the former described as the "art of practice." In his thesis, "knowing how" informs or mediates knowing that, with the latter being incomprehensible without the former. Importantly, he also claims that "knowing that" does not produce "knowing how."

Accordingly, and in a simpler analysis, personal knowledge is the ability, with organizational knowledge representing a process. Organizational knowledge cannot function without the other. The similarities with Duguid's formulation are plain: personal knowledge equates to Duguid's "knowing *how*," which is the implicit ability to know how to act in a given set of circumstances, while organizational knowledge equates to his "knowing *that*," which is the codifiable, explicit dimension that, of necessity, requires knowing *how* in order to function. But, and this is where such comparisons and contrasts become slippery and prone to misinterpretation, Duguid's emphasis is on collectively shared knowledge, with the importance of a Community of Practitioners largely defined by its commonly shared tacit knowledge. Contrastingly, Tsoukas and his colleague emphasize the role of individual human judgment in arriving at "collective definitions." There is a sheet of paper between these two perspectives. Conflating and simplifying both theoretical perspectives, individuals possess knowledge of the world, often held and used without conscious awareness, and which is the essential ingredient in making sense of the world and its contents. Organizational knowledge is the codifiable stuff, which organizations can produce as explicit content, or as enacted in shared understandings of how to behave, for instance, in a given circumstance. In other words, personal knowledge brings meaning to organizational knowledge. Personal knowledge can be unique to the individual, and it can fuel communally shared meanings, but, from a psychological perspective, what a person "knows" is fundamentally singular to the individual.

There are two important points to draw here. First, that personal knowledge or "knowing how" and organizational knowledge or "knowing that," with an understanding of "organizational" in its broadest sense of community or even society, are tightly bound to one another with the latter dependent on the former for meaningful function. Second, Tsoukas and his coworker's theory of the relationship between personal and organizational knowledge can be interpreted as implicating the four thematic categories earlier related to KS: context, identity, trust, and risk. While noting that their ideas draw heavily on the philosophical literature—in this case, Polanyi—which they adopt uncritically, their base of evidence is limited to one single case study with no detail given of the research methods or means of analysis. But as a discussion of the *nature and relationship* of personal versus organizational knowledge, it is a robust piece of rhetoric.

Taking a wider perspective, Robert Grant gives a critical account of the Knowledge-Based View of the Firm (KBVF). According to Grant, KBVF was developed in the 1990s based on the resource/capability analysis of the firm, epistemology, and organizational learning, all of which, he claims, have their focus on the role of knowledge as a "factor in production." He argues that collective knowledge (viz., organizational knowledge) should be seen as an aggregation of the knowledge in people's heads. But he goes on to warn that a focus on organizational knowledge risks reducing knowledge to the status of object. Thus, defining rules, procedures and such like as knowledge runs the risk of muddying the processes by which shared knowledge is evolved through human interaction (socialization). The upshot, he concludes, is of little use to managers in aiding them to "influence" these processes.

This particular perspective can be contrasted with that described by John Seely Brown and Paul Duguid who give primacy to organizational knowledge over personal knowledge. The contrast between these two versions of the KBVF operates at a fundamental level: Grant argues that firms exist to coordinate teams of specialist workers so that their knowledge may be integrated (reminiscent of Peter Drucker's *The Coming of the New Organization*), whereas Brown and his colleague see the hard work of organizing knowledge as the important business of the organization. In their world, it is the firms that generate the knowledge with knowledge and practice inextricably linked. In Grant's view, it is the individual who is the knowledge creator with firms in the role of "knowledge structures." The key difference lies in the view of the organization: Brown and his coworker arguably perceive the organization as a "living system," which echo's Vincent Barabba and colleagues' view of the organization as a system of parts that cannot be reduced to its individual elements. The alternative view offered by Grant is of the organization as a collection of structures that presumably *could* be reduced to its parts. What both impress on is the importance of knowledge to firms' success, and an influencing role for technology.

So this is and is not a "red herring." Arguably, the literature conflates two questions: that of whether knowledge is personal or organizational and that of whether the *unit of analysis*, as the focus of research and theory, should be at the personal or organizational level. In the taxonomy of KM theory included here, the personal versus organizational axis refers to the unit of analysis, *not* the implied or explicit stance of any given theory on the location of knowledge. That being understood, what does the taxonomy reveal about KM theory?

4.5 THE PERSONAL VERSUS ORGANIZATIONAL KNOWLEDGE ON THE SOCIAL ACTION AXIS

This section focuses on those theories classified along the "knowledge as social action" axis, grouping these into themes of inquiry. It would be impossible to exhaustively address all of the theories contained in the sampling, so discussions focus on those that are considered to be of most relevance and interest.

4.5.1 Personal Knowledge as the Unit of Analysis

As discussed earlier, Robert Grant is critical of those who subscribe entirely to organizational knowledge and is one of the few who make a clear reference to the "unit of analysis," arguing that this should be the "person" not the organization. In this model, the goal is not knowledge transfer, but knowledge integration although one could argue that this is merely splitting hairs. Note, however, that Grant does not appear to dispute the existence of organizational knowledge, only that it should not be the focus of knowledge activities at the expense of personal knowledge.

Although the KBVF has been interpreted as a theoretical position, Grant himself questions whether it adds up to a singular theory. Nonetheless, according to Grant, it is the knowledge constitutive of persons that is the valued asset, and this can only be leveraged by integration through teamwork. By (borderline) implication, Grant, somewhat ironically, reifies knowledge as the object of integration mechanisms: rules and directives, sequencing, routines, group problem-solving, and decision-making. There is also a strong implication of the commodification of knowledge: "(K)knowledge is the overwhelmingly important productive resource in terms of market value..." (2002: 136). Yet, if one sets aside those particular references, Grant is also arguably casting knowledge as social action in his emphasis on (social) integration practices as key to managing knowledge.

4.5.2 Knowledge as Practice Contrasted with Knowledge as Possession

Whereas Grant invokes the discourse of possession, Scott Cook and John Seely Brown of the Xerox Palo Alto Research Center in California, in their peculiarly named *"generative dance"* theory, take issue with this whole idea. They argue that such a discourse, with its implication of knowledge as something that people have, is limiting because it emphasizes one type of knowledge (explicit) above the other (tacit), resulting in a growing literature with a habit of explicitly or implicitly labeling knowledge as a typology of one. While there may be some truth in the latter statement, subsequent discussions reveal an opposite analysis to the notion of personal knowledge emphasizing the explicit. While Cook and his coworker's theory is interpreted as approaching "knowing" as social action, their focus is more at *organizational* level in contrast to Grant's approach.

In opposing an epistemology of possession, Cook and his colleague argue for an approach that views knowledge as a tool of knowing, with knowing connected to how we interact with the world. In their thesis, it is the interaction between knowing and knowledge that leads to the creation of new knowledge and "ways of knowing." Thus, the term "generative dance" is coined and which is the source of all innovation. Their prescription is that knowledge is both used and grounded in action. Consequently, more attention should be paid to what knowledge work is done—in other words, practice. In effectively emphasizing knowledge accomplished in social interaction, and the action orientation of knowledge, are they that far apart from Grant's emphasis on social integration practices? Not really. Brown and his colleague do arguably soften their case by proposing that epistemologies of possession and practice, while completely separate, are not incompatible. This immediately begs the question of why one would want to introduce a novel theory while clinging on to the traditionalist view. Nonetheless, the notion of knowing as action done in social contexts with knowledge as the requisite tool is generally consistent with a long line of theoretical development stretching back to the early 1990s and on to the present day. What they do not do is offer a perspective on how those "social contexts" come into being. At the most common-sense interpretative level, this idea implicates both the KS thematic categories of context and identity as a minimum.

There are two other points of interest to draw from the *"generative dance"* work: their criticism of the traditional scientific view of knowledge as something that must be sought, found, and articulated—in other words, knowledge as object—and their strong disagreement with the proposal that tacit knowledge can be converted to explicit and vice versa. This is the conversion process that lies at the heart of the influential theory of the knowledge-creating firm. Yet despite their position on the conversion issue, Cook and his colleague group this theory along with a number of other works, describing them as provocative and insightful.

The "generative dance" framework can be compared and contrasted with that proposed by Gustavo Guzman, of Griffith University, Australia, whose theory is interpreted as focusing on personal knowledge. He investigates the nature of practical knowledge, finding two opposing positions on this question: one approaches practical knowledge as stored in people's heads, while the other sees it as situated in practice. Similarly to Cook and his coworker's treatment of the ideas of possession and practice Guzman reasons that the two positions are not mutually exclusive. His theory, which has the aim of clarifying the confusing diversity of opinion, underlines the synergies between the cognitive and practice dimensions of knowledge using a simple case to make his point: it is the users of rules (as one form of knowledge) who determine when and how to use those rules. Thus, he makes the connection between knowledge how and knowledge that. Perspectives on those two concepts and their relationship are returned to presently.

According to this view, knowledge is seen as a multidimensional concept that can be personal, situated, and socially constructed at the same time. In terms of our KS thematic categories, if knowledge is personal, situated, and socially constructed, then it is bound to context and implicates identity with the aspects of "interpretation" and "determining" invoking notions of trust and risk.

Perhaps a more important contribution of Guzman's proposal is that he treats dimensions of practical knowledge as "fuzzy"—they are not clear-cut categories but rather form a continuum. His aim is to explicate the various "quadrants" of practical knowledge, linking these to learning strategies with the objective of providing organizational managers with the ability to select the most appropriate learning strategy to suit the particular practical knowledge formula. In other words by road-mapping the type of practical knowledge that is to be shared or transferred between persons, the most effective learning approach can be selected and applied. Guzman's theory of practical knowledge has some weight and rational validity, but it is entirely based on a review of the literature and it is not clear if the theory has been empirically tested.

Both of these theories invoke the idea of "Communities of Practice," an influential notion that will be addressed in due course.

4.5.3 Connecting the "Organizational" with the "Personal": Social, Situated, and Constructed

A number of theories that follow the notion of "knowledge as social action" and which are categorized as having a joint focus on both personal and organizational knowledge include those by Spender (1996), Tsoukas and Vladimirou, Boisot, Jakubik, and Crane and Bontis. Max Boisot's "I-Space" theory of knowledge creation, similarly to Guzman's project, emphasizes the importance of social learning as the foundation of knowledge creation, claiming that people do not share knowledge, rather they share *information*, which becomes knowledge once internalized to the individual. In Boisot's model, knowledge is highly personal and relies on shared repertoires between individuals to reach common understandings (thus broadening the focus to the "organization"), which thesis has resonance with J.R. Searle's influential notion of shared rules in speech acts, published in the late 1960s. The model can therefore be interpreted as having a joint focus both on the personal and organizational aspects of knowledge.

Although using different terminology, this theory is also consistent with the earlier account of organizational knowledge proposed by Tsoukas and his colleague, for instance. A divergence is Boisot's leaning toward a cognitive understanding of knowledge with his emphasis on the cognitive effort in the form of abstraction and codification that is required in putting one's knowledge into words such that it may be shared with others. This raises some interesting questions around people's short- and long-term memory abilities, cognitive demand, limits on attention, and so forth, although a discussion of these does not feature in the framework and perhaps deservedly so as these are substantial topics for scientific research stretching back more than 100 years in the field of psychology alone. That aside, Boisot's model, perhaps more strongly than others, foregrounds the role of identity, trust and risk, and context in the idea of "shared repertoires" and "common understandings."

In something of a departure, Maria Jakubik's "transformative teleology framework," where "teleology" relates to a phenomenon's end or purpose, proposes that the individual and social are not separated into different levels of organizational life. Instead, and with echoes of Guzman, knowledge is seen as embedded in human action, interactions, and situated practice. In her investigation of the relationship between knowledge creation and learning, she draws on the social view of learning defined by Etienne Wenger: "…learning is not located in individual heads, but in the processes of co-participation and in experiences. Learning can be seen as a social act, as a process of practice" (2011: 384). Wenger, an independent consultant, researcher, and author and who is credited along with Jean Lave with introducing the notion of "Communities of Practice" during the 1990s, claims that identity is a key structuring element in how we know because knowing is an act of belonging, referring here to Communities of Practice. In his account of these Communities as Social Learning Systems, Wenger also arguably invokes the importance of context. Two of the KS categories are therefore implicated here. What Wenger and Jakubik do not do, in the same vein as that noted in reference to Cook and Brown (1999) earlier and as found in most if not all KM theories, is explain how these social contexts, identity, and so forth come into being.

A fascinating account of the structure of knowledge is proposed by H. Collins. However as this does not really address KM *per se*, although it is included in the taxonomy because of its perceived importance, the commentary on this is restricted to the following. He posits two types of knowledge-relevant human action: regular acts that are normally associated with rule-following or rule-establishing and that can largely function at the unconscious level. Secondly, there are behavior-specific acts that are not really "acts" but more understood as behaviors, which can be articulated and therefore explicitly learned. One way of interpreting this is to apply the tacit/explicit labels, but this is perhaps to dilute the insight that Collins offers—the action-orientated, constructive nature of knowledge. And the implication of both context and identity as influencing factors.

What is beginning to emerge is the idea of knowledge being both inherently socially enacted, and as singular to the individual: it represents each person's unique ability to de-code, interpret and make sense of their world without which socially enacted knowledge action could not and would not exist. Moreover, to a larger or lesser extent, many of the theories discussed so far can be interpreted as invoking categories of context, identity, trust, and risk (implicated earlier in Chapter 3 as factors in KS). Next, we review a number of KM theories located on the "knowledge as social action" axis, most of which focus on organizational knowledge: Activity Theory, the phenomenological perspective, "knowing how" and "knowing that," Communities of Practice, and Creative Abrasion.

4.5.4   Knowledge, Activity Theory, and Activity Systems

Frank Blackler is responsible for some of the most insightful work in the field of KM—and some of the least recognized or understood. Blackler's *Knowledge and the Theory of Organizations* is based on a modified version of Activity Theory, and like several others (e.g., Boisot), he emphasizes the central role of social learning. Activity Theory was originally proposed by the psychologist L.S. Vygotsky, working in the aftermath of the Russian Revolution. This constitutes people's material actions and communications processes as the focus of study of human activity. These ideas locate the context of actions within "activity systems." As Blackler caustically summarizes, "…the theory of organizations as activity systems offers an antidote to simplistic interpretations of the nature of individual knowledge and action, and organizational cultures and competencies" (1993: 882).

In proposing that people construct themselves in action as a historically evolving process, Blackler is advocating a constructivist, action-orientated approach to knowledge. As such, he may be one of the first in this domain to refer to the idea of "identity construction." He is critical of the mainstream rational-cognitive approaches to KM in their reification of knowledge and assumption of the rationality of both organization and individual. Interestingly, Philip Selznick, of the University of California, in his *Foundations of the Theory of Organization*, published in 1948, formulates the organization as a cooperative system of rational action, which is at risk from the "indiscipline" or irrationality of its participants!

As touched on in Section 1.4, Blackler draws on the work of H. Collins speculating a shift away from knowledge as situated in bodies and routines (embodied, embedded) toward knowledge as situated in brains (embrained), dialogue (encultured), and symbols (encoded). In other words, a move from knowledge as objective, tangible, and routinizable, to knowledge as constituted in social action. Thus the unit of analysis should be the socially distributed activity system within which knowing is done. He further emphasizes the importance of language in such systems, referring to it as the "archetypal communal activity" without which action would not be possible. From this perspective, the five-image framework of knowledge that Blackler had earlier seemed to espouse, he now sees as lacking. Instead, Blackler argues that the lens of research, practice and analysis should be on the activity systems in which knowledge is socially done: knowledge as mediated (e.g., through language), situated (in context), provisional (constantly developing) and contested (the subject of power relations). A clear reference can be drawn from Blackler's theory to the KS categories of context and identity, with the implication of trust and risk. Moreover, the connection between these "actions" and language is made explicit.

Blackler is an early advocate of what could be described as a postmodernist approach to KM. (A core tenet of postmodernism is that knowledge is constructed rather than discovered through, for instance, observation, and is the means of power). Blackler positions his theory as a critical reaction to mainstream conventions (the "rational-cognitive" approach), although unfortunately his work has been largely overlooked in the field. Nonetheless, the view of knowledge as socially actioned has many proponents as shown in the taxonomy, and many of which emphasize the pivotal role of communications: these are, for instance, landmarked in the late 1980s by Gaines, the late 1990s by Drucker and in the more recent work of theorists including Tsoukas, which is discussed next.

4.5.5   The Phenomenological Perspective

Haridimos Tsoukas' *Phenomenological View of Tacit Knowledge* quite clearly has a focus on personal knowledge, with its ideas grounded in those theorized by Michael Polanyi. As discussed in Section 1.4, far from theorizing about KM, Polanyi's 1962 work, *Personal Knowledge: Towards a Post-Critical Philosophy*, is in fact an argument for turning away from the traditional view and practice of the exact sciences and its pursuit of objective knowledge and scientific detachment. Instead, he posits the importance of the scientist—the "knower"—in the act of discovery and validation of scientific knowledge. Drawing on Polanyi's reasoning, Tsoukas criticizes the contemporary movement toward the decontextualization of knowledge. In his phenomenological approach to tacit knowledge he argues that explicit knowledge cannot exist without the tacit. This personal co-efficient factor suggests that all knowing—which implies the actual and potential to know residing in the individual's head—is rooted to some context and action. It is important to note here that Tsoukas' theory is centered on personal knowledge as an action-orientated phenomenon as opposed to a global understanding of knowledge (e.g., written knowledge). Resonance with many earlier works is clear. In this, context emerges as essential to knowing action.

Tsoukas is a particular critic of Nonaka's theory of the knowledge-creating firm, devoting a substantial part of his paper to its unraveling. In his criticism, Tsoukas is not alone.

4.5.6   "Know(ing) How" and "Know(ing) That" and Communities of Practice

In his conceptualization of knowledge creation (and scathing criticism of "Nonaka's theory"), Stephen Gourlay stands aside from the mainstream's general acceptance of the tacit and explicit components of knowledge. Instead, he offers an explanation based on the concepts of "know how" and "know that." This sounds familiar: recall, for instance, Paul Duguid's use of similar terms, although there are some differences notably in Duguid's preference for "knowing how/that" (see Section 1.4) and Guzman's theory of practical knowledge. In Gourlay's thesis, "know how" is rooted in and characteristic of everyday life, some of which is not capable of articulation, whereas "know that" emerges from the processes of reflecting and theorizing. A further distinction is that Gourlay views both of these concepts as behaviors. He reasons that in order to manage knowledge one must do so indirectly by managing behavior. This, he warns, raises a new panoply of issues and the potential to destroy that which management seeks to control (see Section 2.6 for a discussion around ethics and KM). Again, an interpretive view implicates the four KS thematic categories of context, identity, trust, and risk: that is, "know how" rooted in everyday life (context), "know that" as an outcome of reflection, and theorizing (identity), which collectively with the notion of behavior gives rise to the potential for trust and risk.

Like Blackler, Gourlay's reasoning is consistent with postmodernist thinking and has particular relevance to the discussions around Implicit Learning in Chapter 7. Note also the synergies with the ideas proposed by, for instance, Tsoukas, through the emphasis on knowing as behavior, connecting knowledge—knowing something—to action. That said, his conceptualization of "know how" and "know that" is no doubt the source of some confusion when the attempt is made to compare this with Paul Duguid's conceptualization, for instance. It is to Duguid and his colleague's work, arguably more influential than that of Gourlay, that we now turn.

Communities of Practice (CoPs) lie at the heart of John Seely Brown and Paul Duguid's architecture for organizational knowledge. In this, knowledge is mostly collective with successful CoPs being informal in nature, resonant of Etienne Wenger's claim for the primacy of the informal over the formal. Ironically their architecture is largely dominated by themes of command and control. For instance, they emphasize the "organizing" work of firms, which contrasts with Robert Grant's view that the organization exists to foster and coordinate an environment in which individuals can integrate their personal knowledge with that of others. Brown and Duguid view the organization as the *means* of knowledge generation and see organizational knowledge as more important than personal knowledge—the sum is greater than its parts, which once again recalls Vincent Barabba and colleagues' systemic view of the organization. Their *Architecture for Organizational Knowledge* is largely about interfirm communications and the establishment of human, technological, and process-based conduits through which a team's knowledge can be shared among other teams. For example, they propose that "translators," people who are attached to more than one team group, are important transports for knowledge between groups in a kind of cross-fertilization process.

Originally introduced in the early 1990s, Communities of Practice theory has proved immensely influential but frequently misused according to Duguid writing in the mid-2000s. Emphasizing the inherently social substance of CoP theory, he conjures the CoP as the stage on which the shared "knowing how" of the community is on display, not just that of its individual members. His explication of CoP theory is largely concerned with dispelling the "myth" that tacit knowledge can or should be converted to the explicit. Equating "knowing how" to tacit knowledge as the "art of the knowing," which he importantly constructs as the action of "learning to be," and "knowing that" to explicit knowledge as the action of "learning about," he reasons that to attempt to transform the former into the latter will likely lead to a transformation of learning *to be* into learning *about*. The profound importance of this lies in the simple analogy: "learning to be" is the art of knowing; of becoming a member of a Community of Practice, for instance; or of assimilating an art from a mentor over time. "Learning about" is equivalent to reading from books. To use Duguid's reasoning, one does not become an accountant by reading an accountancy textbook. One must learn from a master.

Duguid's ideas have considerable significance for the ideas developed here and in subsequent parts of the book. To complete this section, we make a brief visit to the intriguingly named *Theory of Creative Abrasion*.

4.5.7 Creative Abrasion

Dorothy Leonard and her colleague, writing in 2002, are also interested in people sharing knowledge in group work. Their *Theory of Creative Abrasion* frames the different backgrounds, skills, experiences, and understood social norms that individuals have as the factors that generate the melting pot of innovation. In this implied chaotic environment, people will challenge each other leading to an abrasion of different ideas, which in turn give rise to new ones. Their explanation of this outcome is simple: people will search for novel solutions to problems when they are exposed to ideas and perspectives which "challenge" the majority's prevailing wisdom. Moreover, it is the tacit dimension of an individual's knowledge, learned through practice, not capable of articulation, which formulates them as valuable contributors to group work and innovation. From a pragmatist's perspective, this thesis does rely on the majority group within any given organizational community being, in the first instance, open to novel concept: this cannot be simply assumed. But it does have an interesting connection to Chris Argyris' notion of Double Loop Learning (DLL), which we will come to shortly.

As a basic idea, this is not entirely divorced from the concepts of social learning advocated elsewhere. It sits on the organization end of the organization versus personal knowledge continuum through its focus on the organization—teams of workers—as the unit of analysis. From their perspective, the individual is problematic in the tendency to hoard tacit knowledge and reluctance to share knowledge through fear of failure or of looking foolish. A further point to draw is their acknowledgment of the need for a cross-disciplinary approach to understanding knowledge and innovation: "(C)clearly, many different fields of inquiry are relevant, including ones as diverse as design, cognitive psychology, group dynamics and information technology" (Leonard and Sensiper, 2002: 495). It sounds complicated, but this theory does have echoes of Peter Drucker's visionary piece on the future organization comprising teams of specialists dedicated to specific projects. It also has resonance with the KS categories of interest—context (teamwork), identity (team membership), trust, and risk.

An earlier piece of work by Leonard and coworker Susaan Straus takes a more general, higher-level viewpoint arguing that innovation, of necessity, requires a mixture of different styles of human thinking. Accordingly, innovation will not emerge among teams of like-minded individuals. Wenger (2000) makes a similar point. Innovation needs conflict. Consequently, organizations need the means of determining thinking styles and preferences, and for that, psychometric tests are recommended. While their reasoning is logical, the implication that individuals be assessed for thinking style and appointed based on this assessment inevitably raises some ethical concerns. Leonard and Strauss' ideas can be interpreted as orienting to "knowledge as social action" through their emphasis on social interaction, with consequences for knowledge as an action category.

We now turn to the "knowledge as object" end of the continuum, noting how this end of the field is largely dominated by one theory.

4.6 REIFICATION OF KNOWLEDGE: ONE PARADIGM DOMINATES

Those theories that explicitly, or by implication, reify knowledge all focus on the organizational level. This section mainly focuses on the *Dynamic Theory of Organizational Knowledge Creation/Knowledge-Creating Firm*, and its various manifestations ("the theory"). It has been so heavily criticized over the years, with almost no element left unchallenged, that only a brief account of the theory itself is given to begin with. Most of the discussions then focus on an analysis of some of the major points of criticism brought against it.

4.6.1 "The Theory" and the Theorist as Bricoleur

The driving force behind the theory, according to Nonaka, writing in 1994, is a reaction against the then dominant conventional conceptualization of the organization as a static, passive, "input–process–output" system. According to his radical (at the time) reasoning, building an action-orientated understanding of the organization means attending to two key aspects of the organization itself: its interaction with the environment in which it operates (and presumably those in which it would like to operate) and the ways and means by which it creates and communicates knowledge and information. These are ranked as the most important features of the organization. In effect, what Nonaka aims to do is to shift the emphasis from how the organization processes information and knowledge to how it *creates it*. That is surely a worthy ambition and appropriate to the emergence of the "knowledge society."

A noticeable feature of the theory is the number of other theories and philosophical works that it draws on from across a wide range of disciplines (subsequent discussions address several of these): for instance, JR Searle's "Speech Acts" (philosophy of language), John Anderson's "Adaptive Control of Thought" architecture of cognition (cognitive psychology), Polanyi's philosophy of knowledge, Chris Argyris's "DLL" theory (organizational behavior), John Seely Brown and Paul Duguid's (version of) "Communities of Practice" (knowledge management), A.E. Scheflen's work in "Interaction Rhythms" (communications behavior), and introduced in 1998, the concept of "Ba" derived from the works of two Japanese philosophers. Now, there is nothing wrong in drawing on the works of others, and indeed the majority of academic writing does precisely this. But this particular treatment suggests something of the theorist as "bricoleur."

At the heart of the theory is the SECI model that explains knowledge creation as the outcome of a dynamic interaction between subjectivities and objectivities. Accordingly, new knowledge is created in a spiral of interaction between the processes of socialization, externalization (explicit knowledge), combination, and internalization (tacit knowledge). Despite its emphasis on the socialization principle (indeed, Nonaka's theory is one of the very few to make a direct reference to a theory of language, namely, JR Searle's *Speech Acts*), the theory is positioned at the "knowledge as object" end of the axis because of its central tenet that tacit knowledge can and should be converted to explicit knowledge in the fashion proposed by the SECI model. It is for this "conversion" process that it is most heavily criticized. The product of this theory is a view of knowledge reified as an object to be managed and converted. According to David Snowden, Nonaka and his colleagues conceptualize knowledge creation as the output of a process that passes knowledge from the individual onto the group, and from the group to the organization, and thence to wherever else it needs to or can be transferred to. This, he claims, is quite obviously a reified view of knowledge as the object of management that at some point in the SECI process can be rendered explicit. A further question is this: in a theory that sets out to explain and predict organizational knowledge creation, is it not essentially wedded to "process"?

The inherent irony is that while Nonaka and his coworkers emphasize the importance of tacit knowledge, implying its possession of greater value than the explicit variety, the mandate to convert tacit to explicit knowledge signals a consequential devaluation of the former—it is only useful if transformed to the explicit. As Charles Despres and his colleague somewhat dramatically phrase it: "(T)the root idea is that knowledge becomes only useful when it goes into the forge of social interaction" (2002: 93). A dissenting voice to this interpretation is Snowden, who claims that the SECI model does not mandate that *all* knowledge in people's heads and conversations should or could be made explicit. However in this, Snowden stands out from a majority of scholars critical of the SECI model. Note that in later versions of the theory (see, for instance, Nonaka and Toyama, 2007) an explicit reference is made to an "*interaction*" between explicit and tacit knowledge, but the conversion mandate remains at its core, thus arguably diluting the reference to "interaction."

The idea that new knowledge can be generated in this dynamic interaction between two types of knowledge representing the subjective and the objective, and which process is fertilized and promoted in the socially engineered environment of "Ba," has been the target of considerable criticism.

4.6.2 Shuffling Ideas

Critics include Charles Despres and his coworker who condemn theories including Nonaka's for being too prescriptive and, with their ideas based around "transformations and dynamics," imply these represent nothing more than the shuffling of ideas back and forth in structures and systems. According to Mark Thompson and his coworker, the very notion of knowledge transformation leads to a contradiction because "*...the meaning of any objective 'knowledge' will always remain the subjective product of the person in whose mind this is constituted, always relationally defined, and therefore does not transfer easily to others in a form which may be operationalized to the benefit of the organization*" (2004: 726: italics in original).

In this way, they invoke and promote the importance of context, reasoning that attempts to "transfer" knowledge are unlikely to lead to organizational success. Support for this perspective can be seen in Ilkka Virtanen's review of the literature, which reports that most Information and Communications Technologies (ICT) focused KM initiatives aim to convert tacit to explicit knowledge—and most fail.

As well as being criticized for its focus on the organization (at the expense of the individual), coupled with the reification and decontextualization of knowledge, the theory is censured for its ambiguity on the one hand and explicit distinction between knowledge and learning on the other. For instance, many would disagree with his proposal that learning is a static and limited concept (as noted earlier in Section 2.3.3) compared with the more dynamic and conceptually broader idea of knowledge creation. As discussed in Section 3.6, knowledge is elsewhere posited as a *subset of learning*.

Stephen Gourlay, perhaps one of the most outspoken critics of the theory, is certainly not alone in devoting much of his work on *Conceptualizing Knowledge Creation* to dissecting the theory, seeking to demonstrate the shifting sands and miscalculations on which is it is based. He specifically points to the "cracks in the engine" of the SECI model, arguing that this is more a theory of managerial decision-making than knowledge creation. On Nonaka's evidence in support of the validity of the theory, Gourlay comments that this in reality represents nothing more than what managers *believe* to be the source of new ideas.

4.6.3 Misinterpretation and Misrepresentation

Perhaps most problematic is the suggestion that Nonaka and his colleagues have misinterpreted and misrepresented the works of Michael Polanyi in what Haridimos Tsoukas refers to as the "great misunderstanding" (see also Section 1.4 for additional discussions around this issue). As the core foundation of the theory draws on Polanyi's work on the nature of knowledge this is a significant issue. The primary sticking point is over the nature of tacit knowledge. Polanyi proposes that all knowledge is personal, involves judgment, and that all knowledge contains a tacit element, which is often difficult if not impossible to articulate. According to Tsoukas, this establishes the contextual and action-orientated nature of knowing. However, Nonaka's interpretation is slightly— but crucially—different: "Polanyi *classified knowledge into two categories*. 'Explicit' or codified knowledge refers to knowledge that is transmittable in formal, systematic language. On the other hand, 'tacit' knowledge has a personal quality which makes it hard to formalize and communicate" (Nonaka, 1994: 16, italics added).

In his analysis of Nonaka and his various coworkers' interpretation of the works of Polanyi, Tsoukas is critical of their emphasis on reducing practical knowledge (viz., tacit knowledge) to "precisely definable content." In other words, the aim of collecting knowledge located in people's heads and "translating" this to explicit knowledge will achieve little more than reduce the value of that knowledge by converting what is known to that which is representable. This is precisely the argument that Paul Duguid and others imply in their view that 'knowing that' does not produce 'knowing how'. So, while the theory draws on Polanyi's ideas, the interpretation and representation of it—particularly the nature of tacit knowledge and its potential for conversion to explicit knowledge—is allegedly misrepresentative.

A related issue is highlighted by Kenneth Grant, following an earlier piece of work in which Grant and his coworker conclude that Polanyi's theory concerning the tacit/explicit question has been largely misunderstood. Grant hypothesizes that many researchers in the KM field who refer to Polanyi have not actually read the source material, but are instead relying on others' interpretation. This combined with a less than critical approach to the work of Nonaka and his colleagues, suggests Grant, is one of the underpinning reasons for KM's lack of success.

As mentioned at the outset, the theory makes reference to the works of two other leading and influential theorists: Chris Argyris's DLL in Organizations and John Anderson's *Architecture of Cognition* (ACT theory). In both instances, it can be shown that Nonaka *appears* to misrepresent these works in how they are used to support his ideas. Argyris' theory of DLL is essentially concerned with the need for senior managers to continuously challenge organizational policies, procedures, visions, objectives—as people's internal theories of action—and so on in order to ensure progress and development. If not, firms will remain in a status quo and will eventually be overcome by others. According to Nonaka, firms find it difficult to implement DLL themselves, but, fortunately, it is "built in" to his theory. In reality, the *only potential* point of synergy between this theory and the theory of DLL is Nonaka's parole that managers should challenge what *employees* know. However, Argyris is primarily talking about manager's *own internal theories of action* based on organizational dictates, while Nonaka is talking about third parties challenging *knowledge in other people's heads*—and how the latter interpret organizational dictates, for example. Arguably, then, DLL is not "built in" to the theory of the knowledge-creating firm.

The theory also draws on a 1983 version of Anderson's ACT Model, however the later 1996 version published by Anderson suffices for the purpose here. In this, declarative memory (which Nonaka equates to explicit knowledge) is a schema like structure encoding a small bundle of knowledge, whereas procedural memory (equated to tacit knowledge) is applied automatically, is tied to context and can often not be articulated. Anderson proposes that complex cognitions are the result of interactions between declarative and procedural knowledge: "(A)all that there is to intelligence is the simple accrual and tuning of many small units of knowledge that in total produce complex cognition. The whole is no more than the sum of its parts, but it has a lot of parts" (1996: 356). He also claims that production rules that embody procedural knowledge can create declarative structures, but not the other way around. (This has echoes in Paul Duguid's argument that knowing *how* cannot be derived from knowing *that*.) Note the use of the term "interactions" to describe the relationship between these two forms of knowledge/memory.

Interestingly, according to one interpretation of Anderson's model, skill compilation leads to new skill acquisition, making knowledge a subset of learning (consistent with Krathwohl's account of Bloom's Taxonomy), whereas Nonaka's theory constitutes learning as a subset of knowledge. Nonaka also clearly states that in Anderson's theory declarative knowledge is *transformed* into procedural knowledge: "(T)he idea of 'knowledge conversion' may be traced from Anderson's ACT model..." (1994: 18). This is not a strictly accurate account of Anderson's own version of affairs in its introduction of the notion of "transformation" (viz., conversion), which is entirely absent from Anderson's.

Note that both DLL and ACT are absent from the SECI model in versions subsequent to 1994.

4.6.4   More Troubling Observations on the Theory of the Knowledge-Creating Firm

Analogous with Brown and Duguid's and Wenger's conceptualization of Communities of Practice, the theory describes the "informal community" as the location of emerging knowledge. He goes on to suggest that these need to be integrated into the formal hierarchical structure of the organization. This implies a transformation of the informal to the formal. Would this not lead to a loss of the values and benefits afforded through informally organized work groups? Moreover, the scholar Charles Ehin, of Westminster College Utah, in his framework for "unmanaging" knowledge workers, claims that the formalization of communities of practice within a top-down hierarchical structure does not work. This mirrors a view previously promoted by Wenger.

Expanding on this theme of "communities," a key claim made is that the theory is cross-cultural. This is difficult to substantiate particularly in the light of the nature of the theory. Recall that the theory is originally developed based on observations of Japanese firms. As is widely theorized elsewhere, knowledge is inextricably bound to culture (as context). Following H. Collins' *The Structure of Knowledge*, culture undeniably varies from organization to organization, from community to community, from nation to nation, and so forth and so will the following of rules (see Section 3.5 for a discussion of this issue). The "one-size-fits-all" approach does not sit well with this conceptualization.

To complete this critical review, the theory's stance on the temporal/cognitive nature of knowledge raises some interesting questions. The theory proposes that tacit knowledge refers to future events (with the inference that it only can refer to the future), while explicit knowledge deals with the past. Further, only tacit knowledge comprises cognitive elements. There is no evidence for this claim, and arguably, even if one takes the view that tacit knowledge is internalized, comprising skills, difficult to articulate, and the "more than we can tell" element of knowledge, why can tacit knowledge not refer to the past and present as well as the future? Additionally, if, as Polanyi argues, *all* knowledge contains a tacit element, then it is not logical to propose that explicit knowledge is bereft of cognitive components nor that it can only refer to events in the past.

With respect to the KS thematic categories of context, identity, trust, and risk, this theory arguably offers an ambiguous view: for instance, context from one direction is valued (e.g., social interaction, "Ba"), but then devalued from another (culture is irrelevant and can be "crossed," the conversion model). Despite these difficulties, the theory continues to dominate the KM theoretical landscape with numerous other theorists following in its wake in one fashion or another, mainly through an uncritical acceptance and adoption of the tacit/explicit explanation at its heart.

4.7   ROUNDUP OF SOME OTHER PERSPECTIVES IN THE "KNOWLEDGE AS OBJECT" SPECTRUM

Of those theories categorized at the "knowledge as object" end of the axis, the following brief review focuses on four, which are considered to be both interesting and of some value to the organizational manager. (This is a subjectively based selection and is not meant to indicate the inadequacy, in any way, of other theories.) Michael Earl (2001), professor of IM at the London Business School, offers an account of "schools of KM." He uses the analysis of case studies, interviews, workshops, and published materials to develop his "taxonomy of KM strategy." This proposes three schools of KM—technocratic, economic, and behavioral—each of which is designed to apply to different types of organization, including descriptions of how they might work in practice. Despite the selective, subjective, and interpretive nature of his methodology, Earl's work can be seen as a practical aid for knowledge managers which at least acknowledges that there are many "flavors" of KM, in contrast to the "one-size-fits-all" accounts.

In her account, Dorothy Leonard considers ways in which knowledge is transferred within organizations, and the associated barriers. Like many other theorists, she draws on case studies in the literature and her own anecdotes to give substance to her proposals. Leonard is notably one of the few theorists to highlight the difference between knowledge that is transferred and knowledge that is reused. The knowledge that is transferred from its host will not be the same as that which is admitted by the recipient. This is because knowledge will become adapted, claims Leonard, as the recipient indexes it to their pre-existing knowledge and experience. The problem with transferring tacit knowledge, she reasons, lies in its "stickiness"—that is, the difficulty of separating knowledge from its source citing cultural effects, tensions in attempting to apply rigid coding contrasted with ambiguity of knowledge, and the knowledge gaps between transmitter and receiver. The subject matter of Leonard's framework, and her treatment of it, implies knowledge as an object in contrast to her other work mentioned elsewhere that does not. That aside, there is the notable reprise of categories seen in the "knowledge as social action" side of the debate in the idea of stickiness and cultural effects (context), knowledge gaps between knowers (identity), and connotations of trust and risk that these imply.

Leonard's cognitive perspective can be compared with Hong Kong-based Professor Lynne Markus' theory of knowledge reuse. In what is clearly a "systems approach" to KM, Markus advises that KM should only be concerned with explicit knowledge, emphasizing the importance of "organizational memory systems" such as IT repositories. Markus' theory proposes that different knowledge reuse situations require different approaches: so, for instance, producers and users of shared work have different needs, which makes sense. However, this work is an example of what some have insisted is at the heart of KM's issues—a concentrated focus on IT. As discussed elsewhere, many have connected the commitment to KM technologies to the risk of failure (see, for instance, Sections 2.5 and 3.3). That aside, Markus' theory does implicate the influence of context. Rosina Weber, of Dexel University, Philadelphia, admits the construction of enormous organizational memory systems stands as 1 of the 15 factors leading to KM failure. In addressing this issue, she suggests a framework for how technology should be approached, adopted, and implemented in organizations (e.g., design input from end users). This might be of particular use and interest to the organizational manager.

It would be remiss to complete this round-up without a brief review of David Snowden's *Complex Acts of Knowing*. Unusually, this is categorized across all taxonomy quadrants: that is, it treats knowledge both as an object ("thing" to use Snowden's word) and action (a "flow"), spreading its focus across both organizational and personal knowledge. In his Cynefin model, he offers four "domains" of knowledge: bureaucratic, professional, informal, and uncharted. According to Snowden, the model's purpose is to facilitate sense-making as an aid to decision-making, leadership, and so forth. While Snowden's model may not represent a KM theory in the conventional sense, what it does do is step the "convention" beyond the management of knowledge for its self-serving sake to knowledge and its management as a fundamental building block in any organizational activity.

Two pragmatic points raised by Snowden are worth noting: first, he argues that the number of informal and formal communities in any large organization prohibits their formal management, a perspective that can be contrasted with Nonaka's advice to formalize all such communities. Secondly he suggests, perhaps somewhat controversially, that the knowledge that exists within the "informal space" should not necessarily be seen as an asset of the organization. In other words, KM need not concern itself with every workplace community, nor should it attempt to print its ownership on all knowledge that walks in and out of the doors each day. Neither will bring advantage to decision-making, problem-solving, and leadership, for instance.

One characteristic that Snowden's model shares with all other KM theories discussed here is the absence of a specified theory of language despite, in his case, an emphasis on culture. Even those theories and frameworks, which directly emphasize the importance of language, with knowledge understood as accomplished in social action, there is no reference to a theory of discourse—with the exception of Nonaka's theory, of course.

In terms of the thematic categories of context, identity, trust, and risk, most of the foregoing is ambiguous. To a larger or lesser extent, one might arguably suggest a common implication of the notion of "context," but here that is predominantly framed as the context of the environment and its contents (e.g., IT system) influencing the human participants. The exception is Leonard.

Continuing in the pragmatic theme, there is one more feature of KM theory that needs to be discussed: the inductionist basis.

4.8 THE ISSUES OVER THE INDUCTIONIST FOUNDATION OF THEORY

Arguably, KM's most influential theories are in fact largely inductive in nature. Nonaka's theory, for instance, is developed from observations of Japanese firms. This raises the question of their validity. According to Karl Popper, perhaps the most famous critic of inductionism, its crime is to construct "universal truths" based on single instances of experience (observation). In his immensely popular book *What Is This Thing Called Science?*, Professor Alan Chalmers argues that no two observers watching the same scene or object will perceive it in exactly the same way. The logical inference of this is a relational chain of culpability: if observation can be subject to error, what chance for the facts that it produces, and the scientific knowledge that is constructed on those facts? Recall the case of the Royal Astronomer discussed in Section 1.3, and how two observers of the same phenomena are found to record *different* accounts. Professor Thomas Kuhn's equally influential treatise, *The Structure of Scientific Revolutions*, argues along much the same lines. Kenneth Gergen also claims that there can be no such thing as objective observation, subsequently developing his ideas in the direction of universal relational being.

As many KM theories take scientific enquiry and knowledge as their basis, it is appropriate to bring the scientific perspective to bear. If the inductionist approach to theory development involves extracting "facts" from observation, and then developing a theory to explain them, and it can be shown that those "facts" can be wrong, where does this leave the theory? Specific to Nonaka's claim for cultural transcendence, the facts observed and used to construct theory are drawn from firms operating in Japanese culture. Would the same facts be observed in a different cultural environment? Or, for that matter, by American observers of Japanese companies? Would individual observers arrive at different accounts? These fascinating topics are addressed in more detail in Part Two (Chapter 11).

No apologies are made for giving over so much space to a discussion of one single KM theory. As this is the dominant perspective and paradigm, as both influencer and subject of criticism, an understanding of the "Nonaka" phenomenon is essential to understanding the KM theoretical landscape. There are, of course, many more theories in the KM field, but this nonexhaustive review of the theory literature gives a flavor of the ground covered, and issues raised.

4.9 SUMMARY AND CONCLUSIONS

The KM domain of theory is broad, complex, sometimes ambiguous, and often confusing. To bring some clarity, theories are classified into the broad categories of "personal versus organizational knowledge" and a view of "knowledge as object" or as "accomplished in social action." This classification reveals a significant anomaly. On the one hand, the most dominant and influential theory and its various evolutions, collectively grouped as *The Knowledge-Creating Company*, is interpreted as reifying knowledge as object and as having a focus on the organizational unit of analysis, as do a number of other theories. On the other hand, there is a visible trend toward the view of knowledge as social action, but none of its theories or frameworks has achieved the popularity and recognition assigned to *The Knowledge-Creating Company*. Added to this is the perspective that KM has yet to achieve the kind of success that one would expect from a discipline and practice that concentrates on what is widely seen as an organization's most important asset.

It has also been shown how the KM theoretical landscape is often the sparring ring of considerable debate, contradiction and dissent, with accusations of misinterpretation and misrepresentation constituting a characteristic hall-mark. In part, these issues emanate from the substantial assumptions on which many theories rest: that knowledge can be identified as a singular thing or activity, that KM outcomes can be measured in some way, that the tacit can be made explicit and vice versa, that this phenomenon called knowledge resides in people's heads, but that they must be motivated to share it. Many assume that language, communication, and social interaction are important, but how is not specified; that what will work in one culture or organization will—or will not—work in another; and finally, that with the right organizational structure, knowledge can be commanded and controlled.

One question lingers: how and why did the theoretical works of Nonaka and his colleagues achieve such "superstar" status? One can only speculate. Perhaps one reason is that these works are more accessible—more easily understood and more resonant of modern organizational thinking—than some of those on offer.

From the discussions around organizational knowledge, and particularly drawing on the works of Haridimos Tsoukas and his colleague, and Paul Duguid, it is reasoned that personal knowledge and organizational knowledge are tightly connected, with the latter dependent on the former. It is the personal component that illuminates and brings meaning to the organizational experience, as indeed it has been speculated elsewhere that it does with all aspects of life. This is an idea that is developed as we proceed through the rest of this book, culminating in an explication and illustration of exactly how this works in everyday life.

Four final points can be drawn.

First, that the thesis of "knowledge as social action" invokes an understanding of "social action" as discourse (talk and text) in interaction.

Second, that while those theories and frameworks shown to occupy the "knowledge as social action" end of the taxonomy axis can be interpreted as implicating, to some degree, the thematic categories of context, identity, trust, and risk, previously identified (see Chapter 3) as categories relevant to KS, those on the "knowledge as object" axis are far more ambiguous in this respect.

Third, that while some of the "knowledge as social action" based theories explicitly orient to the importance of language—variously understood as communication, discourse, talk, and text in social interaction—and others imply this, none (in this sampling) have optioned discourse in the organizational context as a viable and relevant site for research.

Finally, and extending the latter point, a theory of language is also shown to be all but absent (one exception being, ironically, Nonaka's *Dynamic Theory of Organizational Knowledge Creation* in its reference to Searle's *Speech Act Theory*), in spite of some scholars' emphasis on the import of language.

To conclude, if KM is not perceived to have achieved any significant measure of recognized success in practice—as some have argued—then there is perhaps room for a different approach. If there is a demonstrable trend toward the view of knowledge as constructed in social interaction, along with the implied importance ascribed to language and communication, then it would seem logical to turn in this direction, for the purposes of the research project research project here: language and talk as the site of action.

The next chapter moves the debate in the direction of social psychology, social constructionism, and discourse analysis with a particular interest in discursive psychology. We consider how the latter—the study and analysis of human linguistic actions as accomplished in everyday talk-in-interaction—could represent both a valid, even novel (within the KM field), perspective, and approach to KM. Moreover, this paradigm brings a theory of language into play. The origins and some of the contributions of discursive psychology are discussed, along with those from the wider field of discourse analysis. What could an approach grounded in discursive psychology bring to the study and practice of KM? Moreover, could discursive psychology provide the means to develop, evaluate, and analyze the knowledge sharing thematic categories introduced at the end of the previous chapter?

FURTHER READING

Chalmers, A. (1999). *What is this thing called Science?* 3rd Edn. Maidenhead: Open University Press.

Choo, C. and Bontis, N. (Eds). (2002). *The Strategic Management of Intellectual Capital and Organizational Knowledge.* Oxford: Oxford University Press.

Duguid, P. (2005). The art of knowing: social and tacit dimensions of knowledge and the limits of the community of practice. *The Information Society,* 21: 109–118.

Heisig, P. (2009). Harmonisation of knowledge management—comparing 160 KM frameworks around the globe. *Journal of Knowledge Management,* 13, (4): 4–31.

Ichijo, K. and Nonaka, I. (Eds). (2007). *Knowledge Creation and Management: New Challenges for Managers.* Oxford: Oxford University Press.

Ragab, M. and Arisha, A. (2013). Knowledge management and measurement: a critical review. *Journal of Knowledge Management,* 17, (6): 873–901.

5

SOCIAL CONSTRUCTIONISM AND THE CONSTRUCTIONIST VIEW OF KNOWLEDGE

5.1 INTRODUCTION

This chapter marks a step in extending the discussions around knowledge management (KM) in the direction of social constructionism (SC) for a theory of knowledge, critical social psychology for a view of knowledge and language in action, and a methodology for research.

The aim of the chapter is essentially to lay out the arguments for a discursive approach to knowledge work in social interaction drawing on a constructionist epistemology and view of the world. Laying some early groundwork, the position taken here differentiates between *critical social psychology* and *experimental social psychology*: the former is positioned as a challenge to the latter and its adherence to traditional experimental methods of research (viz., laboratory, also referred to as the "positivist" approach). In using the term "critical social psychology," and following Wendy Stainton Rogers, we refer to developing new perspectives on what social psychology should be, and should be concerned with, and which draws on, among other ideas, SC and discourse analysis. Consequently, all of the following discussions are located within the context of critical social psychology, thus providing some clear boundaries. The objective is to establish the foundations for what follows throughout the rest of this book by fitting together all of the pieces to form an intelligible and relevant picture.

We start with a brief account of SC, which Kenneth Gergen is credited with coordinating in social psychology, and its relevance to KM. This is followed by an account of how the thesis proposed here is simply extending the directions, which many in the KM field have already been shown to be indicating (see Chapter 4 in particular). Next, consideration of

Knowledge and Discourse Matters: Relocating Knowledge Management's Sphere of Interest onto Language,
First Edition. Lesley Crane.

the constructionist theory of knowledge leads into the long-running dispute over knowledge and how it should be researched. This can not only be seen as having a profound impact on what we know about the world, but also on how we generate new knowledge. Henry Markram and his colleague make the point: knowledge from research is the "foundation stone" on which societies stand. That being the case, what happens when two sides of a research community wholly disagree on how and what topics should be researched? Critical and experimental approaches in social psychology are shown to be polar opposites in terms of their epistemologies, which in turn transforms the topic of research method- ology into the proverbial battleground. This debate lies at the center of what is termed the "crisis in social psychology" and raises a question over the "knowledge" that we routinely acquire and use in everyday work. This inevitably, and again, raises the question over what is meant by "objectivity" from the perspectives of methodology, which we have already seen has an impact on how one chooses to approach knowledge and its management.

What we end up with is an alternative theory of knowledge to that adhered to by what is referred to as mainstream KM and a view of language as the "stage" of social interac- tion. Importantly, this results in language being seen as a topic of interest in its own right. In many ways, these alternative views are only extending and explicitly locating directions already taken by many in the KM field.

5.2   SOCIAL CONSTRUCTIONISM AS A WAY OF LOOKING AT THE WORLD

From the outset, it is admitted that SC is not a subject that features prominently in the indexes of organizational management guides. Some might see SC as an example of academic ideas in which, as management consultants and authors Christian Madsbjerg and his colleague note, the business world declines an interest because these are deemed to have little relevance of any practical value to organizations. But, as I hope to make clear, *because* of the issues in KM over the nature of knowledge and its management, SC has something very particular to speak on the matter.

Located in postmodernism, SC has its roots in the 1950s alongside a growing interest in ideas of language as social action. The British philosopher John Austin succinctly captured this idea in his profoundly influential book *How to Do Things with Words*, with its—at the time—radical idea of language not just as words and grammar, but as action-performative. In this view, what we say has function and effect beyond the literal meaning of the words strung in a sentence. This coincided with an increasing dissatisfaction over the reliance on experimental research methods in social psychology. Against this background, SC marked a radical change of emphasis, focus, and epistemology. Often referred to as the "crisis in social psychology," the result is a near schism in the discipline, which persists to this day. Consequently in the field of social psychology, SC and critical social psychology are a counter-reference to and reaction against the positivist-experimental agenda of traditional psychology, a debate that is considered in more detail later in this chapter.

In particular, the SC movement brought about a shift in the focus of research interest from the idea of the "self-as-entity" (which, from traditional perspectives, can be empirically tested and measured) to the self as a construct accomplished in language. Jonathan Potter and Margaret Wetherell, early pioneers in the take-up of discourse analysis in social psychology, summarize this: "…any sociopsychological image of the self, in fact the very possibility of a self concept, is inextricably dependent on the linguistic practices used in everyday life to make sense of our own and others' actions" (1987: 95). Describing the increasing influence of SC, the psychologist Carla Willig points out that SC is concerned with human experience and perception as "mediated historically, culturally, and linguistically." Drawing on both of these accounts, and from a practical perspective, not only did the SC movement bring about a significant change in research theory—what is studied, why, and how—but also coincided with a reconceptualization of language as the site of human accomplishment, that is, language as a topic of study in its own right, as action oriented, constructive, and constructed, with discourse analysis constituting an appropriate methodology for its study. In positioning language as one of the primary mediating factors in the human experience, it axiomatically follows that language should constitute a prime focus of action—and of interest.

How is this relevant to KM? Nelson Phillips, of London's Imperial College, and his colleague, writing specifically about organizational discourse, claim that the study of discourse allows one to get to a greater level of understanding of the organization as a socially constructed reality. Far deeper, they propose, than that achievable through the application of conventional research methods. Taking this at face value should stand as reason enough to warrant a focus of interest and research on the study of discourse in action. In other words, the approach to the organization as discursively constructed in social interaction opens the potential for an understanding of the lived experience of the organization that is not available through more traditional methodologies and theories. Thus a different understanding of the organization and its members' knowledge work similarly promises alternative avenues for approaching KM. While the analysis of discourse *in general* is not a new paradigm in the study of organizations, as may be construed from Phillips and his coworker's comments, such an approach is mostly if not entirely missing from the mainstream KM field and literature.

5.3 SIMPLY EXTENDING EXISTING DIRECTIONS

These claims can be further supported by connecting them to the already existing trends within KM in approaching knowledge as social action. In general, the thesis under consideration here is that knowledge is dynamically constructed in linguistic action: this implies function and consequence. In reality, this is just extending the directions that many KM scholars and theorists have been shown to be leaning in. The reader will no doubt have already noticed that the boundaries of KM are frequently shown to be porous in drawing on other disciplines. This is not surprising given a field with such diverse origins (see Section 2.2) and which is concerned with a phenomenon that is itself the subject of interest within many other disciplines. It is however beholden on the serious researcher to avoid being seen to be merely "cherry-picking." Still, the reader might question why KM's horizons need to or should be broadened in directions, SC for instance, which might seem somewhat irrelevant and perhaps unjustified. Justifying why and how these directions are in fact relevant to KM is one of the aims of the current and all subsequent chapters of this book. A few observations based on the investigations and discussions of KM's primary debates and issues and its theoretical landscape help to make the case.

A recurrent theme that has been seen in all of the previous chapters is the trend toward a conception of knowledge as constituting or as embedded in social action. But what is meant by "social action"? As far back as the mid-1990s, not long after the first publication of *A Dynamic Theory of Organizational Knowledge Creation,* Frank Blackler defined "knowing" as an active process that is mediated, situated, provisional, pragmatic, and contested. He promoted a change in focus from "the kinds of knowledge demanded by capitalism" toward the "systems through which doing and knowing" are accomplished, as the unit of analysis. Blackler's "systems" are similar to the notions of Communities of Practice, for instance. Both his conceptualization of knowing and his proposed unit of analysis are consistent with the idea of knowledge accomplishment in social interaction.

More recently, Ikujiro Nonaka and his coworker, in their 2007 version of *The Theory of the Knowledge-Creating Firm,* although categorized along the "knowledge as object" axis of the taxonomy of KM theory, nonetheless emphasize the notion of knowledge created through people interacting with people. There is also a hint of constructionism in their denial of knowledge as something "out there to be discovered." So, "social action" is the action by and through which the individual interacts with their environment and its contents and which action is largely mediated by the individual's personal understanding and knowledge of socially normative precepts. From all of these perspectives, then, knowledge or knowing is contingent to social (inter)action. That is a constructionist concept.

The idea that the action of knowing is accomplished in social interaction implicates talk-in-interaction ("people interacting with people"). From the perspective of critical social psychology, language is theorized as the site of "knowing," along with all of other psychological phenomena, and as the topic of interest in its own right. Making connections directly, KM's concept of knowledge and social interaction is consistent with the paradigm of discursive psychology and the social constructionist movement in the field of social psychology. While KM's scholars and practitioners may not have overtly walked in these directions, there is a good sense that these are indicated, with justification.

Shifting the perception of the location of knowledge work to language could signify some fundamental ramifications for the study and practice of KM or none at all—depending on one's viewpoint. From the perspective of constructionist social psychology, Stainton Rogers usefully defines "discourse" as both the product and the means of constructing meaning in particular ways. Put another way, language is both constructed (product) and constructive (means). In Section 3.6 discussions on creating new knowledge, the work of Endel Tulving in human memory and consciousness introduced the idea of a person's unique store of knowledge about the world, combined with the "predictability" of language, as the essential prerequisite of making sense of the world and its contents. Synthesizing these two ideas—admittedly drawn from two competing ends of the psychological debate—a person's unique store of knowledge informs and influences both the product and action of making sense of the world and its contents through discursive social interaction. The influencing nature of what might be thought of as "personal knowledge" is a topic that is returned to in detail in Chapter 7.

A further point to clarify here is that when we talk about "discourse," we are referring to both talk and text. While it is obvious to consider talk as socially interacted, what of text? Recall Paul Duguid's proposal that no text can determine the rules of its interpretation, that these are the product of a person's tacit understanding of the ground rules, which they bring to the reading of any text (as discussed in Section 4.3). The action of producing a text, and another reading it, are just as much a form of social interaction as two people engaging in a conversation.

5.4 THE SOCIAL CONSTRUCTIONIST VIEW OF KNOWLEDGE

Knowledge constitutes the very basis of all forms of social cognition, including social attitudes, social identities and attribution, among many other phenomena traditionally studied in social psychology. (Teun van Dijk, 2013: 498)

In contrast to the traditional Western assumption, from the SC viewpoint, knowledge is not approached as something "out there" waiting to be discovered but rather as constructed in social interaction. As we saw earlier, this is partly the idea promoted by Nonaka and his coworker, for instance. From this perspective, knowledge cannot be derived from an unambiguous perception of truth and fact. At the heart of the constructionist perspective is the view that people engage and interact with the world and its phenomena through meaning-making. For instance, Egon Guba, professor emeritus of Education at Indiana University, and his coworker reason that knowledge can never be separate from the knower because what a person knows is bound to their "meaning-making mechanisms," which are themselves inextricably a part of the social, cognitive, and linguistic worlds in which the knower exists. These ideas have some interesting synergies with "sense-making," the study of how people experience life (a brief account of this is given in the next chapter).

Collectively, this view is, of course, at considerable variance to much of the mainstream KM "knowledge as object" theoretical accounts. However, the genesis of the idea that knowing emerges in and through social interaction is frequently implied in those theoretical approaches that are particularly categorized as "knowledge as social action." The influence of SC's epistemology in Guba and his coworker's reasoning is clear: knowledge is constructed by individuals in discourse—it is personal and unique. It is, above all, subjective with "knowing" existing in and through social participation. This notion, it is suggested, has a great deal of resonance with many of the KM theorists encountered in the previous chapter.

Similarly, one can start to appreciate how mainstream approaches to knowledge and its management are, from the SC perspective, founded on doubtful principles. Notice also how, in the SC paradigm, there is no mention of "two types of knowledge, one tacit and one explicit." Knowledge is knowledge, a construction of, and accomplishment in social interaction. This holistic view of knowledge is consistent with the SC view of language: rather than being seen as a conduit to the inner thoughts of minds, language is understood as the constructive site of knowledge and meaning-making. There is, consequently, no real need to think of two or more "types" of knowledge. This notwithstanding, the terms "tacit" and "explicit" will continue to be used here for two reasons: first, to maintain a coherence to KM's terminology, and second, and perhaps more importantly, because of its connections with the "knowing how–knowing that" formulation promoted by Paul Duguid and others (see Section 4.4 for a review), which is already identified as central to the ideas developed here. In the following chapters, tacit knowing (also known as tacit knowledge) is equivalent to "knowing how." True, some might dispute the efficacy of conflating these terms, particularly tacit knowing and tacit knowledge; however, the hair-spitting over such matters is arguably one source of the perception of a confused picture. In this case, I would argue that the devil is not in the detail.

To reprise what was proposed earlier, a person's unique store of knowledge informs and influences both the product and action of making sense of the world and its contents through discursive social interaction.

As discussed in previous chapters, particularly those around the nature of knowledge, it has been claimed that the way in which one conceptualizes knowledge must of necessity direct how one approaches its management. Exactly the same issue lies at the heart of the debate over research methods in science, and this has a profound implication on the nature of research.

5.5   THE DEBATE OVER METHOD

The topic of methodology is covered in far greater depth in part two, so the intention here is to offer some headline concepts and core principles to position a sensible question mark over the assumptions of traditional scientific research methods and the claims of findings. A second intention is to establish some methodological context for the following chapter. A brief detour into history provides some interesting perspectives on the importance of knowledge discovery in societal development.

In his ambitious account of the history of knowledge, Charles van Doren relates three periods of history, which can be interpreted as demonstrating what happens to society when the search for new knowledge—research—is compromised. First, the ancient Egyptians: for thousands of years, the Egyptian dynasties actively boycotted new knowledge as a way of maintaining the order of things. The result, according to van Doren's analysis, was a civilization caught in a time warp, inadequate to the task of responding effectively when external forces threatened their society and its wealth. Second, the Roman Empire: their lack of interest in science and technology, according to van Doren, prohibited new developments and innovation that may well have solved considerable logistical shortcomings. For one thing, the sheer size of the empire meant that sending things from one end to the other was quite an undertaking. Third, the European Middle Ages: van Doren implicates the rise of monastery and cloister as being responsible for the removal of society's most intelligent, imaginative, and creative individuals to lives of piety, solitude, and contemplation. This, he suggests, was an immeasurable loss that could well have been one of the reasons why Europe took so many centuries to recover after the fall of the Roman Empire in the early fifth century.

This may be a somewhat fanciful digression, particularly in the reliance on one single source (something that any reader should be wary of, by the way). However, there is a hint of connection to some of the ideas from KM touched on in previous chapters: recall, for instance, Peter Drucker's vision of the future organization in which teams of specialists will work to generate innovative solutions in task-focused teams. Recall also Dorothy Leonard and her colleague's emphasis on the importance of diversity of background, experiences, skills, and so forth in team members—the "creative abrasion" idea. Shifting the viewpoint back to the macro level, the lesson, certainly at face value, is clear. Knowledge—as an evolving phenomenon—is essential to societal and human evolutionary development and survival. The modern world sadly contains sufficient examples of nations suffering in the wake of decades of autocratic repression, and those which are teetering on the brink as a consequence of years of intolerance to progress, difference, and enlightenment. These are struggles taking place at the national level. Recall Markram and his coworker's notion that the underpinning foundation stone of society is research knowledge: there are struggles here too.

The value of research is not solely determined by its product—knowledge—it is also determined by its methodology. When this is questioned, so is research knowledge. Beginning in the 1970s, the critical social psychology movement evolved as a direct reaction to, and argument against, the so-called "laboratory" methods of discovery common in experimental social psychology along with all of its connotations of statistical averages, probabilities, and so forth. This sets the goal of research as the production of objective truths and knowledge, which can only be gained through the application of the "scientific method," and the discovery of general laws through observation. Both imply what Willig, writing in 2003, describes as a straightforward relationship between the world and the human perception and understanding of it. Moreover, language is valued as no more than a medium, which unproblematically reflects reality *as it is*. In contrast, the methodology of discourse analysis, as one of the principle methods used by critical social psychologists, approaches language as the topic of study, as action oriented, functional, and consequential, as both constructed and constructive. Why, critical social psychology asks, see language as a site of "secondhand" data (the "conduit metaphor of communication" disparagingly referred to by Haridimos Tsoukas, writing in 2011), when one can see it as the place where thought is actively constructed and made live? Where things actually happen.

The social constructionist Kenneth Gergen, writing in the early 1970s, particularly criticizes traditional scientific principles and research methods used in the study of human behavior. Human behavior, he reasons, cannot be empirically tested in the same way as the objects of the natural sciences. He subsequently claims that the modern world's obsession with the need for objectivity, facts, realism, observation, and rationality results in an academia populated by "knowledge factories" churning out objective truths like "so many sausages." In a similar vein, Professor Linda Wood, of York University, Canada, and her colleague diplomatically describe the introduction of the laboratory-based experimental methods to social psychology, with their aim of simulating "aspects of culture," as misguided.

In the field of Organization Studies, William Starbuck is particularly critical of experimental methods. He reports a fascinating study of how a US law firm achieves and maintains its stellar success despite breaking all of the conventional rules constituting what makes a firm profitable and successful. Starbuck is forensic in his dissection of the flaws in traditional research methods. In the rush to produce research outcomes that can be universally generalized, he argues, those properties that signify firms as unique—such as the firm at the center of his study—are actively ignored. This, according to Starbuck, leads to the situations where data is deceptive, findings lack validity, and "formulated rules" are no more than "sense-making ritual." Following his argument leads to the conclusion that social science's addiction to statistical averages risks overlooking all of those oddities, which are exactly those features that determine originality and excellence. In what could be described as the "killer argument," he points out that while scientists in the conventional mold pursue the evidence of statistical averages in order to form rules about what makes success or failure, successful organizations do not achieve their success by imitating others! The altar of statistical averages is to be viewed with suspicion.

This raises an interesting point. According to Starbuck's reasoning, the temporal, demographic, political, economic, geographic, and human contexts within which the successful firm operates are influencing—to a larger or lesser extent—factors. Thus, in his study of what makes the law firm exceptionally successful, the elements of this success, he argues, are specific to this case and this case only. Of course, you can reduce a phenomenon to a set of generic rules but in so doing the context is lost. In this sense, context is the defining factor in a way. Translate this idea to a common organizational practice: the production of "lessons learned" documents. Their objective is to facilitate the avoidance of past mistakes and the furtherance of good practice. But should those documents not be viewed as "historical artifacts" as unique to their temporal context and so forth? It is quite possible to imagine that actions and situations that led to errors in the past could, in a different time, represent good opportunities and not events to be avoided.

Continuing on the subject of context, Kenneth Gergen sees social psychology as a historical endeavor, which should approach the study of human behavior as reflections of situated, contemporary history, rather than seeking decontextualized rules. The context of phenomena in one timeframe cannot be assumed to be identical to that of a different time-frame, and to do so is to risk error. Recall Frank Blackler's theory with organizations seen as "activity systems": he argues that people construct selves as a historically evolving process. Nor does simply ignoring context avoid this issue as phenomena divorced of context are meaningless.

Both lines of argument can be seen in Tsoukas' reasoning that "…to reduce something to allegedly objective information and then to treat that information as if it was an adequate description of the phenomenon at hand, is to obscure the *purpose* behind the information, a purpose that is not made explicit in the information as such" (1997: 830). Tsoukas refers to this misguided practice as information reduction, raising the other contentious topic of objectivity.

It should be emphasized that the perspectives presented here are not meant as a devaluing of conventional psychology. Traditional psychology has made a significant and rich contribution to the understanding of the human mind and behavior for more than 100 years. Of particular significance to the present project is the work of Arthur Reber and colleagues, and others, in the field of cognitive psychology and implicit learning, which claims to reveal the cognitive processes and systems by which tacit knowledge is acquired. This work is explored in more detail in a subsequent chapter.

5.6   ON OBJECTIVITY

The debates around subjectivity and objectivity have already been touched on (Section 1.3) in the context of the definition of knowledge. The following short discussion considers objectivity from the perspectives of SC and methodology. As will become evident, the conceptualization of objectivity is fairly fundamental to the SC theory.

A core argument of the SC case is that no phenomena can be objectively studied. Kenneth Gergen claims that one must abandon the whole idea of objective truth as this simply cannot and does not exist. Stretching this argument a little further, natural sciences, with their laws based on stable events that do not change over time, can be contrasted with the irrationality and unpredictability of human behavior. This leads Gergen to insist that the epistemology and methodology of the former cannot be applied to the latter. Central to this claim is the idea that all social interaction, including the social psychologist's interaction with her subjects, is filled with value judgments, labeling biases, and value-laden terms. On the opposite side of the argument, the essence of the positivist-experimental case is that phenomena in the world can be observed objectively: objective facts may be found, and experimental findings generalized. As noted earlier, drawing on William Starbuck's work, the pursuit of generalizability comes at a cost.

These ideas have currency from many different directions. For instance, coming at the subject of objectivity from the topic of scientific discovery but reaching a similar conclusion, Michael Polanyi reasons that the scientist's participation in the discovery and validation of knowledge is itself a part of that knowledge. As we noted earlier, Alan Chalmers makes the practical point that no two observers looking at the same scene will come away with identical experiences. We encountered an example of this in Section 1.3 in the story of the English Royal Astronomer, Nevil Maskelyne, and his associate who was unfortunate enough to record different astronomical observations from his senior, resulting in his dismissal: individual differences. According to Paul Feyerabend, professor of Philosophy at the University of California, Berkeley, the positivist-experimental viewpoint considers scientific facts to be sterilized of any kind of personal values such as belief or opinion, an assumption, and—as Feyerabend describes it—an almost slavish adherence, which he rhetorically demolishes.

Feyerabend, Kuhn, and Chalmers all fundamentally question and dissect the traditionalist, positivist approach, and methodology adopted by the scientific disciplines. In *Against Method,* Feyerabend singles out "critical rationalism" and "logical empiricism" as misguided practices that result in inadequate accounts of science, which in turn risk their future development. He further adds: "(T)they give an inadequate account of science because science is much more 'sloppy' and 'irrational' than its methodological image. And they are liable to hinder it because the attempt to make science more 'rational' and more precise is bound to wipe it out, as we have seen" (2010: 160).

This review of the debates in and around SC is admittedly eclectic. However, the objective is to draw attention to the fact that conventional approaches to science and scientific discovery are not themselves immune from criticism. Added to this, there is a sense that a view of knowledge as socially constructed, as a basic idea, exists across many different fields of enquiry.

5.7 SUMMARY AND CONCLUSIONS

This chapter has investigated SC and the challenging debates between the respective, critical, and experimental approaches to the world in general and knowledge in particular. This has an obvious impact on and consequence for research—what and how a topic is researched, and why. We have then considered the debates around the concept of objectivity finding this to be a contested area (see Chapter 1 for the KM debates on this particular issue). Two key definitions are offered: discourse, following Stainton Rogers, is understood as both the product and the means of creating meaning in particular ways. Social action is understood as the ways in which individuals interact with their environments and their contents, mediated by personal understanding and knowledge of shared precepts (which idea has connections to Paul Duguid's notion of "knowing how" as mediating "knowing that").

The aim has been to frame SC and discourse analysis as not only having the validity and credentials to constitute an alternative perspective on knowledge and KM but also as one which is perfectly suited to such a project. It is suggested that these proposed directions are only extending those already indicated by many working in the KM field. If nothing else, the strategic management of knowledge within organizations can perhaps now be clearly understood as dealing with something that is far more dynamic and complex than an "object." Even a piece of text, a report, a lessons learned document, a corporate vision statement, are more than sets of ordered letters and words on a page to be read and understood in *exactly* the manner in which they were expressed by the author. They only take on meaning in the context of the reader, and which meaning is singular to the individual.

What we have before us now is an alternative theory of knowledge and a perspective of language as action oriented that constitutes a topic of interest in its own right, which can be studied using the methodology of discourse analysis. In particular, noting the foundational importance of research to the development of societies in the broadest sense, it has been argued that how and what is researched is contested ground, with implications for what knowledge is created.

The next chapter explores research in the discourse analysis field, with particular attention paid to what this reveals and what this means for KM.

FURTHER READING

Madsbjerg, C. and Rasmussen, M. (2014). An anthropologist walks into a bar…. Harvard Business Review, March: 80–88.

Marshall, H. (1994). Discourse analysis in an occupational context. In Cassell, C. and Symon, G. (Eds). *Qualitative Methods in Organizational Research*. London: Sage.

Phillips, N. and Di Domenico, M. (2009). Discourse analysis in organizational research: methods and debates. In Buchanan, D. and Bryman, A. (Eds). *The Sage Handbook of Organizational Research Methods*. London: Sage.

Potter, J. and Wetherell, M. (1987b). *Discourse and Social Psychology: Beyond Attitudes and Behaviour*. London: Sage.

Starbuck, W. (2002). Keeping a butterfly and an elephant in a house of cards. In Choo, C. and Bontis, N. (Eds). *The Strategic Management of Intellectual Capital and Organizational Knowledge*. Oxford: Oxford University Press.

6

DISCOURSE AS THE SITE OF KNOWLEDGE WORK

6.1 INTRODUCTION AND THE TURN TO TALK

"…to *say* something is to *do* something; or in which *by* saying or *in* saying something we are doing something."

(J.L. Austin, *How to do things with words*; italics in original, 1962: 12)

British Philosopher John Austin's work and ideas have been profoundly influential in shaping the development of discourse analysis (DA) and a host of related fields. The crux of his insight rests on the notion that when we speak we do much more than utter words and that these words are received and interpreted by listeners as doing more than conveying a mere description or factual account of some event, for instance. The significance of these ideas is evident in all of the following discussions.

By turning in the direction of talk as the site of knowledge work, the topic of DA, the theory and methodology for the study of the dynamics of human linguistic interaction and accomplishment, takes on paramount relevance. Certainly, as far as the study of the organization goes, there is a growing popularity and credibility in postmodern paradigms and, in particular, DA. Equally, there is evidence that discursive studies are proving significant, not just in terms of the study of organizations but also in contributing to debates around what constitutes an organization, according to a report by Cynthia Hardy, professor of management at the University of Melbourne. This is a conclusion that Nelson Phillips, of London's Imperial College, and his coworkers claim is illustrated in their discursive model of institutionalization: this emphasizes the relationship between text, discourse, institutions, and actions.

DA is located within postmodernism and social constructionism: as such, DA is diametrically opposed to conventional or traditional theoretical and methodological

Knowledge and Discourse Matters: Relocating Knowledge Management's Sphere of Interest onto Language, First Edition. Lesley Crane.

approaches. Recall William Starbuck's relegation of conventional methods of research as particularly useless in the study of organizations. Likewise, DA has attracted its share of criticism in, for instance, the subjective nature of its data. Nonetheless, Egon Guba and his colleague are clear that the "legitimacy of postmodern paradigms" is now well established and considered equal to that of conventional positivist-based methodologies. The growing popularity of these methodologies is described by Jonathan Potter, toward the end of the 1990s, as "mushrooming" across multiple diverse disciplines.

DA comes in a variety of forms and types, partly because it is a methodology adopted by many different disciplines including psychology, linguistics, and organization studies, for instance: see Robin Wooffitt's *Conversation Analysis and Discourse Analysis* for a comprehensive and critical review. Nelson Phillips and Maria Laura Di Domenico also offer a critical review and summary of DA brands from the perspective of organizational studies research, noting their common interest in how social reality is constituted in talk. In contrast, Jonathan Potter and his colleague draw attention to the definitional confusion where virtually all research concerned with language, in whatever discipline and whether in a social or cognitive context, uses the term "discourse analysis" (recall Stainton-Roger's useful definition of "discourse" in the previous chapter). It is perfectly possible, they claim, to have two books on DA with no overlapping content. Generally, though, what different types of DA share is an interest in how discourse displays action orientation, function and effect and a view of language itself as the topic of interest. Within critical social psychology, the most commonly cited are discursive psychology (DP), conversation analysis (CA), membership categorization analysis (MCA), and critical discourse analysis (CDA). In their fascinating study of workplace interactions, Maria Stubbe and her colleagues at the Victoria University of Wellington, apply and contrast five different DA methodologies to the same discourses. While they uncover substantial areas of overlap, they also indicate significant differences and points of tension. The implication is that choice of DA methodology or paradigm is, or should be, determined by the directions of the research and topics of interest.

The focus here is on DP as the preferred paradigm for the study of organizational knowledge work, and there are several reasons for this. First, it focuses on language as action with consequences, and as variable; secondly, it can be applied to all forms of communication—spoken and written—which offers a level of flexibility not available with some of the other types of DA; thirdly, it is both a methodology and a theoretical framework; fourthly, DP approaches language as inseparable from the processes of thinking and reasoning. Finally, and following from this latter point, discourse itself is the topic of interest, study, and action. This positions talk and text as the site of human action, performance and accomplishment in every psychological respect: hence "the turn to talk."

The next section introduces DP in detail, followed by an overview of some of the other dominant DA paradigms in critical social psychology. This is followed by a review of some relevant themes and topics in what is shown to be a substantial, comprehensive, and broad DA research agenda. It has already been claimed that the analysis of everyday discourse reveals quite different phenomena than those reported using conventional research method-ologies: now we can begin to see some substance to this claim. Novel insights, for instance, emerge in the analysis of "identity," "gender," and discourse in computer-mediated com-munications (CMCs). The penultimate section pays a brief visit to the management practice of "sensemaking," drawing out some interesting comparisons and contrasts with the discursive fields. Some early conclusions suggest that shifting attention in the direction of organizational discourse could reveal some alternative directions for the knowledge management project with the suggestion of some concrete benefits.

6.2 INTRODUCING DISCURSIVE PSYCHOLOGY

6.2.1 Origins

> Motives and intentions (vernacularly understood) are built inferentially out of descriptions of actions and events; they are built to contrast with alternatives; they attend to matters local to the interactional context in which they occur; and they attend reflexively to the speaker's stake or investment in producing those descriptions. (Derek Edwards and Jonathan Potter, 2005: 246)

Jonathan Potter and Margaret Wetherell are credited with being the first to introduce DA to social psychology in the late 1980s with their groundbreaking book, *Discourse and Social Psychology: Beyond Attitudes and Behaviour*. DP was developed and formally introduced by Derek Edwards and Potter in their 1992 publication of the same title. The earlier work applies the DP theoretical framework (in all but name), and its distinctive DA methodology, to the study of attitudes and behavior as examples of studying traditional psychological phenomena from a different perspective. By comparing and contrasting this to conventional theory and research, Potter and Wetherell seek to highlight the weakness of mainstream approaches, which they contrast with the advantages of DA in revealing the social world as constituted in language.

Similarly, the later work by Edwards and Potter compares DP with traditional methods of studying human memory in cognitive psychology. An important point to emphasize is that while being critical of conventional methods in psychology, and cognitive psychology in particular, Edwards and his coauthor do not claim that DP represents a "straight substitute" for the conventional paradigm. Nor do they suggest that the conventional paradigm is wrong or invalid as a basis for theory and research. They just advocate a different approach.

6.2.2 Discursive Psychology's Core Assumptions

Discursive psychology's core assumption is that language is the location of the social world—human action and performance—as distinct from behavior. This distinction needs a little unpacking because while traditional psychology is concerned with mind and *behavior*, DP speaks of discursive *action*. Recall JR Searle's *Speech Acts*, which the KM theorist Professor Nonaka claims to draw upon in his theory of the knowledge-creating company. According to Searle's theory, speakers make statements, blame, argue, give commands, ask questions, and so on, and these *acts* are governed by the adherence to certain linguistic rules. Language—speaking—then is action in the sense of behavior governed by rules. This directly connects to DP's second core assumption—that talk and text are locally and situationally organized. What this means is that the meaning of discourse cannot be divorced from the context in which it is uttered. Thus, people use language to create versions of the social world, which may vary from context to context.

Conversely, conventional social psychology approaches language as a transparent medium which reflects reality as it is manifest, evidenced in the use of surveys and interviews, for instance. Here, the topic of interest is *what* people report or say as a route to uncovering some hidden cognitive structure such as attitudes or beliefs, or intentions to act. For instance, discussions in Chapter 3 show the frequent use of such research methods in the context of knowledge management studies although, as seen in the last chapter, such approaches and methods have come in for considerable criticism over the last two decades. Referring to studies using self-reporting questionnaires or semistructured or structured interview methods, social psychologist Charles Antaki, of the UK's Loughborough University, claims that while these rely on memories of past events, such memories are notoriously prone to inaccuracy. Consequently, interviews and so forth are "unsatisfactory sources of evidence." Jonathan Potter also makes the point that attitude scales, as another example of favorite conventional methods, which he labels as "arcane contexts," cannot tell you what people are doing with their evaluations in their everyday environments. The psychologist Michael Billig claims that attitudes in particular, by their very nature, are stances on matters of public controversy not reports of private, internal mental affairs. Rather than study what he describes as "...ghostly essences, lying behind and supposedly controlling what can be directly observed" (2001: 210), if one takes the approach that psychology is constituted in language, then it becomes possible to study the processes of thinking directly.

The assumptions that flow from this understanding of language are what make DP singular: that talk is constructive, functional, consequential, and variant. It is constructive in that people construct versions of the social world ("reality") linguistically in discourse. This in turn implies that all language is functional in that it works to achieve some accomplishment (e.g., persuasion or argument, blaming, or warranting). It is consequential in the sense that discourse construction and function lead to consequences for the speaker and the coparticipant(s). It is variable, in that one person can describe another, or a phenomenon, action or scene in completely different ways to different people.

An ongoing debate that affects not only DP but other brands of DA is the extent to which the analysis of discourse should address, focus on, or even acknowledge "cognition" and "cognitive states." This has been the subject of some confusion and has relevance in particular for DP as a branch of psychology and indeed for the directions of the present discussions: these issues are taken up in subsequent chapters. For now, it is sufficient to note Derek Edwards and his coworker's stance on the issue in their own words: "(D) discourse analysis is particularly concerned with examining discourse for how cognitive issues of knowledge and belief, fact and error, truth and explanation, are dealt with" (1992: 29). That is, cognitive phenomena are constructed and managed in discourse itself.

6.2.3 Emerging Ideas

An aspect of DA that has been developed in analytic practice, and which was originally introduced to social psychology in Potter and Wetherell's *Discourse and Social Psychology*, is the notion of interpretive repertoires. These refer to the individual's stock of words, phrases, metaphors, and so on that are used to give meaning to and evaluate experience of the world and its contents. Repertoires can be linked to themes of attitudes, beliefs, and attributes—the stamping ground of the conventional social psychologist—but are not tied by group boundaries. Thus, repertoires can be specific to the individual or relate to an organization or group. Note that the subsequent formal introduction of DP by Edwards and Potter does not explicitly reference repertoires perhaps because its text is focused on memory, but the idea of repertoires is arguably implicit to their conception.

This idea about "group boundaries" raises an interesting point and topic of ongoing debate: the distinction between ordinary everyday talk and organizational (or institutional) talk. This is something that Bethan Benwell and her colleague address in their investigations of identity from the discursive perspective and in a variety of different environmental settings. Drawing on their reasoning, the characteristics that distinguish organizational talk from any other kind of talk include an orientation to organization-specific goals to be accomplished; speakers' contributions are typically constrained by specialized and restricted contexts (e.g., a meeting agenda); and organizational "leaders" (in the broadest sense) have the right to ask questions and to expect answers.

On this latter point, Benwell and her coworker contrast the rhetorical structure of classroom talk with that of the television interviewer: the former has the normative rights to make evaluations of answers, whereas the latter does not. Faced with the recalcitrant interviewee, the challenge for the interviewer is how to achieve a "critical interview." A further characterizing feature of organizational talk can be seen in the rhetorical devices used by speakers to align themselves with the organization: "we" and "us," for instance, and the use of jargon as well as the display of particular types of knowledge. A recent study of organizational team talk by researcher Jonathan Clifton displays how speakers bring the "hierarchical organizational identity" into being through the negotiation of rights to make role-based knowledge claims. That is, people construct themselves in discourse as possessing this or that role (implicitly or explicitly), with particular roles implicating a shared understanding of rights to possessing knowledge (the role of finance director implicates possession of financial knowledge, for instance), and it this that warrants their rights to bring the organization into being as this or that. In Chapter 15, there is a fascinating example of constructing an organization in social talk, which has considerable consequence for the meeting in which this action takes place. This has synergies with "group construction," which we will see a lot of in Part Two. It is also particularly resonant with the notion of repertoires.

The idea of interpretive repertoires has some consistency with Kenneth Gergen's theory of the "saturated self." According to his reasoning, people construct a myriad number of personal identities dependent on context and circumstance. We are comfortable within contexts and environments of which we have experience—we have the requisite discursive repertoire to make sense of it. Thus, repertoires can be understood as personal lexicons that, in effect, define the individual and their multiple selves, and this notion has some connection with "sensemaking." There are equally clear synergies with, for instance, Paul Duguid's analysis of Communities of Practice where it is the individual's underpinning, uncodifiable tacit knowing that mediates understanding and sensemaking in any given context.

6.2.4 The Thorny Issue of Variation

Unlike traditional approaches in psychology, DP is not about attempting to understand what is said in talk as a means of illuminating some underlying cognitive phenomenon. That is, the view of language as a mirror that does no more than reflect inner thought as contrasted with DP's constitution of language as the site of interest in its own right. This is an important differentiation that highlights a particular problem in traditional psychology's research methods. In the use of questionnaires, scales, and so forth, the conventionalist searches for patterns and consistencies in data with the aim of uncovering phenomena that can be generalized to the world at large. But how does the conventionalist accommodate for the variation in talk and text—the so-called outliers? In this case, the conventionalist must "sort out" any variability in the data or it may impact on results. As Potter and his coauthor note, "(*V*) variability of the kind seen in detailed studies of discourse is thus a considerable embarrassment to traditional attitude theories" (1987: 54). In the DP paradigm, variability in language is sought for and studied for its consequence and function, and it is this feature that is its empirical mainstay.

Next is a brief review of some of the other leading types of DA applied in critical social psychology to provide an even-handed view of the field, starting with CDA.

6.3   OTHER LEADING PARADIGMS IN DISCOURSE ANALYSIS

6.3.1   Critical Discourse Analysis

For the scholar who is attributed with developing it, professor of language in social life at the United Kingdom's Lancaster University, Norman Fairclough, the purpose of CDA is to explain the relationship between language and society and, importantly, the relationship between *what* is analyzed and *how* it is analyzed. The essence of the project is an understanding of a dialectical relationship between a "discourse event" (e.g., a piece of text, or a conversation, meeting talk, and so forth) and the context within which it takes place (e.g., environment, circumstances, institution, and its social structures), claiming that one has transformative possibilities and capabilities for the other. That is, discourse can be shaped by the context in which it is enacted and vice versa. It is this transformative capability that invokes connotations of power, domination, and ideology. As Fairclough and his colleague Professor Ruth Wodak see it: "(B) both the ideological loading of particular ways of using language and the relations of power which underlie them are often unclear to people. CDA aims to make more visible those opaque aspects of discourse" (1997: 258). So, similarly to DP, CDA emphasizes the critical role of context in discourse in action but, unlike DP, constructs that role as bidirectional. This is an important differentiation, and one which illuminates a potential limiting factor in DP. This is returned to in the following chapter.

This particular brand of DA is concerned with how discourse is used to influence the direction of social and political processes using a combination of discourse analytic technique and a critical approach. More specifically, according to Wooffitt, it constitutes a method of analyzing discourse for how political and social inequalities come into being. Note however that Paul Chilton, in his exploration of political DA, makes no mention of CDA whatsoever. Even within the subgenre of "political discourse," there are different definitions. Such notions of power and domination also raise the spectre of researcher bias.

The scholar and editor of the academic journal *Discourse Studies*, Teun van Dijk particularly highlights the role of the discourse analyst, reasoning that there can never be an unbiased interpretive analysis of discourse and consequently the role and position of the analyst must be treated as part of the analysis. Others locate the prospect of bias even earlier in the process in describing the act of transcription of meeting recordings, for instance, as being "inevitably selective." The idea of the researcher's actions connected to bias is one we have encountered in earlier chapters: recall, for example, Michael Polanyi's description of the scientist's participation in the discovery and validation of knowledge as being a part of that knowledge and Kenneth Gergen's reasoning that it takes a "rare social psychologist" to successfully refrain from coloring his or her work with their personal values, methods, and so forth.

6.3.2 Conversation Analysis

Two other types of DA—CA and MCA—both emanate from the work of Harvey Sacks, the American sociologist renowned for his pioneering work in the 1960s and 1970s in the study of how people use language in everyday life. Like DP, CA has the core assumption that talk is locally and situationally organized and as constituting the site of human action. It focuses on everyday "mundane" conversation with a particular interest in the constitutive processes of social action: that is, how actions such as blaming, excusing, and so forth are negotiated and accomplished with the emphasis on the organization of turns at talk— "the system of distribution." So while speakers have a "naïve mastery" of the processes that define social action, they may have limited ability to identify and describe those processes—thus, it is the task of the analyst to dismantle or disaggregate such processes in order to study directly how people perform and understand their own actions and those of others. Paul Drew, a sociologist based at the United Kingdom's University of York, is one of several scholars who offer a detailed explanation of this methodology: he describes it as a naturalistic, observation science of actual verbal and nonverbal behavior. A key feature of CA is that it is data-driven rather than theory driven. That is, completely opposite to conventional methods of enquiry, its analysis does not begin with a theory.

It has become increasingly popular across diverse disciplines. In the late 1980s, for instance, Potter and Wetherell refer to this brand as "youthful." By 2012, Elizabeth Stokoe, professor of social sciences at Loughborough University, likens CA to a "juggernaut" such has been the explosion of work in this paradigm. A brief survey of CA work published in 2012 includes Jan Svennevig's study of agendas and workplace meetings; Cecilia Ford and Trini Stickle's study of how turn taking is managed in work meetings; Hanna Rautajoki's analysis of how TV discussion show participants manage identity and accountability; Mie Femø Nielsen's study of how meeting facilitators use various devices to facilitate innovation in organizational brainstorming sessions; and Jonathan Clifton's study of trust in workplace conference calls, showing how trust is a relationally constructed phenomenon accomplished through the use of various rhetorical devices and practices.

A major area of debate centers on the issue of context or culture: that is, the extent to which the analyst can bring her own a priori knowledge of context to the analysis or whether analysis should be confined solely to the sense of context that speakers make live in their talk. To shed some light on this question, consider the positions of two viewpoints: on the one hand, Emanuel Schegloff, professor of sociology at UCLA, Berkeley, warns against muddying analytic findings through the analyst's application of their own contexts (e.g., gender) to discourse rather than focusing on those constructed by speakers. From this perspective, the artificial application of an understanding of context external to those of the discourse itself would effectively negate analytical findings. On the other hand, scholars Jackie Abell and Elizabeth Stokoe argue that this is too limiting a perspective in restricting the whole idea of culture in the study of socially situated identities. Later in this chapter, we will see an example of what Abell and her colleague mean by this. Nonetheless, once again, context steals the show.

There is a less troubling but ongoing debate over what types of data CA should be concerned with—video and audio and/or written texts. Some claim that the nature of CA limits it to audiovisual materials only. Others take the view that it can be applied to any type of data, including online forums and chat rooms as demonstrated in a study by Mona Nilsen and her coresearcher.

6.3.3 Membership Categorization Analysis

Compared to CA's juggernaut, MCA is a mere "milk float" according to Stokoe. Whereas CA is concerned with conversational sequential practices ("turn taking"), MCA is concerned with the meaning-laden categories invoked in everyday talk, suggesting resonance with the idea of "repertoires" discussed earlier. MCA's insight is that people are referred to using categories and that at any point an individual may be referred to or "labeled" with more than one different category: for example, manager, contractor, father, and brother. Each of these categories carries meaning and mostly come embedded with "category-bound activities," activities considered to be typical or expected of a given category. Elizabeth Stokoe provides a comprehensive overview of the field, proposing that MCA can reveal the commonsense routine workings of society. To underline her point, she includes a number of examples of MCA analysis: "advice giving" in the context of a US television show, "account giving" contingent to the construction of the shared meanings invoked by "common knowledge components" such as "y' know" in the context of a radio interview, call and online support services, and police interviews.

The idea that we live in a world of identity categories, each of which has a bearing on behavior, sensemaking, and discursive repertoires is a foundational theme to Gergen's "saturated self" in which the individual is seen as a multiplicity of selves and where "human significance" is determined by relationship. MCA is consequently concerned with category selection as action with consequences.

According to Stokoe, MCA is at risk of being subsumed into CA. In reality, the two methods are not mutually exclusive, nor do they necessarily overlap with one another. There are, in fact, examples of useful and insightful studies that combine both types of analysis in their methodology (e.g., Stommel and Koole's intriguing analysis of how new members negotiate joining an online help website with some surprising findings).

6.4 TOPICS OF STUDY IN DISCOURSE ANALYSIS

Thus far, the chapter has described and summarized the theoretical and methodological stances of various types of DA, building on the idea that these constitute frameworks and methodologies that have much to offer to knowledge management. To add weight and substance to this, the following sections review and discuss some of the more popular (and relevant) DA topics in critical social psychology with a particular focus on research in DP.

The span of DA research is enormous even within the boundaries set out above. Frustratingly, it also refuses to fit neatly into a categorization of three or four manageable headings. Studies have focused on **gender** (e.g., Charlebois, 2010; Potter and Edwards, 2003; Rhodes and Pullen, 2009; Schegloff, 1997; Stokoe, 2012), **identity** (e.g., Abell and Stokoe, 2001; Ainsworth and Hardy, 2004; Benwell and Stokoe, 2012; Brown and Phua, 2011; Bucholtz and Hall, 2005; Condor, 2000; Crane, 2012; Davies and Harré, 1990; Giles, 2006; Greatbatch, 2009; Gulich, 2003; Hobbs, 2003; Holmes, 2005; Hutchby, 2001; Locke and Edwards, 2003; Mieroop, 2005; Myers, 2010; Rautajoki, 2012; Wetherell, 2001; Whittle, 2005), **attitudes and evaluative practices** (e.g., Potter, 1998a; Potter and Edwards, 2012; Wiggins and Potter, 2003), **occupational roles and good practice** (e.g., Cromdal et al., 2012; Ford and Stickle, 2012; Holmes, 2005; Housley and Smith, 2011; Marshall, 1994; Nielsen, 2012; Svennevig, 2012b; Wasson, 2004), **and knowing as an interactional accomplishment** (e.g., Gulich; Hepburn and Wiggins, 2005; Hutchby; Lester and Paulus, 2011; Marra et al., 2004; Paulus, 2007; Svennevig). *Abbreviated references are retained in the text here to facilitate the interested reader in locating the appropriate reference.*

The intention of this section is to draw upon this body of work to support the argument that DA methods are relevant and could make a valid contribution to the study and practice of KM. Consequently, we concentrate on two of the most popular and distinct themes of DA study—identity and CMCs—plus a brief visit to the topic of gender because of the intriguing findings that DA studies reveal in this area. CMCs are of particular relevance bearing in mind the prominence of technologies within the context of KM. These studies collectively reveal and represent a snapshot of the variety of topics and situations that DA has investigated, and some of the insights they can offer. It is not the intention here to provide a detailed critical review of the literature, but rather to give an idea of the work in this field. We will start with identity, perhaps one of the most significant and enduring topics of interest in DA.

6.4.1 Discourse and Identity

The study of identity is one of the fastest-growing areas in the social sciences. Andrew Brown, at the United Kingdom's Warwick Business School, and his colleague speculate on this growing phenomenon with an interesting perspective in their suggestion that concrete ideas of "who we are" are becoming less certain in a world in which the domination of ideas of commodification and ubiquitous technologies lead to fragmentation, discontinuity, and crisis. This is a perspective encountered before in, for instance, Kenneth Gergen's notions of the increasingly fractured nature of the self, largely in response to the presence of technology in all aspects of human life. It is ironic that in a world in which social media, Web 2.0 and so forth are promoted and positioned as enhancing and transforming our abilities to communicate, others such as Gergen see them as leading to identity fracture.

Debates

In his comprehensive appraisal of the "social science of identity," sociologist James Côté, at the University of Western Ontario, describes the field as filled with debate, much of which is focused on what constitutes identity and how it should be researched. This sounds somewhat reminiscent of earlier discussions around the topic of knowledge management. As noted in the previous chapter, from the social constructionist perspective, there is a shift from the notion of identity as a static, enduring entity with its connotations of equally enduring personality traits that can be studied and measured. Instead, identity is perceived as dynamic, fluid, and malleable and relational to context. The essence of these arguments is that identity is a socially and relationally constructed psychological phenomenon, although perhaps not entirely at the whim of context at any given time. From these perspectives, a person's identity is a far more complex and evolving phenomenon than conventional identity theorists would have us subscribe to. It also throws into question the idea of "measuring" identity or personality with questionnaires, surveys, interviews, and scales.

Côté is drawing out more of a political argument for the streamlining of what he sees as the "Tower of Babel" state of identity research and theory. This, he argues, would result in a more potentially powerful lobbying position with policy makers. He also argues that pure identity research often has no real prescription for the practical utility of its ideas. As we touched on in the previous chapter, Madsbjerg and his cowriter are critical of the human sciences as being "notoriously difficult to understand" and, worse, irrelevant from the perspectives of the "real world" of the organization.

Before reviewing some of the DA work in the identity field, it is worth briefly speculating on what the view of identity as socially and relationally constructed in talk might mean for knowledge management. An immediate observation is that if identities are constructed and made live with function and consequence in discourse, then that function and consequence can be observed firsthand in the discourse itself. Building on this, it is conjectured that a function and consequence of identity work, intentionally or otherwise, is to influence the direction and nature of discourse that has implications for knowledge work as an action accomplished in talk.

Princess Diana, Bill Clinton, Punks, Goths, and Hippies

We begin our review of work in the identity field by focusing on three distinctive studies. First, Jackie Abell and Elizabeth Stokoe use a combination of a social constructionism and CA to investigate how Princess Diana accomplishes the business of constructing and contrasting her "true self" and her royal role as two distinctive identities in a TV documentary interview, highlighting the tensions between the two. They show how culturally situated identities are located in conversation, claiming that social identity does not exist as some private cognitive process. Their study stands as a classic display of how identity is manufactured in social interaction between people rather than being a single, individualistic, enduring and static inner self. A further feature of the analysis reveals how speakers' references to others, for example, Diana's reference to "my husband" rather than "Charles," constitutes a powerful rhetorical practice. "Husband," as an identity category, invokes far more meaning, motive, relationship, and symbols than the use of a Christian name. So, how people categorize others, and the meanings that such labels implicate for the recipient, has a direct effect on the nature and direction of the conversation.

Abell and Stokoe's study has a particular aim in impressing on the importance of importing relevant cultural context to any DA (an argument also brought by Paul Chilton, in his account of political discourse) in order to locate identities as they are constructed. This is something that the CA purist would refute but that Abell and her colleague insist allows them to work with the best of both worlds—the microscopic "word scrap" detail of CA and a broader, more context-driven approach.

In the second example, Abigail Locke and Derek Edwards adopt a DP approach to study former US President Bill Clinton's testimony before the Grand Jury, demonstrating how he uses crafted rhetorical practices to both manage and mitigate the relationship between himself and Monica Lewinsky. A key finding reveals how Clinton, in his portrayal of Lewinsky as unreasonable, overly emotional, and demanding, effectively and reflexively casts himself as the exact opposite: as caring and responsible. This study also demonstrates how Clinton uses memory limitations, combined with an explicit desire for accuracy of recall, as a rhetorical resource to mitigate his accountability for "forgotten actions." In other words, Clinton uses the rhetoric of the law, and its obsession with getting at the facts as they happened, to his own ends. In their analysis, Locke and Edwards show how claims to memory failure can serve as a device for mitigating—or avoiding— responsibility, which is a particularly effective rhetorical strategy and one which has clear consequences for the direction of the discourse. The use of this and other devices works to cast Clinton in the role of being only interested in the evidential facts, consequently as someone to be trusted and believed. These are the sorts of findings that cannot be unraveled through traditional qualitative or quantitative methods.

Clinton's concern with accuracy of recall has interesting parallels with a raft of experimental work in cognitive psychology, which study the inaccuracies of human memory (see for instance Elizabeth Loftus' account of memory faults) and the importance of context in memory retrieval. Also note a recent article in *New Scientist* that announces the development of a new artificial intelligence application that identifies, for instance, the frequent use of phrases such as "as far as I can recall...." as indicators of false testimony![1] This is precisely the type of phrase that Clinton is shown to use.

In the third example study, Sue Widdicombe and Robin Wooffitt use a combination of CA and DA (Potter and Wetherell's 1987 version, *Discourse and Social Psychology: beyond attitudes and behaviour*) to analyze informal interviews with subculture group members, with a particular interest in how social comparisons are used to accomplish "authenticity." According to conventional social identity theory, people innately strive for a positive self-esteem or self-image and that this is a prime motivator in making social comparisons in intergroup and between group contexts. Accordingly, members of one group will often display prejudice against others through drawing on social comparisons.

In their analysis, they diplomatically call into question some of the underlying assumptions in the conventional prescription, arguing that if identities are socially produced and one is interested in understanding how, then the imperative is to locate study in the context of action—discourse. Their compelling analysis of punk-rockers', goths', and hippies' talk draws out a clear "being/doing" distinction, a "shallowness" versus "genuineness" embedded in social comparison talk. Speakers compare groups to an external standard, compare past and present characteristics of their group, and compare new members with older members. In this way, the creation of categories is shown to be connected to the action of social comparison. The analysis also shows the recurrence of "motivation" as a linguistic resource for differentiating between group members in that motives between different members vary from "authentic" to "shallow" or "faddy."

Identity and Categorical Groups

Leadership is a category with a history of research stretching back almost eight decades. In his discursive study of leadership in the context of an organizational meeting, researcher Jonathan Clifton defines the category as the ability to influence the management of meaning, including that of the organization, which is achieved interactionally.

---

[1] "Our laptop says the witness is unreliable" (*New Scientist*, March 8, 2014, No 2959).

He approaches leadership as a "language game" in which the "…rights to assess, and, therefore, to define the organizational landscape are negotiated in talk and the person, or persons, who have most influence in this process emerge as the leaders" (2012b: 150). What his fascinating analysis reveals is the war chest of discursive resources and devices that are made live in meeting talk—negotiation of claims to superior knowledge, for instance—and their effect on accomplishing the coconstruction of the category of leadership. A key finding displays how leadership is dynamically distributed in the moment-to-moment business of the meeting's discourse: leaders can only be leaders in interaction with others who live in the identity of "followers." A further finding shows that while "leaders" claim the rights to assess topics and define meaning for the organization, this latter is not necessarily connected to hierarchy.

Another piece of work uses the example of older workers to demonstrate how CDA can be used to unpick very real social issues. Researchers Ainsworth and Hardy show how meanings associated with "labels" influence behavior and action. CDA is particularly focused on how language is involved in the social relations of power and domination. Ainsworth and her coworker's interest lies in how the identity of "older worker," and its associated meanings, is evoked in discourse showing how this has real consequences for people categorized in this way. Conventional research methods, they suggest, are unable to unlock these subtleties. Their point is that a CDA approach can reveal the ways in which the use of "labels" and "categories" in identity construction can constrain individuals, and how the meanings attached to those labels can influence behavior. Unfortunately Ainsworth and her colleague's work is not a report of a CDA study, but rather a well-reasoned and persuasive argument for the advantages of undertaking such a study.

Categorical groups are constructed in many different ways. For example, a linguistics study of courtroom proceedings demonstrates how a lawyer uses her rhetorical practices and resources to construct an "in group" which includes herself and the jurors, but excludes the opposing attorney. In this study, impression management practices are linked to persuasion. According to the analysis, this "in group" comes into being when the lawyer uses African American vernacular English in addressing the (African American) jury. While exemplifying the practice of impression management, it can also be seen as an example of active, dynamic identity construction with, here, the sole purpose of alignment with the jury. This is shown to be a powerful and effective resource in constructing mutual empathy.

This understanding of impression management is different from that elsewhere in the DA literature. For instance, Susan Condor, of Lancaster University, presents impression management as a device for prejudice avoidance. In her discourse study (note that she does not actually specify which type of DA she uses in here analysis) of how English people formulate their country in an interview context, she rather surprisingly finds that people deployed impression management strategies and devices to actively avoid being heard to have an explicitly national stance, or to overtly display national pride. Condor suggests that one way of interpreting this is that participants "hear" talk of English nationalism as "typical" Anglo-British xenophobia. She does conclude, however, that the apparent correlation between national and prejudice accounting, which seems to be an evident rhetorical pattern in her data, is not necessarily universal to all British citizens. Condor's study uncovers the immensely complex nature of identity work, and the effects and consequences of (un)conscious impression management work. Impression management has close ties to stance (or position) taking, which is considered next.

Stance-Taking and Status Work

Greg Myers, also of Lancaster University, investigates how bloggers use language to take stances in online forums, suggesting that the priority of the blogger is to mark their position relative to others rather than dialogic debate or collective discussion. Stance-taking, Myers claims, is not just about having an opinion on any given topic but also about using that opinion to align or misalign with someone else interactionally. Arguably, the business of stance-taking is fundamentally concerned with identity construction, and both are bound to context and social interaction.

Similarly and drawing on the DP paradigm, my own study of a knowledge managers' online discussion forum investigated how contributors construct their identities as expert with entitlement to be heard as such. The analysis (which forms the subject of Chapter 15) shows how participants use rhetorical devices to actively and relationally construct and accomplish membership of an elite group, and that membership of this group is marked by within-group competitive rivalry. In other words, participants work to establish their expert credentials relationally which, it is claimed, has some synergies with the theory of creative abrasion (see Chapter 4).

This notion of expertise being constructed interactionally and relationally is also evident in an earlier study of knowledge transfer between experts (doctors) and nonexperts (patients). Analysis identifies three devices used in the construction of expertise: self-categorization, category-bound activities such as the use of specialist terms followed by a reformulating colloquial description, and evaluation. The primary contribution of this work however lies more in the identification of *how* experts share knowledge with nonexperts and to what effect. The findings clearly demonstrate how a divergence in perception between these two categories (doctor and patient) often leads to unsuccessful communications. For instance, it is shown how patients describe long-term illness as having a sudden onset, but doctors display it as having a long development and onset. In other words, doctors and patients can often construct two entirely different meanings of the same thing. This finding is reminiscent of Leonard's (2007) claim that gaps in knowledge between two or more people can result in barriers to knowledge sharing.

From this brief review, it can be seen that DA applied to the study of identity can reveal features and facets of human social and interactional life that may not be available to traditional research methods. While it is acknowledged that some of the findings are not entirely relevant to organizational management and studies, and KM in particular, the point here is to show what *can be achieved*.

We now turn to a brief review of some of the discourse work in the area of "gender," which reveals some fascinating and thought-provoking research findings.

6.4.2 Discourse and Gender

> From a discursive perspective, it may be unsurprising that the kind of gender stereotypes found in the lab virtually disappear in actual face-to-face interactions, since lab instruments are designed to find gender and then smuggle it into the language of sex differences. (Neill Korobov, 2011: 462)

What Korobov is drawing attention to here is the blunt difference between the traditional perspective of gender as a measureable, tangible, manageable, and physical part of the human experience and the social constructionist perspective of gender as an artifact that is constructed in human interaction. This, Korobov suggests, means that the relevancy of gender is something for speakers to contextualize and bring meaning to, which may in some instances have no connection to society's reified understanding of "gender." As an artifact of talk, gender is infinitely more dynamic, ambiguous, complicated, and rich in meaning and consequence. Moreover, gender is important in the modern organization. Organizations have a moral and, in some cases, a legal obligation to have effective policies, procedures and rules on gender equality, and sex discrimination, for instance. What if, in designing and implementing such policies, organizations are looking in the wrong direction? One of the core questions that gender studies raise is this: if gender becomes a live issue or context displayed in talk and text in social interaction, then how is this action brought about, and what are its effects on the discourse participants? Who is doing the gendering, and to what effect? The reader will find an example of the construction of gender in Chapter 16's analysis of meeting discourse.

To illuminate this point, Elizabeth Stokoe, in her review of developments in language and gender research, investigates what happens in a higher education seminar involving three male and one female students who are tasked with carrying out a collaborative writing task. Stokoe's analysis reveals how the female comes to take on the role of group "scribe" (secretary), speculating that such a move may well have influenced her resulting intellectual contribution to the task. Thus, how members of a group (e.g., team, firm, community of practice, and so on) accomplish categorization practices, such as gender, is shown to have practical consequences for unfolding events.

A review of two other discourse studies reveals some of the intricacies of gender from a discursive perspective.

Challenging the traditional view of job assignation based on gender, Mats Alvesson, professor of business administration at Sweden's Lund University, reports on a study of a Swedish creative advertising company—which he describes as a "knowledge intensive company"—showing how gender division is extreme. His findings indicate that, on one hand, what are seen as "female gender traits" are highly valued. On the other, identity work done by men places stronger emphasis on workplace sexuality in response to the ambiguous context of advertising work that, he suggests, is strongly linked with "femininity." Thus, his analysis shows that the femininity associated with advertising work affects gender relations and interactions in the workplace resulting in greater emphasis on "doing" masculinity.

Drawing on critical DP, Justin Charlebois, of Aichi Shukutoku University in Japan, reports on a study of how Japanese women construct gendered identities through drawing on what he describes as "gendered interpretive repertoires"—ways of seeing the world. He finds evidence of an emerging gender equality (women are and should have equal rights with men) repertoire amongst young women. This, he suggests, conflicts with the traditional repertoires of "woman as primary parent" and "woman as natural caregiver." He concludes that this signifies a culture in a state of flux where emergent and traditional repertoires compete to construct femininity. This is largely based on his exposé of a "guilty thoughts" phenomenon, which Charlebois claims to be indicative of the inner struggle and tension between desire for equal rights with men (e.g., opportunity and right to work) and societal and parental expectation for the assumption of traditional roles (e.g., as mother, caregiver). Is it possible to embrace gender equality while retaining femininity? Charlebois suggests that it is not.

Charlebois' significant findings demonstrate how DA can be used to explore relational and identity issues and crises. However, there is the suggestion in the study that these claims can be generalized across the entire of Japanese society, although they are based on a very small sample of semistructured interviews with only limited discussion of the ever-present matters of researcher bias and subjectivity. David Silverman is critical of studies, which are based entirely on interviews and the use of selective extracts, although he does concede that "manufactured data" can never be considered to be totally "taboo." In her review of DA in an occupational context published in the early 1990s, Harriette Marshall also makes the point that from a DA perspective even a small number of interviews can yield more valid information than hundreds of traditional qualitative survey-style questionnaires.

Drawing on these ideas, while Charlebois' study may be questioned in terms of attempting to generalize its findings to a much broader population, it does signal two important concepts. First, it is unlikely that, as Marshall suggests, traditional interview or survey scales would be able to reveal such intricacies as this emergent-traditional gender tension. Second, imagine what analysis might uncover in everyday talk and text within an organization. What role, for instance, does gender play in knowledge sharing? While gender is not raised as an issue in the knowledge management literature discussed in the earlier chapters, is this because it is not a factor, or is it because it just has not formed a focus of interest and investigation?

We turn next to review, in detail, some of the issues and research findings in CMC.

6.4.3 Discourse and Computer Mediated Communications

I think therefore I am; I speak therefore and I am; I am perceived therefore I am; I am responded to, therefore I am. Paraphrased from Annette Markham's essay on *The methods, politics, and ethics of representation in online ethnography* (2005)

CMCs have been a topic of interest for researchers for more than two decades. Marked by an explosion in social media and networking sites, online environments have become the magnet in the drive for recognition and status in online communities. Annette Markham, associate professor in communications at the University of the Virgin Islands, describes the "computer-mediated construction of self" as a unique phenomenon for study because in such environments individuals as selves and the "social structures" within which they exist and act are the outcome of mutually shared negotiation. From a critical perspective, this is not so removed from the conceptualization of everyday conversation as to warrant the label of "unique." The true uniqueness of the online environment is, however, perfectly expressed by Markham in the coupling of two phrases: "I am perceived, therefore I am," and "I am responded to, therefore I am." This takes on a slightly darker aspect when understood in the light of Kenneth Gergen's "technologies of social saturation," which, he claims, are leading to an erasure of the individual self because of the increasingly blurred lines between man and machine.

On the one hand, we have Markham's perspective in which CMC constitutes a fascinating and dynamic environment in which the self is constructed through interaction with others, which demands new and different research methodologies to fully explore. On the other, we have the view that technologies are fracturing the "person" through the increasing multiplication of selves needed to compete and interact in a multiplicity of different online (and offline) communities. A further issue relates to the ethics associated with using what are ostensibly public online discussion forums for research data, a topic that is returned to in the subsequent methodology chapter (Part Two).

Taking a more practical perspective, CMC is of particular interest here because of the high profile role that technology, and increasingly Web 2.0 and Social Media apps, play in the knowledge management sphere. While many argue that technology cannot and should not be viewed as the "final solution," it is nonetheless prominent both as a feature of knowledge management and as a target of behavioral study. But, as we have shown elsewhere, focusing study down to the level of actual discourse—in CMC or elsewhere—is not something that has so far been particularly pursued in knowledge management.

Coverage

Research in CMC tends to be clustered around academic sites; online support groups for people with health or mental issues such as eating disorders; self-harming and depression; and blogs. Appearing less frequently in the lens of research are sites such as product review sites and professional practice forums. In terms of online forums, those in higher education are most frequently used in CMC research for obvious reasons—they are the most readily available to the academic researcher. Collectively, studies of CMC have raised a broad spectrum of fascinating findings. Before reviewing a sampling of these, we need to touch on one of the major issues associated with CMC research because of the singular nature of this environment, which has already been touched in during the previous discussions.

Researcher Bias

In her review of methods, politics and ethics in online ethnographic studies, Annette Markham raises the conundrum of the embodied (i.e., the researcher) versus the unembodied (i.e., the forum participants) and the consequences of this in terms of researcher role and bias. While enthusiastically endorsing CMC as a valid and rich vein for research, she warns against what she sets out as the prime pitfalls. With the embodied–unembodied issue, she is referring to the potential transfer of the researcher's own experiences and judgments to her data. For instance, Markham notes that a researcher may unconsciously attribute categories (e.g., gender) to forum participants—that is, assigning them with a body. The risk of this "embodiment" is particularly high, she suggests, with texts that display features such as misspellings or poor grammar: the temptation is to categorize the contributor as being poorly educated, for example. Worse, Markham accuses some researchers of "cleaning up" their data by editing and making corrections. This particular method of treating data is completely contrary to the DA methodologies discussed earlier in this chapter and would likely be considered unacceptable. Bearing in mind the evolution of vernacular linguistic practices specific to mobile devices, for instance, the idea of writing off contributors as poorly educated because of misspellings or even through extensive use of abbreviations would now be seen as somewhat rash.

Note that Markham's discussion of research methods in CMC is generally focused on ethnomethodology research. Originally developed by Harold Garfinkel in the late 1960s, ethnomethodology is a method of studying and understanding the social orders (or "rational orders"), which people use to make sense of their world, and the resources they bring to bear. It is thus concerned with analyzing accounts of day-to-day experience.

For Bethan Benwell and her colleague, CMC data is ideal for researchers who are concerned with issues of authenticity because there is no need for any transcription process. Nor, it can be deduced, is there a need for the researcher to take any active role as contributor in the unfolding discourse. They pursue their case arguing that, with this type of data, the researcher can assume to role of "lurker." The implication is that without the physical presence of the researcher, even as a nonparticipative observer, the potential for influencing the course and nature of participants' actions in any given scenario is removed. These authors devote an entire chapter of their investigation of *Discourse and Identity* to the analysis of discourse in virtual worlds. Thus, we have two quite contrasting views.

While acknowledging the rationale of Markham's argument over this issue, it can also be seen as a double-edged sword in that, clearly, the analyst—consciously or otherwise—brings her own embodied sensibilities to the performance of research. One is necessarily employing embodied senses (perception) and cognition. The issue is arguably more to do with *how* the researcher acknowledges herself as a coparticipant in the study, bringing to the fore an awareness of *what* effect the text is having—what is it making her think, imagine, and see—and how. Following Thomas Kuhn's thesis, what is observed is the consequence of the unconscious alliance of the perception of what is looked at and previous experience. There is a need to accept the subjectivity of analysis while paying attention to factors that might impact or influence the findings.

Orality, Trust, Advice Giving, and Identity

Stepping briefly outside of our focus on DA from the perspective of critical social psychology, it is noted that CMCs have been of particular interest with sociolinguistics workers. One of the areas that research has focused on is stance-taking, encountered earlier in the discussions of identity, and how this is used rhetorically and strategically to gain the attention of others in what is depicted as an overly crowded virtual world.

"Orality" in discussion forums is another topic of interest. Orality can refer to something as simple as underlining a part of a text, which has the effect of "increasing its volume," or using "emoticons" to display cognitive states, or it can refer to more complex actions such as the use of parentheses, which can have multiple effects (an example can be seen in Chapter 15). One study for instance investigates orality in the context of a discussion forum for Spanish students learning English, while another focuses on a knowledge managers' discussion forum located in India. In both cases, however, little conclusion is drawn about the presence of what may be described as actions of orality in the forums. This leaves tantalizing questions around what orality accomplishes, what is the effect on forum contributors and readers/cocontributors, and why people feel the need to simulate spoken language in a written context.

Psychologists Bethan Benwell and her colleague suggest that where there are contexts of shared understanding or experience, CMCs tend to be dominated by an orientation to orality. This echoes the idea that a group of people well known to each other often communicate in a singular form of short-hand known only to themselves. Thus, orality could be seen as a kind of "doing consensus" and "group construction": we come across these actions in the analyses in Part Two. This also raises the idea that orality—or the vernacular—is connected to issues of virtual presence, something which Benwell and her coworker suggest is significant in cyberspace, identity, and status.

Developing this latter point, it is worth noting Jahna Otterbacher's, assistant professor at the Illinois Institute of Technology, linguistics study that investigates online product review sites and the relationship between discursive tactics and self-prominence.

The study is specifically interested in how contributors use available cues to develop judgments about the credibility and utility of others' contributions. Without the presence of visual body language clues, for instance, Otterbacher proposes that reputation becomes key to building and engendering trust, an area that she argues is ripe for more research. The relationship between reputation—with its connotations of identity—and trust, and how these categories are constructed and made live in discourse and with what function and effect, is a key topic of investigation in Part Two.

Turning back to the DA literature in psychology, we find a wider spectrum of topics with a substantial body of work investigating rhetorical practices and their accomplishments in health support CMCs. Community membership is of particular interest. Wyke Stommel and his coworker report a study of contributions posted to an eating disorder support site hosted in Germany. Using a combination of CA and MCA, the researchers are interested in how new contributors to the site negotiate membership in terms of expectations and requirements. The a priori expectation is that membership will be "low threshold"—no particular entry requirements. They use their analysis to show that this is in fact not the case. In forensically unpicking the actions in the postings, Stommel and his coworker uncover three interesting phenomena: first, that entry is dependent upon the newcomer doing "being ill"; secondly, that existing members only ever interact with the newcomer not with each other; and thirdly, that a "sequential misalignment" is evident in the newcomer's rejection of advice given by members. Sequential misalignment refers to a break in expected norms of "sequential pairs" of turns: in this instance, when advice is offered (turn first part), the expectation is that it will be accepted (turn second part), but in their analysis, Stommel and his coworker show how the advice is in fact rejected.

"Advice giving," as a phenomenon of study, is a popular target for the discourse researcher. Similarly to Stommel and his colleague's findings, another study that finds that advice giving is largely ignored investigates postings to a support forum for young people who self-harm. The authors show advice giving to be a troublesome activity in which posters commonly use disclaimers such as "I'd probably…" and "it's been said…" as well as terms of endearment to preface potentially unwelcome advice responses. Upgrading the issues associated with advice giving, Phillip Morrow, professor of English and linguistics at a Japanese University, points to the potentially threatening nature of advice messages. He relates this to the problem-poser's self-image in his study of a support site for depression sufferers. (Note that Morrow's study is linguistic but is included here because of the topic of study, rigorous analysis, and because it includes extracts from the data). He speculates that advice may not be followed by advice seekers because they want to avoid being in the debt of the advice giver. The question is, is this action of advice rejection specific to health support CMCs?

Another interesting feature that Morrow draws out is the use of metaphor by those posting problems: for example, "…it feels like…." His argument is that metaphors are used as imperatives, as opposed to for instance stylistic choice, because of the difficulties in describing complex feelings. Arguably, Morrow does not go far enough in investigating the consequences of this phenomenon. In an earlier and equally fascinating study, Elizabeth Gülich uses a CA approach to examine patients' use of metaphor in knowledge transfer interactions between patients and doctors, showing how metaphors situated the patient's perception of their illness markedly differently from that of the doctor, with consequences for reaching shared understanding.

In a work touched on earlier, Janet Smithson and her colleagues also investigate how advice givers in a self-harm support forum establish their credentials to be heard: "(I)in an online context where people cannot use normal interactional cues to determine the identity of a speaker, the ways in which posters use their posts to demonstrate their validity as members or expert become paramount in whether or not they are accepted" (2011: 489). This is a phenomenon that I explore in detail in a DP study of how knowledge managers negotiate and construct selves as expert in the context of an online professional knowledge managers' forum (see Chapter 15). The findings show how forum participants use rhetorical devices such as consensus followed by elaboration, and elite group construction/membership, to construct themselves as experts. A key finding is that expertise is largely situated in interaction with others, although a superficial analysis would suggest that only limited participant interaction is taking place. The use of disclaimers as a key device to manage accountability is also brought to the fore, a practice described in many other studies.

To complete this review of the discourse literature, we draw on one of the few DA studies that focuses on the construct of "knowing" Taking a DP approach, Jessica Lester and her coworker, of the University of Tennessee, study higher education students' blog postings in response to a course requirement to discuss their beliefs and experiences of dietary supplements. The conclusion of the analysis is that students use disclaimers (e.g., "I don't know much about it") to minimize accountability for their blogs and that such disclaimers are often focused on the action of "knowing." In other words, Lester and coworker are arguing that students are not talking about their lack of knowledge about food supplements, but are rather *managing and protecting their identity as a student and all of the expectations that flow from this category such as intellectual competence.* There is a substantial difference between the two viewpoints.

From this brief review, it can be imagined that many lessons and pointers could be gleaned from studies of CMCs to inform knowledge management strategy, even from those studies that investigate, for example, an eating disorder support site. If one speculates how these findings might be applied to different contexts—with the caveat that this may not always be appropriate or feasible—then these CMC studies, together with those in the areas of identity and gender, represent a rich vein of information for the organizational practitioner and strategist.

6.5 SENSEMAKING

It is worth giving a brief consideration to sensemaking as an organizational practice and topic of study and its synergies and contrasts with DA's framework and methodology. There are, however, two caveats to be drawn. Firstly, sensemaking is a substantial field in its own right, and consequently, there is no intention here to delve into its complexities. Secondly, because the term "sensemaking" is applied quite literally to a blizzard of different, often competing, concepts, care needs to be taken about how the term is used.

Two interpretations of "sensemaking" serve to make this point. David Snowden proposes a sensemaking model, which has the purpose of describing different "domains of knowledge" as diverse contexts, each of which connects to a different model of decision-making. His point is that each decision-making context will be singular and that to attempt to apply a uniform "idealized model" of decision-making to each one will result in difficulties. In contrast, Chun Wei Choo, of the University of Toronto, proposes a model combining sensemaking, decision-making, and the creation of new knowledge based on the perception that sensemaking is the foundation to the shared meanings that define an organization's purpose and the identification of both problem and opportunity. In his thesis, the information that any organization has is in a state of continuous flow between sensemaking, decision-making, and new knowledge creating. He defines "sensemaking" in three interrelated stages: sensing in which organizations scan the horizon, sensemaking that mediates the plausible interpretation of incoming information such that actions may be enabled, and sense giving in which vision and purpose are communicated to organization constituents. Arguably, both are talking about rather different phenomena although using the same terminology. They are, in that respect, almost incommensurable.

Christian Madsbjerg and his colleague offer a quite different understanding of sensemaking, which could be interpreted as more of an ecological, humanistic understanding of affairs. Accordingly, sensemaking draws on phenomenology, which has a focus on the study of how people experience life. Phenomenology was Alfred Schutz's (originally published in German in 1932) attempt to deal with some of the most profound and critical questions facing the social sciences in the early decades of the twentieth century (and probably still do): namely, the role of objectivity versus subjectivity in the social sciences and the nature of human action. In this project, Schutz foregrounds "lived experience."

According to Madsbjerg and his colleague, sensemaking "…reveals the often subtle and unconscious motivations informing consumer behaviour and can lead to insights that enable transformations in product development, organizational culture, and even corporate strategy" (2014: 82). Sensemaking from this perspective is largely occupied in the territory of organizational management and management consultancy, and the claims made for its practice have some synergies with some of those in DA. For instance, Greatbatch proposes that CA, unlike other research methods, can uncover and investigate "seen but unnoticed" or "tacit" linguistic action. Consistent with the social constructionist perspective, the sensemaking paradigm emphasizes and is sensitive to how people interact with the world through meaning making.

In comparison to DP, however, there is a subtle difference. While Madsbjerg and his coworker talk about "hidden motivations" that shape behavior and that can be "revealed" in sensemaking studies, Jonathan Potter argues that DP is solely concerned with social life as "normative and rhetorical" practice, rather than as the end result of an interaction of unspecified patterns and factors. "Norms" do not control actions: they are "orientated to" by individuals in their discourse. In sum, DP does not approach human (inter)action—discourse—as a window providing access to the "ghost in the machine," to quote Gilbert Ryle's famous description of the soul. Instead, it studies the action itself. A point of resonance connects to DP's notion of interpretive repertoires as personal vocabularies of terms that serve to define identity from moment to moment. Similarly, sensemaking studies human experience through action (e.g., through conversation, interview, observation, and so forth) to gain a sense of how an individual "knows" of the world. But, once again, the subtle difference lies in sensemaking's search for what lies beyond the (discursive) action, while DP considers the action itself as constituting the boundaries of interest.

Notwithstanding these differences, there are *some* synergies between the two disciplines, with sensemaking, perhaps, offering DP the organizational management terminology that it currently lacks, and which lacking, in all truth, renders it at risk of being seen as irrelevant to organizational practice. This is a theme that is unpacked in more detail in the following chapter.

6.6 SUMMARY AND CONCLUSIONS

The present discussions began with a look at how the "turn to talk" gained traction through an increasing interest in language as performative and as the topic of study in its own right. The field of DA is shown to be characterized by a wide range of different paradigms, the result of the interest in DA methodologies emerging in many different fields of study. On the most basic level they do, however, share a perspective of language as the site of human action in interaction and as action oriented. In critical social psychology, DA paradigms are also shown to be diametrically opposed to the field's conventional approaches, theories and methodologies. Importantly, DA studies, along with the theories and methodologies that they represent, are seen as credible alternatives to conventional approaches, at least as far as their proponents are concerned. Many argue that this type of research is making significant contributions to, for instance, the understanding of the organization and organizational strategy.

The origins, core assumptions, and emerging ideas, such as the notion of "interpretive repertoires" associated with DP, have been reviewed in some detail. More than any other advantage, it is claimed that DP in particular can reveal phenomena that other more conventional approaches cannot. This is particularly seen in how the paradigm handles "variability" in discourse, claimed to be the subject of concern for the conventionalist but which is actively sought by the DP researcher. A focus on variation in everyday talk is both a hallmark of DP and the foundation of one of its most persuasive criticisms of mainstream methodologies and theories. A further key claim is that the constitution of psychology in discourse itself offers the ability to study the processes of thinking directly as accomplished in discourse while noting that the issue of "cognition" remains the source of some confusion. Brief reviews of some of the other methodologies in critical social psychology—CDA, CA, and MCA—provide points of comparison with DP and give a sense of the richness and contributions of the field as a whole.

The breadth of topics and themes addressed in DA research is extensive and difficult to neatly package. Consequently, three themes (identity, gender, and CMCs) that have some resonance with the debates and interests of knowledge management, to a larger or lesser degree, have been reviewed to provide insight into how these themes are dealt with and how their findings contribute to the knowledge. The research reviewed here is just a tiny sample of the work that has been done in this broad field. While many of these cases are not situated in the organizational workplace context, their meaning for workplace discourse and organizational life is nonetheless valid and potentially consequential. They show how people do the business of constructing everyday realities and how these realities can often be shown to be at odds with *assumed* realities.

Studies in identity have shown how this phenomenon is dynamically constructed and situated in the moment-to-moment action of discourse in interaction, whether it is shifting footing from one identity to another in order to manage personal stake and interest in a public interview or rhetorically accomplishing a positive and moral version of oneself as a reflected mirror image of the negative construction of someone else in a courtroom setting.

The approach to and conceptualization of gender in the discourse field is not only radically different from that in mainstream approaches but also reveals phenomena that would remain hidden to such approaches. In particular, the ability to study and analyze what gender means for speakers and with what consequences and function is arguably of particular value.

The study of CMCs is seen as being particularly relevant to knowledge management and the wider interests of the organization. The curious case of "orality" in online forums, for example, is a topic that has yielded some interesting ideas but warrants much more research. Issues uncovered around the action of "advice giving" also have some resonance: in what circumstances will people accept or decline the advice offered?

To complete the present discussions, a comparison, on an admittedly limited scale, between the organizational field of "sensemaking" and DA reveals some tantalizing potential synergies. On the matter of difference, this is notably centered on whether one considers sensemaking as social practice accomplished by actors in interaction, which is itself the subject of interest, or whether one considers it as methodology applied by the researcher. Either approach would result in radically different outcomes.

So far, we have made the case for relocating the focus of interest, study, and even management to discourse—everyday talk and text—defined as both the product and the means of construction, as an accomplishment of linguistic social interaction. Thus, the argument is that if people's knowledge-sharing actions are accomplished in discourse, then the focus placed here will lead to a more direct understanding of such actions, their function, consequences, and so forth. The review of DA in general, and DP in particular, draws the conclusion that such methodologies, supported by adequate theory, are able to uncover phenomena that are simply unavailable to other more traditional research methods. Consequently, if the research objective is to study the phenomena (identified in Chapter 3) of identity, trust, risk, and context as thematic categories connected to knowledge-sharing practices, which are speculated to operate corelationally, it is reasonable to conclude that the application of DA methodology will fulfill this objective.

For a number of reasons, DP stands out as the preferred method of studying organizational discourse and knowledge work. Perhaps paramount of these is DP's perspective of discourse as psychological action. The approach to language as constructive, functional, consequential and variable as the site of that action, and as having a particular concern with knowledge in terms of how speakers' accounts are explained, described and constructed as factual are further reasons. Of equal interest is the idea that if DP is not concerned with what speakers explicitly state (as a linguistics or content analyst might be, for instance), but rather what they discursively do, then it is the case that DP constitutes a methodology for the direct study of displays of tacit knowing as the influencing and mediating aspect of social interaction, as many KM scholars have suggested that it is (e.g., Duguid, 2005). This question is picked up in the following chapter.

But there is what can only be described as an irritating itch that is hinted at toward the end of the previous section. Is DP at risk of being seen as analysis for analysis' sake, an intriguing and empirically robust program of academic research but with nothing to say beyond pure academic interests? This question—the "so what question"—is met head-on in the following chapter in the search for a singular contribution that this particular paradigm might offer to the field of knowledge management.

FURTHER READING

Benwell, B. and Stokoe, E. (2012). *Discourse and Identity*. Edinburgh: Edinburgh University Press.

Edwards, D. and Potter, J. (1992). *Discursive Psychology*. London: Sage.

Phillips, N., Lawrence, T. and Hardy, C. (2004). Discourse and Institutions. *Academy of Management Review*, 29, (4): 635–652.

Stokoe, E. (2012). Moving forward with membership categorization analysis: methods for systematic analysis. *Discourse Studies*, 14, (3): 277–303.

Stubbe, M., Lane, C., Hilder, J., Vine, E., Vine, B., Marra, M., Holmes, J. and Weatherall, A. (2003). Multiple discourse analyses of a workplace interaction. *Discourse Studies*, 5, (3): 351–388.

Wetherell, M., Taylor, S. and Yates, S. (2001). *Discourse Theory and Practice: A Reader*. London: Sage.

Whittle, A. and Mueller, F. (2011). The language of interests: the contribution of discursive psychology. *Human Relations*, 64, (3): 415–435.

Wooffitt, R. (2005). *Conversation Analysis and Discourse Analysis: A Comparative and Critical Introduction*. London: Sage.

7

THE IMPLICIT FORMULATION OF TACIT KNOWING AND RESOLVING MATTERS OF RELEVANCE[1]

7.1 INTRODUCTION: QUESTIONS AND CONNECTIONS

"...most of a person's everyday life is determined not by their conscious intentions and deliberate choices but by mental processes that are put into motion by features of the environment and that operate outside of conscious awareness and guidance...."

(John Bargh and Tanya Chartrand, 1999: 462)

In their extensive review of scientific research into questions concerning the properties of, and relationships between, unconsciousness and consciousness as mental phenomena, psychologists John Bargh and Tanya Chartrand, of New York University, offer the perfect metaphor: "mental butlers." This refers to those mental processes activated by the environment and its contents, which are simultaneously *beyond conscious control* but which nonetheless *direct action*. This notion has significant correspondence to some formulations of tacit knowledge/knowing/know-how that we have seen in earlier chapters. The present chapter reengages with this topic, approaching it from some alternative viewpoints of which "mental butlers" is one.

Thus far, we have reviewed in detail issues, debates, and theory in the field of knowledge management (KM), followed by a consideration of discursive psychology (DP) within the wider perspective of discourse analysis and the "turn to talk" in critical social psychology. This leads to the conclusion that DP constitutes a valid approach to the

---

[1] This chapter forms the basis for an article subsequently published with Nick Bontis as coauthor, although the article was originally researched and written by the present researcher: Crane, L. and Bontis, N. (2014). Trouble with tacit: developing a new perspective and approach. *Journal of Knowledge Management*, 18, (6).

Knowledge and Discourse Matters: Relocating Knowledge Management's Sphere of Interest onto Language, First Edition. Lesley Crane.

study of organizational knowledge work in discourse, which may lead to insights unavailable to more conventional experimental research paradigms. But this comes with a problem.

The proposal of DP as a theory and methodology for the study—perhaps even practice—of knowledge management in organizations has a potential pitfall. From perspectives beyond those bounded by academia, there is the very real risk of this proposal being seen as irrelevant. That is, there is an unavoidable question over DP's relevance to the practice and concerns of knowledge management in terms of what novel, meaningful and relevant contribution it can bring that would be of interest and practical use to the practitioner. That is the "US$64,000 question," or what some have referred to as the "so-what question." The key to unlocking this issue, it is argued here, lies in the conceptualization of tacit knowledge (TK) or tacit knowing. This has already been shown to have a somewhat checkered history in the field of KM.

The present chapter has the objective of developing some clear arguments for this proposal's relevance, particularly for KM practitioners. The basis of these arguments is the speculation that the study of organizational discourse, drawing on DP, can reveal "tacit knowing" in action, and that this can be directly connected to the thematic categories of identity, trust, risk, and context identified in Chapter 3 as factors in knowledge sharing.

More specifically, the question under discussion in the present chapter is this: does an approach to the study of everyday discourse in organizational settings, drawing on the DP paradigm, have the potential to reveal empirical evidence for how knowledge work is done and with what consequences, particularly how the tacit is made manifest and with what effect ("the tacit question")? Why is this potential important and relevant to KM? There are two reasons: first, that TK is generally regarded in the KM field as possessing beneficial and advantageous qualities, commensurate with organizational success and innovation, for instance, and, second, that TK influences action, in the manner of John Bargh and his coworkers' "mental butlers." Both of these points are returned to in a moment. Proposing the tacit question involves quite a leap of logic and consequently warrants some explanation. How has this speculative question been arrived at, and what issues and opportunities does it raise? It is a complex story that brings together three domains: knowledge management, DP, and cognitive psychology's field of implicit learning (IL).

The discussions begin by addressing the origins of the tacit question, and the connections to KM's social perspectives on knowledge. Next, the subject of TK, from the perspectives of knowledge management, is revisited in detail reviewing its perceived values and definitional complexities. The objective is to position TK as a viable target and topic of research and practice. In pursuing this, disputes over its nature are shown to be centered around two perspectives: conversion versus interaction, and the implicit formulation. It is the consideration of the latter version of the tacit that prompts moving investigations into an area that might, on first sight, appear to be something of a substantial tangent. As it transpires, the field of IL is shown to offer KM a considerable database of scientific evidence in support of an implicit understanding of the tacit and a more robust understanding of the phenomenon. To make this point, a direct comparison is made between the two respective fields' formulations of TK.

Finally, a way must be found to rationally make connections between the two theoretically polar opposite fields of IL and DP. Specifically, from the constructionist and postmodernist perspectives in which the latter has been located (Chapters 5 and 6), drawing on research from IL, with its roots in a positivist view of science and knowledge, could be contested. This leads to the proposal of an extension to DP, specific to its application to organizational knowledge discourse, and the study of knowledge sharing's "mental butlers."

7.2   THE ORIGINS OF THE "TACIT QUESTION"

What prompts the tacit question is a foundational tenet of DP itself. DP is not concerned with what people say but rather what they do with their talk and text: what linguistic devices are employed, what functions are performed, and with what consequences. Discourse is approached as an accountable, action-oriented, and functional phenomenon: what the Cambridge philosopher Ludwig Wittgenstein famously described as "language games." Consequently, the analysis of organizational discourse, from the DP perspective, is not concerned with what might be termed the "explicit."

Yet, to simply state that DP-grounded research looks beyond the explicit nonetheless risks that analysis becoming an end in itself, with findings that are unlikely to be of interest or use to those working in KM's front line. For instance, one can analyze discourse to show how people might formulate this or that rhetorical device with what effect for both hearer and speaker *at that given moment and in that context*, but this does not, it is argued, satisfy the proverbial US$64,000 question—"so what?" Moreover, will this lead to simply telling us something that we already know? If DP is not concerned with the explicit, can it be claimed that it has, instead, a concern with the tacit? "Tacit," in this sense, is understood as referring to the means by which people make sense of their world, which makes the explicit actionable.

In exploring these questions, two assumptions are made. First, that all discourse involves knowledge work: at the most basic level, linguistic knowledge of language and a psychological knowledge of cause and effect, as well as contextual knowledge, are essential to human communication and social interaction. Therefore, DP is concerned with "knowledge action." Secondly, no discursive account can be objective: as the originators of DP, Derek Edwards and Jonathan Potter, propose speakers axiomatically attend to their stake and interest when they construct accounts, reports, and descriptions, as well as to the features of the localized social contexts in which they take place. That is, speakers invent versions of the world in utterances adequate to the prevailing conditions and sensibilities of the speakers themselves, and the context of interaction with all of its implications. Margaret Wetherell succinctly brings the point home: to "speak at all is to speak from a position." In other words, a position or a standpoint is immersed in subjective perception, belief, attitude, and so forth. There really can be no such thing as an entirely objective statement.

As discussed in previous chapters, the DP view of discourse highlights the constructive and action-oriented nature of talk in interaction. It approaches the cognitive as embedded within not separate to discourse. These ideas suggest connections to some of the formulations of the tacit seen in the KM domain. Haridimos Tsoukas, for instance, reasons that one of the principle reasons behind the misunderstanding of knowledge that characterizes management studies is the cognitivist view of language—"communication"— as a "conduit" to people's inner minds and thoughts. The implication of this metaphor suggests that language can be seen as an accurate representation of the mental stuff between our ears. Thus, in Tsoukas' interpretation of the cognitivist perspective, what a person knows can be unproblematically displayed "as is" in linguistic communication.

Add to this perspective another, this time from the field of cognitive psychology and the study of human consciousness, which is concerned with, among other things, the core question of the extent to which we have conscious control over judgments, decision-making, and other behaviors. John Bargh and his colleague's review of this dauntingly enormous field finds that consciousness plays a role in only around 5% of behavior, suggesting that 95% of the time we are all operating on "autopilot." Accordingly, unconscious processes are an automatic perceptual activity, influenced by environmental features and contents but which are nonetheless behaviorally influential (summarized in Fig. 2). And obviously, behavior has an influence on the environment of action.

Recall the core tenet of critical discourse analysis, touched on in the previous chapter, and its view of the relationship between discourse and context (environment) as bidirectional. While Bargh and his colleague do not explicitly state this, is it not obvious that in the same way that "environment" influences perceptual processes, which in turn influence behavioral practices, it is equally plausible that those practices will have an influencing effect on environment? Clearly, what we are about here is to equate the unconscious processes to "tacit knowledge" or "tacit knowing" and to speculate an influencing role for what is often and perhaps mistakenly shut away in the KM strategic drawer.

To suggest that DP can reveal the tacit at work in discourse is *potentially* counter to the central tenet of DP in its *implied* suggestion that analysis opens a channel to hidden mental states. As noted earlier, this is precisely the assumption that Tsoukas criticizes. The cognitivist view, and indeed that of most conventional KM workers, conceptualizes discourse as the expression of thought, intentions, or other underlying cognitive process, thus implicating a mind–behavior (discourse) distinction in which behavior is contingent to mind. By contrast, Edwards and Potter claim that "(R)rather than seeing the study of

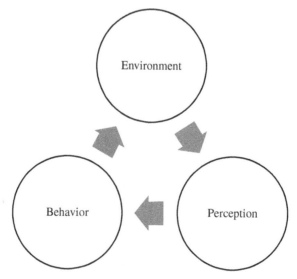

FIGURE 2   The flow of influence in unconscious mental processes.

discourse as a pathway to individuals' inner life, whether it be cognitive processes, motivations or some other mental stuff, we see psychological issues as constructed and deployed in the discourse itself" (1992: 127). There is a subtlety at work here: provided that one formulates TK as a psychological phenomenon that is "done" in discourse and that *only* matters of relevance to the speakers as invoked in that discourse are the subject of analysis, it is argued that posing the tacit question is consistent with Edwards and Potter's approach.

To underline this argument, consider other synergies between this understanding of what DP can reveal and formulations of "tacit" in the KM field. DP's approach to discourse as action oriented corresponds with the notion of TK as action oriented and an influencer of action. The importance of context in the formulation of the tacit is also reflected in DP's approach to context. According to Potter, the "particulars" of any given context of discursive social interaction are important because they are subject to human perception.

In essence, the proposal of adopting a DP theory and methodology to investigate organizational knowledge work, and TK in particular, is only extending in directions that many KM theories are already signposting. Such a proposition should hold some resonance and relevance for the KM practitioner and scholar. The DP project, nonetheless, has its limitations that are returned to toward the end of this chapter. Next, we briefly recall some of the reasons why the tacit is considered to be so valuable in the KM field despite its disputed nature, highlighting the undercurrent of an interesting perspective.

7.3   THE VALUES OF TACIT KNOWLEDGE

The idea that TK (tacit knowing, know-how, etc.; hereafter collectively referred to as TK unless otherwise stated) is crucially linked to innovation and new knowledge in organizations was premiered in the KM field by Ikujiro Nonaka in 1991, in a guide (as opposed to a theory) explaining how Japanese companies are able to generate continuous innovation as knowledge-creating entities. This formed the basis of his future theory, published for the first time in 1994, introducing all of the key and core features of the theory including the SECI model and the imperative to convert TK to explicit (organizational) knowledge and vice versa (see Chapters 2 and 4 for detailed discussions; note that both 1991 and 1994 versions are the basis of Nonaka and Takeuchi's book published the following year, and all subsequent versions). In both guide and theory, Nonaka envisions TK as rooted in action and commitment to specific context, and as comprising skills and cognitive elements. The key to the acquisition of TK is, according to Nonaka, experience *with or without the use of language*. TK quickly became a focal point of debate.

A brief tour of some of the competing perspectives adequately illustrates the tensions over its values. While Nonaka envisions the tacit as the *subject* of amplification, JC Spender contrastingly ascribes the value of TK to its amplifying *agency*. Competitive advantage, from this view, emerges through the integration of tangible (explicit) firm-specific knowledge with the intangible (tacit), leading to outcomes unique to the organization. Unlike Nonaka, Spender stops short of speculating on the nature of this "integration." Robert Grant reports the development of a number of "powerful" information technology tools for knowledge management that are targeted on "tacit knowledge," which, according to his description, is the oldest known form of knowledge. One wonders how such technology would deal with Dorothy Leonard's brand of TK, which she describes as "sticky" and not easily transferable other than through mentoring, observation, and collaborative problem solving.

Preferring to apply an organizational typology, Chun Wei Choo ascribes TK as the personal experiences and expertise of the individual with TK as the principle ingredient in the effective acquisition and application of new knowledge. This headlines TK as not only essential but also intrinsically valuable. This is, of course, reminiscent of Paul Duguid's perspective that TK ("knowing how") makes the explicit ("knowing that") actionable and his claims that the importance of Communities of Practice is contingent on the TK that they share. Rounding up some of its other ascribed values, we find TK described as the well spring of knowledge, as vital to competitive advantage and the explaining factor in expertise, and as the most crucial and challenging "knowledge flow" to acquire. It is also described by Max Boisot as the most valuable component of personal knowledge. In fact, Nick Bontis, while describing its importance to delivering strategic performance, is one of the few scholars who temper the valuation of TK with its limiting characteristics in terms of competitiveness and adaptability.

Thus, irrespective of theoretical perspective, TK is valuable to organizations, and as such requires and warrants some action. But the real issue remains—what is it?

7.4   A DISPUTED PHENOMENON

The enduring issue at the heart of the tacit debate largely centers around two questions: what did Michael Polanyi actually mean, and is Nonaka's imperative to convert tacit to explicit knowledge mistaken?

Without repeating the discussions of earlier chapters, it is worth reemphasizing that despite the disunity over its nature, a substantial portion of the literature draws on Polanyi's work for an understanding of the tacit. One interpretation of this state of affairs suggests that the root of the problem lies in the interpretation of Polanyi's work and even, as the scholar Kenneth Grant claims, a lack of consultation with the source work, relying instead on second or even thirdhand accounts. Another sees this as an appropriate, if ironic, example of what Paul Duguid means when he describes the rules for interpreting texts as residing within the individual reader rather than in the text itself, as we saw in Section 4.3. In this case, understanding is in the eye of the beholder, and from this perspective, one interpretation is as good as any other until shown otherwise.

A further point worth noting is that whereas considerable criticism has been brought to bear on Nonaka's theory of the knowledge-creating firm, very little has been made of Polanyi's work. One exception is Anu Puusa and her colleague, of the University of Joensuu, Finland, who suggest that his perspective of TK is unhelpful and restrictive (so far as research is concerned). So on one hand there is an obvious issue with the interpretation and understanding of what Polanyi meant but on the other, a near unproblematic acceptance of what he is understood to have written as being true.

According to Polanyi, TK is personal, practical, abstract, ineffable, indefinable, unspecifiable, instrumental, and dwelling in subsidiary awareness. There is one characteristic of this account that is the most clearly misrepresented: Polanyi does not divide knowledge into two distinctive, separable entities. In fact, he argues for a quite opposite formula in which every act of knowing contains tacit and explicit components, implying that one cannot exist without the other. Thus, "…the act of knowing includes an appraisal, and this personal co-efficient, which shapes all factual knowledge, bridges in doing so the disjunction between objectivity and subjectivity" (1962: 17). In denying a distinction between the "objective" and "subjective," Polanyi insists that complete objectivity is a "false ideal." According to Ilkka Virtanen and others, many misinterpret Polanyi's thesis by making precisely these distinctions. A further interpretation suggests Polanyi's meaning to invoke a process, not a category of knowledge, and indeed, many criticize the reduction of Polanyi's concept of "tacit knowing" to "tacit knowledge."

While Polanyi did not explicitly describe the tacit as having most value—he was talking about personal knowledge in the context of scientific discovery, not organizational knowledge in a commercial context—his description of it as intangible, hard to articulate, even ethereal, inevitably brings to mind a prize worth pursuing. One could say that it is the "mystic" dimension afforded through the tacit that lends the practice of KM its primary distinguishing feature from information management. Without TK, is KM not simply managing explicit, codifiable, quantifiable, expressable *information*, which recalls some of the questions addressed earlier in Chapter 2: is KM a "trendy" new name for information management, and is it merely a passing fad?

That is not to downgrade the value of explicit knowledge, nor the challenges and complexities of managing it. However, if one follows Polanyi's thesis, all knowledge contains both explicit and tacit phenomena, and one without the other suggests a meaningless state of affairs.

This, once again, links to one of the most contentious debates in the literature: the "conversion versus interaction" question. This question has made an appearance in the preceding chapters (see, for instance, Sections 1.4 and 4.6) so regularly that the reader is, here, sparred any further comment on the matter other than that it remains one of KM's most contested debates. Scrutiny of the debates around the question of TK raises another, and for the present purposes, more interesting notion: the "implicit" formulation of TK.

7.5 KNOWLEDGE MANAGEMENT'S "IMPLICIT FORMULATION" OF TACIT KNOWLEDGE

In his phenomenological framework for TK, Tsoukas argues that rules are of no use in mediating action until it is "assimilated" within the unconsciousness. This is in considerable contrast to the traditional dualism—the "either/or" state of knowledge—expressed in the tacit–explicit distinction promoted by Nonaka. It also indicates a trend toward an implicit formulation of TK in the knowledge management field.

Note that while the term "implicit" in connection to TK is used widely in the KM field, this is generally taken to mean "unspoken" or inexpressible in the sense of phrases such as "they all tacitly understood…" or "when she stated XYZ, she implicitly meant ABC…." The understanding of the implicit nature of TK discussed here is much broader than this, as will be made clear, and is why this understanding is referred to as the "implicit *formulation*."

In a theory that is designed to address the tacit–explicit issue, Max Boisot proposes that new knowledge results from mentally abstracting and coding information from the environment, reckoning this pattern elaboration to a process of problem solving. In this way, Boisot introduces the idea of TK as implicitly acquired: that is, knowledge of the environment and its contents that bypasses a person's conscious mental systems. Similarly,

Dorothy Leonard and her colleague openly state that knowledge can be acquired through IL, again referring to mental actions that are automatic and that bypass conscious awareness. People are not even aware of possessing knowledge acquired in this way, they claim. Stephen Gourlay is another scholar who suggests that "know-how" contains a tacit fraction (incidentally, he resists mapping "know-how" entirely to TK, but any reasonable interpretation would suggest that "know-how" is precisely that!) that can be acquired through IL without the subject being aware of either learning or knowledge. In a similar vein, Davyyd Greenwood and his coworker, preferring to use the term "tacit knowing," characterize this as "hidden understanding," which is difficult to express and which is integral to the active struggle to know how to act in the world.

Offering a slightly different understanding, and drawing on studies in neuroscience, JC Spender suggests that different areas of the brain are responsible for different types of learning, with *some areas being evolutionarily older than others*. This is a concept that will be returned to in more detail presently (Section 7.6.6).

Connections to John Bargh and his colleague's work mentioned at the outset of this chapter are crystal clear particularly in their category of "mental processes that are put into motion by features of the environment." However, have the discussions and investigations around an implicit understanding of TK gone far enough in the KM field? It arguably remains a somewhat vague concept: for instance, in what way is TK "integral to the active struggle to know how to act in the world," and why is this important?

The implicit theme around TK slightly slipped off the KM agenda for a few years, arguably sidetracked by a refreshing of the original "theory of the knowledge-creating organization" by Nonaka and Toyama in 2007. In the present sampling of the KM literature, it is not until 2011 that the "implicit formulation" makes a reappearance with Tsoukas' phenomenological framework.

So far, we have seen that TK is generally considered to be a valuable asset to the organization, and while acknowledging the ongoing disputed nature of its constitution, the "implicit formulation" is a well-established account that is shown to have correspondence with some accounts of the unconscious processes in neuroscience fields. Could the "implicit formulation" hold the key to a deeper understanding of the tacit? If so, then the proposal that an approach drawing on DP has the potential to directly study TK in discourse as implicitly accomplished action with effect and consequence would acquire some rationale.

One of the few scientific domains that has explored and studied TK, with a particular focus on its acquisition and use, is that of IL, a branch within cognitive psychology. This is a substantial body of research that has been at best only briefly referenced in the field of KM. The link, somewhat appropriately, is Polanyi, and this link is shown to have consequences for KM. The following section investigates IL, its leading theory and key debates, together with its experimental methodologies and findings. A comparison between this body of evidence and theory and perspectives from the KM literature proves revealing.

7.6   THE IMPLICIT LEARNING PARADIGM

The study of IL from a cognitive psychology perspective finds its origins in the mid-1960s in the work of psychologist Arthur Reber, who is also credited with coining the term. According to Reber, in his essay on implicit and learning and its resulting base of tacit knowledge, IL is the process by which complex knowledge about structured stimulus displays in the environment is largely induced without awareness or the use of conscious learning strategies. Knowledge acquired in this way is unconsciously encoded and stored as abstract mental representations mainly of structural relationships. In Reber's theory, these abstract mental representations are rule governed, and most importantly for the arguments being developed here, they are unconsciously deployed in modifying behavior appropriate to the environment. Recall John Bargh and his colleague's thesis that, for the most part, everyday life is guided by unconscious mental processes that are triggered in accordance with prevailing features of the environment: the notion of "mental butlers."

Before going any further, it is important to emphasize that the interpretation given here to Reber's (and others') terminology in IL studies is given the broadest understanding: for instance, his reference to "structures in the environment" is understood as contexts in the sense of the environment and its contents, and "rules" is taken too include shared "social norms," for instance.

Referring directly to Polanyi's work, Reber calls these mental representations "tacit knowledge": "(I)it is this induction process that the philosopher Michael Polanyi referred to when he describes the essence of the work of the creative scientist as building up a 'personal knowledge' that resisted verbalization but nevertheless was the driving force behind the ultimate attempts to understand the 'knowable reality' that was out there"(1993: 117). As Reber and his coworker, writing in the late 1970s, conclude, "…implicit learning is a naturally occurring, unconscious, cognitive act, an automatic process of a human mind operating in any complex environment with a rich underlying structure with which it must interact" (1977: 355). This is the launching pad of Reber's clever but controversial *theory of IL* and its formulation of tacit knowledge (see Reber's 1993 detailed essay on the theory, its evidence base, and debates). Importantly, the theory is concerned with both *acquisition and application*, consistent with the core concerns of KM.

At this early stage of the discussions, it is essential to lay down some boundaries for what follows. IL is bound to questions of consciousness and unconsciousness that modern scientists have wrestled with for more than a century. As one of the founders of cognitive psychology, George A. Miller, writing in the early 1960s, describes it, "consciousness is a word worn smooth by a million tongues." It is not the intention here to enter into the debates over what the psychologist and cognitive neuroscientist Endel Tulving counts as among the most closely guarded of Nature's secrets. But, while the present discussions stay focused around Reber's theory of IL, it is important to view the IL project as sitting within the unresolved—perhaps unresolvable—questions of the nature of consciousness and unconsciousness.

A brief exploration of the Polanyi connection lays the foundations for an understanding of the potential importance of IL for knowledge management.

7.6.1   The "Polanyi Connection"

The "Polanyi link" takes its significance from the argument that while Reber's appears to be the only work in IL to make a *direct* reference to Polanyi, most if not all studies in the IL field are arguably testing Polanyi's conceptualization of tacit knowledge. The evidence in support of this argument becomes clearer in the following discussions of theory and experimental findings. As we have already seen, much of the KM literature draws on

Polanyi's work for its theoretical basis. Consequently, if these arguments are persuasively made, the substantial bank of IL research can be seen as a vital empirical basis for KM's understanding and theorizing on the tacit, with potential implications for the study and practice of KM.

If Polanyi's work is so relevant to the IL field, an obvious question concerns why it is only Reber who appears to reference it. There are two possible answers to this. First, Reber began his work in IL around a decade after the first publication of Polanyi's work in 1958, and both share a certain liking for arguing against the prevailing wisdom. Secondly, Polanyi is a philosopher (and a scientist), and psychologists in the 1960s "lacked a consideration" of philosophy compounded by a prejudice against cross-disciplinary working. Psychology was originally a subset of philosophy and when it finally emerged, armed with its new precise and objective methodologies (borrowed from the natural sciences, as we saw in Section 5.5) and accounts of its subject matter, psychologists worked hard to claim identity as a serious field of scientific study in their own right. Thus, the mere mention of the works of a leading philosopher in the context of psychological enquiry must have been somewhat risky during the 60s. But then, Reber is not one to shy away from controversy.

While it is not surprising that Polanyi's work finds little citation in the IL literature, what is surprising is that the KM field has not happened on IL's rich vein of empirical work other than the occasional passing reference. This is particularly striking when as Carol Seger, in her comprehensive review of the IL field, concludes that IL could well be of fundamental importance to developing practical knowledge of how the real world in all of its complexity actually works. Echoes of the ideas of Paul Duguid, Haridimos Tsoukas, and many others in the KM field are inescapable. The following critical review of research in IL impresses the relevance for KM to an even greater extent, using an account of Reber's theory serving as a backdrop and narrative against which to view this data.

7.6.2 The Challenge of Researching the Unspeakable: Research Paradigms in Implicit Learning

To state that the study of IL and its product, TK, is a challenge is something of an understatement. One is in effect attempting to observe and record a phenomenon of which the performer is allegedly unaware, and cannot speak of adequately. This challenge has been met with some of the more ingenious research paradigms in cognitive psychology. The most frequently used is the artificial grammar learning (AGL) task (see Emmanuel Pothos' comprehensive review of AGL research, published in 2007).

Originally devised by Reber in the mid-1960s, this test uses a finite-state artificial grammar to generate letter strings of various lengths. So while they have the appearance of random nonsense, the strings are rule-governed. Participants are typically shown between 15 and 25 strings. Participants are tasked with learning them having been instructed that they are engaging in a test of memory. On completion of the "learning stage," participants are informed that the strings are rule governed, but not what these are. Then they are presented with a set of novel letter strings, some grammatically consistent with the rules and some not: participants have to judge their rule conformance. As Diane Berry and her colleague, at the University of Oxford, concede participants' performance is shown to be well above the chance level despite their apparent inability to express knowledge of the rules, with success rates typically around 65%. While this suggests that participants have, somehow, learned something of the grammar rules they are, nonetheless, shown to have difficulty in expressing the rules by which they make judgments. Numerous variations to this basic research paradigm have yielded mixed results.

An important contribution to IL evidence comes from studies of patients with mental impairments (see Michael Abrams and Arthur Reber's review, published in 1988), particularly patients with amnesia. In the case of the latter, patients' episodic (explicit) memory is impaired, but their IL abilities are shown to be intact, which implicates separate systems. Another study found no difference between the control group and patients in the ability to differentiate between compliant and noncompliant letter strings in an AGL task. In a study involving a serial reaction test, amnesiac patients were able to learn the visual sequence even though they were subsequently unaware of the learning task, and shown to retain this knowledge after a week's delay. Amnesia is associated with damage to the hippocampus region of the brain in amnesiac patients resulting in impairment to episodic (explicit) memory, but not to implicit systems. This explains some of the findings, for instance, where patients are shown to be as capable of IL tasks as controls, but not in explicit learning tasks. Despite some misgivings over data consistency, Pothos' review concludes that "(O)verall, the neuroscience data corroborate a view of separate implicit and explicit components in competition with each other" (2007: 238).

There is, however, one awkward question that these studies in particular raise. If, as has been shown, IL task performance is unaffected by mental impairment—commensurate with controls—while explicit learning performance is degraded, with the implication of separate mental systems, how can the widely held conclusion that all knowledge, including task performance, contains *both a tacit and an implicit component* be explained? This underlines the deeply complex nature of human consciousness–unconsciousness: as Reber attests, "...implicit perception, learning, and memory.... are complex processes whose properties are delicately intertwined with those of more familiar processes that operate largely within the control parameters of consciousness" (1997: 137).

Four core features of IL theory can be picked out as having relevance to KM: "unconscious and natural," "abstractionist," "automaticity and influence," and "an ancient evolved system."

7.6.3 Unconscious and Natural

The essence of IL theory is that the acquisition—and application—of tacit knowledge is an unconscious and *natural* process. Drawing on Polanyi, Reber proposes that whereas the implicit acquisition of knowledge is a natural process, the attempted verbal explication of that which is acquired is not and consequently that "...what is held or stored exceeds what can be expressed" (1989: 231). This is almost identical to Polanyi's frequently cited account.

Contrast this with the influential imperative to convert the tacit to explicit in the KM field. This approach to TK appears overly simplistic and illogical according to IL's empirical evidence base. For example, in their experimental study of the role of TK in intellectual competence in real-world pursuits, Robert Wagner, of Yale University and his coworker find that while TK is integrally important in competent behaviors, it is not related to verbal intelligence. Drawing from this, they argue that much of TK is "...probably disorganized, informal, and relatively inaccessible, making it potentially ill-suited for direct instruction" (1985: 439). "Ill-suited for direct instruction" and, perhaps, ill-suited for direct management?

Unsurprisingly, there is some dispute over the unconscious nature of IL and TK, and some studies have found at least a partial ability to communicate implicitly acquired knowledge. Nonetheless, the relevance for conventional KM perspectives on tacit are clear: if there is a type of knowledge that cannot be adequately expressed, but that is unconsciously applied to making sense of the environment and that mediates behavior, then it cannot be managed in the conventional sense. The attempt to do so is to embark on an "unnatural" course. However, this does not mean that the value of TK is in any way reduced.

It is worth pausing to compare Reber's formulation of TK, as the product of IL, with Polanyi's. Polanyi suggests that we are only subsidiarily aware of personal knowledge, thus TK is subsidiary to other knowledge. Subsidiary knowledge, he explains, "…is not known in itself but is known in terms of something focally known, to the quality of which it contributes: and to this extent it is unspecifiable" (1962: 88). The key to understanding this account lies in "to the quality of which it contributes." TK is, quite simply, essential to (explicit) knowledge, howsoever it is manifest. If one is subsidiarily aware of something, it is barely noticed; it does not enter into attentive consciousness—*but it can influence behavior and indeed is essential to it*. But, this does not entirely "square" with the evidence from studies of patients with amnesia, for instance, referred to earlier and the awkward question that these implicate for an appraisal of knowledge comprising both explicit and implicit components.

Reprising some similar ideas from the KM field, recall the notion of "knowing how" (tacit) as the facilitator to "knowing that" (explicit) being actionable. Likewise, Scott Cook and John Seely Brown's account describes TK as a tool that aids, but is not part of, the action of knowing. In contrast to this latter, and according to Polanyi's thesis (and that of Reber), TK is very much a part of the action. One potential explanation for the difficulty in articulating TK lies in Reber's account of the nature of stored TK.

7.6.4   An Abstractionist Model

In Reber's theory, the TK acquired through the implicit processes is stored in the form of abstract representations of structures in the environment with the emphasis on the structural relationships, and covariance. In terms of probability, covariance refers to the measure of how variables correspond to and vary together: where, for example, the greater values of one variable relate to greater values in the other, their smaller values will also be related, and they will tend toward similar behavior. In the case of the AGL task, for instance, it is not a snapshot of the string that is stored, but a set of rules that represent the structural relationships within the letter strings. These abstract representations—which can be equated to an unconsciously stored personal theory of the world's contents—are automatically and unconsciously "triggered" by novel stimuli in the environment with which the representation shares covariance.

This notion underlies the "abstractive" nature of the theory and is, according to Reber, core to its ability to explain the transfer of knowledge from one stimulus domain to another. Further, it is rapid and a key feature to "effective performance." This notion has considerable correspondence with Daniel Kahneman's proposal of a dual neurological processing system, specifically sharing equivalence with his formulation of a "System 1," which is automatic and rapid, involving little or no effort or control, as well as his view of humans as innately pattern seeking. This is also analogous to Polanyi's prescription of what he terms a "well-known" notion that "...the aim of the skillful performance is achieved by the observance of a set of rules not known as such to the person following them" (1962: 49). This explanation illuminates what might otherwise be described as Polanyi's mystical hypothesis that "...we act and see by the light of unspecifiable knowledge..." (53). In KM terms, this formulation of the tacit emphasizes the inevitability and contingency of context, which lends support to, for instance, Mark Thompson and his colleague's understanding of the underpinning role of context.

In their claims for the necessity of implicitly learned content as well as declarative content in the creation of expertise, cognitive psychologists Pawel Lewicki and his coworkers extend the "abstractionist" hypothesis. They propose that mental representations result from an interaction between a stimulus' objective characteristics and preexisting, internally stored algorithms. It is these algorithms that give the stimulus semantic meaning—subjectivity—and that formulate the rules by which the stimulus is encoded and represented. Thus, they conclude that it is a biased encoding system and subject to error, consistent with Kahnehman's System 1. Echoing Reber's concept of the importance of covariance, Lewicki and coworkers interpret the evidence from studies as demonstrating the human innate ability to detect and store data about contingencies and covariation between stimuli in the environment, with or without awareness. Note the similarities between these conceptualizations and Haridimos Tsoukas' proposed structure of TK with functional, semantic, and phenomenal components. So, even if one could articulate TK in its pure form, it would probably make no sense, and yet paradoxically, it has sensemaking properties.

Like most other aspects of IL theory, the abstractionist view is not without its critics. A robust argument against the abstract nature of TK comes from Don Dulany and colleagues at the University of Illinios who replicated one of Reber's earlier AGL experiments. Though some of their results are consistent with those of Reber and others, they offer a different interpretation. They insist that what their data shows is the use of conscious rules of informal grammars in grammaticality judgment. Consequently, they conclude, performance is not the result of the use of abstract, unconsciously held representations. Somewhat unsurprisingly, Arthur Reber and colleagues' riposte counters that Dulany and his team have made a significant adaptation to the research methodology, rendering it ineffective as an IL test. They have a point: in their "grammaticality test" part of the experiment, Dulany and his coworkers changed the procedure from a simple button selection task to making explicit marks on written novel letter strings with a strikethrough or underline used according to whether a string part violates or not the grammar rules. This arguably transforms the task from a rapid hunch or intuition-based judgment of the *whole* string into a targeted decision-making task of *parts* of the string. That is an explicit decision task based on explicit memory recall.

Criticism notwithstanding, if one accepts the abstractionist model this raises the potential for automaticity and, perhaps of most significance to KM, the ability of TK to influence action, both of which are discussed next.

7.6.5 Automaticity and Influence

Logically, a process that operates by automatically inducing knowledge of the environment would result in an equally automatic deployment of that knowledge given the right context, which is precisely what the theory of IL proposes. This is reminiscent of

Polanyi's account of "skillful performance" and Ryle's earlier concept of "knowing how": "(W)e learn how by practice, schooled indeed by criticism and example, but often quite unaided by any lessons in the theory" (1949: 40). The result is a construction of TK as experiential, derived from experience, and performative in being automatic and active. Recall how Ikujiro Nonaka's theory of the knowledge-creating firm describes experience as the source of TK. Not everyone subscribes to the 100% automaticity attribute: Richard Shiffrin, of Indiana University, for instance, speculates that all tasks involve a mixture of both automatic and attentive processing.

This leads into perhaps one of the most significant claims made by IL theory, and one with most relevance for KM practitioners: the influencing nature of TK. If it can be shown that people routinely, unconsciously induce and encode abstract representations of complex environmental structures, which unconsciously and automatically affect action—behavior—then TK can be said to have an influencing effect on that behavior. As Reber summarizes, "...memories can be established that resist attempts at conscious retrieval, but, nevertheless, display their effects on behavior" (1993: 89). Fundamental to Polanyi's prescription for personal knowledge is the idea that we "feel our way" to success and discovery in ways that cannot be readily articulated, but which account for "an immense mental domain": we know how to use it but know nothing of its contents.

This notion has a reasonable weight of evidence. Moreover, it adds further kindling to the fire already set around attempts to apply conventional management practices—and research paradigms—to the tacit. The combination of the "unconscious and natural," "abstractionist," "automatic," and "influential" characteristics of implicitly learned TK raises a fundamental question over the conventional characteristics attached to it. But, at the same time, this does further emphasize the importance of focusing on discourse as the site of knowledge work: if discourse is envisioned as action, then it must be subject to TK influence.

7.6.6   An Ancient Evolved System

A final key element in Reber's theory describes the IL system as an evolutionary system, more ancient than its explicit counterpart, although this is a speculative element in the story. This evolutionary perspective on IL emphasizes the primacy of the unconscious mental processes as the foundation on which conscious actions and behaviors are made. Recall JC Spender's reference to some parts of the human brain as being more ancient than others.

Evidence for this hypothesis is principally drawn from studies of neurologically damaged patients in which it is claimed that while explicit mental functions are shown to be impaired, the IL system is not (as in the studies with amnesiac patients noted earlier). It is speculated that implicit systems—being more ancient and stable—are more robust in the face of neurological insult. Has KM practice and study been pursuing a phenomenon that predates consciousness and that has been shown to be present in both human and nonhuman species?

7.6.7   Some Spanners in the Implicit Learning Theory Works

The attempt to "measure" something as nebulous as unconscious learning spotlights the research methods used. The importance of methodology rests on the commonsense notion that research findings can be disputed, even rejected entirely, based on the researcher's methodology. Indeed much of the criticism laid on IL theory turns on methodologically related issues: namely, the interpretation of findings, the verbalization criterion, and the conscious versus unconscious controversy.

The issue with interpretation is demonstrated in the scholarly arguments between Don Dulany and coworkers, and Arthur Reber and his colleagues, each disputing the interpretation of the other's findings, as we touched on earlier. Zoltan Dienes and his coworkers at the University of Oxford point critically to the lack of participant transcripts in published reports (by Reber and colleagues), which prohibits any attempt at an independent interpretation of findings. This is a serious flaw as the *interpretation* of findings is often in part based on participants' reports.

A "major blunder" in interpretation is raised by Arthur Reber himself concerning the scientist confusing his rules of artificial grammar, for instance, with those that participants induce implicitly as abstract representations and then use in classification tests. The error is thus to assume a formal equivalence between the two that, as Reber acknowledges, simply may not exist. This explains why participants, when shown the actual grammar rules following learning, do not demonstrate improvement in test performance. This is a classic example of misinterpretation based on misleading assumptions.

Turning to the verbalizability criterion, Reber confesses that work in IL has been largely criticized over the issue of the experimental participants' ability to describe their knowledge of "rules" that they have acquired during the learning phase of any experimental study. The entire house of IL theory cards stands on the argument that if people cannot articulate the knowledge underlying their decision-making, then they do not know what they know and consequently that knowledge is implicitly learned and held tacitly. Dienes and his colleagues speculate that the failure to freely report decision-making bases could be a consequence of having to learn a large number of associations during the learning phase, suggesting a far more complex explanation than that offered by Reber's thesis.

Referring to Reber's position as "tenuous," Jonathan Schooler and his colleague criticize him for, on the one hand, emphasizing the importance of the verbalizability criterion as a marker for implicit processes, while on the other, the "…slippery relation between verbalizability and consciousness leads Reber to suggest that the 'verbalizability criterion is a red herring' " (1997: 242). They suggest that the distinction between conscious reportable experiences and nonconscious unreportable experiences lies at the core of issues central to consciousness. In support of their position, they point to studies that show how people can report being unaware of experiencing a particular stimulus but are still able to describe it. Dealing what could be seen as the "crunch blow" to Reber's IL theory, Schooler and his colleague argue that even if one is unable to state or report a particular "cognitive event," this cannot be taken as firm evidence of the event having been experienced at one level of consciousness or another, and presumably vice versa.

Ironically, if Reber and his colleagues had included verbatim excerpts from participant report transcripts along with their analysis—in the manner of DP or most other types of discourse analysis study—they might have been spared this forensic examination.

The automaticity property of the tacit, raised earlier, is disputed and bound to a wider and more complex debate around unconscious versus conscious, which, after more than a century of study, is unlikely to be resolved in the near future. As Shiffrin suggests, there is no accepted method for distinguishing between attentive and automatic processing, nor, as John Bargh and his colleague summarize, is there a consensus over the definition of "automatic mental processes." That being the case, one can sympathize with the debates in the IL literature and the relentless pursuit for the perfect experimental paradigm that measures that which—and only that which—one seeks to measure. Suffice to conclude that the territory is sufficiently prone to shifting sands as to put any research paradigm at risk of considerable criticism.

Despite these various disputes and criticisms, IL studies constitute a substantial and authoritative set of empirical findings reaching back several decades. This offers KM some alternative perspectives on the tacit: in particular a view of "tacit knowing" as action oriented and influencing. A direct comparison of key features of TK drawn from the fields of IL and KM supports this argument.

7.7 COMPARING KNOWLEDGE MANAGEMENT'S PERSPECTIVES ON THE TACIT WITH THE IL FORMULATION

The admittedly selective sampling in Table 3 demonstrates how closely some KM scholars come to expressing a theory of implicit processes, consistent with the IL literature. Common denominators include the articulation issue, the abstract property, automaticity, unconscious and influencing properties, use in problem solving, being rule based, and the formulation of both tacit and explicit as a "knowledge continuum." This is an important conjunction and one that justifies drawing on the IL empirical evidence in the context of KM.

The points of departure highlight perspectives in KM that cast TK as rooted in action yet not part of action (3) and that TK can be converted to explicit knowledge through social interaction with others (9). Of these, the second has been shown elsewhere to be the subject of considerable dispute, while the first only requires an element of flexibility to become consistent with a theory of IL.

Three speculative points for KM practice and research can now be underlined. First, one could set aside the label "tacit knowledge," preferring instead "tacit knowing" as more reflective of the action oriented and influential nature of the phenomenon. Second, the "trigger" for TK action is not mediated, facilitated, nor choreographed by management imperative or IT device: it is context—environment—driven, pure and simple. Third, TK's value lies first and foremost within the individual, only becoming useful to the organization in the execution of performance. But it does have value.

The following section touches on philosophical underpinnings of KM, DP, and IL, and issues around theoretical incommensurability.

7.8 PHILOSOPHY, METHODOLOGY, AND INCOMMENSURABILITY

The theory of knowledge (epistemology) and the nature of reality, or ontology, are both concerned with how the world and its contents are perceived. Consequently these provide the philosophical foundations for theory and research methodology. As we saw in Chapter 5, in these matters we find two opposing agendas. On one side, positivism approaches facts and knowledge as out there in the world to be observed, discovered, and objectively acted upon. On the other, the constructionist perspective sees knowledge and reality as socially constructed and consequently mental representations are unique to the

TABLE 3   Comparison between Implicit Learning and Knowledge Management on the Features of Tacit Knowledge

	KM Domain	Implicit Learning (Cognitive Psychology) Domain
1.	Ineffable, difficult to articulate, and unspecifiable (Polanyi, 1962)	Difficult to express (e.g., Dienes et al., 1991; Lewicki et al., 1997; Reber, 1997; Shiffrin, 1997)
2.	Rooted in action and context, comprising technical and cognitive components (Nonaka, 1991)	See (7) below. "The form of representation of the tacit knowledge base that is induced here in is large measure functionally determined by the context within which it was acquired..." (Reber, 1997: 152). TK *is* a "cognitive component." Arguably a "technical component" is implied by a "cognitive component"
3.	A tool that aids—but is not part of—the action of knowing (Cook and Brown, 1999)	Influential and integral to action (e.g., Reber, 1993)
4.	It is abstracted from the environment and encoded, with pattern elaboration leading to problem solving (Boisot, 2002)	Abstracted from the environment, coded and stored as abstract, and rule-governed representations, which can be (unconsciously) used in problem solving (e.g., Reber, 1993, 1997). This coding relies on interaction with preexisting inferential algorithms (Lewicki et al., 1997)
5.	Automatic, unconscious, and cannot be easily articulated (Leonard and Sensiper, 2002)	Acquired automatically and unconsciously and deployed in the same way (e.g., Lewicki et al., 1997; Reber, 1993) but cannot be readily articulated (see 1)
6.	Bound to context (Thompson and Walsham, 2004)	Can be inferred as bound to context in that stimuli in the environment, similar to that which gave rise to the TK, and will elicit that knowledge (e.g., Reber, 1993), even if that "context" is not available to memory as shown in studies with amnesiac patients (e.g., Nissen et al., 1989). Evidence suggests TK is abstract enough to be modality independent (e.g., Lewicki et al., 1997; Pothos, 2007; Reber, 1993)
7.	"Hidden understanding"—difficult to express and facilitates the struggle with knowing how to act in the world (Greenwood and Levin, 2005)	IL is implicated in developing understanding of how to deal with complex real-world systems (e.g., Seger, 1994), and implicitly held algorithms are vital in social interactions where social stimuli are often ambiguous (e.g., Lewicki et al., 1997)

(Continued)

TABLE 3 *(Continued)*

KM Domain	Implicit Learning (Cognitive Psychology) Domain
8. "Knowledge how" contains a tacit fraction that is acquired through implicit learning (Gourlay, 2006)	Acquired implicitly—not a consequence of explicit knowledge (e.g., Seger, 1994)
9. Can be made explicit in interaction. Only through social interaction can new knowledge and TK be generated. Emphasis on interaction of objectivities and subjectivities in social interaction (Nonaka and Toyama, 2007)	Cannot be expressed adequately (see 5). Shown to be generated in implicit learning studies, involving no social interaction (e.g., Berry and Broadbent, 1988; Reber and Lewis, 1977)
10. Exists as rules in the unconscious (Tsoukas, 2011)	Encoded and stored as rule-governed abstract representations (e.g., Reber and Lewis, 1977) and interacts with preexisting algorithms (Lewicki et al., 1997)
11. Necessary to make explicit knowledge usable (Puusa and Eerikainen, 2010)	"...knowledge about relationships (between features and events) acquired outside of conscious awareness can be much more complex than the knowledge that the person is able to detect or even comprehend on the level of consciously controlled cognition" (Lewicki et al., 1997: 166). One is foundational to the other
12. A knowledge spectrum with TK at one end, explicit knowledge at the other, and both ends combining elements of the two (Leonard and Sensiper, 2002)	Reber argues that the "...implicit-explicit distinction is not between two isolated cognitive modules but between two poles on a continuum" (1997: 145) and, moreover, the two operate synergistically

individual and cannot be known entirely to another. This is a debate that largely centers around the subjectivist versus objectivist debate. What will shortly become clear is that the field of IL and the academic discipline of DP both operate to opposite agendas. This is not conceptualized as a "spectrum" of debate as this would suggest a scale with two extreme points and an implied "middle ground": in this debate, there is none. Drawing on both schools of thought consequently creates a problem of incommensurability.

7.8.1 A Divergence of Approach

The field of IL adopts the positivist, modernist convention with its emphasis on understanding human behavior and discovering "truths" through objective observation (see Chapters 5 and 11 for a discussion on these and related issues). Discourse is not approached as the location of action and performance but instead is viewed as a transparent medium that reflects reality as it is, as a conduit to inner minds. Accordingly, the focus is on what people say, assumed to reveal hidden, private inner thoughts, and cognitive states (e.g., beliefs, attitudes, intentions, and so forth). That is, discourse and cognition are treated as separate.

By contrast, in the DP agenda, discourse and "thought" are viewed as one and the same in the fashion of what Daniel Kahneman describes as the "what you see is all there is" approach. This conceptualization of language owes much to Ludwig Wittgenstein's influential book, *Philosophical Investigations:* "(W)when I think in language, there aren't 'meanings' going through my mind in addition to the verbal expressions: *the language is itself the vehicle of thought*" (1986: 329; italics added). Equally influential, according to Jonathan Potter, are the ideas of British philosopher John Austin in his simple but profound observation that utterances make statements about world, but they can also perform action. Thus, in its formulation of the homogeneity of talk and thought and conceptualization of talk as action oriented, DP is a constructionist, subjectivist-postmodernist account.

The lobby against the positivist–objectivist account has increased in volume over the last five or more decades. Michael Polanyi, as we have already seen in earlier discussions, is particularly critical of science's insistence on a "mistaken ideal of objectivity." While he does not dispute its existence, what he does disapprove of is science's overly simplistic clear-cut distinction between the objective and subjective. In his project, independent objectivity, separate from subjectivity, cannot and does not exist. He quite clearly leans toward the subjectivist end of the philosophical spectrum—and a postmodernist agenda.

7.8.2   Reconciling Two Opposing Fields

It is already suggested that IL and DP represent two opposing philosophical foundations, with competing methodologies, thus creating the difficulty of incommensurability. The question is, how can both be drawn upon to inform a perspective on knowledge and knowledge work? Fortunately, there are what might be termed "mitigating circumstances" allied to DP's potential limitations.

1. First of all, DP could be criticized for being an extremist approach, with the risk of analysis becoming an end in itself rather than a field of study that can reveal knowledge of human mind and behavior. Teun Van Dijk, for instance, is particularly critical of DP's anticognitive stance, implying that DP risks being a "mindless endeavor."

2. Second, while one can readily criticize conventional experimental work on a number of methodological fronts, one should be able to draw—albeit critically and selectively—upon what is more than a century of psychological investigation. Derek Edwards and Jonathan Potter, the originators of DP, claim to have no intentions, in their own words, "…to undermine what we see as entirely reasonable theoretical and empirical concerns" (1992: 1).

3. Third, DP could be interpreted as being limited in not possessing the ability—or apparent desire—to explain various psychological phenomena such as theory of mind and IL. Yet, DP claims to address "psychological" topics.

4. Fourth, as we saw in the previous chapter, critical discourse analysis approaches the context in which discourse is located as having a bidirectional role. That is, discourse and context occupy a dialectical relationship. This can be compared with

DP's viewpoint that holds context to be an essentially influential phenomenon on discourse in so much as discourses are situated and occasioned in the context within which they take place. There is a suggestion then that DP has a limiting perspective on context.

5. Ultimately, the major mitigating argument lies in the nature of IL methodology. AGL experiments in particular observe and measure participants' *physical actions* in decision-making. Participants' reports are used as a measure of the so-called verbalizability criterion. If the basic premise of the IL project is to seek a performative demonstration of IL, then where is the inconsistency and tension between this and DP's agenda? In fact, the inclusion of a DP methodological approach to a conventional IL research study, certainly as far as an analysis of participants' accounts are concerned, would ironically represent a prospectively more robust method of interpreting and reporting findings.

For these reasons, it is argued that drawing on DP, along with studies and theories from IL, is a valid project in the study of knowledge discourse. IL's theory focuses on the acquisition and influence of unconsciously held knowledge, whereas that of DP is based on knowledge as something that is constructed in discourse. There is no need, from DP's standpoint, to hypothesize about what is going on in the mind of the participant because the participant (according to the IL theory) largely *does not know what they know.* In other words, IL is interested in "what goes in," while DP is concerned with "what comes out."

Despite the case presented here, many purists may undoubtedly view such a connection as unacceptable. The issue lies at the philosophical level—it is unlikely to be resolved completely here. The argument, then, is principally made at the methodological level, as outlined earlier. Chapter 11 returns to questions of methodology in much greater detail. For now, however, our purposes are served by proposing an extension to DP.

7.9 SUMMARY AND CONCLUSIONS

(C)contexts—defined as mental constructs of relevant aspects of social situations—influence what people say and especially *how* they say it. (Teun van Dijk, 2006: 165)

This chapter started with a problem, namely, that to simply embrace the DP paradigm uncritically and unreservedly could lead to an approach whose product risks being of little interest or use to the KM practitioner or researcher. In attempting to address the "US\$64,000 question"—what can an approach from the theoretical and methodological groundings of DP offer that would be of value and use to KM—the answer is found in a one of DP's basic tenets and the conceptualization of tacit knowing.

In KM, the subject of TK invokes considerable disunity over definition but there is nonetheless a widely held perception of its importance and values. It has also been suggested that this disunity is the result of variation in understanding and interpretation of Michael Polanyi's thesis that can be seen in, for instance, the "conversion" debate. But what is also evident among many KM scholars is the conceptualization of the tacit as an "implicit formulation." If TK is valuable, implicitly acquired and deployed, yet is influential to action, then a proposal for a method of specifically targeting the tacit in action will surely yield relevant and valuable insights into organizational knowledge work.

An investigation of cognitive psychology's IL finds decades of experimental research and theorizing. This also offers a more precise account of TK, including its acquisition and deployment, which is shown to have currency with at least some accounts in the KM field. Thus, implicit formulations of TK can be seen as being supported by IL's empirical evidence. Admittedly, Reber's theory of IL and research across the board are subject to considerable criticism, but despite this, there is arguably sufficient evidence to suggest its plausibility as a perspective on TK. "Plausibility" is a key measure here because there can be no objective and unbiased "truth" on what constitutes TK, nor any other aspect of knowledge for that matter. The truth is whatever is commonly shared at any given time. The idea of the tacit as the product of natural processes, unconsciously acquired and deployed, contingent to the environment and its contents, an influential mediator of action, and one component of what we call "knowledge" is consistent with many of the accounts discussed in this chapter, which are drawn from diverse fields: John Bargh and his colleague and their notion of "mental butlers," Polanyi and his idea of the "personal coefficient," Kahneman and his idea of "System 1," Duguid and his notions of the contingent relationship between knowing how and knowing that; and so on and so forth. To add support to these arguments, a direct comparison between theoretical ideas in KM and IL reveals considerable compatibility.

With this conceptualization of TK in mind, it is suggested that an approach to the study of organizational knowledge work, drawing on DP, can uncover tacit action and influence. Thus, we propose drawing on Derek Edwards and his colleague's DP for a constructionist theory of knowledge, a theory of language and methodology for the study of discourse. In directly addressing the issue of relevance and the US$64,000 question, the DP paradigm is here extended in two ways: first, the conceptualization of TK drawn from IL theory and some in the KM field is acknowledged and made the focus of research. Second, it is explicitly claimed, based on the arguments and evidence discussed here and elsewhere, that in applying a DP approach to studying organizational knowledge discourse, one is studying directly tacit knowing (knowing how) in action, that is, the end product or "output" of the IL process—tacit knowing as an influencing factor in that discourse—with no need to speculate on the mental processes that result in such discursive displays.

In this way, knowledge is approached as constructed in discourse that is itself occasioned and situated, within which the "tacit fraction" is understood as action oriented and influential and contingent to the environment (context). The crux of the matter is the proposal that the influence, or footprint, of tacit knowing *as an aspect of discursively actioned knowledge* can be revealed through the analysis of organizational discourse for how speakers make sense of the world.

The point is that in any given account, a report to a meeting, for instance, a version of the world is actively constructed, which is influenced by tacit knowing. By examining discourse for how people talk and what actions they accomplish (e.g., managing risk, accountability, attribution, identity, claims to be heard as expert, and so on), rather than the explicit contents of their talk, an understanding of speakers' lived in experience and interpretation of their world—their orientation to context—can be studied directly.

What all of this suggests is that a tacit/explicit dualist understanding of knowledge is not only inconsistent with the constructionist approach promoted here, but is also irrelevant. Tacit knowing is that aspect—or coefficient, to use Polanyi's description—of knowledge that underlies, influences, motivates, affects, and drives discourse: it serves the functional, consequential, and variable actions in the construction. A further feature to underline, and drawing on Kenneth Gergen's notion of "relational being," is the view of knowledge as corelational or coactioned: it is always constructed in relation to someone or something else, which links back to Reber's notion of covariance. The understanding of tacit knowing expressed here is very similar to the notions of Daniel Kahneman in his essay on intuition: "…the mystery of knowing without knowing is not a distinctive feature of intuition: it is the norm of mental life" (2011: 237).

Two further points to note that are relevant to the practice and study of KM are as follows: first, a preference for the term "tacit knowing" because this is more reflective of the active, processional, and influential nature of the phenomenon. Second, the "trigger" for TK action is not subservient to some management imperative: it is context driven, pure, and simple—with context understood as the actor's interpretation and understanding of their environment and its contents.

The penultimate chapter in Part One brings these ideas together with the thematic categories of knowledge sharing identified in Chapter 3.

FURTHER READING

Bargh, J. and Chartbrand, T. (1999). The unbearable automaticity of being. *American Psychologist*, 54, (7): 462–479.

Cohen, J. and Schooler, J. (Eds). (1997). *Scientific Approaches to Consciousness*. Mahwah: Lawrence Erlbaum Associates, Inc.

Gourlay, S. (2006). Conceptualizing knowledge creation: a critique of Nonaka's theory. *Journal of Management Studies*, 43, (7): 1415–1436.

Kahneman, D. (2011). *Thinking, Fast and Slow*. London: Penguin.

Nonaka, I. (1994). A dynamic theory of organizational knowledge creation. *Organization Science*, 5, (1): 14–37.

Pothos, E. (2007). Theories of artificial grammar learning. *Psychological Bulletin*, 133, (2): 227–244.

Reber, A. (1993). *Implicit Learning and Tacit Knowledge: An Essay on Cognitive Unconsciousness*. Oxford: Oxford University Press.

Seger, C. (1994). Implicit learning. *Psychological Bulletin*, 115, (2): 163–196.

8

THEMATIC CATEGORIES OF KNOWLEDGE SHARING

8.1 INTRODUCTION

The critical appraisal of the knowledge management (KM) field reveals knowledge sharing (KS) to be one of the most significant organizational imperatives, frequently nominated as a key marker of success in the strategic practice of organizational KM (see Chapter 3 for discussions). There is also a notably strong theme of the "social world" in accounts of KS, which connects to the crucial importance of language accomplished in social practice in *all* aspects of the organization. This is a theme that is making more and more of an appearance in the "toolset" of the KM consultant, for instance. Consequently, person-to-person meetings, physical proximity, shared narratives, the idea of "Ba," and all other conceivable mediators and facilitators of social interaction are, according to this contemporary perspective, given a central role to effective KS. Building on this theme, links can be unambiguously formed with notions of the social group, networking, and of course learning. These are fundamental organizational practices that in turn invoke the foundational nature of KS. From the behavioral perspective, there is also the claim made by psychologist Thomas Suddendorf that KS is an innate aspect of human nature and behavior.

Yet, as we discussed in Chapter 3, KS is also widely seen as problematical. According to Gee-Woo Bock and his colleagues, who study influencing factors on intentions to share knowledge, examples of extensive KS are somewhat absent. Given the weight of evidence and common sense for the importance of KS to the effective management of knowledge and to organizational success and innovation, this has inevitably prompted the question, "what's going on"?

Knowledge and Discourse Matters: Relocating Knowledge Management's Sphere of Interest onto Language,
First Edition. Lesley Crane.
© 2016 John Wiley & Sons, Inc. Published 2016 by John Wiley & Sons, Inc.

To find some answers to this question, investigations resulted in identity, trust, risk, and context being identified as important and influencing thematic categories in KS (see Table 1, Chapter 3). While these themes are claimed to be important and influential, it is not clear *how*. But the implication is that a study of KS practices would show these themes as affective, bound to and influencing of those practices. On a point of conjecture, these themes are also considered to be corelational: "risk," for instance, will likely go hand in glove with "trust."

While these thematic categories are shown to be present in the KM literature, they are also present in those relating to discourse analysis. Developing on this, it is speculated that the analysis of everyday organizational discourse, drawing on an extended version of discursive psychology (DP; see previous chapter), will show how these categories mediate KS and with what consequences for speakers and discursive transaction. Of key interest is the potential that these categories, from the DP perspective of their constitution as psychological phenomena constructed in discursive action, can be shown to be "tacitly" accomplished in discourse. Such phenomena can and are routinely constructed explicitly in everyday discourse, but, in drawing on DP (extended), their influence on KS actions can be made the subject of research. There is one more point to make in support of the arguments made here and throughout earlier chapters, and this concerns the matter of definition.

It has been frequently shown that debates around the definition of concepts such as knowledge, even "KM," are the source of considerable complexity and confusion. There has also been the suggestion that such issues underlie perceptions of KM's success or failure. In other words, by far, the majority of research and theory in the field of KM adheres to a common theme of the search for meaning from the perspective of the concerns of the researcher. According to Jonathan Clifton, this is to adopt an etic approach: that is, the concerns and categories of the researcher take precedence over those available and observable in the data in the form of the meaning-making of participants, speakers, and actors themselves. In contrast, Clifton's study of "doing" trust in the workplace takes an emic approach, which is concerned with how people perceive the world and its contents and how they make sense of it. As Clifton describes it, the etic approach is potentially irrelevant because it seeks an explanation that may in fact have no correspondence with that of actors in their discourse in social interaction. DP can be considered as an emic approach. This is particularly relevant: as the following discussion will emphasize, the thematic categories of identity, trust, risk, and context are not themselves immune from definitional debate by scholars.

All of this provides some firm and clear boundaries for the primary research that is reported in Part Two. Before moving on to a summary for Part One, a brief sketch of each of the four thematic categories of identity, trust, risk, and context—drawing variously on the three literatures of KM, discourse analysis, and organizational studies—serves as background.

8.2   IDENTITY

The topic of identity is particularly high on the discourse analysis agenda (see Chapter 6 for a review of discourse analysis studies). Similarly to the discussions around the nature of knowledge (Chapter 1), identity is a term that comes wrapped in a myriad of meanings leading to what sociologist James Côté evocatively describes as the Tower of Babel of the social sciences. Some scholars propose that identity is closely tied to how people make sense of their world, while for others, motivation, stability and change, loyalty and commitment, leadership, and decision-making are approached as central to its concept.

Earlier, it was noted how the social constructionist movement marked a change toward a view of the self as discursively constructed (Chapter 5) in contrast to the traditional view of identity as a static and monolithic entity, the "self-as-entity." The thrust of the interest in identity from the discourse analysis perspective tends to concentrate on how people go about the business of managing their identities in the context of what social actions are being accomplished, with what linguistic resources, and what effect: Susan Condor's study of identity management in terms of "nationalism," for instance, and Jackie Abell and her coworker's study of culturally situated identities located in the conversational context are good examples. Few if any are drawn into the to-and-fro of the debate over what constitutes identity: from the DP perspective in particular, "identity" is precisely that which *speakers* make live as matters of self and others in their talk and text.

For the purpose here, a useful understanding of the concept can be drawn from Bronwyn Davies and Rom Harré's notion of "positioning," according to which theory people routinely "position" themselves through discursive practices. That is, people implicitly or explicitly cast themselves in a role in discourse and that such moves accomplish actions with consequences. This is synonymous to Derek Edwards and his colleague's "role discourse" and "category entitlements." Positioning in organizational discourse is particularly meaningful in its connections to power, influence, and persuasion, for instance. As one scholar notes, power is an important consideration in the construction of workplace identity. Margaret Wetherell, in her account of the construction of identity based on an analysis of Princess Diana's famous Panorama television interview, sums it up: "(T)to speak at all is to speak from a position" (2001: 23).

Drawing connections to KS, an intriguing conversation analysis study of KS between doctors and patients (noted in Chapter 6) reveals identity to be interactionally emergent— that is, relational and evolving—and bound to context. That being the case, it follows that KS is work accomplished from a subject position in a given context and that such positions are inference rich, which combination undoubtedly influences the directions and outcomes of this sharing. Another study shows how displays of status-based knowledge not only connect to the discursively enacted identities of speakers, but are also shown to "talk the hierarchy of an organization into being." It is further proposed that all of the other thematic categories considered to be influential in KS can be related to identity in the sense of identity as inevitably, often unconsciously, socially constructed in talk in interaction.

8.3   TRUST

Organizational theorist Chris Argyris reasons that an absence of trust within an organization will likely lead to a lack of communication. However, the concept of trust is a problematic one, as noted earlier in reference to Clifton's study of trust in the workplace. Professor of management at Purdue University F. David Schoorman and colleagues, for instance, highlight a schism between the conventional conceptualization of trust as dispositional and "trait-like" (an example is a study of coworker trust by Australian researchers Natalie Ferres and her colleagues) and a more ecological approach such as their own that locates trust in relationships. In their multidimensional and relational model, trust is defined as the measure of willingness to be vulnerable to another. Accordingly, dimensions of trustworthiness—presumably the focus of the measure of willingness—are the individual's perceptions of another's ability, integrity, and benevolence: "(A)as the perception of each of these factors increases, we would expect an increase in willingness to take a risk in a relationship" (2007: 346), and vice versa. Thus, in this model, trust is very clearly aligned with risk and, by extension, with identity work and context, *which can all be seen as phenomena accessed and mediated by perception.*

Recall the debates in the KM field around KS and trust discussed in Chapter 3. Here, it is argued that what is missing from these accounts is an explanation of *how* trust mediates KS (other than as a help or hindrance).

In the discourse analysis literature, reputation is considered to be an important identity factor in online communities' sense of trust, while trustworthiness is shown to be enhanced when contributors to online forums demonstrate a concern with saying no more than they can be sure of. Sociologist Ian Hutchby of London's Brunel University studies callers to radio talk shows with an interest in how they construct themselves as "authentic firsthand witnesses" to the events they describe. In scripting themselves as being in possession of firsthand knowledge of a particular event, Hutchby claims that speakers invoke rights to authenticity of experience, emotion, and legitimacy as a narrator. Firsthand accounts are also a way of constructing what Jonathan Clifton terms "epistemic primacy"—superior knowledge, which he links to category bound rights to knowledge.

In one of the very few discursive studies of trust per se, Clifton offers a fascinating and revealing investigation of displays of epistemic primacy, showing how speakers orient to these as displays of trustworthiness in an organizational setting. The analysis makes explicit how epistemic primacy is accomplished in discursive action using a variety of rhetorical devices such as displays of firsthand knowledge (like Hutchby's radio callers), objective and unmitigated statements, and declarative statements worked up in juxtaposition to previous utterances marked by "hedging." In the context of discursive studies, "hedging" means exactly what it suggests—hedging bets: that is, people very commonly frame their statements, claims, and descriptions in terms that would afford a means of face-saving in the event that they are contradicted.

Central to DP is, in Derek Edwards and Jonathan Potter's words, the everyday "… dilemma of presenting factual reports while being treated as having a stake in some specific version of events or some practical outcome" (1992: 3). That is, when people report factual accounts, they routinely work to mitigate against being seen to have a vested interest in the contents of those accounts and may even invoke "instructions" as to how accounts should be understood by cospeakers. This suggests that trust is not accomplished in isolation but rather in relation to other psychological phenomena and actions.

8.4 RISK

There are good arguments for KS to be understood as instinctive and innate behavior in humans, yet the evidence in the KM literature suggests that there are significant barriers and inhibitors to this practice (see Chapter 3 for a detailed discussion). Among these, KS is particularly associated with the threat of reputational damage, low values assigned to mentoring and sharing, cost, and the threat of industrial espionage. Arguably, all of these factors index to risk, that is, risk as a phenomenon constructed by social actors consequent to their personal knowledge and understanding of situated context.

As we saw earlier, F. David Schoorman and colleagues' multidimensional model of trust makes a clear contingency connecting trust and risk, with risk as a measure of one's perception of others' ability, integrity, and benevolence. This, in turn, invokes the categories of identity and context, which are connected directly to matters of stake, interest, and accountability.

As we saw earlier, discourse studies show that speakers routinely orient to stake and interest in everyday conversation. This is a frequently visited topic of investigation in the discourse literature. Speakers are shown to work to protect their accountability against potential criticism and accusation of bias: note that the term "inoculate" is frequently used instead of "protect" in the discourse analytic context, although it is a mystery why analysts should appropriate a medical term linked to disease to describe the action of discursively mitigating against criticism! The way in which people deal with accountability is one of the most basic and pervasive forms of discursive action and very much concerned with risk—risk to self and to others.

8.5 CONTEXT

From the discussions around the nature of knowledge, recall Varun Grover and his colleague's emphasis on the importance of context to the values of knowledge. Elsewhere, context's importance lies in the argument that knowledge is meaningless without it. Charles Despres and his coworker argue along similar lines, insisting that the meaning of knowledge—and by inference, its value—is not contained in the knowledge itself but rather knowledge in some context. Accordingly, context is not only inseparable from knowledge, but it creates and defines it, and hence knowledge is always knowledge in some context in much the same way that to speak is to speak from a position.

There have been several KM studies of the effects of culture (viz., context) on knowledge-related activities. Jin Tong of the UK's Cranfield University and her colleague, for instance, argue that if "…the tools and processes designed to manage the knowledge and facilitate the sharing do not take into account the differing national cultures represented by the different parts of the organization, there will be severe impediments preventing the vital circulation of the modern enterprise's life's blood—knowledge" (2009: 421). Their detailed case study explores KM practices in Chinese manufacturing firms, finding that factors specific to Chinese culture such as fear of losing face and a sense of modesty can represent barriers to KS. This has some synergies with Despres and his coworker's conclusion that organizations vary so considerably in structure, scope, culture, and so forth that a "one-size-fits-all" approach to KM will never work. It is clear that within the KM literature, the notion of context comes with all the obfuscation of a foggy day! What KM scholars do not do is approach language—discourse—as the site of context.

From the DP perspective, context according to Derek Edwards and his coworker is approached as a phenomenon made live by speakers in discourse. Analysis is then concerned not with the analyst's own sense of context but with what speakers themselves orient to as context in the interactional procedures of discourse. This is the topic of some debate in the wider discourse analysis field. Professor of sociology Emanuel Schegloff, for example, warns that the analysis of discourse is frequently at risk of being driven by the analyst's sense of context rather than that constructed by speakers. For instance, in response to arguments made for the use of "talk-extrinsic data" in conversation analysis-based research, Charles Antaki reasons that "…conversation analysts are happy to use the word 'context' in the sense of things visible to the analyst or made live by the people in the scene themselves. Otherwise, not" (2012: 493). To contrast with this stance, Hutchby makes an interesting point in his (membership categorization analysis) study of radio talk show callers. One caller raises the subject of dog mess in the streets, mentioning that she is the mother of young children. Hutchby notes that around the time of the radio show, there was a news story about the risks of disease from dog mess. He argues that knowledge of this story and its "importing" into the analysis result in an important context for the caller's account, which would otherwise be missing from the analysis.

An account of context given toward the end of Chapter 7 summarizes the approach taken here. In describing the "trigger" for TK action, it is concluded that this is context driven, pure, and simple—with context understood as the actor's interpretation and understanding of their environment and its contents.

8.6   A FINAL PROBLEM TO RESOLVE

The discussion around context raises a very particular and important point that comes with a problem. If it is acknowledged that, for the most part, research in KM—including that noted earlier—takes an etic approach, then this would suggest that the thematic categories associated with KS are in fact a researcher's fabrication rather than an understanding displayed by any research participants. The reason that this problem comes to the fore now is because of the singularly broad and even nebulous meaning of "context". The problem becomes even more clear when looked at from the DP perspective and its emic approach to research: from this standpoint, trust, risk, and identity can be understood as "contexts" that speakers construct as live concerns in their discourse in social interaction. So, when context is mentioned from a discursive viewpoint, what is meant is the context that the speaker invokes in his or her utterances—and that context could be anything from a context of gender tension to one of leadership, for instance. Consequently, to state that risk, trust, identity, and context are themes consequential to KS is to state, from a discursive perspective, that context, context, context, and any other context you care to mention are consequential to KS. How can this be resolved?

Fortunately, this problem can be squared relatively easily without making any major changes in direction. Trust, risk, and identity are contexts that speakers invoke in their talk, which are recognized as such from a discursive research perspective: consequently, they can be considered to be valid topics for research as consequential to KS actions, as indicated in KM research and theories. Context is the generic category label used to describe phenomena that speakers invoke and construct in their talk and text. In other words, context can be seen as a "corroborating" thematic category: if it is the case that the analysis of organizational discourse in KS activities finds the contexts of trust, risk, and identity, then it logically follows that a focus on what contexts *in general* speakers conjure as live concerns in KS actions will locate the same phenomena. So, we have a focus for research and a means of, potentially at least, corroborating the findings.

Thus, from this point forward, the thematic category of "context" should be understood to represent "context in general," which comes with the potential to add a measure of confirmation to the present research and its findings.

8.7 SUMMARY

In summary, these four thematic categories represent relevant themes for the analysis of organizational discourse, where the primary goal is to explain *how* these phenomena affect the practice of KS. The speculation that an emic approach to the study of organizational discourse drawing on DP (extended) could display tacit knowing in action is arguably a valid one, which comes with the potential to realize findings of interest and value to the KM field. A further point to draw is this: if a DP approach can show how these thematic categories are invoked and made relevant by speakers in their discourse, then it could be conjectured that these themes will have an equal influence on organizational knowledge creating and innovation, both of which are connected to KS.

FURTHER READING

Clifton, J. (2012). 'Doing' trust in workplace interaction. In Mada, S. and Saftoiu, R. (Eds). *Professional Communications across Languages and Cultures*. Amsterdam: John Benjamins Publishing Co.

Davies, B. and Harre, R. (1990). Positioning: the discursive production of selves. *Journal for the theory of social behaviour*, 20, (1): 43–63.

Grover, V. and Davenport, T. (2001). General perspectives on knowledge management: fostering a research agenda. *Journal of Management Information Systems*, 18, (1): 5–21.

Gulich, E. (2003). Conversational techniques in transferring knowledge between medical experts and non-experts. *Discourse Studies*, 5, (2): 235–263.

Hutchby, I. (2001). 'Witnessing': the use of first-hand knowledge in legitimating lay opinions on talk radio. *Discourse Studies*, 3, (4): 481–497.

Schoorman, F., Mayer, R., and Davis, J. (2007). An integrative model of organizational trust: past, present, and future. *Academy of Management Review*, 32, (20): 344–354.

Tong, J. and Mitra, A. (2009). Chinese cultural influences on knowledge management practice. *Journal of Knowledge Management*, 13, (2): 49–62.

9

THE CASE FOR DISCOURSE AS THE PRIORITY

9.1 KNOWLEDGE AND DISCOURSE MATTERS: SUMMARIZING THE CASE

The preceding chapters have engaged with the immense, complex but absorbing topics of knowledge management (KM), discourse analysis, and, to a lesser extent, that of implicit learning. All three, in their own ways, make claims for the delivery of considerable benefits in the pursuit of knowledge.

The field of KM is something of a curious paradox. From one perspective, proponents claim that KM can deliver what are described as considerable organizational benefits through the pursuit and management of knowledge within the organization. From a commonsense position, this is hardly something to disagree with. Moreover, there is probably sufficient evidence, mostly in the form of case studies and anecdotes, to be able to mount a reasonable case in favor of these claims. However, the other side of the paradox is strewn with the substantial issues and debates concerning the definition of knowledge, shown to underlie questions over the constitution of KM itself, and the business of creating and sharing knowledge, for instance. The central issue, then, concerns the "how" (how do we manage our knowledge) and the "what" (what should our actions be focused on) rather than the "why" (why should we manage knowledge). The "how" and "what" are precisely the types of questions that discursive psychology (DP) is concerned with.

The organizational practice of knowledge sharing has been variously described as the source of innovation and the key to improving organizational performance among many other attributes. The detailed analysis of the critical factors (barriers and enablers)

Knowledge and Discourse Matters: Relocating Knowledge Management's Sphere of Interest onto Language,
First Edition. Lesley Crane.
© 2016 John Wiley & Sons, Inc. Published 2016 by John Wiley & Sons, Inc.

associated with knowledge sharing maps these to four thematic categories—identity, trust, risk, and context (see Table 1, Chapter 3, and 8 for a discussion over what is meant by "context"). It is emphasized that the source of these critical factors is the KM literature with the concession that the thematic mapping is the outcome of the interpretation and analysis made here. An additional point of emphasis is that while scholars in the KM literature implicate these critical factors as consequential to knowledge sharing actions, there is little explanation of *how*.

The review and analysis of KM theory find a confusing landscape of competing paradigms as one would expect in a field characterized by so many issues and debates. Against a background of one dominant theory (e.g., *The knowledge-Creating Company*, Nonaka and Takeuchi, 1995), the categorization of KM theory into a taxonomy (see Section 4.3) of *personal versus organizational knowledge* and *knowledge as social action versus knowledge as object* reveals a persistent theme of knowledge work located in social interaction, with some scholars explicitly implicating language. This theme precedes the earliest publication of aforementioned theory with Peter Drucker writing in the late 1980s (original version of his 1998a article), and persists through to the present. However, this review shows a near absence of locating research, theoretical, or management interest directly in organizational discourse—talk and text—and a similar near absence of a theory of language.

A further key finding of the KM theoretical review claims that those theories located on the *knowledge as social action* taxonomy axis can be interpreted as implicating the themes (critical factors) of knowledge sharing referred to earlier. Those on the opposite end of the axis are interpreted as being more ambivalent in this respect.

These two findings—the lack of attention to organizational discourse allied to a near absence of a theory of language combined with the identification of the themes of knowledge sharing—are interpreted as suggesting both a clear location and a purpose for research. According to this, research should focus on organizational discourse as the site of "knowing" action, with the objective of investigating how these themes impact and influence knowledge sharing actions. But a location and purpose for research are of little use without a relevant and appropriate research methodology.

Discourse analysis, it has been argued, represents the solution (see Chapters 5 and 6) making the case for approaching the study of organizational discourse within the paradigm of DP. This draws on a constructionist theory of language, with its methodology based on discourse analysis. DP frames discourse as a topic of study in its own right, with language seen as action oriented and locally situated. It is particularly concerned with knowledge—how events are explained and described and accounts constructed as factual. Any reasonable analysis might well have parked the matter there. However, the "so what?" or US$64,000 raised an issue over DP's relevance for KM practitioners and the KM field in general, and the risk of DP being seen as an academic's tool, and no more.

Chapter 7 tackles these questions head on with speculations that DP's methodology can connect directly with "tacit knowing." This, in turn, prompts an investigation of implicit learning, a branch of cognitive psychology, and its focus on the "tacit" phenomenon. Attention is drawn to what turns out to be a substantial field of theory, research, and evidence focused on the idea of tacit knowledge as the product of the mental abstraction of information from the environment.

The mental process of acquiring this type of knowledge is both automatic and unconscious but nonetheless guides action—the notion of "mental butlers." The neurological systems associated with implicit learning are also claimed to be ancient and evolved, more robust than their conscious counterparts, and less susceptible to damage. This latter point raises a question over the idea that all knowledge comprises both tacit and explicit components, as many KM scholars have argued. Does it, in fact, add support to those who follow the tacit–explicit dualist conceptualization? There are two points to draw to diffuse this particular line of reasoning: First, implicit learning's theoretician Arthur Reber himself describes this "evolutionary" approach as no more than speculation. Second, as we saw in Chapter 7, the field of the human mind, consciousness and unconsciousness, is subject to competing theory and interpretation (much like KM), and so concrete attestations of this or that case are far from likely.

The comparison between the account of tacit knowledge from the implicit learning field and KM's "implicit formulation" displays surprisingly high levels of consistency between perspectives. So, although the KM field has largely bypassed theory and findings in the former, it is argued that research in the implicit learning field is of considerable relevance to KM.

This does, however, raise the issue of incommensurability in attempting to draw on DP to research KM themes and issues in the light of implicit learning's theory and evidence. While the incommensurability issue is perhaps not fully resolved here, the proposed solution discussed toward the end of Chapter 7 suggests an extension to DP. This extension allows for a conceptualization of tacit knowing drawn from implicit learning theory, which in turn leads to two significant points of departure:

First, the rationale now stands as follows: the "knowing how–knowing that" formulation in KM is seen as the most important theory in KM among those classified as approaching knowledge as or embedded in social action; this formulation explains knowledge as consisting of (and always consisting of) two principal fragments— the tacit and the explicit—with the former described as the unspecifiable "substrate" (to use Paul Duguid's term), which makes knowing that actionable, with the implication of the influencing qualities of knowing how; implicit learning theory, while acknowledging the criticism leveled in its direction, describes the "input" and "output" process relevant to tacit knowing; thus, the research proposed here has its focus on knowing how or the tacit fragment as displayed by speakers in their discourse ("the output").

Second, it is made explicit that in applying this methodology to organizational knowledge discourse, one is directly studying tacit knowing in action. There is, it is argued, no need to speculate about the contents of inner minds.

In summarizing the case, this chapter considers two further questions in the light of the preceding discussions. The first of these tackles the question of whether the adoption of a discursive approach to organizational knowledge work leads to a fundamental change of direction for KM. The second, already touched in the previous chapters, asks what and how will such an approach contribute to KM. The chapter concludes with the only reasonable outcome to this and the previous investigations and discussions: that research in the context of organizational knowledge work drawing on the (extended) paradigm of DP is warranted.

9.2 CHANGES IN DIRECTION?

At first glance, the application of the DP paradigm extended or otherwise to the study and practice of KM conjures the prospects of a significant change in direction. From a practical perspective, the majority of studies in the KM field involve conventional research methods—quantitative surveys, qualitative surveys, semistructured interviews, and case studies, for instance. As noted earlier, little evidence has been found of any discursive approaches to KM studies although elsewhere in the wider organization studies field they are very much in evidence (see Chapter 6 for examples). Consequently, the application of an *analytic methodology* focused on discourse potentially constitutes a radical departure: a shift in focus onto action and accomplishment in discourse. But new methodologies seldom lead to paradigmatic shifts in thinking: they are more likely to lead to polarized sides of debate, as has been seen time and again in all of the disciplines covered here.

In contrast, on a *theoretical* level, many KM theorists, academics, and practitioners consider knowledge and knowledge work to be constituted in social interaction—in conversation, informal and formal meetings, mentoring practices and other learning events, and so forth—suggesting the primacy of talk and text (see Chapter 4). But there the rhetoric tends to get parked with few stepping further into engaging with discourse itself from an analytical perspective. Moreover, it has also been shown how many KM theorists are within a sheet of paper of advocating an "implicit learning" theory of tacit knowledge. This, as mentioned earlier, opens up the opportunity of drawing on the work of Arthur Reber and many others in the field of cognitive psychology for both ideas and empirical research. Thus, in reality, the thesis made here is extending existing and current directions rather than radically changing them. One of these directions concerns theory of language, which is shown to be all but absent from the KM field. Why is this so important?

To unpack and add conviction to this line of reasoning, consider how the work of scientist and philosopher Michael Polanyi, writing in the 1950s and 1960s, has such a wide constituency in the KM field as an underpinning theory of knowledge. While his ideas focus on personal knowledge in the context of scientific discovery, those same ideas arguably transformed the KM landscape although, as has been shown, not always in directions consistent with the original. Similarly, linguist and philosopher Noam Chomsky, together with language philosophers John L. Austin and John R. Searle, writing in the same time period, produced work and ideas that revolutionized the way that we think about language and laid the foundations for the development of a discursive analytical view of language. Austin is credited with creating the simple but pivotal notion that speech is not a passive medium but rather is active, constructive, and consequential. In his theory of "speech acts," John R. Searle develops this work with his hypothesis of language as a rule-governed form of behavior. Also working in the 1960s, the sociologist Harvey Sacks and his colleagues developed what would become one of the most widely used discourse analytical methods—conversation analysis. (By curious coincidence, the 1950s and 1960s also witnessed the "birth" of cognitive psychology and cognitive science. It was working within this discipline that Reber and colleagues, starting in the mid-1960s, developed their ideas for implicit learning and tacit knowledge.)

The point is that if one wants to draw upon a theory of knowledge as located in social interaction, is it not essential to draw upon a theory of language? It can also be argued that *all*

KM theories, not just those that cite knowledge in social action, emphasize and underscore—overtly or otherwise—the importance of communication in the accomplishment of knowledge work. Consequently, approaching the study of knowledge work drawing on the paradigm of DP, and its theory of discourse, will allow a more complete picture to be contemplated. This leads into question of how this approach might contribute to KM.

9.3   MAKING IT WORK: IMPLICATIONS AND CONTRIBUTIONS

To begin with, a reminder of the core questions that KM asks: how, and in what circumstances, can new knowledge be created, innovation inspired, and knowledge shared between people? According to most workers in the KM field, a reliable and realizable answer to these questions will lead to sustainable organizational success, innovation, competitive edge, and organizational wealth. However, to date, successful outcomes from KM initiatives seem thin on the ground (see Chapters 2 and 3). It is true that this apparent lack of universal and predictable success can be questioned from the perspective of a limited arsenal of valid methods and tools of measurement, an exception being those proposed by Pieris Chourides and his colleagues at the University of Derby and researchers Mohamed Ragab and his coworker (see Section 3.4). There is also the matter of debate over the definition of knowledge: how can a phenomenon be measured if its object is not well defined? Added to this is the matter of defining what is meant by success. Or failure for that matter.

In DP terms, measurements of success are invalid. They are not the issue because the objective of discourse analysis is not to *evaluate* content and outcomes but rather to uncover accomplishments and their effects *for speakers*. With respect to the issue of measuring KM activities, linked to success or failure, the present study's contribution is not to determine probabilities and so forth, but rather to represent a different way of understanding these issues.

Briefly referring to some of the main issues in KM discussed in the first three chapters, it is suggested that the directions proposed here add a further explanatory dimension to the debate over what KM is and what it should be concerned with. In contributing to the KM debate over the nature of knowledge, the approach advocated here brings an explicit constructionist conceptualization of knowledge and a methodology for its study. In this project, we are able to "sidestep" the commodification–reification of knowledge issue, for instance, as being irrelevant. Considering the questions over ethics and culture, the proposed approach, again, offers an alternative understanding to the types of questions that could be asked. For instance, instead of asking, will "one approach transfer across different cultures, be they national, organizational, or operating at the group level" (referring to a KM theory or strategic approach), from the DP perspective, one might ask, "what shared understandings are evident and how can they be built on?"

Borrowing from Etienne Wenger, organizations can be considered as Communities of Practice whose members represent individually held unique stocks of competence and experience—their personal "art of knowing" or, in our terms, tacit knowing. It is this that mediates learning and teaching, which is the active catalyst in a community's meaning of existence and terms of boundary. It is highly unlikely that conventional methods could measure that. It is also hard to see how such entities can be wrapped in rule and procedure without risking the essence of the asset (tacit knowing). But what such a perspective does do is bring discourse in social interaction to the forefront as the primary location for study if what one seeks to see is tacit knowing in action.

A primary argument made by workers in the discourse analysis field is that their methodologies can reveal phenomena that other more conventional and traditional research methods would leave obscured and untouched. A good example is Hariett Marshall's study of the discourse of health workers, in which her analysis reveals *how* they construct their work and relationships with others as opposed to self-reports about what they do (in an ideal world). A problem is revealed, which Marshall claims could not have been made visible to conventional methods of research, meaning that actions can be taken to address it. Other examples include a conversation analysis study by researchers Mary Horton-Salway and her coworkers, which finds that telephone tutorial conferences are shown to be functionally comparable with tutorials (in higher education) in which students and tutors are physically present. The finding has some resonance for organizational settings and organizational learning and could aid in improving training and learning strategies and practice. Note also Jonathan Clifton's work in organizational trust and leadership, both revealed as the discursive accomplishments of speakers working interactionally. There are many such examples of social phenomena being uncovered through the application of discourse analysis that conventional methods would simply not have exorcised.

With particular reference to organizational knowledge sharing, the main contribution to KM is the explication of how such actions are accomplished and with what influencing factors and consequences. It is speculated that if the influencing and impacting circumstances can be identified through the analysis of organizational discourse drawing on DP, then this opens the potential for a different conceptualization of knowledge sharing as an interactional accomplishment. In the simplest sense, the present study contributes to KM by providing support to those who promote the importance of language in knowledge work and the notion of knowledge accomplished in social interaction. By the same token, it also supports those who are critical of the adherence to and emphasis on the use of technologies as the bedrock "silver bullet" strategic solution to delivering KM success.

9.4 CONCLUSIONS

A number of conclusions can be drawn. First, we can conclude that the domain of KM has a significant difficulty over the nature and definition of knowledge and that this difficulty arguably underscores the myriad other issues identified, including the commodification and reification of knowledge, the muddy water around success and failure, and strategies for its measurement. Clearly, the way that knowledge is defined and understood has a significant implication for how KM is theorized, researched, and practiced. While we have identified some common denominators running through the various debates—for instance, a preference for the tacit–explicit duality of knowledge—there are differences of interpretation over what these are and how they can be managed.

A second conclusion to be drawn is that while there is a demonstrable trend toward theory that approaches knowledge as social action or as accomplished in social action, conventional approaches continue to dominate the field despite a persistent number of critical voices. What is not in dispute is the legacy that scholars including Ikujiro Nonaka and his colleagues give to the KM field in drawing attention to and highlighting the importance of knowledge and tacit knowledge in particular. Notwithstanding this state of affairs, most KM theories can be criticized from one direction or another—and largely have been. What they mostly have in common is a commitment to communication as the most critical ingredient in the pursuit of knowledge, yet a theory of language—of discourse—is nearly absent from the literature. This common ground is interpreted and concluded as a clear approbation for a theoretical and research approach, which positions discourse as the topic of study.

Developing this, one of KM's debates holds particular interest for the present study: the formulation of tacit knowledge, or "tacit knowing" as some have preferred to call it. Specifically, it is concluded that a study of organizational discourse drawing on DP will reveal tacit knowing as an action accomplishment of discourse, which is distinct from what Derek Edwards and his colleague, writing in 2005, refer to as the mistaken idea of "minds" revealed or expressed in what people say.

Fourth, it is concluded that whereas the KM literature indicates various factors as having influence on knowledge sharing, a study drawing on DP has the aim of investigating how these factors (themes), approached as corelational in discourse, influence and with what effect.

Indicative research questions, then, are concerned with the themes of identity, trust, risk, and context, implicated as consequential to knowledge sharing activities. Can they be shown to be corelational, how do they influence knowledge sharing, and with what effect? In particular, can these phenomena be shown to be suggestive or indicative of tacit knowing?

This concludes Part One. Part Two begins by addressing the issues around epistemology, ontology, and methodology as the foundations for reporting the findings and analysis of organizational discourse.

PART TWO

10

INTRODUCTION TO PART TWO

Part Two of this book is concerned with reporting and discussing the findings of a study of organizational knowledge discourse with a focus on the indicative research questions sketched out at the end of Part One. These can be elaborated on:

- In the environment of organizational knowledge sharing, how are matters of identity, trust, risk and, context constructed as live issues and concerns of speakers?
- It is suggested that such matters or themes influence knowledge sharing—how and with what effect for speakers and their business?
- It is also suggested that these themes work corelationally—how is this displayed in discourse in social interaction, and with what effect?
- It is proposed that these matters are accomplished tacitly as psychological phenomena, with the implication that speakers orient to them as live matters consequent to their tacit understanding of what is going on in the environment (analogous to the automatic, unconscious abstraction of structures and patterns in the environment): how is this displayed and oriented to in discourse?

We begin with a discussion of research methodology followed by a detailed explanation of the specific methodology and procedures adopted in the present study. The themes of knowledge sharing identified in Part One—identity, trust, risk, and context—each form the primary topic of analysis in the five subsequent chapters ("identity" is split over two chapters).

The research draws on recordings of routine organizational "knowledge-sharing" meetings and an online discussion forum. Linda Wood and her colleague offer a useful

Knowledge and Discourse Matters: Relocating Knowledge Management's Sphere of Interest onto Language, First Edition. Lesley Crane.

overview of the directions for the analysis: "(T)the overall goal of the analysis is to explain what is being done in the discourse and how this is accomplished, that is, how the discourse is structured or organized to perform various functions and achieve various effects or consequences," (2000: 95). Consequently, the five analytic chapters present both analysis and discussion of findings at a fine-grain level with attention paid to how and what actions speakers accomplish, and with what effect for both speakers and cospeakers. Our overall emphasis is on knowledge sharing actions as discursive accomplishment. The analysis and discussions are supported through the inclusion of relevant extracts from the research data. Note that the reader will find a key to the coding used in the included data extracts, as well as a summary table of the extracts, in the Appendix.

The findings are discussed in Chapter 17, with the combined findings largely structured around the indicative research questions posed here. This is followed by a consideration of how the findings relate back to some of the relevant key debates and issues around knowledge management raised in Part One. What is found is that the research broadly supports the notion of knowledge sharing activities being contingent to the themes identified here (see Section 3.7 and Chapter 8 for discussions of these themes). The themes are shown to be discursively and collaboratively constructed by speakers as corelational phenomena. Further, these discursive actions are shown to influence the scope, directions, and substance of knowledge sharing action.

The purpose of the following chapter on Methodology is essentially to lay the detailed foundations for the research findings reported here. As previous discussions have shown, research methodology is key to what is researched, why, and how, with the results and findings, and their interpretation, being entirely contingent to the elected methodology (see for instance Section 5.5). So, while readers who are uninterested in matters and issues in research methodology could arguably skip or skim what follows without any significant loss of comprehension of the analytic findings, it is nonetheless emphasized that methodology made explicit acts as a blueprint and dictionary (to mix metaphors) to the research itself.

The topic of methodology is, in its own right, a fascinating and much contested topic. It is, however, beyond the scope of work here to enter too deeply into its centuries of debate. But this does raise an interesting question: if research methodology drives what is researched, if method axiomatically influences findings and their interpretation, then what does this say of the knowledge that we know? Or think that we know?

To prepare some initial groundwork, the present research is located as an interpretivist and qualitative approach, drawing on a view of knowledge as socially constructed in everyday discourse. A detailed explanation of the research methodology and design serves to establish the precise parameters and actions of research in terms of what was done and how. Matters of research strategy—including a discussion of the questions associated with the measurement of quality of qualitative studies—are also addressed. As part of our data comes from a public online discussion forum, brief consideration is given to the ethics of using this type of data in research. Chapter 11 concludes with a discussion of the limitations of the research approach in this particular case.

11

METHODOLOGY

11.1 INTRODUCTION

Why should we be interested in research methodology? In simple terms, methodology is concerned with the way in which the researcher frames questions for research and how that research is carried out using a project designed to provide reasonable answers. However, this simplistic description masks a significant underlying complexity. Setting that aside for the moment, there is one main reason for having an interest in methodology and in developing an understanding of its core concepts, questions, and debates. Here it is: if one does not have even a rudimentary notion of research methodology as the determinant of what is asked, what is researched and how, how findings are arrived at, and how they are interpreted and reported and if one does not understand the view of the world and its contents that the researcher is working within and influenced by, then one is not in the position to do any other than accept research at its face value.

This is, admittedly, what most people do when watching the television news for instance. But, just occasionally, a broadcast news report will prompt the response: "that's not right!" "that's not how it is!" and so on. In these cases, the viewer has personal knowledge and understanding of the matter being reported and is consequently in a position to take on the role of critical reviewer. The implication of this analogy is that the reader of research—casual or otherwise—is just as much a participant in the research as the researcher herself. That is the importance of methodology from a research consumer's perspective, but what of the researcher's?

For the researcher in particular, the importance of methodology rests on the argument that research findings can be criticized or dismissed out of hand (as noted in Section 7.6.7 in

---

Knowledge and Discourse Matters: Relocating Knowledge Management's Sphere of Interest onto Language,
First Edition. Lesley Crane.
© 2016 John Wiley & Sons, Inc. Published 2016 by John Wiley & Sons, Inc.

relation to implicit learning theory) on the basis of the researcher's methodology. Consider for example, the arguments ranged against the methodologies of cognitive and experimental social psychologists by scholars such as Derek Edwards, Jonathan Potter, and David Silverman. Silverman, for instance, describes conventional qualitative research design in social psychology, and its assumption that this involves researchers asking questions, as a "blunder" that risks simply not studying behavior. This raises questions over what they are studying and what their findings really report on (recall the brief discussion around researcher bias in Section 1.4, for instance). On the subject of quantitative methods in general and the pursuit of statistical averages on which a scientist's rules are based, William Starbuck is particularly scathing, claiming that such an approach is more based on "stylized sensemaking ritual" than science. Of course, others would argue for the complete opposite case.

The many issues associated with methodology are not so much concerned with the technical skills of the researcher in designing and implementing a study but rather with something more fundamental to science as a whole—the underlying complexity referred to earlier. They concern positions on ontology and epistemology as the philosophical foundations to methodology. Like most other aspects of scientific endeavor, these topics are not immune to considerable debate—often heated and personal; for instance, Kenneth Gergen's condemnation of traditional methods in social psychology for their abandonment of matters of culture and history, Charles Antaki's criticism of experimental research's reliance on laboratory-based simulations of real life, Potter and Edwards' response to criticism on their stance on cognitivism, and Teun Van Dijk's arguments for a sociocognitive account of context, describing the approach adopted by Edwards and his colleagues as anticognitivist and bordering on being "mindless." All these examples concern debates over methodology, but what underlies them is the conceptualization of "reality" and "knowledge." In fact, it may not stretch facts too far to see the field of modern social sciences as largely split by a schism of philosophy.

This chapter proceeds with a brief discussion of ontology and epistemology as determinants in methodology with the aim of locating the present study. A consideration of the nature of the debates reveals two opposing perspectives: positivism and social constructionism. As a qualitative and interpretive methods study, the present work aligns with the latter.

This is followed by an explanation of the research method—discursive psychology (DP)—to add to that already described in Chapter 6. This section includes a consideration of the criticism that has been made concerning discourse analysis (DA) in general. The troubling question of how the quality of qualitative research can be measured, if at all, is given particular consideration. Next, based on Jonathan Potter and coworker's 10 stages of DA, a detailed description is given of the present research design, data, and participants. The latter includes a brief discussion of the ethics associated with the use of data from publicly available online discussion groups (some of which is used in the present research). This is followed by a consideration of the potential limitations of the methodology proposed here. Discussions conclude with a summary and reprisal of the indicative research questions.

11.2   LOCATING THE PRESENT STUDY

At the root of what scholars Dvora Yanow and her colleague describe as the "paradigmatic wars," epistemology, the theory of knowledge, and ontology which is concerned with the nature of reality are both characterized by similar tensions. Experimental social psychology typically adopts a positivist epistemological position that understands knowledge as objective, knowable, and discoverable, where reliable facts can be discovered about the social world as it really is. This is congruent with the realist ontology, located in the philosophy of modernism. In contrast, critical social psychology adopts a social constructionist epistemology (see Chapter 5 for an introduction to this topic), located in the postmodernist philosophical perspective that approaches both knowledge and reality as socially constructed in social interaction. Mary Holden and Patrick Lynch of the Waterford Institute of Technology offer a very accessible guide to choosing research methodology: they caution that because philosophical stance dictates methodological choice, the absence of philosophical clarity can lead to use of research methods that are inappropriate to the research questions. Silverman makes exactly the same point from the more pragmatic perspective of the "fit" between the research question and the chosen methodology. The reader is referred to Chapter 5 for earlier discussions on critical social psychology as a reaction and counterreference to, and criticism of, the research methods adopted by the experimentalists. Brief discussions on both the positivist and constructionist positions make the point.

The positivist position rests on three principal assumptions, according to Alan Chalmers: that facts are perceived via the senses through diligent and unbiased observation, that facts precede and are independent of theory, and that facts constitute a firm and reliable basis for scientific knowledge. Its epistemology and ontology consequently assume that facts can exist as objective phenomena and that as such they may be objectively discovered, observed, attended to, and acted upon. This of course relies on the assumption that what one perceives is an accurate mirror of reality. It is also generally associated with an inductionist approach to scientific discovery through its emphasis on facts discovered through observation. This idea is returned to in a moment.

It is precisely all of these assumptions that social constructionism categorically rejects. Kenneth Gergen, whose work we have regularly encountered throughout previous chapters, was among the first in the social sciences to criticize the positivist position in social psychology, later referring to the "crisis over beliefs in objective knowledge." He argues that whereas positivism relies on observable facts that can be transmuted into laws and that are stable over time, human behavior is not historically stable. Moreover, on the subject of methodology, and as noted in Chapter 6 in the discussions around the role of the discourse analyst, Gergen is skeptical of the social psychologist's ability to divorce their values from the subject of their research. There cannot be, in consequence, any kind of objective representation of the "truth" in the study of human behavior, and that what we perceive cannot be a mirror image of reality as it is. We have previously engaged with debates on the subject of objectivity (e.g., see Section 5.6): Thomas Kuhn sums up the perspective that is subscribed to here, noting that "(W)hat a man sees depends upon what he looks at and also upon what his previous visual-conceptual experience has taught him to see" (1996: 113).

The present study, in drawing on DP, is described as qualitative and interpretive and is located in constructionism. Jonathan Potter, writing in the late 1990s, clarifies this constructionist position with two salient points: first, that speakers' accounts, reports, and descriptions construct versions of their world and, second, that those accounts are themselves "fabricated in occasions of talk." The key point is that DP takes an anticognitivist approach (i.e., contrary to the tenets of the cognitive sciences) and in particular takes exception to the cognitivist formulation of language as a superconduit to inner mental thought. According to Potter's treatise on making psychology relevant, a key difference between DP and other types of DA lies in its focus on psychology: DP treats psychology as practical, accountable, situated, embodied, and displayed.

Positivism is such an influential account of science that a short perspective on its historical roots and development provides some useful insights. (The reader is referred to Chapters 5 and 6 for accounts of the origins of social constructionism and DP.)

11.3   A BRIEF DIGRESS INTO THE POSITIVIST ACCOUNT OF SCIENCE

The idea of science deriving its facts through observation has the longest history of all scientific methods. It is not hard to see why. When the ancients first began attempting to understand and control the world around them, their principal scientific instrument was their eyes. So the observation of phenomena, with the development of more and more sophisticated instruments for investigation rendering these abilities even more powerful, has been more or less the principal delivery channel of what we know: everything from (to pick some highlights) the fact that the earth revolves around the sun in a system of other planets, usually credited to Copernicus (1473–1543) but which Charles van Doren argues is more justly ascribed to Galileo (1564–1646); René Descartes' (1596–1650) idea that the mind and body mutually interact, with the mind having one single purpose and that is to think, thus introducing the enduring question over physical–psychological duality; and the invention of the laws of motion by Isaac Newton (1642–1727), which came with a downside for countless generations of schoolchildren—the invention of differential and integral calculus. What all of these achievements in human knowledge have in common are (i) the ability to build on the knowledge of those who had gone before, (ii) an unbridled curiosity about the world and its contents, (iii) the ability to observe, and (iv), for whatever motive or reason, the desire to share that knowledge.

The rival to this idea of facts derived through observation, certainly up until (and perhaps even including) Newton's time, was religion and its emphasis on the written word. This is admittedly something of a sweeping generalization to make, and the reader is recommended to "Further Reading" at the end of this chapter for texts that deal with this topic in detail.

The invention of positivism is credited to the French philosopher Auguste Comte (1798–1857). According to chroniclers of psychology's history, Duane Schultz and his cowriter, Comte's systematic survey of all human knowledge rigidly adhered to the rules by which only knowledge that is objectively observable and indisputable could be considered: "(E)verything of a speculative, inferential or metaphysical nature he declared illusory and rejected" (2004: 44). Comte's notions of science based on observable facts, and the move away from explanations grounded in religious beliefs, for instance, proved highly influential on European thought. Along with materialism (the notion that the facts of the universe can be described in physical terms and explained in terms of matter and energy) and empiricism (a concern with how the mind acquires knowledge, which can only be acquired through sensory experience or observation), positivism was adopted as the foundation of modern psychology and, indeed, by most other sciences.

A more recent influential paradigm comes in the form of Karl Popper's *The Logic of Scientific Discovery*, first published in 1935. It is in this work that he presents the logic of the case for a deductivist approach to scientific research and discovery and introduces the concept of falsification—the idea that in order to be valid, scientific theory must be capable of being tested and falsified. Aware of the potential for criticism that his arguments might attract, Popper notes an inherent problem with his falsifiability criterion and its implication of a program of "ad infinitum" testing: accordingly, a theory could never be said to be valid as it will always be subject to testing. He has a solution to this: "… I do not demand that every scientific statement must *have in fact been tested* before it is accepted. I demand that every such statement must be *capable* of being tested" (1959: 26: italics in original). Accordingly, observations that form the basis of scientific knowledge must be both objective and subject to falsification. In essence, Popper's thesis is a criticism of the inductionism seemly bound to the positivist position.

Without going into further detail, suffice to state that Popper's logic, in particular his account of falsification, while becoming profoundly influential in the natural and human sciences, also became the target of many critics. Among these, Thomas Kuhn proposes that falsification is simply incompatible with the normal way that science progresses; Paul Feyerabend brands the enterprise as "silly"; and even Michael Polanyi is critical of the insistence that a theory cannot be regarded as a theory unless it can be tested and shown capable of falsification. Arguably, what sits at the center of all of these various debates and criticisms is the question over objectivity. This is a topic that has, I suggest, been adequately covered elsewhere (e.g., see Section 5.6). But the point made here, drawing on this brief account of positivism and the importance of scientific observation, is that even within this there are debates over what is and is not objective truth. The discussions now give a detailed account of the research method adopted in the present study and grounds for criticism.

11.4 RESEARCH METHOD

11.4.1 An Explanation of the Method

To begin with, a reminder of Stainton-Rogers' useful definition of the term "discourse" from the perspective of constructionist social psychology: "… a discourse is defined as the product of constructing and the means to construct meaning in a particular way" (2003: 81). Stainton-Rogers is not alone when she notes that the field of DA is characterized by numerous methodological types and definitions of discourse. Her version is however ideally suited to the present purposes and is consistent with DP as a methodology for research.

For its core ideas, DP draws on DA, conversation analysis, rhetoric, and ethnomethodology. It takes its theoretical and analytical origins in, for instance, the pioneering works of Michael Gilbert and Nigel Mulkay who were the first sociologists to apply a discourse analytic methodology in their field. They investigated how scientists "do knowledge" in discourse: in an intriguing study, which uses interviews and written texts, they report an asymmetry between scientists' treatment of "correct belief" as derived unambiguously from experimental evidence (which therefore has no need of explanation), and errors that must be explained away as these are invariably seen as the result of nonscientific influence. Gilbert and his coresearcher's interest lay particularly in the latter phenomena, finding that scientists used a far more elaborate repertoire in their accounting for error (recall the discussion of interpretive repertoires in Section 6.2.3).

DP is concerned with the action orientation of language (talk and text), specifically the rhetorical construction and organization of versions of affairs, their social organization—how it works—and what it is designed to do. In Derek Edwards' and his coworker's own words, DP is "… concerned with the nature of knowledge, cognition and reality: with how events are described and explained, how factual reports are constructed, how cognitive states are attributed" (1992: 2). It is, in other words, a functional approach to the analysis of discourse with a particular interest in epistemology, and its core assumption is that language is constructive/constructed, functional, consequential, and variable.

A simple example will, it is hoped, illustrate these points. The conceptualization of DP, in the most basic sense, draws a distinct difference between the contents of what a speaker utters and what the utterance actually accomplishes as linguistic action:

it is statistically safer to travel by airplane

In this short statement, the speaker, on the "contents level," is simply reporting a fact. From the analytic perspective, the speaker is using scientific accounting ("statistically") to persuade the listener of the factuality of their version of affairs. The upshot is to imply that all other forms of travel are risky and that to ignore this version of affairs is to take action (decisions, purchases, intentions, and so forth) which is risk laden—even foolish—with the consequences "on your own head." Alternatively, as what Jonathan Clifton describes as "competent members of the same community of speakers," we know that this is a commonly issued statement (Superman said something similar to Lois Lane after a near helicopter disaster in the 1978 film), so it must be true. But—and it is a big "but"—we cannot be sure that either perspective is anything other than the researcher's own interpretation in the absence of evidence of how the listener formulates their understanding of its contents. This raises two points that are returned to subsequently: the idea of the "next turn proof" and the role of the researcher.

In Wooffitt's analysis, DP is "… focused on the ways in which cognitive notions can be treated analytically as situated practices which address interactional and inferential concerns in everyday circumstances" (2005: 116). By locating psychology in language, it makes possible the direct study of the processes of thinking. Contrast this with the traditional experimental method that, from this perspective, is reduced to the study of secondary or indirect phenomena in the form of, for instance, reported recollections of past events. This difference is significant: DP studies psychological phenomena as constructed in everyday talk and text and as "noticed" by both speaker *and* recipient (the idea of "next turn proof" mentioned earlier), while conventional methods treat discourse as the *pathway* to what a person is "really thinking." This inevitably treats phenomena as secondhand.

A further significant difference lies in DP's focus and interest in what is *not* said. Robin Wooffitt provides the perfect example to illustrate this: he describes a comparison between transcripts of interviews with a mentally ill patient and people talking about their Psi experiences. Both report strange phenomena. But the Psi reporters linguistically work to "display" themselves as normal ("I was just coming into the kitchen when…": "I was getting out of the car and then I saw …") as a preface to their account of a weird happening, whereas the mentally ill patient uses no such rhetorical devices: "the god appeared holding a sword and shield" (*paraphrased*). The omission is suggestive of abnormal behavior.

The kinds of questions that DP focuses on are then: *how* is the account constructed to appear, for instance, factual and objective, *what* resources are used, with *what* function, and *how* these connect to topics in social psychology. Again, this contrasts with traditional methods that focus on "why" questions.

The DP project draws its data from everyday talk and text that can take the form of audio and/or video recordings, interviews, and any kind of written text. Following Edwards and his colleague, the focus of analysis is on the social and rhetorical organization present in the data, as opposed to linguistic organization, for instance. It is thus an observational science that seeks to describe and document phenomena in order to support broader theoretical claims. But this does not necessarily make it an inductionist approach, as understood in Karl Popper's interpretation of the term. In summary, DP is a theoretically informed analytical approach that seeks to investigate and understand social psychological phenomena as they are enacted as located ("situated") in the speakers' understanding of how talk normatively and progressively unfolds (the "procedural discursive interaction").

An approach that locates knowledge work in discourse and takes that discourse as the topic of study has the potential to lead to a greater understanding of how knowledge work "works." As argued at the end of Chapter 9, such an approach simply extends an existing trend to conceptualize knowledge as social action subscribed to by many scholars in the knowledge management (KM) field.

11.4.2 Grounds for Criticism and the Issue of Measuring Quality

It is usual in scientific research reports to discuss matters of bias (both researcher and participant), validity, and reliability (e.g., the extent to which findings can be generalized to wider phenomena in the real world) in the context of the research methodology and its findings. However, the nature of the present research makes such topics invalid—although this status is itself the subject of some debate—with the possible exception of "validity," which is returned to later in the chapter. Of more relevance is the question over the extent to which the quality of qualitative research methods may be measured, which is what we turn to now, beginning with a brief perspective on the wider grounds for criticism.

In considering what criticism has been made concerning DA, an interesting viewpoint is expressed by Stainton-Rogers: she suggests that studies in critical social psychology have been largely (as of 2003) ignored by researchers in the experimental tradition. Consequently, there is a perspective that criticism of DA methodologies are often raised by its own proponents (e.g., see Charles Antaki and coresearchers, 2002, for a discussion of analytic standards: Emanuel Schegloff, 1997, on the issue of context: on the issue of cognition, see Teun van Dijk, 2006; Jonathan Potter and cowriter, 2003; Linda Wood and cowriter, 2000: on the omission of considerations of experience, unconsciousness, subjectivity, etc., see Bethan Benwell and cowriter, 2012: for the subjectivity of analysis, see Maria Stubbe and colleagues, 2003; and see Charles Antaki, 2012, on the subject of using mixed methods). The reader will have already seen how researchers in critical social psychology also frequently direct criticism in the direction of experimental methods research, despite the apparent lack of reciprocation.

Arguably, the most obvious and problematic issue concerning qualitative research in general, and one that can be understood as underlying many other points of criticism, concerns the question of how to measure the quality of qualitative research methodologies. This is the principal focus of the following discussions.

The question of how to measure the quality of qualitative research methods is the topic of a substantial debate among qualitative researchers (see, e.g., an interesting study by Peter Cooper and Alan Branthwaite, published in the 1970s, which argues for the maturity of qualitative methods by comparing the findings of a qualitative and quantitative study of the same phenomena, finding similar overall results). This evidently concerns the issue of how to determine the values of qualitative research. The problem can be condensed into three of its interconnected characteristics: first, the diversity of method; second, the perspective that conventional criteria of measurement such as reliability and validity, so well established in quantitative methodologies, are irrelevant; and third, the profound difference in epistemology between quantitative and qualitative researchers and their methodologies, which some researchers suggest is the source of the problem. In particular, Lucy Yardley, a psychologist at the UK's University of Southampton, claims that the first two combined have led to a situation in which there is an absence of firm *general* guidelines relevant to the work of the qualitative researcher. It is this omission that Yardley, and Robert Elliott and his colleagues seek to address with their "evolving" proposed guidelines.

Specific to the field of DA in psychology, there is a further matter that impacts on the quality question, which concerns the use of the term "measure." While many scholars debate and propose methods for addressing the quality question, the term "measure" does not seem to feature. The term is absent from relevant discussions offered by, for instance, Wood and Kroger, and Potter and Wetherell, in their respective accounts of how to do DA. There is perhaps one simple reason for this: the term "measure" implies a scale or a benchmark, a mark out of ten, which in turn implies "quantification." Emphasizing the limited role for "quantification" in DA in general, Linda Wood and her colleague propose more appropriate phraseologies (how research claims can be warranted) as does Potter (how research claims can be validated), for instance.

Examples of how one can strategically approach the quality issue in DA methodologies (in general) are detailed by both Wood and Kroger, and Potter and Wetherell, with the former drawing on the latter. Wood and her colleague propose that the issue concerns warranting—how to give justification to and grounds for analytic claims. They question the application of the traditional notion of "validity" on the commonsense grounds that an analytic account can only ever represent one version of many possible versions of affairs, so it can never be considered as either true or false. If validity is traditionally considered to be the measure of research claims' "fit" with the world as it is, then clearly DA studies cannot be evaluated on this basis. An alternative conceptualization of "validity" is needed.

Wood and her colleague's solution for "warranting" centers on two principal components: the trustworthiness of the account, which can be addressed through ensuring that a clear and detailed description of all stages of research is included in the account, and the soundness of an account, which principally concerns the analytic section of the research report. A number of factors need to be adhered to include the grounding of analysis in speakers' orientations (addressing the speaker's understanding as displayed in discourse vs. the analyst's interpretation), which refers to the "next turn proof" analytic tool encountered earlier; the coherence of analysis (a claim should satisfactorily account for exceptions and deviants in a discourse); the plausibility of an account in, for instance, how it relates (can be grounded) to other research work in similar areas; and the notion of "fruitfulness" (Potter and Wetherell's term), which addresses the implications of a study's findings for other work and what questions it might raise in terms of future research.

Specific to DP, Jonathan Potter, writing in the late 1990s, provides a set of four pragmatic guidelines. Interestingly, Potter describes his guidelines as "validation procedures" and wastes no time on debates around whether this term should be used in this type of research methodology or not: he quite simply reformulates it. Potter's procedures start with the analyst's attention to grounding their claims in speakers' own understandings as displayed in discourse, which also serves as a check for interpretive claims—the "next turn proof" aspect. This has correspondence to Yardley's "sensitivity to context" principle. Second, attention to what Potter describes as deviant cases can be useful in assessing the sufficiency of claims—do deviant cases in a discourse, for instance, support an analytic claim or weaken it? This has far less synergy with Yardley's principles probably because the explicit search for and importance assigned to "deviant cases" is very particular to DA, particularly DP. Potter's third procedure concerns an account's coherence with respect to previous studies in similar areas, which can be clearly related to Yardley's first principle as well as her third, "impact and importance," but which varies from Wood and her coworker's understanding of "coherence."

The last procedure concerns the reader, which Potter describes as the most important of the four. This refers to the inclusion of extracts of data (the "real" data) in research reports so that the reader is able to make their own judgment of the analyst's interpretation. Although he does not elaborate on this point here, this is an interesting notion: it potentially makes the reader part of the analytic work as an active contributor and implicates the role of the researcher as interpreter. This can be contrasted with Yardley's emphasis on a study's impact and importance in the sense of how a study markedly contributes to the knowledge (does it tell us anything new, does it make a difference?). While it is certain that Potter has this as an objective for research, there is a suggestion that this is made more personal to the individual reader rather than the academic research community as a whole.

The present research reported here draws on Potter's validation procedures, the application of which is discussed in the following section. As a final point, Potter creates a caveat: in his own words, "… none of these procedures *guarantee* the validity of an analysis. However, work in philosophy and sociology of science over the last 30 years has cast doubt on the possibility of such bottom-line guarantees in science, whether provided by observation, replication or experimentation" (1998a: 241: italics in original). Even "the independent audit" and "interrater reliability approach," as outlined by Jonathan Smith and Linda Wood and her coworker, for instance, are no guarantee for an account's warrantability according to this caveat.

11.5   RESEARCH DESIGN

11.5.1   Design

This section of the chapter turns attention from discussions around topics in methodology to those around how the present research was actually carried out.

A first point to note about the DP methodology is that there is no straightforward prescription for analyzing discourse. That is, there is no check box list of actions to take that will lead to the perfect analytical outcome. Derek Edwards and his coworker, in their book introducing DP, synthesize various features of discursive action and the relationships between them in a conceptual scheme referred to as the *Discursive Action Model*. It is organized into three principal themes: action (e.g., a focus on action rather than cognition), fact and interest (e.g., negotiating the dilemma of stake and interest), and accountability (e.g., the speaker's displayed sense of accountability in reports). It establishes some useful guiding principles as well as some potential areas on which to focus research (such as, e.g., how speakers construct and manage their remembered accounts of past events as factual and authentic).

More practical as a framework for guiding methodology, Jonathan Potter and Margaret Wetherell map out a 10-stage guide to DA: research questions, sample selection, data collection, interviews, transcription, coding, analysis, validation, report writing, and application. This is not meant as a strict order of business for undertaking DA: the order in which these "actions" are engaged is entirely dependent on each specific research case. Both the *Discursive Action Model* and the 10-stage guide are used to inform our research, with the latter providing points of discussion here. Note that both sample selection and data collection are addressed in the following subsections, "Research Data" and "Participants and Ethical Considerations," and that the topic of "interviews" is not relevant to the present study. "Validation," in the following discussions, addresses how the present study approaches matters of validation procedures. "Report writing" is not relevant to our present purposes, and "application" is addressed in the final chapter of the thesis.

Research Questions
In DP, the use of research questions is more a matter of opinion and preference than prescription. Some, including Robin Wooffitt from the perspective of conversation analysis, are persuaded that even indicative research questions are unnecessary and potentially limiting to the analysis at hand. Where they are used, Carla Willig advises that these should be focused on how accountability and stake are managed in real everyday life. Accordingly, DP asks "what" and "how" questions rather than the "why" questions which are the hallmark of experimental methods as noted earlier.

As with any research project, an important part of formulating research questions is researching relevant literature. This has two practical outcomes: first, it enables the researcher to understand how particular topics are dealt with and to identify any gaps in the literature. Second, it enables the researcher to ground analysis in existing research. Both support the drive for coherence. In other words, a piece of work that contributes to and builds on existing work will likely be seen as more plausible than one that does not. Consequently, based on the themes evident in the KM literature review (e.g., trust), the DA literature and in particular those that are relevant to DP formed the basis of primary research. This led to a relatively broad purview that can largely be categorized as (i) those literatures concerned with DA/DP as a methodology and a theoretical approach and (ii) reports of studies relevant to the matters in hand. To facilitate such a broad field of research, a computer-based research database was created in which details of all papers/books (including those from KM and related fields) were recorded, along with links to the source publication and research notes. To date, this database contains some 500 entries. A further action that was taken was to create a minidatabase of DA terminology ("jargon") used in research reports, which, during the analysis, greatly facilitated the discovery of studies compatible with, or in other ways supportive of, or indeed contradictory to the analysis and its findings reported here.

Based on the research reported in the previous chapters, the indicative research questions are proposed as:

In the environment of organizational knowledge sharing, how are matters of identity, trust, risk, and context constructed as live issues and concerns of speakers?

It is suggested that such matters or themes influence knowledge sharing—how and with what effect for speakers and their business?

It is also suggested that these themes work corelationally—how is this displayed in discourse in social interaction, and with what effect?

It is proposed that these matters are accomplished tacitly as psychological phenomena, with the implication that speakers orient to them as live matters consequent to their understanding of what is going on in the environment (analogous to the automatic, unconscious abstraction of structures and patterns in the environment): how is this displayed and oriented to in discourse?

Transcription

Transcription as a preparatory step to analysis involves transforming spoken (as opposed to written, such as online forum contributions) texts into written form suitable for analysis. It also involves annotating the transcript with symbols indicating pauses (often including duration), intakes of breath, rises or falls in tone, increase or decrease in volume, overtalk, laughter, speech repairs, and so on. The aim is to produce a written version that is, as far as the research aims require, as accurate a representation as possible of the spoken words while acknowledging that a literal rendering is impossible. A key to transcription conventions used in the present study is contained in Table 5, which is based on that developed by Gail Jefferson.

Any transcription's level of detail is determined by the research question. In our case, the process began with a "gist" transcription noting what each meeting recording covered in terms of explicit topic, action (e.g., argument, agreement, persuasion, etc.), speaker, indicative timings, and so forth, as a first step in becoming familiar with the data. The aim was to produce a transactional description of each meeting's discourse. Each meeting recording was then transcribed in detail, using the appropriate transcription conventions, using the "gist" version to discard any meeting talk considered to be wholly irrelevant to the business at hand, for example, unintelligible talk, pauses for passing traffic, or reference to technical difficulties with IT systems used in the meeting. As well as representing a practical stage in preparation for analysis, the process of transcription is also an invaluable way to get very familiar with the data, to "dwell in it" as Michael Polanyi might have described it.

The following is a short example taken from the analysis contained in the subsequent chapters:

1. Steve: Wa::ay. (.) Okay so we have Ade, Damien and Manoj.
2.   (2) ["yeahs" via conference call]=
3. Steve: Yep, yep, yep. Good. Okay. Ummmm. (0.5) Right=
4. Bob: = Shall we go through the list ↑first?
5. Steve: Ye::ah Mark why don't you—why don't you wheel us through the list?
6. Bob: Alrighty so starting in alphabetical with (names). So, (project name)?

The ":::" in Line 1 indicates the word is elongated, while the bracketed number in Line 2 indicates a length of silence. The "=" shown in Lines 3 and 4 indicates no discernible gap between utterances, while the "↑" displays a rise in intonation.

So far as possible, the aim is to act in the role of "objective observer" in the transcription, coding, and analysis stages, for instance. It is however clear that no such research can ever be immune from the presence of the researcher—even acknowledging that the way in which a particular utterance might be heard is always open to the possibility of being heard differently by another researcher.

Coding

Not to be confused with the application of transcription conventions or with the analysis itself, coding is the process by which the researcher searches for and selects instances in the transcript relevant to the research question or theme under investigation.

The indicative research questions lead to a particular interest in the themes of identity, trust, and risk and what contexts in general speakers make live in their discourse. The research is concerned with whether and if such themes are invoked and oriented to by speakers as psychological phenomena with influence and effect on the scope and content of knowledge sharing actions. Consequently, the process of coding involves trawling through the data—working iteratively between the transcripts and the recordings—to identify the presence of these or related themes as discursive actions: "instances of interest." In their 10 stages of DA, Potter and Wetherell advise that such a process should be as inclusive as possible—that is, even instances that are considered to be "borderline" in relation to the themes of interest should be included.

Analysis

Analysis is an iterative process in which the researcher must continuously move back and forth between analytical concerns, the corpus of relevant published literature, and the data itself, both the transcripts and the source recordings. It was, for instance, felt necessary to return to the original recording from which an instance of interest was drawn to experience over and over again its whole context and the actual performance of the speakers.

The core principle is that the topic of interest is language itself. While there is no set procedure for doing analysis, there are some key questions to be borne in mind: why am I hearing/reading the text in this way, what are the features that lead to this way of hearing/reading it, what is the recording/text making me feel, and so on. The researcher is specifically looking for both patterns and variation in the data.

Analysis focused specifically, one after the other, on each of the four identified themes related to knowledge sharing. Note that the purpose of the meetings in the dataset, in each case, is understood knowledge sharing: for instance, a routine sales and marketing meeting has the purpose of sharing past, present, and predicted activities and experiences.

The analysis begins by identifying the patterns within the organizational structure of the data: what is its nature—is it agenda driven, for instance? This is followed by a stage that investigates the rhetorical practices evident in the data: what discursive work is being done, and with what effect? Next, the analysis considers matters of construction, evaluation, and function: what is being constructed, how is this negotiated, for instance, and with what function? In examining the instances of interest identified earlier in the data, their general context is addressed: why this extract, what is happening, what precedes it, and what are its major features? Throughout all aspects of the analysis, exceptions or deviant cases are sought, with the analytic purview focused on what speakers themselves orient to or construct as "consistent and different." Thus, following Potter, analytic descriptions that are "careful and systematic" lend themselves more to constructing claims of a theoretical nature. The analysis also focuses on rhetorical effects and consequences: what are the effects of the discourse on speakers, and has anything changed? Throughout, the analysis is carefully grounded in the relevant literatures where possible.

Analysis is concerned with the ways in which speakers manage issues such as blame and accountability, the action orientation, and rhetorical organization of talk and how people construct particular versions of reality and what these accomplish for the interaction. Specifically, and drawing on the theory of language (discourse) represented in DP, the study considers the question of how people, in everyday organizational settings, go about the business of constructing and accomplishing actions in discourse, with what function, and what consequences. In particular, the analysis is interested in how speakers orient to the identified themes associated with knowledge sharing and with what effect for speakers and recipients. Each instance of interest identified in the coding stage is forensically dissected for action, function, and effect, and compared with other instances, with an iterative process of testing used to identify features of interest to the focus of the study and in turn to compare and contrast these with features in the extant literature.

Validation
Jonathan Potter's four validation procedures specific to DP, discussed earlier, are applied in the research: (i) analysis pays attention to speakers' own understanding as displayed in discursive interaction (not just the researcher's interpretation), (ii) the adequacy of a claim is assessed against any "deviant cases" in the data, (iii) analysis and claims are grounded in previous studies, and (iv) the inclusion of data extracts allows the reader to form their own interpretations and judgments. Taking each of these procedures in turn, we can now look at how these are applied in the present research.

The analysis is concerned with those issues that the speakers themselves make live and relevant in their talk. That is, the analysis attends to what sense speakers and recipients are shown to construct and orient to in their discursive interaction and not just how the researcher might interpret a particular utterance. Following Edwards and Potter, reports and descriptions are "… examined in the context of their occurrence as situated and occasioned constructions whose precise nature makes sense, to participants and analysts alike, in terms of the actions those descriptions accomplish" (1992: 2). So, where, for instance, analysis suggests a particular contextual matter such as "trust" is made live by a speaker, evidence is sought for this as an understanding displayed in subsequent speaker turns: the next turn proof procedure. If such evidence is absent, the researcher's interpretation is either excluded from the analysis or explicitly marked as potentially speculative. An example of this can be seen in the analysis of "risk" (Chapter 13).

Deviant cases are particularly sought: that is deviant to the perceived dominant pattern, for instance, seen in the data or in a meeting recording as a whole event. An example of this can be seen toward the end of Chapter 13, along with a discussion of its meaning to the analytic claims. Deviant cases can either support analytic claims or serve to weaken them. The objective is not to ignore them as irrelevant to the business at hand but rather to notice these for what they accomplish and how they relate to analytic claims. As Jonathan Potter and Margaret Wetherell advise, exceptions can often "dredge up" important features and problems.

From the outset of the research and analysis, the present study approaches existing DA studies as a major source of knowledge to inform and provide a source of coherence for analytic claims. This can be seen in how the analysis reported in the following chapters is, for instance, grounded in the literature where relevant, showing how the analysis and claims made here either support or vary from existing work.

Extracts (see Table 4 for a summary of these) from the data are included in the reported analytic findings to both support analytic claims and allow the reader to formulate their own interpretation and judgment of the data. This attends particularly to the ever-present possibility that talk and text are open to more than one analysis and conclusion. In the following chapters, extracts are placed alongside detailed descriptions and accounts of how the analysis is grounded and developed. Following Linda Wood and her colleague, the demonstration of analysis in the inclusion of extracts is understood as a key requirement of warrantability.

11.5.2   Research Data

The size and content of any sample selection are driven by the research question. Potter and his coworker emphasize that, in DA, the size of the research sample is not a determinant in a study's success. The analyst's priority is an interest in the language itself, how it is used and what it accomplishes, not the speakers. Most DA research generally samples a corpus of data from different sources or from the same source (e.g., see Robin Wooffitt's intriguing 2001 study of verbal interaction between mediums and their clients finding "reported speech" to be a commonly used linguistic device, which, he claims, works to invoke "favorable assessments" of the psychics' authenticity).

When collecting data, many of the same principles of conventional research methods are relevant: a consideration of ethics, for instance, and ensuring the appropriate permissions are gained. Preference is always for using naturally occurring language in interaction (i.e., with the complete absence of the researcher). But the use of surreptitious recordings would, for instance, be ethically questionable. This raises a particular question concerning ethics in respect of some of the data used here (public online discussion forum), which is addressed in the following subsection, "Participants," as part of a general discussion on the ethical approach of the present study.

Firms were selected for the study based on the researcher's prior relationship with their senior management and the nature of their business as having an emphasis on sharing and developing knowledge. This prior relationship transpired to be an essential factor in gaining the cooperative participation of both organizations. Several other organizations, where no prior connection or relationship existed, were also approached as potential participants but, while expressing support for the research project and its aims, all declined to become involved as participants. This suggests a sobering lesson and potential limitation for future research: the nature of the research methodology is such that, without a prior relationship of trust, potential participating organizations are unlikely to agree to take part.

Individual participants were not selected by me as the researcher: instead, these represent, in effect, an opportunity sample in that they happened to be present in the meetings that took place at times and dates when I, with the agreement of the organizations' senior management, happened to be present at their respective premises (but not physically present in the meetings themselves). Nor was there any deliberate selection made of the meetings to be recorded or influence upon their topics of discussion. In this sense, while the organizations themselves are actively selected by me as the researcher, the actual participants are not. Nor was I physically present in any of the meetings themselves, not even in the guise of observer. I can claim, then, that this data can be considered as naturally occurring language in interaction.

The principal empirical basis for the present study comprises digital audio recordings of 13 individual meetings, collectively representing more than 15 hours of recordings, taking place in two different London-based organizations during March and May 2013. These meetings are regular, scheduled meetings in each case.

No instruments were used in the data capturing part of the project apart from a small digital audio recording device, which was positioned in meeting rooms in advance of meetings to be recorded. All participants were briefed in advance, verbally or via written instruction, of the nature and purpose of the study.

11.5.3 Participants and Ethical Considerations

This section of the chapter focuses on the ethical conduct of the study, with particular consideration given to the use of online discussion data. This is followed by a description of the participating firms. A description of the online data and its source is given at the start of the analysis in Chapter 15.

In compliance with ethical standards for research, two documents were prepared: a participant consent form and an information/briefing form. All participants were given both documents prior to any recording being undertaken. In most cases, participants were given a short verbal briefing on the nature of the research, in particular of their rights to withdraw from the study at any point. Participants, comprising organizational employees, contractors, and/or associates of two independent London-based private sector consultancy firms, were required to sign individual consent forms. All participants and their organizations are treated as anonymous in all aspects of the research.

With respect to the online discussion forum data, no overt permission was sought by the researcher from forum participants. Participants made their contributions voluntarily to a publicly available discussion forum, which is part of an international professional networking website: that is, access to this forum is not restricted to registered forum members only, although in order to access the site users must first register with the website itself. Note, though, that there is no restriction, fee, or qualification required in order to register with this website. A further important point to note is that this group, which is a networking group, publishes no explicit rules, guidelines, or other considerations in respect of members' contributions and their use thereof. To post a contribution, one must register with the group, but access to its contents is available to any website member.

Was it ethical to sample and use this data collected in this way? The review of studies using data from computer-mediated communications (Section 6.4.3) gives an idea of the widespread practice of using such data in research. On the advantages of using this type of data, in their book on *Discourse and Identity*, Bethan Benwell and her colleague describe this as particularly "authentic and pure" because it requires no transcription and places the researcher in the position of a "lurker" as opposed to the traditional perception of the "scientist as observer" where the presence of the researcher can influence that which they observe. They, in fact, make no reference to any ethical issues with using data from such sources. In reality, the general thrust of research is more focused on the values and advantages of using this data rather than on any ethical issues that this might raise (e.g., see a study by Charles Antaki and colleagues, published in 2006, which compares everyday conversation talk with online forum discursive interactions). Moreover, in their account of the "revolution" of "Big Data," Viktor Mayer-Schonberger and cowriter recently describe in some detail how large Internet businesses including Google, for instance, routinely "scrape" the Internet for content as data for their algorithms. There is no indication of any permission being sought from individual contributors.

To answer the initial question, is it ethical: it is claimed here that the use of such data—because of its circumstances in terms of accessibility to wider audiences and the implied acceptance by contributors that their data may be used for purposes other than they intended, together with the practical problems in attempting to gain permission from individual contributors, and the impact that such a requirements would have on the growing and valuable contributions from research in computer-mediated communications—is ethically acceptable. As a caveat, however, it should be noted that this is a gray area to say the least.

What follows is a brief description of each participating organization. Note that the context of individual meetings, where they form the basis of subsequent analysis, is described in each case of use:

Organization A

Organization A is located in Central London although the business also has offices elsewhere in the United Kingdom and in mainland Europe. It has a full-time staff of around 80. The company describes itself as a learning and communications specialist, with a particular focus on the design and application of learning technologies and software to facilitate the transformation of client organizations into successful (learning) businesses. While the organization operates in a competitive marketplace that can be described as highly knowledge focused, the organization itself does not have any formal KM policies or practices in place (like Company B). Also similarly to the other participating organization, the work environment is a large, airy open-place space. People largely work at long banks of desks, and there is a lot of "hot desking." There is a centrally positioned coffee area with a small sitting area where ad hoc meetings take place and where informal chat happens. Both meeting rooms are screened off from the main working area. The working space is relatively quiet and informal.

Organization B

Located in the center of London, Organization B describes itself as a services innovator and aggregator, which provides specialist professionals on permanent or contract basis to the public sector in the United Kingdom and which has a core staff of around 60. The core business is, in effect, a contract bidding "machine." The working environment is a large open-plan office, surrounded by spacious, glass-fronted meetings rooms. These are used for formal, scheduled meetings as well as ad hoc ones when available: that is, they are in use virtually all the time. Another noticeable feature of the environment is the low noise level despite the perennial presence of one or more "floorwalkers" talking on a mobile phone. The organization is team driven. There is an interesting contrast between the heavy use of internal email to communicate with colleagues (across the room, for instance) and occasional impromptu problem-solving or idea-generating interactions, which take place by, for instance, the coffee facilities. In fact, the researcher particularly observed that ad hoc meetings often took place around a counter in front of the centrally located kitchen area, which suggests that the design of this area in a prominent position was deliberate.

11.6 POINTS OF LIMITATION

As noted earlier, an obvious and very practical limitation to the present work is the difficulty in gaining the trust and agreement of organizations to take part in studies of this type. This clearly has ramifications for future research. This issue is not so much concerned with sample size, but rather with sample variety. The present study is limited to two organizations, and while they operate in quite different fields, they are both involved in the private service sector. It would have been preferable to have been able to include, for instance, organizations from the public sector and some from radically different business sectors.

A further limitation (of necessity) of the present study is that the research and analysis is entirely done by one person. Experience suggests that research of this nature would benefit from the involvement of more than one researcher in order to be able to bring different perspectives and knowledge to bear (ironically, much as Dorothy Leonard and her colleague claim in their theory of creative abrasion in the KM field). These matters draw attention to the interpretive nature of the study and its methodology. It is always possible that another researcher might arrive at different findings and conclusions, particularly if using a different analytical methodology. There again, that topic of objectivity versus subjectivity reemerges. Suffice to state that the adherence to Potter's validation procedures mediates, as far as is possible, the consequences of these types of research limitations.

We have elsewhere discussed potential limitations specific to DP (see, e.g., Section 7.8.2). One point is worth reemphasizing, and this concerns the relevance of this type of research and its findings specific to the business world in general and the KM practitioner in particular. In Chapter 5 and the discussions around social constructionism, we noted the warning given recently by Christian Madsbjerg and his colleague that studies in the human sciences are often seen by those in the business world as of little practical relevance, as being academic and notoriously difficult to understand. The onus is consequently on the shoulders of the researcher to find and promote the relevance of research work specific to the audiences to whom it may or should be of interest.

There is one last issue to address in terms of potential limitations, and this concerns the decision to focus on the thematic categories of knowledge sharing—trust, identity, risk, and context. Is it possible that in looking for how these matters are invoked in discourse, one simply finds what one seeks? That the act of looking brings these interpretations to the fore? When looking for instances of how and what speakers invoke as context, is the analyst unawaredly conjuring a context by applying her own categories? In mitigation, careful and methodical attention was given to seek, not just for instances where speakers invoke this or that context, but also for evidence of cospeakers orienting to the same phenomena, thus displaying shared understanding, as next turn proof.

To complete this chapter, a brief summary and a reprise of the research questions of interest are given in the following.

11.7   SUMMARY AND INDICATIVE RESEARCH QUESTIONS

A consideration of a complex tangle of issues and questions encountered in all of the fields of interest in Part One's discussions leads to some indicative research questions. These are included in their "long version" in the earlier discussions on "Research questions" (Section 11.5.1). These can be shortened to:

> Using the DP approach, discourse in organizational settings is analyzed for how the thematic categories of trust, identity, risk, and context are made live and with what, if any, influence and effect on what are understood as knowledge sharing meeting/forum contexts. In particular, will such an analysis inform an understanding of these thematic categories as tacitly invoked phenomena, and can these themes be shown to be corelational?

To summarize, then, the present research is a qualitative and interpretive methods study located in constructionism, which approaches knowledge and versions of reality as socially constructed in everyday discourse. The methodology draws on DP, with its design informed by Jonathan Potter and his coworker's ten stages of DA, Derek Edwards and Jonathan Potter's *Discursive Action Model*, and Potter's four procedures of validation. In addition, matters of measuring the quality of DA studies and ethical concerns have been addressed, and the limitations of the present study noted. The following analytic chapters report the study's analytical findings, based on the preceding description of method and design, with analysis particularly focused on knowledge sharing activities.

On a final note, it is conjectured that by extending the directions and boundaries already taken by many in the KM domain, the present study has the potential to contribute alternative ways of conceptualizing KM, knowledge work, and knowledge sharing in particular.

FURTHER READING

Buchanan, D. and Bryman, A. (Eds). (2009). *The Sage Handbook of Organizational Research Methods*. London: Sage.

Chalmers, A. (1999). *What is this thing called Science?* 3rd Edn. Maidenhead: Open University Press.

Holden, M. and Lynch, P. (2004). Choosing the appropriate methodology: understanding research philosophy. *The Marketing Review*, 4: 397–409.

Mulkay, M. and Gilbert, G. (1982). Accounting for error: how scientists construct their social world when they account for correct and incorrect belief. *Sociology*, 16: 164–183.

Potter, J. and Wetherell, M. (1987). *Discourse and Social Psychology: Beyond Attitudes and Behaviour*. London: Sage.

Silverman, D. (2007). *A Very Short, Fairly Interesting and Reasonably Cheap Book about Qualitative Research*. London: Sage.

Wood, L. and Kroger, R. (2000). *Doing Discourse Analysis: Methods for Studying Action in Talk and Text*. London: Sage.

Yardley, L. (2000). Dilemmas in qualitative health research. *Psychology and Health*, 15: 215–228.

12

TRUST AS AN ARTIFACT OF KNOWLEDGE SHARING

12.1 THE IMPORTANCE OF TRUST

The importance of trust in knowledge sharing (KS) and its status as the lubricant of an organization's operations are two good reasons to justify trust as a phenomenon of interest. Without trust, organizations would simply not be able to function. We can all easily imagine the chaos that would ensue if everyone in work suddenly decided that no one and no thing could be trusted. Fortunately, we are not only a highly collaborative species, an essential ingredient to human progress and development as Thomas Suddendorf notes, but we are also quite trusting.

Yet ironically and as has been seen time after time with other phenomena of interest, the definition of trust is a troubling concern. The scholar Jonathan Clifton is one of the few in the discourse world who has investigated "trust" in the workplace: pointing to the substantial body of conventional research on trust in organizational settings, much of which wrestles with the question of definition, he argues that it is futile to attempt to pin words onto what is essentially a human accomplishment in social interaction. According to this interpretation, trust takes its meaning from the context in which it is embedded or locally situated. Recall F. David Schoorman and colleagues' model that locates trust in relationships as a measure of willingness to be vulnerable, defining trust as acceptable risk contingent on perception of ability, integrity, and benevolence. In this model, trust is consequently approached as an aspect of relationship and as a function of perception.

Further evidence of the phenomenon's importance comes from a recently published empirical study of trust in organizational KS by Max Evans. As a starting point, Evans indicates the conditions necessary for effective KS as being a willingness to share,

Knowledge and Discourse Matters: Relocating Knowledge Management's Sphere of Interest onto Language,
First Edition. Lesley Crane.
© 2016 John Wiley & Sons, Inc. Published 2016 by John Wiley & Sons, Inc.

willingness to use, and perceived receipt of useful knowledge: KS, from this perspective, occupies highly complex social interactions and relationships. His study reports trust, shared language, and vision as the most important influencing factors in a willingness to share knowledge. Trust, he concludes, is particularly identified as a prerequisite for KS, which is fairly consistent with much of the rest of the knowledge management (KM) literature on the subject (see Chapter 3). From the discursive psychology (DP) perspective, "shared language and vision" can be readily mapped to shared understanding of context operating at the tacit level.

It is speculated that analysis of the data will show trust and related themes in action, providing the opportunity to explore how trust is made live in discourse, and with what effect, relevant to KS activities.

The data analyzed here comes from a recording of a meeting in which the activity of KS is understood as implicit. This is not a meeting in which one person deals out tasks and action: instead, it is regular event with team members coming together to share knowledge of actions and activities of mutual interest and concern. It is anticipated, then, that analysis of the data will display trust and its related themes in the interaction, providing the opportunity to explore how trust is made live in discourse and with what effect relevant to KS activities.

How do people "do trust"? If KS is concerned with producing accounts and descriptions, versions of affairs, with the aim of sharing this with others ("a willingness to share"), then it is a commonsense understanding to link trust to "factual accounting." That is, people routinely serve up their accounts or reports as factual, authentic, and free of personal stake and interest, hence objective and trustworthy. For instance, Jonathan Clifton's research shows how speakers invoke actions of "epistemic primacy" (the "I know more than you do" strategy: note that the word "superiority" is subsequently frequently used in place of "primacy" as the former is considered to more commonsensically indicative of the meaning applied here). This can be seen as a kind of action in which actors display the possession of access to unique and preferential knowledge. In scripting factual accounts, speakers orient to the trustworthiness both of account and of self, arguably contingent one to the other. In the terms of the research discussed earlier, in accepting and agreeing with versions produced by others ("a willingness to use and perceived usefulness of shared knowledge"), speakers index others' trustworthiness—that is, a willingness to be vulnerable to others, as a measure of others' ability, integrity, and benevolence. This consequently sets the directions of the present discussions, and, as the analysis shows, the business of factual accounting, epistemic superiority, and displays of access to privileged knowledge are routinely used. Moreover, these actions are seen as the foundation on which competing accounts are shown to be constructed.

Speakers Orient
The term "orient" or "orienting" is commonly used in discourse analysis to refer to that which speakers make relevant in their talk, whether consciously or unconsciously. Think of it like "notice" or "understand." When I orient to something (object, subject, action, emotion, whatever), I am making this a live concern of my talk.

Speakers Index
Utterances are said to be "indexical" in that the meaning depends on the context of its use. For instance, a speaker might be said to be "indexing" to skepticism if the tone of

their utterance emphasizes a downward movement suggesting a dismissing action. In the wider understanding, indexicality refers to speakers' displays of their understanding of the meaning of other speakers' utterances.

Turn-by-Turn Interaction
Typical conversation or meeting talk is structured according to "turns": a turn is the conversational "slot" that each speaker fills with their utterance, with the turn structure implicitly understood by speakers according to the circumstances of the discourse interaction. In normal conversation, one speaker takes a turn, which is completed before the next speaker takes a turn. In meetings, speakers' turns may be controlled by the meeting chairperson. The way that speakers construct and tacitly understand the turn structure of a discursive action is of particular interest to conversation analysts.

Relationally Situated
Something is relationally situated when its location (in time, context, spatial reference, etc.) works in relation with other features of talk.

We start with a brief discussion of the data and its context that forms the topic of analysis. This is followed by the analysis and discussion that shows trust to be a multidimensioned phenomenon, constructed in the turn-by-turn interaction of discourse, and as a relationally situated underpinning construct to KS. In this and all of the following analytic chapters, references are shown as embedded within the text to underline how the analysis and discussions are grounded in relevant research. The chapter concludes with some preliminary reflections. The findings are further discussed in Chapter 17, combined with those from subsequent analytic chapters.

12.2 DATA

The data under analysis comes from a Company B meeting recording. This is a regular team meeting, involving five participants, all male. Two are located in a meeting room in Company B's London offices, with the others joining in via conference call. It is assumed that the virtual attendees cannot see the others, and vice versa, for the simple reason that there is no suggestion of such visual availability.

The context of the meeting is a weekly exchange of team activities, responsibilities, future actions, and issues arising. The subject is the development of data handling services (software application) for discrete units of a major public sector organization. There is a further meeting immediately following this one that some of these actors will also attend. It becomes clear that this second meeting has the business of decision-making and is the source of some tension. This largely emanates from "Steve" who mandates a speedy pace for the present meeting from the outset. There is also the almost continuous sound of fast, often furious, typing that can only emanate from the meeting room in London.

Patterned Sequential Organization
Episodes of discourse—whether ordinary conversation, meeting, or whatever—generally display a pattern of sequential organization—that is, the way that the speakers progress their turns one after the other, which establishes an implicitly understood set of speaker

rules governing how, when, and what speakers should contribute. A simple example would be how a speaker's question generally sets up an anticipation and expectation of another's answer, so the structure and expected interaction is "question–answer."

While a substantial part of the meeting follows the patterned sequential organization of "topic announcement," "participant report," and "team leader evaluation," its choreography is marked by regular disagreements—competing accounts of affairs. There are six extracts presented here, five of which orient variously to challenge and persuasion, rivalry centered on competence, attribution, and claims to superior knowledge, all of which are shown to have implications for trust. This, in itself, is not an unusual feature of everyday talk: as Robin Wooffitt, a sociologist at the UK's University of York, explains in his book comparing conversation and discourse analysis (incidentally, essential reading for those interested), people routinely argue and disagree. He also makes the commonsense observation that disputes cannot be resolved by referring to the "facts of the matter" as it is precisely the facts that are usually in dispute. The first extract serves to set the scene, with participants orienting to their status in the context of the meeting, and a very particular imperative—the need for speed. Each extract is presented in the order in which it appears to illustrate the sequential unfolding of themes, challenges, and respective understanding of context that participants make live in their discourse in interaction.

12.3   CASTING THE CHARACTERS AND SETTING THE SCENE FOR ACTION

The meeting is initiated when the three remote actors dial in to the meeting using conference call technology. Extract 1 shows what happens.

Lines 1–9 script what would be colloquially known as the meeting "pecking order" while at the same time invoking the need for speed, setting direction, and the business at hand. Steve clearly orients to "doing leadership" in his rights to summon participants to the meeting confirmed with a roll call (Line 1) and in invoking his rights to be the first to formulate an assessment ("first turn assessment"; Clifton, 2012b: Line 4). The meeting callers are reflexively constructed as the "summoned," therefore subject to command. Steve further works up his identity as leader through claiming rights to make decisions (Line 8) and to establish the pace of the meeting in his reformulation of Bob's proposal

---

EXTRACT 1   130319_005 COMPANY B

1. Steve: Wa::ay. (.) Okay so we have Ade, Damien and Manoj.
2. (2)
3. ['yep', 'yep', 'yep' via conference call]=
4. Steve: =Yep, yep, yep. Good. Okay. ↑Ummmm.
5. (2)
6. Steve: ↓Right=
7. Bob: =Shall we go through the list ↑first?
8. Steve: Ye:: <u>ah</u> Bob why don't you why don't you wheel us through the list?
9. Bob: ↑Alrighty so starting in alphabetical with [names]. So, [project name]?

(Line 7) with a sanction to "wheel us through the list." This can be heard as a sense of time pressure with the need for speed, which Bob indexes with his "Alrighty ..." (Line 9). Bob's implied possession of the "list," coupled with his claimed ability to suggest actions, casts him in a secondary role to Steve's leader status.

Notice the 2 second delay in the three virtual attendees responding to Steve's statement of who "we have" (Line 2): in a face-to-face meeting, such a delay would be understood to suggest troubles in interaction (Drew, 2003b), but as Steve does not orient to this understanding in his assessment (Line 4), it cannot here be analyzed as such. It could simply just be a case of the nature of "virtual meetings" being more tolerant of such delays.

First Turn Assessments
In his discursive study of leadership, published in 2012, Jonathan Clifton argues that when a speaker claims the first turn in an assessment sequence, that is a sequence designed to provide an assessment or evaluation of what another speaker has just said, for instance, this works on the level of a claim to overriding rights to set and manage the meaning of the discussion as a whole. This, he suggests, is a rhetorical hallmark of leadership.

Reflexively Constructed
When a rhetorical action by an actor has the function and consequence of scripting something or someone as its opposite. For instance, Abigail Locke and Derek Edward, in their fascinating analysis of former US President Clinton's Grand Jury testimony, show how "(I)in portraying [Monica] Lewinksy as irrational, emotional and motivated by personal problems, Clinton reflexively defines himself, in contrast, as rational, behaving properly..." (2003: 249).

Steve hesitates over what topic to start with—the extended "ummm," brief pause, and carefully spoken "Right" invokes a display of searching (Potter, 1998a) among competing topics (Lines 4–6). Bob steps in with a tentatively spoken suggestion formulated as a question with a candidate answer (Potter and Edwards, 2012), orienting to Steve's control of the "agenda" as leader. Steve's stretched affirmative ("Ye:: ah") indexes the candidate answer but scripts reluctance—going through the list would not have been his preferred course of action. Subsequent analysis shows how this actor frequently uses the stretched "ye:: ah" to signal difficulty, disagreement, or reluctance. Instead of producing an alternative course of action, he reformulates Bob's suggestion, and the "list" becomes topicalized as the first business of the meeting, albeit one to be dispensed with at speed, with its imperative for participants to share knowledge.

Questions with Candidate Answers
When formulating a question, speakers will routinely include a possible answer embedded within the question. Thus, speakers offer a "candidate answer" to cospeakers on the expectation that this will be adopted and issued by the next speaker, in which turns-in-interaction have the effect of scripting consensus and collaboration.

The sense of speed invoked in this extract arguably has an interesting effect on subsequent transactions. In three of the following extracts (2, 3, and 4), the action of argument—competing accounts—is shown to be triggered at the point at which Bob, as the possessor of the list to be "wheeled through," is attempting to effect topic closure and transition to a new topic. Also, Extract 3 contains a call for a "bigger discussion" on a particular topic. All of this suggests that the imperative for speed is not only creating a tension, but is also being resisted. The normative and appropriate place for topic discussion and comment would be between topic opener and closer. Thus, the action of initiating further discussion on a topic during or after the issuing for its closure indicates troubles, suggestive of dissatisfaction with time allocated to topic discussion, with its inference of a potential for decisions based on less than adequate discussion or debate. There is, in fact, only one instance of argumentative actions taking place within the appropriate topic discussion space, and that is initiated by Steve himself.

A final point to raise is the team's mutual familiarity: roles are not explicitly established as they are already tacitly known. Thus, the mutual roles are cast and shown to be tacitly understood, the objective of the interaction is made live, and the team's familiarity with one another made contingent.

12.4 WORKING UP TRUST THROUGH EPISTEMIC SUPERIORITY AND AUTHENTICITY

12.4.1 Emerging Challenge

The next extract comes less than three minutes into the meeting and displays the first evidence of emerging challenge in the form of competing accounts offered, respectively, by Steve and Ade. The latter, in his role as "commanded," has a normatively understood imperative to couch his account in the actions of persuasion, trustworthiness, and so forth. Steve, on the other hand, as leader, has no such imperative: he has the rights to make decisions on behalf of team members without recourse to any form of warranting. Nonetheless, he is shown to accomplish many of the same actions in his account, making "team buy-in" to his version live and accountable. The difference between the two is that while Ade's competing account reflexively conjures Steve's as untrustworthy (in contrast to his own), Steve effectively wins the argument by simply reformulating the issue and removing it from the team's control, which actions are made possible by his access to privileged knowledge. That is, he is able to resolve the disagreement without disputing Ade's version of "the facts," allowing the trajectory of the meeting to move on. Trust, then, comes to the fore. This is how the action plays out.

This action involves three actors, Steve, Ade, and Bob. In Lines 43–45, Bob works to close down a list item with a two-part action: he serves up the classic topic boundary marker, "Ok" (Svennevig, 2012b), combined with a projected future action ("… leave it on the <u>list</u> just to keep ↓chasing …": Line 43). These collectively work up a topic closing component (Drew and Holt, 1988). But, rather than producing a new topic, Bob issues a topic extension with an assessment component ("but it's good to know": Line 44) combined with a knowledge component ("y'know"). The latter is typically used to project assumptions of shared knowledge and intersubjective agreement (Clifton, 2012a). Specifically, here, he is orienting to Ade's account in the previous turn. This is the first occasion that Bob has offered an evaluative assessment, not formulated as a question directed to Steve. In interrupting Bob (Line 46), Steve effectively deletes any warrant that Bob might have to make evaluations, with the implication that only he has the entitlement to perform such actions. What happens next is a seesaw of competing assessment, with issues of trust being made live and under threat.

EXTRACT 2   130319_005 COMPANY B

43. Bob: Ok well we'll leave it on the <u>list</u> just to keep ↓chasing them on VPN and
44. dongles but it's good to know that we're (.) y'know that we're we can keep using the
45. desktops as]
46. Steve: [Yeah I wou(ld) I <u>do</u> want to get off the desktops as poss- as fast as
47. possible but (0.5) for the moment we-uh we ↓don't have much choice.
48. Ade: Yeah]
49. Steve: [we do need to keep]
50. Ade: [that worries me a bit (.) the only part that worries me
51. about it is if we go onto ( ) and it's the same set up as we used t'ave then (.) it's
52. not good. We might as well stick to desktops.
53. Steve: Yeah well it- I-I –I think the conversation at 4 o' clock will prove that it's
54. only an intermediate anyway.
55. Bob: Yeah, there's things we may not]
56. Steve: [I think we're gonna be getting out of out of ( )
57. fai::rly <u>rapidly</u> anyway
58. Ade: Okay.

Topic Boundary Marker
These are devices that are particularly noticeable in agenda-driven meetings where a participant might use the term "okay" to display closure of one topic, leaving the field open for another to be initiated. Jan Svennevig of the University of Oslo, Norway, has published some interesting work that investigates this action in workplace meetings.

Contrast Devices/Markers
These are rhetorical devices—phrases or single words—which have the effect of marking a contrast between two or more different accounts or descriptions. So, for instance, "I could go to work on Monday but I would rather not." According to analysis by Ann Widdicombe and her colleague, such devices are usually associated with and used in talk designed to persuade.

Preferred Turns
An account that starts with a weak agreement with the previous speaker, followed by an account that works at variance to this, thus constituting the speaker's preferred state of affairs.

Footing
Someone is said to shift footing when they change from one stance, perspective, identity, or position to another. Examples include changing from talking about "I" to talking about "we." For instance, Jackie Abell and her colleague explore how Princess Diana linguistically shifts position from that of her "royal role" to that of her role as a private individual, and with what consequences.

On the surface, the disagreement in Lines 46–57 is over nothing if Steve's account that "…we're gonna be getting out of …" (Line 56) is accepted, so why argue? To draw on

Clifton's (2012a) analysis of trust in workplace interaction, this is about jockeying for position, through making claims to rights to knowledge. But these can only be considered as a form of "trust work" where recipients orient to the knowledge claims as such.

12.4.2 Competing Strategies for Conjuring Trust

There are two clear stages—and two different strategies—to the unfolding disagreement. In the first part, Steve receipts Bob's assessment with a weak agreement and then replaces it with his own assessment (Line 46). Such turns are known as "preferred turns" (Edwards and Potter, 1992). The signal for an alternative version on the way is given by the repair ("I would" is replaced with "I do"), which is hearable as a contrast device. Such devices, usually taking the form of "but" or "that said," for instance, mark the end of any conces-sionary material and the start of a competing assessment. According to Widdicombe and Wooffitt (1990), these devices are associated with persuasion talk: in this instance, it for-mulates the action of "I hear what you're saying but ...." So while he does the business of accomplishing a correcting account of affairs to that proposed by Bob, he reduces the strength of the correction, thus invoking his sensitivity to the potential for sounding rude or unreasonably argumentative (Wooffitt, 2005).

Notice how Steve serves up his version of future events formulated first as what <u>he</u> would like to see and then deftly shifts footing (Abell and Stokoe, 2001) from first person to group collective ("... we don't have much choice": Line 47). This has the effect of projecting a mutually shared team status in respect of desktops: in other words, he scripts team consensus. Consensualism is shown to work up stake inoculation, against, for instance, criticism for having personal interest in one's account, and in factualizing accounts (Edwards and Potter, 1992). Thus, it is not just a case of what Steve wants: he projects what he wants onto being what the team wants, and in this respect, they are collectively thwarted by external factors. This is "persuasion talk," designed to elicit trust in Steve's version of affairs on the part of hearers, and this is precisely what Ade orients to with his minimal agreement token (Edwards and Potter: Line 48). Perhaps indexing to the insufficiency of Ade's assent, Steve plows on with his version (Line 49).

The second part to the unfolding disagreement talk occurs in Lines 50–58 and is ini-tiated by Ade's interruption that talks over Steve's continued account of affairs as being inclusively imperative ("we do need to keep": Line 49). Ade's self-selected floor grab comes with a strong orientation to professional care and responsibility, in which he dis-plays a different rhetorical strategy in constructing his version as trustworthy. He con-jures the cognitive state of "being worried" but which is downgraded ("... a bit ... the only part ...": Line 50), a practice that Jonathan Potter and his colleague (2003) describe as an activity of disclaiming responsibility. Thus, it is not Ade's fault that he is worried, but rather the consequence of an external state of affairs. In Line 51, he invokes collab-oration and consensus in scripting an inclusion pronoun (Abell and Stokoe, 2001) twice ("we go" and "we used"), which shifts the onus for worry onto the team as a whole: they should all be worried. This is followed by an explicit warrant for worry, framed as a conditional proposition ("if ... then": Chilton, 2004). In scripting himself as possessing knowledge about cause and effect, he serves a warrant for the authen-ticity of his claims (factual accounting), reflexively scripting Steve's version as unacceptable–untrustworthy.

Conditional Propositions
These devices, typically structured as "If X, then Y," are often used by politicians, according to professor of linguistics Paul Chilton, to make claims to possessing knowledge about cause and effect. Events thus described are displayed as having particular consequences. These can also be seen as a form of factual accounting, based on their conditional predictive attributes.

Empiricist Accounting
This type of accounting is particularly associated with talk that has the design of serving up facts. The term was arguably first used in sociology by Gilbert and Mulkay in their study of the discourse of scientists (e.g., 1984), although they refer to "empiricist repertoires." Derek Edwards and his colleague argue that such accounts have the action of removing the speaker from responsibility for the facts, framing facts as independent from the speaker and as available "out there" as objective phenomena.

Ade completes his turn with an assessment ("not good") in the form of an "unhedged" declarative assertion that works to frame accounts as uncontestably in stone (Clifton, 2012a), which is linked to a projection of future action in what "we might as well" do. "Might" is interesting here because it would usually be associated with scripting a "hedge" or mitigation against criticism in its acknowledgement of the possibility of other candidate actions. However, here, it works up the commonsense nature of what might be done, conjuring a sense of tacitly known background knowledge (Clifton, 2006). Consequently, Ade's description of affairs is displayed as emanating from concrete facts, with the future course of action cast as a reasonable one that the team would agree to, which reflexively further implicates Steve's version as having untrustworthy status. Thus, Ade's is designed to be an acceptable account, based on superior knowledge, orienting to status as trustworthy, and hard to challenge. There is also the suggestion of an invocation of risk—Ade clearly conjures Steve's version as being risky ("not good") and with the potential to lead to poor outcomes for the team. Thus, Ade can be said to have scripted himself as unwilling to be vulnerable (Schoorman, Mayer, and Davis, 2007).

12.4.3 Avoiding Direct Challenge by Reformulating the Problem

According to authors Wood and Kroger (2000), prefacing an account with "Yeah, well," as Steve does in Line 53, works as a weak token of agreement, which is a classic signal of forthcoming disagreement (Clifton, 2012a). However, Steve does not directly disagree with Ade's account. Rather he discards it with empiricist accounting (Edwards and Potter, 1992), accomplishing a neat reformulation of the issue: the future predicted conversation is concretized temporally and will "prove" Steve's reformulation of affairs. In other words, he retains the topic problem (Chilton, 2004) but reforms it in the light of his claims to privileged access to knowledge (Willig, 2003), thus avoiding a direct challenge to the authenticity of Ade's account. Ade's version is shown to be consigned to history, as irrelevant to the here, now, and future. Note how he also works to downgrade (Locke and Edwards, 2003) the problem ("…only an intermediate…": Line 54).

Thus, Steve predicts a new set of affairs, which are beyond the decision-making powers of the team, which is carefully hedged as having conditional status (Wooffitt and Allistone, 2008). In this way, he works to downgrade the status of the problem raised by Ade and to diffuse the potential for further dispute.

A three-part turn sequence completes the interaction. Bob's aligning report that there are "things we may not" (Line 55) is interesting in what it does. Firstly, it can be heard as orienting to knowledge ("things") out there, which is beyond the reach of the team, but, secondly and crucially, it is argued here that Bob, in conjuring the team consensus, is orienting directly to the three virtual attendees. There is also a suggestion of lack of trust in external agents who know things and make decisions that impact on the team, which works reflexively to index Steve's account as having trustworthy status. In Lines 56 and 57, in contrast to Bob's account of lack of knowledge, Steve interrupts with a confirmation that he does have access to "things" out there actioned through his claim to knowledge served as news. That is, it is news to the other speakers, but not to him. The interactional accomplishment is trust: there are people out there who may not be trustworthy, but as Steve has access to knowledge of "things," his account can be trusted, and Bob's account in Line 55 can now be seen as an endorsement of Steve's trustworthiness directed to the team. This can be unpacked a little more.

Warrant
People normatively use "warrants" and "warranting" to mark something as being satisfactorily explained, according to David Silverman. Simply, a warrant is an excuse or justification for some action. For instance, "I am not able to go to the meeting because I will be in New York": not being able to go to the meeting is accountable (i.e., requiring an explanation), but comes with a warrant of being in New York, thus excusing the absence.

Steve's turn in Line 56 is prefaced with the conjuring of a cognitive state ("I think …"), which, in contrast to his earlier stuttered "I-I-I think …" (Line 53) that marks his account as open to doubt, works here as an explicit opinion marker (Chilton, 2004). By linking Steve's two utterances (Lines 53/54 and 56/57), the persuasion work becomes clearly evident as Steve conjures his version of affairs as being more and more authentic, and predictable, with the second part building on Bob's admission of the existence of "things we may not know," marking this as a version of affairs that only Steve can predict. The veracity of his opinion—and therefore its trustworthiness—can be seen in his confident emphasis on timescales ("fai::rly rapidly": Line 57). His claim to privileged access to knowledge also works as a warrant in linking to his earlier stance over "getting off desktops" (Line 46). The risk is downgraded and that which Ade has conjured for group worry is effectively deleted but without challenging its authenticity. Steve, then, claims what Clifton (2012a) terms "epistemic primacy," scripting self as trustworthy. Ade orients to this interpretation of affairs with his token of acceptance in Line 58. The entire interaction, then, is a delicate balance between offering competing accounts of affairs and sensitivity to others' concerns displayed particularly by Steve, despite Ade's initial inferred resistance to the trustworthy status of the latter's account of affairs.

The following two extracts display disagreement taking a more confrontational and combative turn.

12.5 RISK AND COMPETENCE AS CONTINGENT FACTORS TO TRUST

12.5.1 Calling on Witnesses to Work Up Persuasion

Extract 3 comes some 5 minutes into the meeting. Just prior to this, Bob has raised a topic from his list, which is directed to Ade for comment. What follows next can only be described as a mutual questioning of ability by Steve and Damien, with implied risks to

---

EXTRACT 3   130319_005 COMPANY B

78. Ade: Yeah I've not had a look at that yet.
79. (1)
80. Bob: Okay hhhh]
81. Steve: [it- it's something that (.)every time I talk to a [Client] they do go 'ooh
82. four months that's a long time
83. Bob: °yeah°
84. Damien: [Clients] always say that but I'm nuhhh ( )]
85. Steve: [I know]
86. Damien: [( ) I think we need a bigger
87. discussion about whether to use ( ) or not but I don't think realistically it's only
88. gonna be a month better (.) in terms of actually being usable. The first the first
89. month's returns (0.5) patchy at best=
90. Steve: = Yeah it's what ↑[name of Competitor firm] use.
91. (2) [sound of rapid typing]
92. Bob: Okay
93. (2.5)
94. Bob: so do we want em is this something for Manoj to look ↑into? Or is]
95. Steve: [Yes please.

---

trust. Recall that Schoorman and colleagues (2007) posit "ability" as one of the three dimensions of trustworthiness, the calculation of which influences perception of acceptable risk in others. In the context of the following discussion, "ability" is understood to infer "competence" and "reputation."

What is interesting about this particular extract is Steve's formulation in Line 90, issued in a sarcastic tone of voice, and referencing the name of a competitor company. In his study of political interview discourse, sociologist Ian Hutchby (2011) shows how such "skeptical rejoinders" constitute nonneutral moves. Here, what the competitor company "uses" is precisely the software product that Damien calls into question (Lines 86–89). Steve's response in Line 90 is not issued as a news item—that is, it is not designed to inform coparticipants of some new state of affairs. Rather, it can be heard as a strong rebuke. Does this signal a crumbling of trust between the two actors?

Skeptical Rejoinders
These are linguistic devices that invoke skepticism on the part of the speaker in response to a prior turn at talk and are usually terms that would otherwise have a nonskeptical connotation. The ways in which an utterance can be shown to be transformed into an action of skepticism include a downward movement of intonation, for instance, rendering the utterance as hearably dismissive. Thus, such devices are not neutral and can be linked to taking a position on some topic.

Reported Speech
Speech that is attributed to some other by the speaker is called "reported speech," and this can be direct or indirect. Direct speech is where the reported words are framed as a direct quotation or citation. It is indirect if the reported words are offered as an

approximation or summary or other representation of the actual words spoken. With direct reported speech clearly being the more powerful linguistic device, both are important, routinely used structures in talk. Their effect on both speaker and hearer is dependent on context, but an obvious function is to effect persuasion work or to bolster the factual nature of what is being reported.

Extreme Case Formulation
Originally studied by Anita Pomerantz, extreme case formulations such as "extremely," "very," "every," "everyone," and so on take an evaluation to its extreme. These devices have multiple functions and consequences. They can "up the ante" of a particular argument; they can be used to "normalize" something that might otherwise be considered to be unusual (e.g., a knife carrying youth explains that "everyone has one," suggesting the carrying of knives is normative behavior). Jonathan Clifton notes that they can leave a speaker exposed to potential criticism in that all that is required to dilute what is being claimed is one exception, the idea that all swans are white until you find a black one!

The sequence initiates in accordance with the now established sequential organization: Bob issues a topic, which is commented on by the relevant actor, followed by an assessment scripted by Steve. Here, we see a variation. In this instance, Ade receipts the topic issue with his habitual "yeah" and then reports the issue status: no progress has been made, thus bouncing the topic straight back to Bob (Line 78). The latter's slight hesitation in picking up his slot ("Okay": Line 80), followed by the start of something more [unfortunately unintelligible], suggests surprise, but nonetheless signals topic closure. The expectation that is established here is that as the topic has not been looked at yet, there will be no need for an assessment by Steve, making a topic transition (Wooffitt, 2005) relevant. What happens next is contrary to this expectation.

Overriding Bob's attempt to mobilize a topic transition, Steve marks Ade's response as insufficient by stalling topic closure. His utterance across Lines 81–82 effectively performs power-persuasion: first, he displays rights to prevent topic closure, and then he works to upgrade the task's importance, which he does using a direct reported speech device. In reporting what the client says ("… every time I talk to a [client] they do go …": Line 81), he neatly works up a warrant for maintaining the topic and ramping up its potency. It is "direct" in so much as it conjures a quotation of what others have said. Such devices serve to strengthen claims, rendering them more credible as fact (Wood and Kroger, 2000). Note how also, in using what others have said to issue a warrant for his version of affairs, Steve effectively disposes of any personal stake or interest in the version (Wetherell, 2001).

What this also suggests is that Steve acknowledges the need to persuade others on this point, with this persuasion talk directed to Ade. Note that he makes no reference to the task itself, instead invoking the negative consequences of the task not being done. This can be seen as a direct admonishment to Ade: it is his lack of attention to the topic that risks negative consequences, but there is no hint of questioning Ade's competence, only his *priorities*. Also note the extreme case formulation prefacing the reported speech ("every time;" Line 80), used here as an instrument to upgrade the "ante" (Schegloff, 1997). This formulation powerfully and persuasively works up the routine and predictable nature of what "clients" will say: this does not just happen once or twice, but each time he engages with clients. It is so routine and part of the course, then, that this is cast as "common knowledge" (Edwards and Potter, 1992). The stakes associated with the task that Ade has reportedly not "looked at" are thus heightened, and risk is made live, to which Bob aligns agreement (Line 83). The nature of the task, at this point, is not the topic of dispute. Things then take a surprising turn.

12.5.2 Two Competing Versions of the Same Witness Accounts

Despite not being the agent of the task under discussion, Damien self-selects with a turn designed to shift risk from "not doing the task" to the task itself. He directly challenges Steve's account and its warrant by rescripting what clients say as inconsequential: it is the very "routineness" ("always say": Line 84) of what clients say that renders it not worth listening to. This is a classic example of variability inherent in talk: in essence, both Steve and Damien use a similar account of what clients say, emphasizing the routine frequency. But Steve's account upgrades the importance of what clients say, while Damien's does precisely the opposite. As Robin Wooffitt succinctly notes, "(T)the possibility of variation in and between versions of events is built into the fabric of everyday life" (2005: 16). Consequently, an appeal to the facts will not resolve the issue. The contrast marker ("but") signals the preferred nature of what is about to follow (Edwards and Potter, 1992). Steve's talk-under ("I know": Line 85) orients to what is about to now emerge as being a known-about account. Damien does not concede his turn to Steve's interruption, but continues to press his version of affairs, summoning a broader picture with a call for a "bigger discussion" (Line 86/87).

12.5.3 Issuing Challenges to Competency and Undermining Trust

This call works on two levels: First, it indexes back to his account of what clients "always say" framing this as irrelevant, and beside the point, thus deleting any risk associated with what they say, reflexively working up criticism of Steve's use of such evidence. Second, the call for a bigger discussion, formulated as a decision-making event ("whether to use [] or not": Line 87), implies that the decision has already been discussed, but not thoroughly enough with the suggestion that its decision outcome is flawed. Risk is thus made live along a new trajectory. Collectively, Damien's account serves as a competency challenge, which effectively undermines the previous speaker's competence to comment on a given issue (Hutchby, 2011).

Declarative Assertion
When a speaker asserts a particular version of affairs as fact, which is not hedged in any way with, for instance, a qualifier such as "I think" or "it's possible that," then this version is said to be constructed as a representation of concrete reality. In asserting such an actual state of affairs, the speaker is said to be making self accountable for being right. It thus works on the level of an appeal to trust.

The decision-making process is further called into question through the issuing of a declarative assertion (Clifton, 2012a) in Line 88/89. In his study of trust actions in workplace interactions, Clifton shows how such assertions work up states of affairs as concrete reality, thus formulating the speaker as accountable for being right. The action of holding oneself publicly as accountable is a marker for trustworthiness. In this instance, Damien scripts a prediction of minimal benefits to be gained if Steve's course of action is adopted. Thus, Damien's account works as a display of superior knowledge as authentic, which is nonetheless accountable. It is accountable in the sense that future events could prove him to be right—or wrong. Such claims are inherently risky, so in making a concrete prediction about "the first month's returns," Damien rhetorically and reflexively scripts himself as knowledgeable and competent expert, with integrity (in nonetheless reporting such a negative projected future action). Consequently, his display of possessing superior knowledge, of ability to predict, and of accountability, integrity, and authenticity all work interrelationally as a display of "doing trust." In other words, he constructs his version of affairs as hard if not impossible to dispute. But this is precisely what Steve does.

Orienting to the implicit competency challenge (Hutchby, 2011), Steve's rejoinder is immediate—a tapering off and lowering of voice tone—issuing a discard by scripting the evidence of what another company (later identified as a competitor) does. It can also be heard as a call to common knowledge of facts out there (Edwards and Potter, 1992): this is what everyone knows. This arguably conjures a question over Damien's ability and knowledge, with its implication that Damien's account is biased in favor of his own interests. Thus, he reverses the competency challenge, scripting Damien's account as not to be trusted, and that others know more, with all of associated consequences for reputation. Trust becomes undermined, and Damien makes no further contribution at this point. The impact of Line 90 can be seen in the two second delay and repair in Line 92, in which Bob attempts to "line under" the debate with a tentative formulation of a question on future projected action, issuing this with a candidate answer (Hepburn and Wiggins, 2005). He clearly makes live a context of discomfort, initiating a turn transition.

In this exchange, ability and reputation are shown as tacitly managed, as accountable and contingent to trust, authenticity, and trustworthiness. Actions are recipient designed (Potter and Edwards, 2012) to invoke warrants (e.g., claims to superior knowledge) for the trustworthiness of accounts. In this way, trust can be seen as implicit to KS, as well as working corelationally with ability and reputation.

It is claimed that Extract 3 shows trust breaking down; however, this is not the end of the matter.

12.6 TRUST BREAKDOWN CONNECTS WITH KNOWLEDGE SHARING BREACHES

12.6.1 Factual Accounting as a Warrant for Trust

Extract 4 comes a few lines later, following the selection of Manoj to "look into" the task (the subject of Extract 3) and the latter's acceptance of the work.

To all intents and purposes, the topic has been closed, a resource assigned to the task, with agreement that it should be carried out. Bob actions a topic boundary marker (Svennevig, 2012b), "Kay good" (Line 101), with the rapid typing suggesting that the decision just made is being concretized in the form of meeting notes. It can be speculated that this concretizing action is what drives Damien to reopen it in what is essentially a breach of the meeting's procedural norms, something that it is assumed that only Steve, as Leader, is warranted to do. The claims to witness evidence constructed by Steve in Extract 3 have not persuaded Damien to change his opinion.

It is suggested here that Damien orients to his breach of meeting norms with a metaphorical "hand in the air" suggested by his opening particle "Uh" (Line 103), working up a claim to a turn. Note how his opening utterance contains markedly heavy exhalations of

---

EXTRACT 4   130319_005 COMPANY B

101. Bob: °'kay good°
102. [Rapid, noisy typing)
103. Damien: Uh it's gonna (.hhhhh) it (.hhh) that's gonna
104. be a ↑lot of work so do we need to before we get Manoj doing y'know
105. (0.5) two weeks work ( ) package to put in the cos there's basically a-at
106. least one rule for every single field=
107. Steve: =No no tha-that's]
108. Damien: [( )
109. Steve: [that-that's not what I'm asking for at
110. the moment what I'm as::king for is simply for Manoj to get his head
111. around what we would need to do to ( ) data (.) to create ( ) that we
112. can ↑use um and then report back on (.) feasibility and scale of the
113. task (.) not to actually ↑do it=
114. Damien: =right yeah okay (.) ↓no problem.
115. [lots of rustling]

---

breath and a repair: "… it's gonna … that's gonna …." This invokes frustration—the proverbial "banging of the head against a brick wall." His concerns have moved from issues around what the client can expect (Extract 3, Lines 87–89) to those around a team member who has just been tasked with "a lot of work." This is tonally emphasized, making it hearable as derived from expert knowledge. His orienting to a concern for others is designed to inoculate against potential criticism of having personal stake and interest (Edwards and Potter, 2005). His claim is thus serving up facts that are out there for any reasonable person to see.

He further embellishes the factual nature of his account with quantification: "two weeks' work" (Line 105). The actor treats this piece of "fact" as accountable (Silverman, 2007), wrapping it in a two-part warrant. The scripting of "y'know," prior to the quantification "fact," typically works to project shared knowledge and intersubjective agreement (Clifton, 2012a); the team already jointly know this to be the case—thus, shared consensus and corroboration are invoked (Edwards and Potter, 1992). The second part of the warrant lies in the appeal to a self-evident level of common sense (Thompson, 2004) concerning what the task will specifically require ("… there's basically at least one rule for every single field": Lines 105/106), formulating this as obvious to everyone (but perhaps not Steve) and therefore undeniable. Notice also the absence of any references to cognitive states (e.g., I think) that might conjure a doubt marker or epistemic downgrade (Clifton). This absence increases the strength of the account as a warrant for an objective and therefore authentic state of affairs.

Doubt Marker and Epistemic Downgrades
Use of phrases such as "I think" and "I'm not sure" can serve to conjure doubt over whatever claim or account is being constructed, thus orienting to uncertainty. Likewise, "I think" and similar phrases can also perform the action of downgrading or diluting the knowledge that the speaker claims to possess. However, "I think" can also signify an

expression of opinion as the personal possession of the speaker. How such phrases are understood depends on the context in which they are performed.

Quantification Rhetoric
This refers to utterances in which numerical and nonnumerical descriptor (e.g., "small," "large") phrases are used to construct accounts as factual and as designed to argue. The way in which such phrases are deployed is also significant in effect: for instance, half a million "sounds" more than 500,000 because the former refers to "millions," while the latter invokes "thousands."

Damien's turn works up Steve as being unreasonable, perhaps not even being in possession of the most basic facts (e.g., the rule for every field). It also orients to pressures of time, with the heavy emphasis on "a lot of work" quantified as being "two weeks," with the risk that this implies in rendering valuable resources unavailable for other, perhaps more important work. In their study of quantification rhetoric in a media environment, Potter and his coworkers (1991) argue that such accounts are not simply accounts of some "robust reality" but are specifically designed to argue. The upshot is a second attempt by Damien to serve up a version of Steve's "task" as being inappropriate and risky. However, it now transpires that Damien has entirely misunderstood the nature of the task.

12.6.2   A Breach in Knowledge Sharing Comes to the Fore

Steve is quick to discard Damien's version of affairs (Line 109) for the second time. The stuttering repetition of "tha-that's" coming at the start of his turn suggests a measure of surprise. Damien's description of the task is not what Steve is asking to be done, thus working up a classic form of counter argument. However, Steve does more than simply correct Damien's understanding of what is being asked for. He orients to the implicit "accusation" contained in Damien's turn. Not only does Steve rebut the charges, but he also deflects the conjured "unreasonableness" back at Damien. The task is downgraded to "simple," with a rhetorical boundary parked around its scope (Line 110). The requirement for a report on feasibility and scale of the now future projected task (the action that Damien has been concerned with), contrasted with "not to actually ↑do it" (Line 113), scripts Damien's version of affairs, in which Manoj is understood to be tasked with doing the "actual" job, as being wholly irregular and something that Steve would never sanction. Steve, in this fashion, successfully retakes the moral high ground, arguably eroded as a result of his "quip" in Line 90, while simultaneously dismantling the position scripted by Damien. Damien's position—his ability and reputation—is thus undermined. What Steve displays is a constructed context of lack of trust.

The upshot of the interactions in Extracts 3 and 4 is a significant climb-down by Damien (Line 114) and arguably a breakdown in trust. The gap of silence indicated in Line 115, with its audible sounds of papers rustling, suggests discomfort among team members.

There is one question that remains unanswered: how is it that Damien misunderstood the task that Steve (and Bob) refers to at the outset of the discussion? While it cannot be known or even speculated what is going on in the minds of speakers, what can be speculated is that the breakdown in trust between Steve and Damien, inaugurated in Extract 3, clouds the issues for the speakers and the business of sharing knowledge. Damien formulates the task of migration from one software database to another as (i) a lot of tedious work, (ii) not likely to give more than minimal benefits in return, and (iii) as a topic that needs a much broader discussion, with its suggestion of insufficient and even poorly informed discussion to date. That, by any standards, is an entrenched position. Steve, on the other hand, orients to what the clients want, what the competitor company does (and knows), and to himself as competent manager who would not require a task to be actually done before it is understood fully in terms of scope and feasibility. They are almost—but not quite—arguing about different things. Note how Steve does not orient to Damien's concerns: he effectively discards them. A breakdown in trust has, it is conjectured, resulted directly in a break in communication, as Argyris (2009) predicts will happen when communications deteriorate, and hence a breach in KS.

12.7 KNOWLEDGE, TRUST, AND BLAME

12.7.1 Issuing the Call to Account

The following two short extracts appear in a further disagreement interaction between the same two actors—Steve and Damien—occurring around 20 minutes into the meeting. These extracts are different from the rest because, in this case, the disagreement is not issued at or during topic closure but is located in its normative and expected position in the discourse structure. Steve is coming to the end of a short descriptive report of another meeting at which he presented the team's software product for review, receiving a good reception. This leads him into a relatively lengthy and technical description of navigation through the software application, which ends with Line 200, and the formulation of a problem.

Steve is referring to layers within the navigational system of the team's software application, one of which is claimed to be missing (Line 200). The topic is issued as an assessment formulated as a question through a raised voice tone at the end. Although he uses the inclusive pronoun "we," typically having the effect of projecting or presupposing agreement in meeting contexts (Clifton, 2006), it is hypothesized that here, the pronoun serves to separate "we" as a group that includes Steve, the members of the previously

---

EXTRACT 5   130319_005 COMPANY B

200. Steve: ... so we're <u>missing</u> the middle level which is u::m which is
201. ↑[label name]?
202. (1.5)
203. Damien: We're not mi- no we're not missing any- it's just uh the only way
204. it couldn't be worked there's only jus' one thing it jus' automatically
205. collects it
206. Steve: Ye::ah=
207. Damien: =So it's there it jus' doesn't show=
208. Steve: =That's a ↓problem
209. (1.5)
210. Damien: ↓Yeah it's a problem but there's nothin' that could be done
211. about it unless you wanna (.) hire someone for the software. It sho- it
212. ↑should display at top of the chart that—it should (.) <u>show</u> it at the top
213. of the chart in the title of the chart.

reported review panel, and possibly the other three meeting participants, from Damien himself. It can thus be heard as "we have a problem, and it's your responsibility"—as a blame action, but with the raised tone at the end, making it hearable as a question.

What is the effect of serving an assessment in the form of a question? A question is one part of an adjacency pair, with an answer forming the other. The two are discriminately related in that the first defines an appropriate response in the second (Silverman, 2007). Thus, Steve's turn makes an answer from Damien conditionally relevant (Wooffitt, 2005). He is publicly calling him to account.

Adjacency Pair
This term is drawn from the terminology of conversation analysis, and it refers to two conversational items that naturally and inevitably belong together. Greetings, for instance, are examples where if one speaker issues a greeting, it is incumbent on the other to respond similarly. Questions and answers are another example: if a person asks a question of another, the expected response is an answer to the question, not, for instance, a further question. Thus, these are "ordered pairs" such that the first part sets a requirement for a particular second part to be delivered, so it is made "conditionally relevant." If a required second part is not forthcoming, it is generally treated by the first part speaker as a non-normative absence.

Intensifier
An intensifier is a word or phrase that works in the same way as an "extreme case formulation" in its effect of upgrading a given feature of the topic under discussion. So, for example, one speaker might say that a recently watched film is pretty good, and the subsequent speaker might describe the same film as well worth watching. This description is not an extreme case formulation because it is, evidently enough, not extreme, but it intensifies the previous description.

The rhetorical pattern displayed in Lines 200 to 206 is a repeat of "yes it is" contrasted with "no it's not": Ian Hutchby (2011) refers to such devices as "polar contrastives," typically used in argumentative discourse. Damien bluntly denies Steve's account of the software ("nothing is missing": Line 202), formulating this denial as accountable by wrapping it with a warrant (e.g., "… only way … couldn't be worked …": Lines 202–203). This is stake management work in the sense of scripting one account while simultaneously undermining another (Edwards and Potter, 2005) and in fact undermining any potential alternative in the formulation of "only way." In displaying his knowledge of what is not missing, he orients to self as technical expert, reflexively constructing Steve as inexpert and even irrational in his suggestion that "something is missing." He bolsters his account in Line 206 by scripting an upshot ("… it's there it just doesn't show"), with "just" working to downgrade the issue (Abell and Stokoe, 2001). This is delivered in response to Steve's stretched receipt token (Line 205)—which can be heard as a skeptical rejoinder (Hutchby)— in the attempt to formulate an acceptable end to topic in its dealing with Steve's initial question over "something missing." Instead of closing the topic, Steve ups the ante in the form of an intensifier (Schegloff, 1997), upgrading the issue to "a problem," with "that's" working as a metaphorical pointing of the finger. Blame is thus made live and attributed.

In the final part of Extract 5, there is a short delay before Damien responds, which makes his initial acceptance of the label "problem" hearable as an admission, and thus Damien orients to the blame work done by his colleague. Note, however, how Damien's construct of "it's a problem" contrasts with Steve's version ("that's a problem"), which can be seen as initializing a strategy of depersonalizing the problem. The "but" in Line 208 signals the start of a disclaimer (Potter and Wetherell, 1987), an acknowledgement that attribution has been made live and must be deflected.

12.7.2   Managing Blame

He first deselects himself as the subject of blame ("there's nothing that could be done") and then offers a contradictory set of affairs that explicitly sets the trajectory of attribution back in Steve's direction ("… unless you wanna …": Line 209). The warranting work for this redirected attribution is formulated in the implicit understanding that Steve, in his leader role, is responsible for project budget, with the rights to spend money on a novel solution ("(hire) someone for the software": Line 209). There is a solution available out there, but it requires money to be spent, and Steve owns the responsibility for this, with the reflexive implication that it is Steve's fault for not spending appropriate sums of money. His absolution work is completed in his subsequent proffering of his solution as the only one reasonably available, with the implicit understanding that his account of affairs can be trusted as an accurate description of reality: he has done as best as he can.

12.7.3   Question over Competence or Simply not Sharing Knowledge?

What is interesting about this interchange, with all its connotations of blame and attribution, is that Damien is not only aware of the "problem," but has already taken steps to resolve it in the only available way. However, until now, that is a state of affairs unknown to Steve. Knowledge of the "problem" has only come to communal light as a consequence of the competing accounts. This is unusual given the attention to detail that, elsewhere, Steve in his role of leader is shown to display. This understanding of events becomes explicit in Extract 6.

EXTRACT 6   130319_005 COMPANY B

220. Steve: C-can you have a conversation with <u>David</u> and see if there's
221. some way to <u>trick</u> it.
222. (1.5)
223. Damien: D-hm::mm=
224. Steve: =Y'know put something ↑else in that has no data
225. in or <u>something</u> ↓I don't know.
226. (2)
227. Steve: Y'know put in a second]
228. Damien: [( )the thing is the only thing you can do
229. is to put a blank to put a blank [] in but then
230. (1)
231. Damien: [] [software tier label] and then a blank underneath
232.   it]
233. Steve: [this is (.)this is the kind of thing that makes me
234. think I don't like [Software]↑.

In the intervening lines, Steve and Damien continue to discuss the problem and its implications for the software. Just prior to this, Damien has repeated his assessment that "it's a problem" but one about which nothing can be done. (It is also worth noting that, throughout all of these exchanges, the rhetoric is largely spoken in reasonable tones—the tones of voice one would expect in a professional business meeting.)

Steve's turn in Lines 220 and 221 can be seen as orienting to a lack of trust in the account given by Damien ("nothing to be done"). Not only does Steve persist in the existence of potential other solutions out there, with the implication that either Damien does not know of them or has not considered them, but he now introduces another character in his "suggestion" that Damien "have a conversation" with David. This conjures "David" as more competent and implicitly more trustworthy than Damien, scripting a competency challenge (Hutchby, 2011). This, in contrast to his earlier issuing of the problem in Line 200, is not formulated as a question. The nonquestion status can be seen in Damien's response with its noncommittal utterance: that is, as it is not a question, an answer is not conditionally relevant. Steve scripts such a projected future event as having the ability to realize devious solutions ("way to trick it": Line 219), with the implication that these will come from David. Damien is reflexively scripted as either lacking in such knowledge and imagination or, possibly, holding it back. This latter understanding stems from Steve's subsequent turn (Lines 224–227).

With no articulated response from Damien, with instead his nonlinguistic utterance suggesting disdain at the proposal of "tricking," Steve continues to conjure knowledge of solutions "out there" with his repeat of "y'know" projecting intersubjective agreement (Clifton, 2012a) shared with Damien. That is, Steve scripts Damien as being privy to knowledge that he has not shared, which may hold an acceptable solution to the problem ("something"). So the work done here is persuasion, with Steve's own claims to knowledge mitigated by "I don't know." This phrase is shown to be a way that people handle or downplay stake or interest in reports and descriptions (Edwards and Potter, 2005). This formulation works in sharp contrast to the project knowledge that Steve scripts Damien as having, but not sharing. The issue of trust is again made live, with attribution work setting its trajectory.

Unfortunately, Damien's turn at talk in Lines 228–232 is all but unintelligible, but there is enough of a gist to gather that, again, Damien is scripting "only one solution," and this has already been considered (and possibly implemented). The final turn in this extract (Lines 233/234) marks a radical change in rhetorical trajectory. Once again, Steve uses a rise in tone at the end of the utterance, which, here, does not script a question but rather an appeal for consensus. He issues a subjective assessment of the software that is being used to create the team's software product as problematic and prospectively unlikable. This not only displays his claims to rights to make such an evaluation, actions that are linked to, for instance, persuasion and blaming (Wiggins and Potter, 2003), but also constructs his evaluation as not being voluntarily made, but rather as a consequence of the "offending" software application—and presumably, its creators.

Thus, Steve's "game-changing" evaluation of affairs erases blame from Damien and from himself and works to reestablish trust through orienting to consensus. The upshot is an evaluation of a state of affairs that is shared by everyone, so it must be true (Edwards and Potter, 1992), and as something that they will all just have to live with. In shifting blame to the software, Steve effectively changes rhetorical strategy. Damien's subsequent turn (not included here) orients to this in offering a more detailed account of the problem and what he has done to resolve it, which raises the question of why he did not do so earlier in this exchange. The exchange concludes with Steve accepting things as they are, but leaving options open.

12.8   PRELIMINARY REFLECTIONS

The starting point of the present analysis has been the speculation that KS is contingent to trust and that this, as a phenomenon invoked by speakers in interaction, can be shown to work corelationally with the other KS themes of identity, risk, and context. We further speculated that trust will be shown to have an influencing effect on KS activities in discursive action and that trust as a KS theme can be shown to be tacitly accomplished by speakers as psychological phenomena. These speculations are explored in the context of an organizational meeting. One meeting was selected for analysis over examples from multiple meetings to ensure that developing relationships could be brought to the fore. Consequently, the six extracts are included in the order in which they appear in the meeting transcript.

What the analysis shows is that KS practices are inextricably bound to matters of trust, as made contingent and live by the meeting participants themselves. Trust is shown to be a dynamic, constantly changing pattern of rhetorical action: it is invoked by one speaker then dismantled by another and then reestablished. Displays of trust also vary from context to context: for instance, in his interaction with both Ade and Damien, Steve deals with matters of interrelational trust in different ways. What is also clearly seen is how trust works corelationally with risk as a live concern for speakers: for instance, in Extract 2, Ade conjures Steve's proposed plan of action as risky invoking its untrustworthiness, displaying tacit knowledge of background facts as a warrant. Steve mediates this state of affairs by simply discarding the issue which he is able to do because he has access to privileged knowledge (epistemic superiority) which Ade does not, and which is superior to Ade's. Ade displays acknowledgment of his colleague's superior knowledge through his acceptance of Steve's version. Risk is thus managed as a contingency to trust.

We have also seen how trust works corelationally with identity—particularly visible in the collaboratively conjured contexts of reputation, competence, and authenticity, for instance. In the last extract, for example, Steve is shown to negotiate his understanding of Damien as either incompetent or obstructive with his sharing of knowledge. It is almost as though he is testing first one theory and then another in order to reach a view of Damien as one or the other. Of course, both options come with a problem that must be managed, and the blame that has been conjured and made live must be attributed somewhere. Moreover, we can also argue that risk can also be shown to be corelational with identity, as well as trust. In the latter example, Steve can be understood to be carefully working to mediate the risk of a breakdown in trust and attribution left unresolved, which he does skillfully by relocating both attribution and distrust onto the software at the root of their conversation.

On a point of general observation, knowledge displays, as a function of doing trust, are linked to persuasion rhetoric, authenticity, factual accounting and attribution, as well as risk. Trustworthiness of self and account are shown to be mutually contingent: it is difficult to have one without the other.

On the question of trust as an influencing factor in KS, it has been shown how in the moment-by-moment turns of discourse, trust erosion is implicated in KS problems, with consequences for mutual displays of competence and reputation. Breakdowns in trust are speculated to lead to a clouding of issues. It was noted earlier how trust can work relationally with attribution (in this case, of blame), linking this to risk: analysis shows that the explicit removal of blame leads to a reestablishment of trust, which in turn reengages KS actions as voluntary. We see similar outcomes in the analysis of another meeting (Chapter 16; extract 2) in which two speakers volunteer additional and important accounts when the meeting lead exonerates them from any criticism or blame.

Extract 6 particularly displays speakers' tacit understanding of the importance of trust to the business of sharing knowledge and the goal of solving problems. In working to resolve the trust breach-attribution problem, Steve and the other participating speakers index to their tacit sense of the meeting's purpose and what will and will not facilitate and mediate its business of KS. A further display of tacit knowing can be seen in Extract 1 in which speakers invoke both mutual familiarity and the sense of mutual status and rights. Thus, and in effect, the meeting's norms are made live and displayed as collaboratively shared. Some of the subsequent actions, however, are shown to be deviant to these norms in, for instance, Damien's introduction of argumentative alternative claims after a topic closing action has been initiated, and contrary to the meetings norms in respect of Steve's status as the only speaker with rights to breach these rules (Extract 3).

What is missing from the analysis, though, is an explicit example of Schoorman and his colleagues' model of trust being contingent on perception of another's ability, integrity, *and* benevolence. Understood as the human characteristic of being well-meaning or kind, benevolence, as a discursive construct of speakers themselves, does not appear to feature in the present discourse, which is otherwise shown to display concerns with trust, reputation, and so forth. It is possible that a further and deeper analysis might hint at its presence, but, alternatively, it might simply be the case that benevolence is not a constructed action here because the action of constructing and displaying trust and trustworthiness in organizational settings is not contingent to perception of another's kindness, for instance.

The next chapter continues to develop these lines of exploration by focusing particularly on the phenomenon of risk.

FURTHER READING

Clifton, J. (2012). 'Doing' trust in workplace interaction. In Mada, S. and Saftoiu, R. (Eds). *Professional Communications across Languages and Cultures*. Amsterdam: John Benjamins Publishing Company.

Evans, M. (2013). Is trust the most important human factor influencing knowledge sharing in organizations? *Journal of Information & Knowledge Management*, 12 (4): 1350038 (17 pages).

Schoorman, F., Mayer, R. and Davis, J. (2007). An integrative model of organizational trust: past, present, and future. *Academy of Management Review*, 32 (20): 344–354.

Wooffitt, R. (2005). *Conversation analysis and discourse analysis: a comparative and critical introduction*. London: Sage.

13

KNOWLEDGE SHARING IS A RISKY BUSINESS

13.1 THE RISKY BUSINESS OF SHARING KNOWLEDGE

Knowledge sharing is particularly associated with the threat of reputational damage (see Chapters 3 and 8 for detailed discussions), which suggests that knowledge sharing is a risky business. Recall David Schoorman and his colleagues' multidimensional model of trust, with trust existing in relationships and contingent to perception of risk, a connection that was shown to be displayed in the analysis of trust discourse in Chapter 12. Now, whether or not one subscribes to this model, what can be argued from a commonsense standing is that people make routine evaluations of risk every day (e.g., Shall I have one more slice of toast before heading out to catch my bus? Shall I carry an umbrella in case it rains?), but what we rarely do is pause to calculate the affordable risk. Risk construction and assessment are, from this perspective, largely accomplished implicitly.

It is also argued that matters of stake, interest, and accountability are concerned with risk (see Chapter 8 for a brief discussion). Developing this idea, and central to the view of the organization, is the notion that people are motivated to act by goals, implying that actions are never entirely random. Consequently, as Andrea Whittle, of the Cardiff Business School, and her colleague conclude in their essay on the *Language of Interests*, people have stake and interest in actions that they orient to as being accountable. And, of course, when discursive actions are accountable, they are subject to the risk of a counter claim or alternative version from others. It can be speculated, then, that people are continuously engaged in the routine business of assessing the risk in taking this or that action, and that most of this is accomplished tacitly. Risk, in the everyday sense of the phenomenon, is a tacitly understood appraisal of the world and its contents and as such is likely to be influential on action.

To gain an understanding of how risk is played out in organizational discourse, and the impact on knowledge sharing, this chapter analyses weekly sales and marketing meetings recorded with both of the participating organizations. The environment of such meetings, as a knowledge sharing forum, offers a fascinating vehicle for studying accountability. It is speculated, for instance, that in such meetings, there are tensions between desires to announce good news and the need for caution, between the need for truth telling and desires to avoid issuing bad news. How do participants protect stake, interest and reputation when called on to make reports and predictions of sales activities? What is uncovered is a far more complex, intricate, and multilayered phenomenon than that seen in conventional knowledge management (KM) research. The analysis reveals connections between risk and identity, in the invoked contexts of reputation and authenticity for instance, and also trust in collaborative interaction. Perhaps of particular importance here, the analysis builds on the findings in the previous chapter specific to the ways in which participants discursively construct and orient to the context of their meeting and which influences action outcomes.

The analysis begins with a discussion of sequential and rhetorical organization finding some intriguing points of variation between the two team meetings. The focus then moves to high stakes and truth telling, with their subthemes of stake, authenticity, and challenge. This is followed by an analysis and discussion of two rhetorical constructs—"narrative" and "consensus–corroboration"—as particular to the high-stakes context. The theme of narrative is carried over into the final part of the main analysis, featuring an instance of discourse that seems to deviate considerably to those in the rest of the analysis. To complete the discussions, some preliminary reflections highlight a point of variation between the two meetings, which, it is argued, has significant impact on the procedural business of knowledge sharing. The main meaning of the findings for KM is discussed in Chapter 17 along with those drawn from the other analytics chapters.

13.2 SEQUENTIAL AND RHETORICAL ORGANIZATION: GROUP NORMS AND REPUTATION

The sequential and rhetorical organization of both meetings is, on face value, identical, and bound to tacitly understood group social norms. Both comprise members familiar with one another, with neither exhibiting the kind of "roll call" seen in Chapter 12. It is important to emphasize that it is the participants themselves who construct context (Silverman, 2007): this idea is tackled head-on in a subsequent chapter. The chair launches the meeting, controls the opening and closing of agenda items, and offers evaluative assessment for each participant report that is made. The chair controls when and how attendees may make a contribution, either by calling "to the floor" for self-selecting accounts or by calling on a participant by name. In floor calling, the chair is not necessarily opening the floor to any elective: the content of the item can work as a "tacit form of addressing" by placing a limit on the potential contributors qualified to contribute (Svennevig, 2012b). We see a variation of this in Chapter 16, in which "historical accounting" is shown to potentially limit contributions to interaction. Thus, a tacitly understood group social norm concerns the chair's authority over the interactional trajectory of the meeting, but this is shown to be mediated by the collaborative, negotiated nature of the talk. So while a meeting chair might on the face of it seem to be controlling the business of sharing knowledge, this is in fact an interactional, social activity.

Interactional Trajectory
This refers to the directions and pace of change in the unfolding discourse interaction. For instance, the turn taken by one speaker might change the topic of the current discussion to a new topic, thus effecting a change in direction of the discourse. Another use of the term "trajectory" is linked to emotions, meaning the movement or change from one emotion to another—laughter turning to sadness, for instance. The term can be used to mean a change within one person's utterance or across a number of speakers' utterances. To identity the interactional trajectory of a discourse is to pay attention to its choreography and its effects.

Epistemic Modality
When a speaker makes an explicit qualification of their commitment to the truth or credibility of their own account or that given by another speaker, they are said to script "epistemic modality." For instance, modal adjectives such as "maybe" and "probably" or modal auxiliaries such as "can," "may," and "must" all work up an overt note of qualification to the proposal in hand. Thus, to speak of some state of affairs as being "probably correct" projects a sense of probability over the level of correctness.

Candidate Repair
A "repair" is the term given to a linguistic correction given in an utterance. That is, one starts to say one thing, then corrects with something else. People so routinely and frequently effect linguistic repairs that they almost slip past normal notice. A candidate repair is where one speaker offers a proposed reinterpretation of what another speaker has said, which remains a "candidate" until receipted and accepted by the original speaker.

An example of the intricacies of this type of interaction can be seen in Extract 1, from Company A, just over ten minutes into the meeting. The chair is closing one topic, in preparation for another. He has fielded several questions directly to one contributor (John), followed by an "open floor" invitation that is initially responded to by John, then others, the last of which opens this extract.

In Lines 88–90, the chair makes arrangements to engage with Sam at an unspecified future date. Topic closing sequences have been shown to typically contain such follow up plans (Svennevig, 2012b). The chair, then, can be seen to be signaling a topic transition. However the business is shown to be incomplete in Sam's turn (Lines 93–94), which initiates immediately following the chair's nonlexical noise. Contrast his reference to future plans ("I will") with the chair's use of the modal adverb "probably" (Line 90): the latter conjures epistemic modality that, according to researchers Petra Sneijder and her colleague, displays "…the speaker's assessment of probability and predictability" (2005: 678). Further analysis suggests that this "probability" is interpreted by Sam as not only referring to future arrangements but also to a question mark over the value of what Sam has to impart.

Sam's turns (Lines 93–94, 96–98) can be seen as "filling in" vague probability on future arrangements. He is working to establish the publicly available value of his future account, effecting a candidate repair (face-saving) to an unsatisfactorily left state of affairs that, if left unattended, might represent a risk—albeit a mild one—to his

---

EXTRACT 1   130520_003 COMPANY A

```
88. Chair:   A::h I-I did ↑wonder about that actually
89.          when you were talking about it
90.          so I'll- I'll probably talk to you about
91.          that one off-line () find out more about
92.          that one heh=
93. Sam:     =I'll fill you in later- in on
94.          that ]one
95. Chair:      [O::K↑ then ] OK
96. Sam:                     [same subject – same
97.          subject, different client, different
98.          technology [heh]
99. Chair:   Yes – yeah [heh] OK. Different world
100.             Sam I think, different ↓world. [Sam :
101.             heh heh]. Uhhh..uhhh that's cool tha-
102.             tha- uh well that was that was it in
103.             terms of uh items to go out uh soh-
104.             any-any new ones to add in? [silence]
105.             Sounds like a (.) silent no uh] uh/
106. John:                            [There'll
107.             be s-sorry Dan the uhhh the [company
108.             name] one that we sent out uhmm
109.             [makes a noise of 'searching'] about
110.             a week ago? Uh they've come back
111.             and said they're pretty much tha-they
112.             want to go ahead with that (.) I think
113.             we need to do another (.) iteration of
114.             the proposal if you put that in again for
115.             the 31st of May …
116. Chair:   OK=
117. John:    =Uhhh we should get confirmation to start
118.             that (.) project by then.
119. Chair:   OK. Thank you very much↑.
```

---

reputation. In this sense, Sam orients to reputation as a live issue, which is understood to be a context of identity work. The chair's repeated "OK" in Line 95 serves to both receipt and confirm (Rautajoki, 2012) Sam's reformulation of future plans and report values, reinvoking topic closure. However, Sam disallows topic closure (Lines 96–98), displaying his desire for a more explicit response from the chair.

The reputational face-saving now becomes mutually done with matching humor (Lines 98–99), which is elsewhere shown to influence social cohesion and group solidarity (Greatbatch, 2009). The chair's direct orientation to Sam's contrast structure ("same," "different": Lines 96–97) scripts ratification (Hepburn and Wiggins, 2005), strengthening what Sam has said with the upgrade "world" (Potter, 1998a). Sam signals consensus with the chair's reformulation of his contribution with reciprocated humor (Lines 100–101). Jonathan Potter and his coworker's case study of an institutional meeting notes how "… laughter and humour can be used to 'soften' troubling or critical actions" (2010: 60): in this instance, it works to smooth the reputational face-saving actions. Later on in this chapter, we come across a different analysis of the function of humor in organizational meetings. The interaction is thus shown to be a complex and delicate, collaboratively accomplished management of mutual stake and interest.

With a final evaluation of the preceding exchange as being "cool," invoking a satisfactory conclusion to the topic, the chair moves into a more explicit topic winding down sequence (Lines 102–104). Despite no response to his call for any "new ones," the chair scripts the collaborative nature of the meeting interaction in still not being in a position to bring about topic closure, instead seeking consensus on the matter (Line 105). His choreographed reluctance to use his authority as chair to move the meeting on becomes clear with the interruption from John (Lines 106–115), suggesting interruptions are consistent to the meeting's "business as usual." John, nonetheless, orients to his breech of the chair's attempts to effect closure with an apology (Line 107), which could be seen as both justifying the interruption and heading off rejection (Potter and Wetherell, 1987), but the real stake management work (Silverman, 2007) is done in John's subsequent report.

The display of searching (Potter, 1998a) in Line 109 emphasizes the just recalled nature of the account given, indexing the need for accuracy. The function and consequence of this action is different to that seen in a previous account given an actor (Steve: Extract 1, Chapter 12) where the display of searching was linked to an indecision over what topic to begin the meeting with. Similar actions by different speakers can work with variable effect and outcome. Note how John hedges his claims with "pretty much," "I think," "if you," and "should get" (Lines 111–117): these have exactly the opposite effect to Jonathan Clifton's (2012a) "declarative assertions," which work up states of affairs as concrete reality. Thus, while he is delivering welcome news in Line 117 in predicting a new contract, the entire claim is made contingent on three of its features: the client, the proposal to be written, and the temporal factors, two of which he has no control over. According to Linda Wood and her coresearcher (2000), hedging is a negative politeness strategy that has the function of constructing statements as provisional, which are particularly noticeable in actions of stake management.

Matching Humor
Displays of matching humor or laughter (e.g., two speakers simultaneously, or in close proximity, laugh or giggle as joint action) are shown to display interpersonal affiliation or rapport. That is, such actions represent ways of displaying alignment with what a speaker has said, for instance. These matching actions have collaborative function.

Stake Inoculation
A speaker's private or personal desires (their personal agenda) can operate crucially in establishing or violating versions of events (accounts). To suggest that someone has a vested interest in the claims they have made is to potentially discredit those claims: the "well he would say that wouldn't he" accusation made so famous by Mandy Rice-Davies! Consequently, people routinely and mostly unconsciously work to couch their versions and accounts as "disinterested," as separate from their own personal agenda—this is stake inoculation.

In this way, John inoculates his stake (Wetherell, 2001), not so much against potential accusation of having a vested interest in his account, but more rising from his tacitly displayed understanding that future events may not transpire as he predicts. That is, there is a risk that things might not turn out as he hopes. The chair receipts this with a positive token, accepting the contingent nature of the claim, with a move to close the topic and his rising intonation in Line 119 sounding a note of finality. Further interpretation of this interaction would suggest that, similarly to the earlier collaborative work between the chair and Sam, here both actors are orienting to and delicately comanaging the potential risk of accepting "welcome news" at face value.

A second tacitly understood group norm is introduced by the chairs at the outset of both meetings, and this is particularly important in respect of the research focus: "risk," "high stakes," and "truth telling." In the following analysis, the influencing role of this context starts to unfold.

13.3   HIGH STAKES AND TRUTH TELLING

Both meetings are initiated by their respective chairs with an account of financial position that, it is claimed here, invokes the high-stakes nature of the meeting's business, making risk a live contextually situated issue. With Company A, financial position is constructed as the collective property of the team, whereas with Company B, the chair invokes an interteam competitive component, delaying the collective team financial results until further into the meeting. A further important difference between the two in terms of rhetorical practices can be seen in the Company A team's patterning of often voluntary, self-selected turns and vivid accounting compared with Company B's team interaction where people are mostly chair-selected for turns. Moreover, turns are shown to be, for the most part, limited in their details. These two points are important, and are returned to in the final section on preliminary reflections.

Contextually Situated
For something to be "situated," it is seen as located or embedded in some phenomenon: an utterance can be contextually situated, for instance, in its orientation to the given context of the situation in which the discourse takes place. An utterance can be "culturally situated" in, for instance, the use of shifts in footing (position/role/identity) according to the cultural context.

Temporal Deixis
Deixis is the term given to markers of reference, and these can be temporal (e.g., "now"), proximal (e.g., "on the spot"), or distal (e.g., "over there"). The important point to note about deixis is that their meaning (for speakers) depends on the context in which they are uttered. Hence, they depend on speakers' shared understanding of context or experience of events. So, for example, if one speaker said, "he's not coming until after 9' to another in an evening context," they might both understand that this can be understood as being inconveniently late; contrastingly, if the same utterance was made in the context of the morning, it might be collaboratively understood to be convenient in locating the prospective visit after the business of breakfast and so forth.

Why does financial accounting invoke contexts of high stakes and risk? From an observational point of view, it is suggested that foregrounding an account of finances foregrounds the financial health of the firms as contingent on the sales teams' activities. In constructing reports of financial status, the chairs effectively script participants' reports as accountable with a mandate for truth and accuracy, which have direct consequence to the organization's economic success. The present analysis shows how participants orient to this context in their reports. As participants formulate accounts, they employ a range of rhetorical practices to construct selves as knowledgeable and accounts as factual, objective and unbiased by self-interest or motivation. Such actions work as a fundamental layer of management of stake and interest (Sneijder and te Molder, 2005). That is, speakers routinely inoculate descriptions against alternative or counter versions, for instance, or criticism (Abell and Stokoe, 2001). In the previous discussions around trust, the actions of invoking epistemic superiority (Clifton, 2012a) and authenticity are frequently displayed as rhetorical strategies for factualizing and concretizing accounts. In the present analysis, we see speakers accomplishing a slightly different set of strategies in their scripting of accounts as authentic, acceptable, and therefore trustworthy in what they themselves construct as a high-stakes context.

13.3.1 Stake and Authenticity

Extract 2 shows how the chair of Company B orients to stake and authenticity.

This extract comes at the start of the meeting. Just prior to this, the chair has called for "quick scores" relating to three levels of sales achievement (bronze, silver, and gold), conjuring a between team member competitive element. Her account opener (Lines 8/9) accomplishes two key actions: first, her formulation of "this information," rather than "the information," can be heard as a possessive scripting of her ownership with authority to deliver, interpret, and evaluate the information—which is exactly what she does. This raises issues of stake and interest, and potential credibility problems (Silverman, 2007) associated with bias and subjectivity. Second, the "up to last Thursday' temporal deixis (Benwell and Stokoe, 2012) conjures the sense of "latest

---

EXTRACT 2   130319_003 COMPANY B

```
 8. Chair: Uuum this information is up to last
 9.        Thursday.
10.        So in terms of who has done the most
11.        placements so far this year (.) ↑Scotland!
12.        You're comin' in in first ↑place um Bob's
13.        actually made um 13 placements ah so
14.        far this year totaling in excess of
15.        £[amount] so I think that actually
16.        deserves a round of applause – whoo
17.        whoo (applause – cheers – whoops
18.        round the table)… well done Scotland.
19.        Long may that continue um
```

available" and "beyond dispute" nature of the forthcoming account. This combination implicates a tension. How does she resolve it?

The headline news is delivered with a repeated extreme case formulation invoking positive assessment (Lines 10–15): "done the most" and "first place." As Derek Edwards and his colleague Potter note, and as shown in the previous chapter on trust, such formulations can work "…to make a report more effective by drawing on the extremes of relevant dimensions of judgement" (1992: 162). This is combined with an attention to accuracy and veracity with "Bob's actually made," with the slight pause before referring to numbers of placements made suggesting a glance at paperwork in hand, scripting the authentic nature of the account. Note also the repeated reference to "so far this year" in Lines 11 and 14: this effects the positive nature of the reported news and its accuracy. Perhaps most importantly for the ensuing transactions, it works to raise the stakes for other participants with its suggestion of more placements to come, something that others on the team must compete with.

The news evaluation (Lines 15–19) does the work of attempting to resolve any unfolding tensions and the chair's own potential stake and interest in these affairs. She invokes demand for consensus with a call for a shared "loud news receipt" (Hepburn and Wiggins, 2005), thereby sidestepping the implications of her stake and interest. The use of "actually deserves" strengthens the call in scripting a warrant of authenticity. On a more tacit level, what may also be heard is an appeal to group corroboration that contrasts with the competitive component introduced at the outset; is the chair now working to invoke team affiliation and mutual support? The analysis cannot show if this is the case as the chair continues with her monologue for some time, with no further calls for cheering. Indeed, the first occurrence of a different speaker takes the form of a brief, factualized statement in response to a direct question. The analysis cannot therefore reveal how the participants understand this speculated "group construction" versus "team member rivalry" other than through the action of their cheers when called for.

In this short extract, then, the chair is shown to accomplish two primary actions: first, she establishes the high-stakes nature of the meeting (with its implication of risk), while foregrounding team member competition and rivalry. At the same time, she orients to authenticity of account—"truth telling"—as a necessary response to high stakes, and resolves as acceptable the team's coshared stake and interest in these proceedings.

13.3.2   Authenticity and Challenge

Company A's chair accomplishes the same in a comparatively different way, shown in the following extract that also comes from the start of the meeting. Just prior to Extract 3, John (assuming temporarily the role of chair) refers to an email that he has sent to all participants with the month's financial data, which he has asked to be checked. Note how he scripts a version of events in which he is not the source of the financial information, but rather its monitor.

There is a considerable amount going on in this extract: the contrast, for instance, between John's scripting of what "we" have done (Line 12) with Brian's account of what "I've done" (Line 24), both referring to the same topic. The first works up an inclusion account that can be heard as constructing consensus (Abell and Stokoe, 2001), shown by Derek Edwards and his coworker Potter (1992) to be a factor in establishing the factual nature of affairs. In the second, Brian formulates an account of possession, effectively

---

EXTRACT 3   130520_003 COMPANY A

 8. John: so-umm wh-when we finish the what-ifs
 9.   sometime this morning (.) uh that should
10.   put us at <u>about (.)</u> the same situation we
11.   were in last month which was great
12.   what we've done I think is <u>move</u> some
13.   of the [client name] revenue from this
14.   year into <u>next</u> (.) which is ↓probably
15.   prudent. Uhmm so we can um we-we'll get a
16.   <u>truer</u> picture of what's gonna come in
17.   this year (.) I think by the end of today.
18. Brian: Yeah.
19.   [cough]
20.   John: heh heh that was-that was Brian ↑<u>violently</u>
21.   agreeing (.) with the previous comment
22.   (1) Good stuff ↑uuum=
23. Brian: =It-it might (.) just-jus' as a <u>positive</u> note
24.   uhm what-what I've done I've <u>moved</u>
25.   an <u>amount</u> into next ↓<u>year</u> with the idea
26.   that if I move just a little bit too much
27.   into next year it can only be a good
28.   thing when we claw it back to () the
29.   other way around=
30. John: =yeah (.) So all good stuff.
31.   ↑So um rather than dwell on the numbers
32.   that are in <u>here</u> um/

---

reattributing ownership for the reported action, perhaps one reason why John moves to dismiss "the numbers"—and any further claims by Brian (!)—in Line 31.

Constructing Consensus
Speakers can construct the consensus of others in many different ways, perhaps the most obvious of which is to use the inclusive pronoun "let's." Invoking consensus also serves as a way of describing some state of affairs as common knowledge to others, thus warranting its truth. If everyone thinks "x" is the case, then it must be true. Such actions can be explicit or implicit.

Evaluative Expressions
As a discourse analysis term, this has its origins in the English Philosopher John Austin's influential book, How to do things with words, *published in 1962. Evaluative expressions come in two types: justifications and excuses. The latter involves admitting something but offered with extenuating or influencing circumstances, while the former involves no denial of responsibility. In a wider understanding, phrases are said to be evaluative expressions or inferences when they invoke some property not explicitly included in the phrase itself. One example of this would be to describe how people come and go at all hours of the day*

and night from a particular house in a street, in which the context of the utterance might suggest that the resident is dealing in drugs, for instance. At their basic level, these expressions make plain a speaker's sense of entitlement to express an opinion on some topic.

Turn Transition
A turn or topic transition is simply the point in the discourse that affords an opportunity for a different speaker to take up a turn or for a new topic to be introduced. Transition points are typically signaled by markers such as pauses by the current speaker, or nonlexical terms, or the clearly described closure of a topic.

Keeping the eye on the present line of inquiry, the "high-stakes" work is done by implicating the collective participants in the business of establishing financial position for this month (Lines 8–11) and the year's end (Lines 16–17). The vivid level of detail afforded in John's account, including the reference to moving money, works as fact construction (Edwards and Potter, 1992) and as a warrant for the truth of the given version, which is evaluated as "probably prudent" (Line 15), with the search for the "truer picture" made explicit in Line 16. Here, the use of "probably" works to distance John as the agent from the probability of the claim (Myers, 1989) should future events transpire otherwise, thus attending to accountability. Sally Wiggins and her colleague (2003), at the UK's Loughborough University, propose that evaluative expressions serve to work up the speaker's entitlement to express an opinion, and from this perspective, John can be heard as scripting not just the money move as being "probably prudent," but reflexively himself too. The high-stakes nature—and prudence—of the enterprise is further strengthened by John's account being laden with "hedging" (Rasmussen, 2010) over the probability of events ("should put," "about the same," "I think," "probably prudent") and laced with discourse of accuracy and truth with their connotations of authenticity and trustworthiness (Lines 15–16).

In these actions, then, John raises the importance of accuracy, truth, and caution as foregrounded contexts to the subsequent meeting. When such matters are constructed as live to the enfolding discourse, what is also implicitly constructed is the opposite—inaccuracy, lies, recklessness—and all its associated risks. What happens next is intriguing.

Brian gives a subdued token of agreement (Edwards and Potter, 1992) to John's initial report (Line 18). John's reaction is to verbally identify the speaker (obviously dialing in and not visible to all participants). He could have simply ignored Brian's "yeah" and cough—no one would have been the wiser. But here, he reformulates Brian's token with an extreme case formulation (Abell and Stokoe, 2001): "violent agreement." One of the effects of such formulations is to "up the ante" and the accuracy of a claim (Edwards and Potter). However, here, it works up irony (contrast this with Ian Hutchby's, 2011, "skeptical rejoinder," which serves to dismiss accounts), implicating an invitation bordering on demand for an explanation. Brian's token turn cannot be ignored, and he is thus held accountable. This conjures John's awareness of accountability for his previous turn, as well as indexing his concerns with truth—trustworthy knowledge. Thus, John arguably interprets Brian's turn as working up doubt over John's description of affairs, as a challenge to its authenticity that must be resolved.

Understood in this way, John constructs the latter's turn as a competency challenge (Hutchby, 2011). By casting Brian in the role of violently agreeing, raising connotations of Brian's personal stake and interest in the affairs being reported, John neatly and reflexively indexes his own concerns with objectivity, thus working to protect his own stake (Edwards and Potter, 2005). Note also John's laughter preface (Line 20) to his account of "violently agreeing": unlike the example seen earlier, here, laughter orients to a potential problem with Brian's brief response. Thus, John is scripting a call to account and the next turn would be normatively taken by Brian in response.

John makes a turn transition opportunity available to Brian (Line 22) with a pause after "previous report," which Brian does not take up, in contrast to expectations. John proceeds with a topic closing token ("Good stuff") and a brief display of searching (Potter, 1998a) for the next topic item ("ummm").

An alternative interpretation might suggest that this "pause" works up a second turn transition opportunity: the topic has been insufficiently reported due to Brian's lack of contribution. Robin Wooffitt offers a good discussion and explanation of turns and how speakers "...orient to, and display to each other in the design of their turns, what they understand to be the salient features of their context" (2005: 64). Thus, John has issued a call to account, making a turn transition opportunity available, which is not taken: John then creates a second opportunity through his delaying tactic, and this time Brian responds. Consequently, we can suggest that Brian effectively displays his orientation to this particular interpretation as it is at this point that he finally takes up a turn. Moreover, Brian displays his tacit knowing of the meeting's concerns with accuracy and knowledge to be trusted with his account of "what has been done," which he scripts as "positive" (Line 22), effecting a contrast to John's description of "probably prudent." Brian, in other words, displays his orientation to a need to offer a clearer and more positive picture than that reported by John, with his delayed and hesitant utterance conjuring troubles with John's preceding account—particularly its precision (see Paul Drew, 2003b, for a fascinating analysis of precision in discourse).

Although he appears to repeat the account made by John, there is a subtle but significant difference. While John's version of affairs is hedged with contingencies, Brian's is assertive and shown to be accountable by the issuing of a warrant (Silverman, 2007) in the form of a conditional structure (Potter and Wetherell, 1987): "if I move … (then) it can only be …" (Lines 26–28). Thus, the account is pragmatically occasioned (Edwards and Potter, 1992) and conditional. Brian rescripts the state of affairs, orienting to his knowledge of cause and effect (Chilton, 2004), which is privileged to him and only him but which he has shared in a display of willingness and concerns for accuracy. In so doing, he upgrades the "probably prudent" evaluation to an undoubtedly ("it can only be a good thing") prudent one. John effectively issues a concession marker (Wood and Kroger, 2000) in Line 30, conceding to the evidence introduced by his colleague: he upgrades his previous evaluation in Line 22 to "So all good stuff," which also works to presignal the forthcoming topic closing sequence, marking the topic as adequately covered (Lines 31–32).

Pragmatically Occasioned
An utterance is said to be pragmatically occasioned when it is clearly driven and influenced by a speaker's personal interest (their agenda).

Concession Marker
Concession markers are words or phrases that concede evidence in some way, with examples including "granted that XYZ," "XYZ fair enough …," "XYZ can or could be the case …."

If this is to be shown as a valid analysis of the data from both meetings, accounts given by other meeting participants should orient to similar concerns with truth and accuracy, and an understood context of high stakes, through their turns. Derek Edwards and Jonathan Potter (1992) show how two discursive strategies, narrative and consensus–corroboration, routinely work to formulate accounts as factual. This is shown in the next extract.

13.3.3 Narrative and Consensus–Corroboration

Extract 4 comes roughly halfway through the meeting (Company B), after the chair has delivered a report on the team's joint financial achievements. The chair is now "going round the room" calling on individuals to provide accounts of current and future predicted "orders."

The first thing to notice is the narrative construction of Ann's account: good news contrasted with its opposite (Line 240), an interpretation of these events, and the formulation of a candidate solution (Hepburn and Wiggins, 2005) to the problem of lack of feedback (Lines 244–246) through getting to know the hiring managers. The proposed solution is confirmed in her future plans to "go up there" with her colleague. The chair's turn in Line 250 is what Robin Wooffitt (2007) calls a "minimal or nonlexical continuer," which is typically interpreted by speakers as a request for more information. What is interesting about these nonlexical minimal continuers is not just their signaling for more information but also their effects on the prior speaker's next (expansion) turn. Wooffitt's study robustly shows how these speech tokens typically lead to next turns marked with hesitation and circumspection. This is precisely what can be seen here.

EXTRACT 4   130319_003 COMPANY B

```
238. Ann:   S::o th::ey are continuing to come out
239.        for a lot of ↑roles um which is really
240.        good um but they're not (.) being (.)
241.        fantastic at coming back to us with
242.        feedback so I think that's something
243.        em that we obviously need to work
244.        on. I think the only way we're go-we're
245.        gonna work on that is by ge(tt)in' to
246.        know the hiring managers directly
247.        yeh um obviously it's gonna help that
248.        me and Tom are going up there
249.        next Thursday]
250. Chair:              [yup]
251. Ann:                     [uuum yeh just need to
252.        Keep (.) keep going ↑really=
253. Chair: =↑Yep=
254. Ann:   = but we are
255.        having some (.) success with them
256.        obviously um ][hearable sniff]
257. Chair:              [Indeed! Just need to
258.        have some ↑more!
```

Minimal (or Nonlexical) Continuer
Continuers, which typically include utterances such as "hmmm" or "mmm," signal to the current speaker, or the speaker who has just offered a turn transition, that they should continue with their account or report. Thus, these act like "permits," in giving permission to another speaker to carry on or to take up another turn.

In contrast to the precise narrative work done in her first turn part, Ann now searches for something more to say ("uuum yeh"), finally resorting to what might be described as stating the obvious—the imperative to "just keep going" (Lines 251–252). This combination scripts a classic "doubt marker" conjuring the conditional status of the statement (Wooffitt, 2007): it acts like a sort of "watch this space." Again, the chair gives a minimal receipt, standing in for a second call for further elaboration. Arguably, Anne indexes to the upbeat tone with a further expansion turn formulating a more positive evaluation: "we are having some success," which is scripted as being tentatively cautious, but obvious, and therefore beyond criticism or doubt.

Ann's work to effect a warrant (in "having some success"), combined with her earlier account of difficulties to be overcome in a particular way, is tacitly endorsed as a "direction of travel" in the chair's call for "more" (Lines 257–258). It could also be interpreted as an admonishment to Anne that she needs to do more, that enough is not being done. However, in the context of risk, high stakes, and truth telling in general and the trajectory ("yup," "yep!," "Indeed!") of the chair's turns in this extract, a more plausible explanation is the chair orienting to endorsement and motivation and that having "more" will not be such a big task or challenge, with "just" doing the downgrading work (Abell and Stokoe, 2001).

According to Derek Edwards and his colleague (1992), narrative accounting scripts claims as more plausible, and factual. The narrative construction here has the effect of bolstering the authenticity of the claim, thus orienting to the tacit understanding of the need for truth telling. This reflexively also has the effect of scripting avoidance of overstated or exaggerated claims, which could run the risk of being shown by subsequent events to have been issued as unwarranted claims. The discursive effect is similar to Petra Sneijder and her colleague's study of participants in an online veganism forum who are shown to use modal constructions (e.g., "certainly," "in my opinion"), which, they argue, "… allows speakers to display a concern for saying no more than they can be sure of, thus enhancing the trustworthiness of their accounts" (2005: 675). We will see an interesting contrast to this in Extract 6.

Ann's consensus–corroboration work accomplishes further "truth-telling" actions and particularly orients to the high-stakes nature of the business in effectively "sharing" the risk among colleagues. For instance, in Lines 242 and 243, Ann's own account of what needs to be done is obvious to "we"—her colleagues. Also, it is not just her that is going to meet the hiring managers, it is also Tom, which has the effect of calling a witness.

Extract 5 shows how participants in Company A interpret events: but do they orient to concerns with truth and accuracy? This extract comes just before midway through the meeting as part of the meeting agenda item "presentations" and follows a fairly extended two-way positively themed conversation between the chair and John with limited input from anyone else.

There is a slightly accusatory note in the chair's call to Mark to provide an account: there is no date in his list, and this, combined with his account of being absent the previous week (given earlier in the meeting), leaves him in the position of not knowing, which he constructs as an unsatisfactory version of affairs. Mark orients to the discrepancy with a hesitant start before delivering his account (Lines 175–181). The first part

---

EXTRACT 5   130520_003 COMPANY A

171. Chair: Ok eh [name]! [name]! Eh Mark that's
172.   the next one on the list but it doesn't
173.   got a <u>date</u> so it did-has it happened
174.   ↑yet or↓
175. Mark: Uh Jim and I were meant to
176.   go there last week and ↓they
177.   postponed and they're coming back ţo
178.   me <u>this</u> week with a new date and it's
179.   at it's down at [name] in [place name] so
180.   it's-it's in [name] itself rather than
181.   [name] which is go]od
182. Chair: [Mm↑m]
183. Mark: [I'll let you
184.   know the date when it comes through=
185. Chair: =ok-I'll
186.   ju- I'll put it to the bottom of the
187.   table there n' with a TBD on it []
188.   still keep it in there] ↑ok
189. Mark: [()]

---

indexes the discrepancy over the missing date with a mitigating (Abell and Stokoe, 2001) description of affairs: the date *was* for the previous week, but the client postponed (as opposed to canceled) with the warrant that they (the client) will be in touch this week with a new date. He emphasizes "this," which upgrades the veracity of the account, neatly erasing his accountability for the lack of meeting and date. The final part of his account (Lines 179–181) works to upgrade the news value by issuing new information (change of meeting location), which Mark positively evaluates as "good." The action of delivering this evaluation—with its potential to be called into question—displays his expectation that the chair and others are sufficiently knowledgeable (Svennevig, 2012b) of the meaning of the change of venue to concur with his evaluation. He is, in other words, orienting to the knowledge held by other group members.

The account and warrant are receipted by the chair with a nonlexical minimal utterance. Mark does not actually pause in his account, but continues across the chair's turn (Line 182). The chair's utterance in Line 182 can be interpreted in either of two ways: first, it could be understood as a "minimal continuer" (Wooffitt, 2007), as a sanction for further clarification, or it could be interpreted as a skeptical rejoinder (Hutchby, 2011). In both Mark's continuation of his account and in the marked rise in tone in the chair's "mm↑m" (Hutchby), it is shown to be mutually understood as agreement for further elaboration.

Mark's turn and that of the chair in Lines 185 to 188 work as contrasting descriptions (Hepburn and Wiggins, 2005). Mark orients to his previous account of a new date being issued <u>this</u> week, and the currently incomplete list, with a firming up of his belief in his prediction—he will issue the date <u>when</u> it "comes through," thus working up his version as authentic and trustworthy—and accurate. This is slightly risky in that future events might show him to be wrong about the date: he is laying himself open to future criticism. It also reflexively indexes his role in managing client action, which is a running theme to both meetings. Clients do not fall out of trees: it is the job of the sales and marketing team to find clients and business opportunities and manage these into effect. Mark's account at this point could also be heard as a further apology for the missing date, with an affirmation that this will be rectified.

The chair's turn effectively works as a repair in the sense of orienting to Mark's account confirmation but working to downgrade (Abell and Stokoe, 2001) potential future credibility problems by receipting the report with "ok-I'll ju." He will "still keep" Mark's meeting on the list but placed at the bottom and marked with a "TBD." Thus, it is the chair who works to remove risk to Mark's accountability through the construction of a hedge on the probability of future events. Truth, accuracy, and the potential for risk are consequently shown to be live concerns that are constructed and oriented to interactionally.

13.4 DOING "UBER AUTHENTICITY" THROUGH VIVID NARRATIVE ACCOUNTING

Compared with the other extracts and the rest of the meeting discourse in general, Extract 6 is hearable as an exaggerated, even glamorized embellishment of events. It also includes an explicit display of subjective bias toward the speaker's own stake and interest in the serving of extreme case formulations as evaluations (e.g., "it was absolutely brilliant," and "I loved it": Line 200). Moreover, his account of enduring "two hours" of being the target of questions formulated as putative weapons ("firing questions at me": Line 206) aimed by PhDs no less has the reflexive effect of scripting the speaker as clever, intelligent, knowledgeable, and trustworthy to succeed in exceptional circumstances. Unlike Extract 5, no-one takes action to collaboratively manage any prospective threat to his stake and interest. As such this account would represent a breach of the shared understanding of a mandate for truth and accuracy as mitigation against risk: in other words, it looks like a deviant case (Potter, 1998a). Stake and authenticity can be seen as live issues.

There are a number of key features of this account that allow for a different analysis. The extract comes around 19 minutes into the Company A meeting, and a few moments after Extract 5. It involves the same actor as the previous extract (Mark) and is initiated by the chair in a casually framed request for an update on other meetings. What the detailed analysis suggests is that Mark is doing a form of "uber authenticity" in his vivid narrative accounting (contrast this, for instance, with that contained in Extract 4), couched in a delicate management of stake and interest. This can be seen in three features: the issuing of a news headline, "doing being ordinary" as the preface to an account of extraordinary events, and quantification rhetoric.

13.4.1 Issuing a News Headline

Marks's account is initiated by a question from the chair concerning whether two other scheduled meetings have taken place. He does not explicitly ask for any further information. In Extract 5, Mark's reply to a similarly framed question orients to accountability in so far as the negative response (the meeting did not take place) requires an explanation in the form of a warrant. Here, the answer given is an affirmative, but again,

---

EXTRACT 6   130520_003 COMPANY A *('UM' = UNKNOWN MALE)*

187. Mark: Yes they both happened [heh heh] the [*name of city*]
188.   One (.) was like a- a – a-sor-sor- it was like an <u>interview</u>=
189. UM: =oh ah
190.   ↓yeah]
191. Mark: [I turned up e::hh thinkin' I was meetin' one person an'
192.   I was meeting the vice uh the pro-vice chancellor of the
193.   education for the whole of the university=
194. UM: =brilliant=
195. Mark: = plus <u>six</u> other PhDs]
196. Female: [.hhh!]
197. Mark: [that were all heads of um [heh]
198. heads of various departments *(uttered laughingly)*
199. [*general noises in the background*]
200. Mark: It was ↑absolutely ↓brilliant I loved it they they were uh they
201.   were brilliant]
202. UM: [m]mm
203. Mark: [I I I sat in the <u>middle</u> (.) with a <u>herd</u> of them round
204.   me]
205. John: [heh]heh
206. Mark: [firing questions at me for <u>two hours</u> a herd of PHds]
207.   [*general laughter*]
208. Mark: [a herd
209.   of PhDs I <u>loved</u> it u::h a::nd they want to talk to Line about uh
210.   a potential business partnership on ↓all their programs
211.   ↑their <u>MBA</u> (.) uh turns over 20 million a year (.) their department
212.   for just one of their small departments which is the business (.)
213.   department turns over 4<u>9</u> million a year u::mm and they want
214.   to ↓make quite a lot of their stuff online and so I've
215.   arranged another meeting for myself and [name of company CEO]
216.   cos the first (.) the first th- (.) the <u>first (.)</u> step is to talk about
217.   a business partnership as opposed to what they're actually going
218.   to be doing. *(He goes straight into an account of another meeting.)*

Mark issues a detailed report that on the face of it has not been requested. Thus Mark displays his tacit knowing of the meeting norm of sharing knowledge that is more than simply issuing bare facts. The way that Mark prefaces his account, and the actions that this accomplishes, is unusual compared to the other extracts.

The account is prefaced by two actions in Lines 187–188: laughter followed by the scripting of a news headline. In their study of interaction in an online discussion forum, Charles Antaki and his colleagues (2006) show how prefaces work as routinely used but powerful devices to "key" the reader to apply a particular understanding to what follows. Similarly, Smith (1978) shows how an interviewee issues "instructions" as a preface to her account of her friend's mental illness, which works to orient the interviewer to a particular interpretation of events. Here, Mark's formulated preface works in much the same way. According to David Greatbatch and his coworker (2002), in their study of laughter in the context of "gurus," public speaking, and audiences, laughter can be used to express solidarity among speakers and to accomplish group cohesion, enhance self-esteem, gain approval, and manage embarrassment. But, in this case, it is only Mark who laughs and as such, stands as a signal that what is about to follow is unusual; thus, it is doing the work of calling attention—rather like the "town crier" who rings his bell before issuing the news proclamation.

The news headline, which works up a different interpretation of the preceding laughter, takes the form of an evaluative inference (Hepburn and Wiggins, 2005). That is, the description ("... was like a- a- a sor sor it was like an <u>interview</u>") is loaded. Combined with the laughter, it underlines the "out of the ordinary nature" of what is to come. The comparison to an interview is quite deliberate, which can be seen in the repair and the emphasis given: this is not working as metaphor (although it has the linguistic construction of a metaphor in "it was like"). As the account unfolds, the category of "interview" is shown to be a compatible descriptor. What this category does invoke, however, is a sense of "confrontation," job and performance appraisals, or discomfort. So, the headline suggests that what is about to follow is not just unusual but also has a potentially negative outcome with the laughter serving *at this moment in time* to manage its potentially embarrassing nature.

This is precisely the interpretation that the "unnamed male" displays in his downbeat token of empathy ("yeah"). The second action that the formulation accomplishes is to establish the start of a narrative—a story—not just a report and as such works to capture the floor for an extended turn without interruption. With the exception of minimal, mostly nonlinguistic, tokens, Mark is able to unfold his story without pause. The upshot of the preface formulation, then, is to signal the "out of the ordinariness" of what follows, which is described in terms of an everyday common occurrence ("an interview") albeit out of context and which is served up with mitigating laughter. In this way, while signaling a forthcoming unusual account, this is nonetheless issued with a claim to authenticity.

A further point to draw out concerning prefaces is the common practice of restating the opening preface at the end of the account, which signals that whatever it is that the preface has "promised" has in fact been delivered (Antaki *et al.*, 2006). This suggests that the absence of such a repeat would leave an unsatisfactory account, perhaps even calling into question its authenticity based on the accusation that "you have not done what you said you were going to do." We find the repeat in Lines 206–209: the action of being the target of fired questions serves as an "interview" scene. Noticing this draws attention to the construction of the account as a whole: the vivid narrative accounting is accomplished in Lines 187–209, which is punctuated by unobtrusive minimal continuers (Wooffitt, 2007)—that is, permits to the speaker to continue. The second part of the account (Lines 209–218) does the business of factual accounting. It is quite clearly an account in two halves.

13.4.2 Doing Being Ordinary

The second feature that suggests that Mark is doing "uber authenticity" can be seen in Lines 191–195. This is a good example of "doing being ordinary" (Line 191: "I turned up e::hh thinkin' I was meetin' one person..."), which is followed by an account of extraordinary events (Lines 192–195: "...was meeting ... the pro-vice chancellor..." and six other PhDs'). Thus, extraordinary events are framed in the context of an ordinary person going about their ordinary, usual business. According to Robin Wooffitt, such rhetorical displays establish the speaker's normality and social competence, which "… is a central feature of warranting the factual basis of our claims" (2005: 107). What is equally interesting about this particular part of the account is the repair seen in Line 192: Mark starts to say that he met with the chancellor, but then self-corrects with "vice-chancellor." In the hierarchy of the higher education establishment, the latter is subordinate to the former. This could be seen as a downgrading of the importance of Mark's encounter. Contrastingly, the repair is seen in the context of the warranting of factual claims: it is doing "authenticity" in the display of attention to detail and accuracy. As we saw in the previous chapter's discussions around trust, these types of actions routinely have the function and effect of constructing trustworthiness on the part of the speaker (Clifton, 2012a). Note the evaluative token issued in Line 194 ("brilliant"), which suggests not just acceptance of the account thus far but positive evaluation with a permit to continue.

The extraordinariness of the circumstances as they transpire is compounded in the reference to "plus six other PhDs', with the number tonally emphasized. This is subsequently further upgraded to a "herd of PhD's" (Lines 203 and 206). Note how Mark uses the category "PhD" and *then* offers a second category of "heads of various departments" (Line 198), with the latter delivered with a sprinkling of laughter. The reference to "PhDs" causes a sharp intake of breath on the part of one hearer, while the second category causes, not matching laughter that one might expect at this point in the account and with a direct indexing to Mark's own laughter tones, but rather general positive murmurs. Why refer to PhDs over department heads (a job category that is more likely to be the routine business of the participants) and why upgrade from "six" to "herd?"

It is suggested here that the category of "PhD" has the effect of, firstly, underlining the unusualness of events in that PhDs may be a common resident at higher education institutions, but 7 (including the pro-vice chancellor) in one place and time is unusual. Secondly, the term "PhD" comes with strong category inference (Silverman, 2007), which is quite different from that of department head, and the *way* in which this is used has a very important function in terms of the speaker's own identity and self-esteem. That is, PhD invokes studiousness, intelligence and knowledge, academic ability, teacher, and so forth: it invokes the sense of the daunting, and this invocation can be seen in the deliberately audible sharp intake of breath by one of the hearers. Having conjured a very particular category, Mark then effects what can only be described as a "mirror action": by placing himself in the middle (Line 203) as the target of a firing line of questions (Line 206) by a "herd of PhDs" for "two hours," and which trial of endurance has a positive outcome for the speaker. The effect is to construct himself as clever, intelligent, knowledgeable, trustworthy and able to cope with the unexpected. It is the narrative of a "David" who finds himself compelled to do combat with "Goliath" in the face of seemingly insurmountable odds.

Notice how Mark repeats the collective noun "herd" three times (Lines 203, 206 and 208), with the second two occurrences arguably orienting to the laughter initiated by John in Line 205. By any analysis, Mark appears to be on the brink of getting carried away by his own performance. This brings a serious risk of being seen as exactly the opposite to that which he has earlier scripted (i.e., clever, authentic, etc.). Consequently, the third repeat (Lines 208/209) can be construed as quite deliberately used to reprise the preface as a signal of the end of the narrative account, with the ensuing "u::h" flagging a change of business. Such linguistic scraps may also be interpreted by hearers as marking a turn transition point (Wooffitt, 2005), a point in someone's talk that allows for a new speaker to step in. However, in this instance, Mark is quick to follow with a stretched "a::nd": stretched words like this are routinely used to retain the floor (Hutchby, 2011) in arguments. The contrast between the first half of the account and the second part could not be more stark.

13.4.3   Whose Counting? Quantitative Accounting

Sprinkled throughout the account as a whole, Mark uses quantification rhetoric (Edwards and Potter, 1992; Potter, Wetherell and Chitty, 1991). He meets with the pro-vice chancellor and "6" other PhDs, leaving the listener to do the arithmetic; he was questioned for two hours, which precision contrasts nicely with "a herd," which invokes a numberless quantity but which is nonetheless substantial; he refers to turnovers of "20 million a year" and "49 million a year." As shown elsewhere, quantification rhetoric constructs accounts as factual, as making "… a specific version appear independent of the speaker and thus a fact rather than an interested account" (Potter, Wetherell and Chitty: 336). That being the case both parts of the account are therefore laced with factuality framed as beyond the manipulation or influence of the speaker and consequently free of his personal stake and interest.

Coming as it does after the repeat of the narrative preface and containing two "meaty" economic numbers, one would expect that this is the part of the account that does the upshot, providing the warrant for the earlier vivid narrative. This is also the only part of the account that contains vague accounting—"a potential business partnership," "they want to make quite a lot of their stuff," and "the first step is to talk about a business partnership"—which is contrasted negatively with "they're actually going to be doing" (underlining added). Notice that the referred to discussion will not address what "they" will be doing, implying that this refers to what the client will be doing. Any sensible interpretation would suggest that discussion of a business partnership in the absence of its purpose (what they will be doing) would run the risk of being a nebulous one. This is clearly reporting a business opportunity for the organization but it is vague and insubstantial. Arguably, Mark himself orients to this turn of events with a triple repeat of "the first" in Line 216, suggesting both unease at referring to "first steps" and perhaps recognizing that the events in which he has engaged thus far, and that which he has reported here, represent no steps whosoever. As if to consign his just delivered account to history, Mark swiftly and smoothly moves on to an account of another meeting with a different client. Note also the complete absence of any interaction from any other member of the team at this point.

Collateral Information
This refers to a rich situated or contextual description that is used to evidence the factuality of an account. These expressions offer a vivid and graphic account of a believable state of affairs.

Taken as a whole, it is proposed that Mark orients to the lack of substance in the actual report of business opportunity. His vivid narrative accounting, shown to be explicitly theatrical, combined with factual accounting accomplished through for instance quantification rhetoric, works to obscure this lack. It can be conjectured that if asked subsequently about Mark's account, what hearers would recall would be the "herd of PhDs," not the announcement of a potential business partnership opportunity. One could further speculate that it is the narrative accounting, as a form of "collateral information" (Edwards and Potter, 1992) that is doing the real "uber authenticating" work, serving to cloud a report that is otherwise risky in its potential to lead to nothing more than talking. The practice of vivid accounting, and emphasis on accuracy and authenticity, as a strategy for masking difficulties is reported in studies of courtroom discourse (e.g., Locke and Edwards, 2003), and other forms of testimony.

13.5 PRELIMINARY REFLECTIONS

Both of the meetings analyzed here represent classic examples of knowledge-sharing meetings within a participant-constructed high stakes context. It is argued that in orienting to this context, with its implications of risk, the trajectory of the interactional meeting discourse becomes driven by matters of stake and interest. This is evidenced in the emphasis given to displays of truth telling, accuracy, authenticity, trustworthiness and concerns with reputation. The hallmarks of the meetings analyzed here are consequently similar to those displayed in the previous chapter's focus on trust. Building on this, one could then make the case that risk is shown to be a corelational phenomenon with trust, which are both shown to be factors in knowledge sharing action. It is also possible to claim that identity is just as much a feature of knowledge sharing discourse as trust and risk and that all three are corelational. The knowledge sharing theme of context, originally determined as factor based on the KM literature, begins to look like vehicle for or category to describe all impacting themes because these are the contexts that speakers themselves invoke as live concerns.

Of particular interest here is the effect of the high-stakes context invoked by speakers in their knowledge sharing actions. One of the key questions for the present research concerns how matters of risk and so forth influence knowledge sharing, and with what effect for speakers and the business at hand. While the analysis reveals similar discursive practices in both meetings in displaying high stakes as a live concern, what can also be seen is a significant difference in how this plays out in their respective patterns of accounting. Recall Extract 4 in which Ann displays apparent reluctance to provide any further elaboration beyond her initial narrative construction. A reminder of the meetings' purpose sets some further background.

The purpose of the meetings is to share accounts of sales and marketing activities against the backdrop of the drive for organizational financial health and success. Participants have a vested interest in giving positive reports, but orient strongly to the need for report accuracy, authenticity and trustworthiness. Derek Edwards and Jonathan Potter (1992) argue that people routinely work to construct "preferred versions" of accounts as "disinterested"—that is, to use objectivity, for instance, to decouple self-interest and accountability, to construct mitigating circumstances as a way of warranting or justifying versions of affairs, or to hedge accounts as contingent on factors that can be scripted as beyond their control. The high-stakes nature of the meetings, linked to the taken-for-granted assumption that accounts can be accepted as realistic versions even though the actor is often the only witness present to the version being related, makes the business of managing stake and interest more acute and complex.

It is claimed that the introduction of the category of finances at the outset of both meetings (Extracts 2 and 3), with its implicit connotations of organizational health and success, is what triggers high stakes as a live concern for speakers. This, it is claimed, in turn sets in motion the meetings' imperative for truth telling and accuracy. In Extract 3, this category is formulated as a group accomplishment—that is, financial reports are given based on how the group has collectively performed. In the other extract, the category of finances is displayed as team member competition and rivalry. With respect to this extract (2), as it only features the chair as speaker, it was noted that it was not possible to determine how this formulation is oriented to by other speakers: that is, whether they display mutually shared orientation to the competitive component of the financial account, *at that point.* But this can now be unpacked.

While both meetings can be considered to display similar features in their overall organizational structure and meeting goals, a comparison between them reveals a subtle but significant variance. In the Company A meeting, the discourse throughout is shown to be more collaborative with contributors often volunteering and elaborating on accounts as self-selected turns. By contrast, Company B's meeting is characterized by contributions being called for by the chair, with minimum details reported and few taking up elaboration turns (Extract 4 being one of the—albeit limited—exceptions). Also, although not included here, the longest account in Meeting B, and probably the most important in terms of the scope of business opportunity described, comes right at the end of the meeting, with consequences for available time to afford appropriate levels of discussion. To illustrate this point of variance, the following extracts from both meetings serve to display their respective characteristic patterns of accounting.

Without going into an in-depth analysis here, the collaborative nature of Company A's meeting discourse is clearly shown in Extract 7 in the extended and detailed accounts of activity given by Tom in response to a call to account made by John. Note how John's call

---

EXTRACT 7   130520_003 COMPANY A

228. John: Tom you went to th::e uh (.) you went to meet the (.)]lady
229. Tom: [yeah]
230. John: from [*company name*]]
231. Tom: [Yeah ( ) the lady from uh the lady from ↑[*name*]'s
232. ↓interesting actually cos she works in [*name*] <u>HR</u> (.) so she knows all
233. the ↓people they're working with there ↑um they they talking about
234. doing some pilots in HR on mobile actually I ↑actually think it was
235. more for their u::m (.) it was more sponsored by the unions actually]
236. John: [mm?]
237. Tom: [quite
238. interesting yeah so that kinda ↓be a interesting project and the lady
239. from [*name*] that ↓didn't turn up but I'm gonna see uh ↑in fact
240. strangely I got call the next day from one of <u>her team</u>=
241. John: =yeah=
242. Tom: ↓so (.) about the HR learning [*product*]( )]
243. John: [That's <u>excellent</u>

EXTRACT 8   130319_003 COMPANY B

301. Chair: <u>Yes</u> she did. Fa::n↑tastic an' <u>last</u> but by <u>no means least</u> (.) <u>Jane</u>!
302. Jane: . hhh
303. Chair: What's happenin in <u>your</u> world?
304. Jane: Got an <u>awful lot</u> of em CVs (.) outstanding both the ( )]
305. Chair: [yup!]
306. Jane: e::mm but I've
307. got one interview for the same BA role that Ben's predicted on so I'm
308. not goin' to predict on that e::mm so ↑yep there we go yep ( )
309. Chair: ↑OK ↓zero this ↑week. So the scores on the doors [*name*] are

---

is not formulated as a question, but does contain a candidate topic (the meeting). Note also how Tom's accounting is punctuated with tonal work, and laced with opinion and assessment. The extract from Company B is occasioned by a call in the form of a question, with no indicative candidate answer other than a reference to the location of activities ("your world"). Jane's is more tonally neutral than Tom's and is carefully factual with the only assessment given to describe "an awful lot em CVs" (Line 304). What can be concluded from this?

Based on the detailed analysis of the two meetings, and this admittedly high level comparison of Extracts 7 and 8, it is proposed that the way that the finances category is introduced to each meeting is the source of the effect that can be seen here. In this sense, what the financial category does is activate existing tacitly known and understood context, mutually shared between members. In the case of Company A, the high risks context is formulated as a context of collaboration, assessment and knowledge elaboration. With Company B, it is formulated as between team member competition, which can be seen in how members carefully hedge their accounts in the form of "summary" or "headline" accounting. Thus, even though collective financial results for the group as a whole are presented part-way through this meeting, the first part of the discourse invoking between team member competition remains foregrounded as the activated context.

This chapter has raised what might be considered some contentious issues and findings in relation to risk and related contextual matters. These are returned to in the discussions of all of the findings in Chapter 17. Next, we turn our attention to the subject of identity, a topic of particular interest to the discourse analyst and, as will be shown, a phenomenon of discourse that has some interesting and unexpected consequences for the business of knowledge sharing.

FURTHER READING

Drew, P. (2003). Precision and Exaggeration in interaction. *American Sociological Review*, 68: 917–938.

Greatbatch, D. (2009). Conversation analysis in organization research. In Buchanan, D. and Bryman, A. (Eds). *The Sage Handbook of Organizational Research Methods*. London: Sage.

Potter, J., Wetherell, M. and Chitty, A. (1991). Quantification rhetoric—cancer on television. *Discourse & Society*, 2, (3): 333–365.

Smith, D. (1978). 'K is mentally ill' the anatomy of a factual account. *Sociology*, 12, (23): 23–53.

Wooffitt, R. (2005). *Conversation Analysis and Discourse Analysis: A Comparative and Critical Introduction*. London: Sage.

Wooffitt, R. (2007). Communication and laboratory performance in parapsychological experiments: demand characteristics and the social organization of interaction. *British Journal of Social Psychology*, 46: 477–498.

14

NEGOTIATING POSITIONS OF AUTHORITY

14.1 KNOWLEDGE SHARING ACCOMPLISHED FROM A SUBJECT POSITION

The concept of identity, like trust, is wrapped in layers of debate and competing definition. The confusion can be seen in the various phenomena theorized and studied under the title of identity: for instance, stance-taking, positioning, and impression management. These can be approached as *categories* of identity as constructed in discursive social interaction. As noted in Chapter 8, Bronwyn Davies and Rom Harré's version of positioning theory is useful in offering a basic perspective of identity, and identity work, as the product not the source of linguistic and semiotic practices. This goes back to one of the fundamental points of variation between postmodernist and modernist approaches to language: on one side, social constructionism constitutes language as constructive and action oriented, as the site at which actions are accomplished, and is consequently an appropriate topic for the study of human action and behavior in its own right. The conventional, modernist perspective, on the other side, approaches language as merely a conduit linking the contents of minds to the outer world with its implication of language as a mirror of mental reality. Thus, each of these perspectives would approach the study of identity in very different although perhaps not entirely incompatible ways. Throughout this chapter, these category terms are used as appropriate to the context of the actions of speakers but are collectively considered to constitute "identity."

Knowledge and Discourse Matters: Relocating Knowledge Management's Sphere of Interest onto Language, First Edition. Lesley Crane.
© 2016 John Wiley & Sons, Inc. Published 2016 by John Wiley & Sons, Inc.

Positioning Theory
According to positioning theory, originally developed by Rom Harré, the moment-to-
moment constructions of identity are conceptualized as positions brought into being in
one's own talk and that of others and the narratives we construct as part of the process of
sensemaking—that is, the practice of making sense of the world and its contents at any
given time. From this perspective, "identity" or rather "selfhood," to use Harré's term, is
a constantly shifting, linguistically orientated phenomenon, which stands in considerable
contrast to the conventional view of identity as static, formal, and ritualistic.

Drawing on the discussions in Chapters 6 and 8, identity is approached as socially and
relationally accomplished and very much bound to context. Recall Bronwyn Davies and
her colleague's notion of people accomplishing the action of positioning through rhetorical practices. This leads to the speculation that knowledge sharing is accomplished from
a subject position in a given context, that such positions influence its direction and outcome, and that most if not all of its thematic categories will emerge relationally when the
analytic focus is on identity. It has already been shown, for instance, in Chapter 12, that
identity is undoubtedly bound to matters of trust.

Perhaps unsurprisingly, identity, as a phenomenon of interest in relation to knowledge
management (KM) theory and practice, has not really been in evidence in the KM
domain. It can, however, be regarded as an "implied" factor. Ikujiro Nonaka's 1994
theory of the dynamic knowledge-creating firm, for instance, emphasizes knowledge
creating as a social activity with interaction between actors having a vital role in its
development. The theory places an equal emphasis on individual beliefs and commitment. Consequently, it does not require much of a stretch of imagination to see identity,
constructed in the moment-by-moment discursive actions of people in social interaction, as an influential factor in knowledge work as it is in almost every other aspect of
human life. However, in conventional approaches to knowledge work, including
Nonaka's, for instance, identity is implicitly conceptualized as a static mental state
operating behind and influencing what people say rather like Gilbert Ryle's "ghost in
the machine." In contrast, identity is here conceptualized as a dynamic psychological
phenomenon that is invoked in discourse in social interaction. (For a more detailed
account, see Bethan Benwell and Elizabeth Stokoe's excellent and comprehensive book
Discourse and Identity.)

This chapter investigates the relationship between identity and knowledge sharing in the
context of a meeting between a client (Company B) and a contractor. (Chapter 15 focuses
on contributions to an online KM discussion forum from the perspective of identity
construction and knowledge sharing.) The present analysis uncovers complex identity work
in which the anticipated subject positions become almost reversed and where this reversal
leads to a breakdown in knowledge sharing and a breach in client–contractor etiquette. In
this action, matters of trust, reputation, and authenticity come to the fore, shown as worked
up relationally in discursive actions. Speakers do not just "do identity," but they work up
complex layers of phenomena, which collectively bring a category of identity into being.

The analysis is preceded by a brief discussion of the event's context, the participants,
and expected norms in terms of actions, motivations, and roles. The meeting is split into
two parts, with the second marked by the arrival of a new participant. In the first part, the
investigation focuses on how unexpected positions are shown to be invoked and the
impact this has on the directions of knowledge sharing. In the second part, the arrival of

the other actor is shown to have consequences for positioning actions, knowledge sharing transactions, and, in particular, what happens when this actor introduces a "bombshell." The analysis and discussions conclude with some preliminary reflections.

14.2 CONTEXT, PARTICIPANTS, AND EXPECTATIONS

The meeting in the client company's (Company B) offices is a prearranged appointment and has the purpose of discussing a brief for the design and installation of a promotional exhibition stand. The first part of the meeting involves two people: the client representative (Elaine) and the contractor (Mike). We can reasonably assume that the contractor has already been contracted to do the stand work: he makes references to a preexisting quotation already being accepted. Consequently, the meeting is not a "sales" occasion but rather a "brief-taking" exercise. Part way through the meeting, a third person (Peter), a director of the client company, joins in. His arrival considerably changes the meeting's dynamics. Unlike the meetings featured in Chapters 12 and 13, there is little evidence of preexisting familiarity between the contractor and his clients, and although the two employees of Company B are obviously familiar to one another, the hierarchical nature of this familiarity is far stronger than that seen in other chapters.

A second reasonable assumption that we can make is that all participants have a vested interest (stake and interest) in sharing knowledge: the client representatives as owners of the client's requirements and possessors of the project budget and the contractor as the possessor of knowledge and experience of exhibition work. The meeting's purpose requires both parties to share knowledge to accomplish a mutually shared understanding of the business at hand. Thus, a mutually shared and implicit understanding of the client–contractor relationship can be speculated as motivating joint interest in ensuring that the client's requirements are satisfactorily met, that all (potential) issues are addressed, and that a favorable outcome is assured.

Developing this latter point, the categories of "client" and "contractor" invoke a number of taken-for-granted norms, collectively described as the "client–contractor etiquette": the client is in charge, makes decisions on what is to be done, knows what they want and need, and will disclose authentic information that can be trusted. The category of contractor invokes notions of compliance, trusted expertise allied to reputation, and the provider of solutions. It is the contractor who has been selected for the project with the client as the agent of selection. The anticipated actions are that the client will list their requirements, with the contractor suggesting ways in which these may be realized. But, in the first meeting part, the analysis reveals an anomaly to this, causing a shift in the normatively expected positions. This has an impact on the anticipated directions for knowledge sharing leading to a breach in client–contractor etiquette, which becomes activated in the second part of the meeting.

14.3 PROBLEMS, COMPLEXITIES, AND APPEALS TO COMMON SENSE

The first extract is chosen because it does not comply with the expected sequential pattern of accounting. As the analysis shows, role positions become the subject of delicate interactional negotiation, with the categories of "client" and "contractor" becoming blurred and the expected primary direction of knowledge sharing (client to contractor, setting the agenda for the contractor's response) being all but reversed.

At the meeting's outset, the client (Elaine) and the contractor (Mike) swap mundane pleasantries before jointly agreeing that, despite a lack of information from the exhibition organizer, they may still proceed with their discussions for which Elaine confirms she has "a brief." The brief does not exist in written form. The possession of a brief nonetheless occasions an agenda for the meeting, and as we have seen in previous analysis work, this possession (in theory) casts its owner in a dominant position with rights to set the discussion directions, topic transitions, and so forth. No mention is made of a third participant yet to arrive. Getting down to the business at hand, Elaine informs Mike of a set of circumstances concerning the stand of which he is unaware: the stand will not just feature the client but will also include up to three of its partners. She predicts a forthcoming "huge meeting" involving all parties at which expectations for the stand—branding, collateral, and staffing—are to be discussed and agreed. This future meeting will not involve Mike. The first extract comes immediately following this disclosure:

EXTRACT 1   130320_02 (E = ELAINE; M = MIKE)

1. E: Uhmmm (.) so (.) ↑if they want branding on the stand as <u>well</u> (.) is that going
2. to be a hu::ge…
3. M: .hhh the <u>only</u> thing I think you need to be aware of is the fact that uhmm
4. [intake of breath] looking at the stand (.) and the size of the one that we did
5. uhmmm which is the same size [*he mutters about pulling up an image on*
6. *his laptop*] is the uhmmm [*mumbles about his laptop 'deciding to stop*
7. *working'*] it's the ↓size. I mean you've got a-a fairly big stand in re- in
8. regards to uhmmm (.) the exhibition itself. [*mutters about his laptop*
9. *having thousands of images*] On the other hand yo-you've got to
10. consider that if you've got yourselves and three other companies]
11. E: [Yeah]
12. M: [you're all
13. vying for the same amount it's the message is gonna get re[ally, really
14. E: [really]
15. M: complic]ated
16. E: [yeah, that's what I think too as]well
17. M: [Uhmmm you know (.) it..it..
18. yes you want people to contribute towards the actual stand itself but
19. ultimately um]
20. E: [The thing is we want it to be a [Company name] (.) a
21. [Company name] piece of work—it's more that they're working with
22. ↑us and all of the (.) products or services that they're gonna be (.) promoting
23. they do (.) through us anyway so I think we can kind of get away with
24. bit of a]
25. M: [well that-that's the size stand that you've got]

[… Lines 26–44 omitted]

45. M: (*coughs*) Yes you ↑can do ummm (.) <u>my</u> advice
46. will be↓ [*gap*] if you .hhh if <u>you</u> .hhh if you have too many <u>screens</u> if you
47. have too many people on the ↓stands if it looks too complicated=
48. E: =↓people won't come over (.) ok=
49. M: =It's gonna be i- you're gonna ge- you're gonna get a confusing
50. message=
51. E: =Yeah
52. M: ↓A::d what's gonna happen is is that ahhhh wh- people just
53. <u>aren't</u> gonna be attracted to it=
54. E: =yeah
55. M: = .hhh you don't want to have too many people↓on the stand (.) um
56. as I did when I worked with Thomas before ummm (.) we actually went
57. through and I- I sorry yeah

[...Lines 58–62 omitted]

63. M: but th::e (.) the problem that you might have is the fact that uh ↓well
64. you probably will have if you've got that it's going to be too crowded and
65. people aren't gonna get the message there's gonna be .hhh <u>four</u> different
66. names up there and it's all gonna get well who is it]
67. E: [who is this], yeah]
68. M: [y'know
69. it's going to get really really confusing=
70. E: =OK=
71. M: .=hhh I↑<u>think</u> (.) <u>yes</u> you want to get these people to buy into it
72. yes it would be great if they could (.) help to contribute towards the
73. costs a bit uh but ultimately (.) ↓I think you need to probably put your
74. foot down a bit and say look, yeah well we do want your contribution
75. but it is a [Company name] sta]nd
76. E: [yeah]
77. M: [If you've got loads of screens going
78. on who-who's looking at]what
79. E: [at what, yeah. Can we have ↑<u>one</u> ↓computer
80. screen si-simply because one of <u>our</u> Directors has said that he wants to be
81. able to-o ummm he's launching an online product and he wants to be able
82. to have-show people it interactively=
83. M: =I've come up with a fe::w layouts initially

14.3.1   Invoking Positions of Authority

The evolving subject position discourse (Davies and Harré, 1990) is characterized by three features: Mike's (i) repertoire of bad news, (ii) persuasion and trust, and (iii) scripting of professionalism and claims to epistemic superiority (Clifton, 2012b). All of these features work up Mike's position as authoritative and authentic, with a stake in both his client's and his own reputation, and as guardian of what the client wants. All of this sounds suspiciously like the concerns and features of what would be expected to be the hallmark of the meeting's dominant actor—the client. We have already encountered many of these features in the previous discussions on trust and risk, which are shown to punctuate the repertoires of meeting leaders. An important consequential feature of Mike's version of affairs is how this reflexively works to cast Elaine in the role of "amateur" in need of strong advice and to which Elaine is shown to display resistance. Each of these three features is considered in turn.

Negative Repertoire

The negative repertoire can be seen in Mike's description of "too many screens" (Line 46), "too many people" (Line 47), "four different names" (Line 65), and "loads of screens" (Line 77), all of which conspire to a confused message with visitors not being attracted to the stand. This is a version of a projected future worked up as something to be obviously avoided. When people predict versions of future events, they are displaying their knowledge of cause and effect (Chilton, 2004) drawn from experience. Note the use of quantification rhetoric. As we saw in the chapters on trust and risk, quantification accounts are not only designed to argue but also serve to formulate accounts as immune from the speaker's stake or interest (Potter et al., 1991). Thus, Mike scripts commonsense facts indexed as obvious (Thompson, 2004), which are not influenced by his own agenda of "clutter avoidance"—his stake and interest. The upshot is to formulate an account that would be difficult for anyone to dispute without appearing incapable of seeing the obvious and fond of mess. This is all indexical and consequent to how Elaine proposes to deal with the involvement of the client's partners in the stand, which is clearly constructed by Mike as a problem in the making.

Across the trajectory of the extract, Mike escalates the "problem" from the inference that the stand's size is not appropriate for "yourselves and three other companies" (Line 10) to a problem that Elaine "might have" and then "probably will have" (Line 63/64), which is rounded up as leading to a "really, really confusing" message (Line 69). The repeat of "really" works as an extreme case formulation that scripts his case as cut and dried and not open to negotiation (Edwards and Potter, 1992). One can readily see this if one thinks of the conventional alternative to "really" in such a phrase—"very, very con-fusing": the use of "really" brings the added sense of reality, concreteness, and unavoid-ability, if his advice is not heeded. Interestingly, when used as a stand-alone utterance, say, in response to some account given by another speaker, the term "really" invokes a charge against the truthfulness of what the other speaker has said (Silverman, 2007). Context is everything.

This negative repertoire works so effectively that it causes Elaine to almost "beg" for "one computer screen" (Line 79). This is charged and comes armed with a warrant (Silverman, 2007)—a Director is launching a new product and needs to be able to demonstrate it (Lines 81/82). The emphasis on "our Director" works to call attention to the title of the person needing the screen—this is not Elaine wanting a screen, but a Director. She uses the title to emphasize her argument for having a screen, with the associated implication that Directors are not to be denied. The addition of the inclusion pronoun ("our") effectively implicates (Abell and Stokoe, 2001) Mike in the business of not denying Directors. There are three repairs in this one utterance suggesting that Elaine is treading very carefully (Hepburn and Wiggins, 2005). There is a sense here that Mike may have taken his rhetoric too far.

He is also explicitly driving the agenda, and setting the direction for knowledge sharing, in opposition to that expected.

Repairs
"Repair" is the term used to identify a part of an utterance (or a whole utterance) in which the speaker has, for instance, started to say one thing and then produces something else. Everyday talk is quite literally littered with repairs. They can also appear in written text. Particularly in talk, words uttered cannot be erased—we cannot "wind the clock back"—so repairs are seen as accomplishing significant actions worthy of the analyst's close attention.

Candidate Solutions
When a speaker formulates a question or indicates a problem, for instance, he or she is described as offering a candidate solution when the utterance contains a prospective solution, similarly to a "candidate answer." In accomplishing such actions, speakers can be seen to orient to two extremes: either the candidate solution is conjured as their preferred solution or framed as ironic or sarcastic, for instance.

Accountability of Descriptions
Descriptions are said to be accountable when the speaker offers a warrant—a justification—for their claim, account, or report. If a speaker orients to the accountability of their description, they are signaling their often tacit understanding that descriptions may be open to criticism, counterclaims, or alternative versions.

Persuasion and Trust
Despite scripting what can be seen as a robust, noncontestable argument, Mike's tone of voice is friendly, concerned, and warm. This seems at odds with the apparent warning work that he is doing with, for instance, his prediction of dire future events (Lines 46–53). Note, however, that the candidate solutions (Hepburn and Wiggins, 2005) to these problems are contained in the warnings: avoid too many screens, avoid too many people, and the message becomes decomplicated. This display of epistemic superiority (Clifton, 2012b) is served as the warrant for the "warning" work being done: that is, the display of possession of knowledge in how to avoid future disasters works as the justification for issuing warning. Such actions index the accountability of descriptions (Silverman, 2007) and an awareness of the potential for criticism (Antaki et al., 2006). So superficial analysis would suggest that he is orienting to the client–contractor etiquette in providing the advice and solutions—required of contractors in such situations—as factual descriptions that are accountable. However, closer investigation of his claims to professionalism and superior knowledge suggest a different understanding.

If there is potential for criticism, the mitigating action is persuasion. Everything about Mike's discursive actions orient to persuasion, displaying knowledge of these problems based on previous experience, as we saw earlier with his prediction of future events. This can be seen more directly in Lines 52 and 53 in which Mike's utterance is initiated with a marked drop in tone and volume to the level of near whisper. This can be understood in two ways: first, as a sharing of confidence and second, as an appeal to common sense. Sharing confidences invokes trust work while conjuring the self-evident nature of common sense (Thompson, 2004) as unproblematic and obvious to everyone.

The cleverness of these types of action lies in their effect of issuing a version of affairs to which every reasonable person would subscribe, but which is nonetheless *his* version of affairs. In appealing to common knowledge that reasonable people would have, Mike is thus managing his own stake and interest in the account through the actions of persuasion linked to trust. Elaine's orienting to the trustworthiness of his account can be seen in Lines 67 and 79, for instance, in her speech mirrors of Mike's utterances. That is, she displays acceptance of Mike's claims.

Claims to Professionalism and Superior Knowledge

Mike makes claims to knowledge of what Elaine will get, wants, or does not want (e.g., Lines 49, 55, 71). This works to script what she *should* want and need as imperatives, with the reflexive inference that Elaine lacks possession of the *right* aspirations. This, in turn, issues Elaine—and her brief—with a potential credibility problem (Silverman, 2007), bilaterally constructing Mike as the owner of a more appropriate "brief": the positions are thus reversed.

According to Andrew Brown and his coworker, one of the ways in which people display professionalism is through making claims to knowledge and expertise, which is an obvious enough notion. Perhaps less obvious is their argument that these kinds of claims work reflexively to "…position relevant others as naïve, neophytes, amateur and inexpert" (2011: 86). Arguably, at this point in the conversation, this is precisely the identity to which Elaine orients with her acquiescent minimal utterances (e.g., "yeah": Lines 51, 54). By contrast, Elaine's speech mirrors (Lines 14, 67, 79) do something more than this. This partial echoing—in three places—of Mike's preceding utterance, and mostly almost simultaneously with his talk, suggests that Elaine is resisting the "unknowledgeable" role being formulated into being by Mike. Working together, the minimal acquiescence and the speech mirrors display not just agreement (Abell and Stokoe, 2001) but also corroboration. Elaine is not just accepting the other's claims as trustworthy (as noted earlier), but she is invoking a position of experience (Rautajoki, 2012), which is in contrast to the role construction that Mike orients to. This reveals the moment-by-moment delicate identity negotiation work.

It is further suggested that Mike's claims to superior knowledge serve as the warrant for his displays of concern for his client's reputation, which invokes the potential of a risk. The progenitor of this risk is the fact that it is Elaine, and not Mike, who will be present at the crucial forthcoming meeting with partners to discuss the stand. Having made these positions of authority and its opposite live concerns, what does Mike do with them? The next part of the analysis demonstrates how this role construction is crucial to accomplishing the action of "creating a script"—in effect, conjuring a position that Elaine is to adopt at the future partners' meeting.

14.3.2 Formulating a Script for the Client

What is it about this extract that suggests that what Mike is doing is conjuring a "script" for what Elaine should say at the future partners' meeting? Toward the end of the extract, Mike makes an explicit statement of what she will need to do in respect of the partners (Lines 74–75): "(you) say, look, well …," which Elaine receipts with a minimal affirmative. Completing the narrative, Mike invokes the further weight of evidence against "loads of screens," which again, Elaine's echo in Line 79, serves to corroborate, with the latter working so effectively that Elaine immediately follows this with an appeal, with its subject ("computer screen") uttered almost subvocally as if working to hide its presence. It is also the case that Elaine's turn (Lines 79–82) serves as the first indication of a "brief" being shared: the Director's specific requirements. The point made here is that the prior actions in the extract are all carefully choreographed to this point and designed to make public all of the reasons and arguments for why Elaine should adopt a particular stance with the partners and what she should say. This can be unpacked.

A comparison of Lines 17–19 and 71–73 shows how the latter repeats almost exactly the former. The earlier utterance is interrupted by Elaine, but the repeat serves to complete it. As the scene setter for this action, Mike orients to the necessity of bringing the "problem" into sharp focus—making it real—with vivid accounting, which works to factualize his claims (Lines 3–10, 12–13: Edwards and Potter, 1992). Note, for instance, that the word "problem" is missing from Elaine's inaugural question (Line 2), although its presence can be heard in Mike's responding audible intake of breath. Elaine positively receipts and partly echoes Mike's utterance (Line 14), scripting consensus, and alignment with his stance (Schegloff, 1997), and even making an explicit claim to similar opinions (Lines 16: "… that's what I think too aswell"). To all intents, Mike's persuasion work has succeeded and trust is invoked—at least, on her part in respect of the contractor's experience and know how.

Vivid Accounting

Vivid accounting or description is one of Derek Edwards and Jonathan Potter's discursive fact construction formulations. People typically construct vivid, richly detailed accounts or descriptions of objects, events, people, and so forth, which give the impression of firsthand witnessing or of perceptual reexperience. This has the reflexive effect of scripting the speaker as possessing good skills of observation and their account as being authentic and accurate.

Mike's continued escalation of the problem (Lines 17–19) invoking the mental state of "what you want" infers that what Elaine thinks "aswell" is insufficient to ward off risk. So, while Mike works to script himself as trustworthy, he reflexively formulates Elaine as being the opposite. Her interruption (Lines 20–24), spoken quite rapidly, can he heard as an attempt to downgrade and reclaim the escalating problem. Turns of talk typically demonstrate the speaker's sense of the previous turn (Potter, 1998a): here, Elaine orients to discomfort with the contractor's problem escalation actions and also arguably his formulation of what she can and cannot do. In other words, is Mike "overegging" the scale of the problem? She works up a careful stamp of ownership (Lines 20–21: "… we want it to be a …."), with the company's name repeated as the owner of the stand. In this way, she conjures a mitigating circumstance (Abell and Stokoe, 2001) for the potential problem: it can be managed ("we can kind of get away with," Line 23), which downgrades its seriousness.

In thus recharacterizing the nature of the problem, Elaine attempts to reclaim the floor. In response, Mike prefaces his utterance with the particle "well" (Line 25), shown to signal the insufficiency of the previous turn (Wood and Kroger, 2000), conjuring Elaine's account as an insufficient strategy and as the source of risk, potentially to reputation. Also, in otherwise explicitly avoiding orienting to Elaine's account (starting in Line 25, he offers a factual description of the stand and its features), he compounds the potential credibility problems

(Silverman, 2007) of her strategy. Thus, a potential tension is created with the scale of the invoked problem, its ownership, as well as strategies for dealing with it made live issues. This interaction works up the two sides of an argument, which need to be resolved. Recall Robin Wooffitt's (2005) reasoning that arguments cannot be resolved through reference to the facts, as it is the facts that are in question. Someone has to give way.

Subsequently, Mike issues all of the reasons and arguments for why his client should adopt a particular stance with the partners, using a number of key rhetorical resources. These have the effect of working up the factual *and persuasive* status of his account, reflexively orienting to his claimed position of knowledgeable expert with a concern for reputation—that is, self and account as authentic and therefore trustworthy, immune from self-interest. The description of the stand, for instance, begun in Line 25, serves as a form of empiricist accounting, which Derek Edwards and his coworker (1992) explain as constructing a constrained neutral record of events. He also uses three-part listing in two places, shown to be effective in persuasion discourse (Edwards and Potter): (Lines 46–47) "too many screens," "too many people," "too complicated," and (Lines 64–66) "too crowded," "people aren't going to get the message," and "it's going to be four different names up there." Additionally, he uses a contrast marker (Lines 45–46), with the "ummm" serving to mark the end of concessionary material (what Elaine *can* have), and the direction of his advice in avoiding "too many screens."

However, the most powerful warrant for his claimed position (Line 55–57) comes with the invoking of past experience with this same client with similar problems to those predicted here. Mike scripts privileged access to knowledge (Willig, 2003), which he does delicately and with attention to avoiding specific allocation of blame. As the only actor able to invoke this previous experience, how can it be disputed? The meaning of this previous experience as being problematical is not made explicit, but rather is worked up in shared meaning through the familiar use of the phrase "too many people." What this clever utterance accomplishes is an unbalancing of the facts in his favor. What is also implied is that the client did not heed his advice on this previous occasion.

Now Mike moves to complete his scripting work, with the earlier contingent status of the problem hardened to predictable fact and with Elaine displaying fully shared consensus through her echo in Line 67. Note how this works as indirectly reported speech of imaginary future stand visitors: it is not just what she thinks, or what Mike says, but what *other people* will problematize.

With these moves, the trajectory of the discourse is shown to lead to a repeat of Mike's earlier warnings, this time encased in an explicit "script" for Elaine to use at her partners' meeting. Again, the anticipated position norms of "client" and "contractor" are blurred.

14.3.3   Influencing Effects of "the Script"

From this point on, part 1 of the meeting largely follows expected norms for a meeting of this type, with a far more equivalent, interactional, and collaborative sharing of ideas and options. Nonetheless, the "script" worked up by Mike continues to influence the direction of the discourse. He twice explicitly reissues the problem, the first reiterating the theme of "clear message," with its opposite leading to people simply walking past the stand. The last few lines of this exchange are included here as they generate an account that is directly contradicted by the third participant when he joins the meeting. The claims invoked in Extract 2 are not just contradicted, but are shown to be wholly wrong. As becomes clear when the third participant joins, Elaine has omitted to pass on one vital piece of knowledge:

EXTRACT 2   130320_02

141. M: ...or something along those lines (.) underneath so-o (.)people see
142. [Company] name]
143. E: [yeah]
144. M: [that's what they see [Company name] right across the
145. top (.) people are gonna co- gonna ↓want to see you there and they're
146. gonna look at that and think ↓'ah there's [Company name] stand=
147. E: =we know who they are=
148. M: = we know who they are

Note how the company's name is made the dominant subject of this transaction, with the name scripted as the "big attractor," that visitors will "know who they are." This idea is cocreated by both participants, with both working up what imaginary exhibition visitors will think (Lines 146–148) with the client referred to in the third person. Like "reported speech," this has the effect of rendering accounts vivid and dramatic (Wood and Kroger, 2000) but here also done objectively ("they" rather than "we"). What is cocreated here is an imaginary version of future events, scripted as authentic and mutually understood.

By the time that the third participant joins in, Mike and Elaine have completed discussions on the stand's brief, with the key features and requirements worked up as a mutually agreed business. The closing stages of the meeting are signaled by Elaine's summation of the core requirements and a move to trivia such as the organization of dishes of confectionary. The third participant comes with something of a "bombshell."

14.4   "SEASONED EXHIBITIONISTS" AND BOMBSHELLS

Recall that the primary purpose of the meeting is to share knowledge so that knowledge of the client's requirements can be "matched" by knowledge of exhibition work with the objective of realizing a successful exhibition presence. So far, Elaine and Mike have negotiated a set of criteria for the exhibition stand, with the interactional trajectory (Wooffitt, 2007) shown to be heavily influenced by Mike. It has been shown how he works to effectively reverse the entitlements of the categories "client" and "contractor," such that the knowledge transaction work is driven by him. They have also mutually invoked reputation, trust, authenticity, and epistemic rights as live issues. Peter now enters the meeting. He is introduced by Elaine as "Peter," "our Services Director" who is "very heavily involved" in the event, a description that Peter confirms. Elaine initiates a review of the discussions thus far. During the course of the next sequential interaction, it is shown how Peter explicitly scripts his position as highly experienced in stand work, just prior to sharing knowledge of a novel circumstance, which serves both as a "bombshell" in the light of previous discussions and which brings to light a breach of client–contractor etiquette.

Category Entitlement

Categories such as "client" or "mother," "father," or "business manager" invoke particular meanings and consequences for speakers. Category entitlements refer to the characteristics and understood meanings of a given category. As such, the authenticity of an account can be justified—warranted—by the entitlements of the category membership that the speaker scripts in their discourse. For example, categories come loaded with certain types of knowledge or expertise that a person claiming membership of a particular category is understood and expected to have.

14.4.1 Shifting the Position of Authority

The first part of the review is largely a two-part interaction between Peter and Elaine, with Elaine doing the describing of the "arrived-at" solution for screens and Peter contributing minimal continuers, comments, and suggestions. The dynamics start to change when Peter asks Mike to "give an indication of what the whole space will be like," with the subsequent interactions predominantly involving Peter and Mike only. Mike's discourse, once again, becomes impregnated with directives toward what "you've got," what "you're gonna have," what "you're gonna want," and what "you can't have." Extract 3 displays what happens as he moves through a list of mundane features such as doors, storage space, and charging laptops:

EXTRACT 3   130320_02 (P = PETER)

554. M: Um-m (.) put your coats, your collateral,]all that type of st-
555. P: [all yeah yeah I've do<u>ne</u> a
556. ↑<u>huge</u> amount of stand work heh heh so]so totally agree heh heh
557. E: [He's a pro by me heh heh]
558. M: You're a seasoned eh]exhibitionist aswell
559. P: [I am yes I am yes]

This is the first time that Peter scripts himself as possessing knowledge relevant to the topic under discussion. He interrupts Mike's listing of features with a double receipt ("yeah, yeah," Line 555), with its suggestion of "OK, I know all this," and then gives tonal and descriptive emphasis to the volume of his experience using an extreme case formulation, "huge" (Line 556), which works up indisputable fact (Edwards and Potter, 1992) as authentic. His orienting to experience bilaterally works as a warrant for his interruption of the other speaker. That is, he explicitly establishes his position as knowledgeable such that Mike does not need to continue with his line of detail, hence the interruption. This is precisely how Mike displays his understanding of Peter's action in that he forgoes any further listing. Note the spontaneous matching laughter by Peter and Elaine, which works collaboratively to accomplish alignment and affiliation (Wooffitt and Allistone, 2005). Interestingly, while Elaine works to upgrade (Potter, 1998a) the claimed stance made by Peter (Line 557), he continues to talk over her, invoking a sense of her claim being unnecessary. The upshot is that Mike orients to this change in positioning by reformulating Peter's claims with the explicit category title "seasoned exhibitionist" (Line 558) with all of the rights, themes, and images—its context—that this normatively invokes (Silverman, 2007).

During meeting part 1, Mike is shown to work up his rights to direct the discourse trajectory, warranted by his expertise and experience (epistemic superiority: Clifton, 2012b)—his authority. Now he has a rival, in so much as he is now not the only one present with such epistemic entitlements. Also note how he neatly conjures the category (Abell and Stokoe, 2001) of "seasoned exhibitionist" as being the joint ownership of both himself and Peter in the scripting of "aswell," affiliating Peter's position to his own. Peter's overtalked response (Line 559) both receipts and scripts category recognition (Peräkylä, 2005) with Mike. Thus, both work interactionally to cocreate status for each other to the notable exclusion of Elaine. The upshot is that from this point on, Elaine is largely sidelined until Peter leaves. These discursive actions place Peter in the position of a dual status: client with a warrant to be heard as a decision-maker and as experienced exhibitor with rights to all of the understood entitlements of that category (Edwards and Potter, 1992). What transpires next would not have had the same trajectory and impact if it were not for this dual status.

14.4.2   Issuing a Bombshell and Working to Save Face

EXTRACT 4   130320_02

655. P: [the other the other very po::werful brand that we've got available is the
656. Acme Jobs
657. E: (spoken in a whisper) which is part of the]Job Centre
658. P: [and I would – no-no-no-no that's
659. that's effectively our na- (.) that is ↑ours]
660. E: [So are ↑we-e](*carries on talking*)
661. P: [So what↑ I was think
662. ↓yeah alri what I was thinking was ↓yes we have [Company name]
663. up but if you were—if you're having something here I would say that o::ur
664. either the same size as ↓[Company name]
665. E: [uhum]
666. P: [Or close to it—it's the Acme Jobs]
667. E: [Acme jobs, yeah]
668. P: Because all of the [prospective customers] it's just such a recognisable
669. Brand]
670. E: [hmm]
671. P: [they will gravitate to it ↑more than they will much more than they
672. will to [Company name]

Immediately before Extract 4, Peter has raised the subject of the client's partner companies, triggering the other two to rehearse their previous discussions on the need to avoid confusing messages, with imaginary visitors once again called upon through indirect reported speech by Elaine. Peter interrupts Mike with his utterance in Line 655, dropping the "bombshell." There is a fifth brand to be displayed ("Acme Jobs"), and moreover,

Peter constructs this brand as having more "attractor" power than the company's own name. Contrast this with the contents of Extract 2. In a subsequent utterance, Peter goes as far as to work up a contrast between exhibition visitors' reactions: while they will "register with Acme Jobs" as they "wander past," their eyes will "glide over" the company's name. Extract 4 thus highlights a breach in client–contractor etiquette in that Elaine has omitted the "Acme Jobs" aspect from her earlier (attempted) brief-giving and consequently both she and Mike have just invested their previous discourse in a false set of stocks. Consequently, while Elaine is seen to have not given an "authentic" brief, Mike, in spite of his prior knowledge of the client's stands, is now understood to have persuaded Elaine to the potentially false belief that the client's name will be the attractor for visitors. How this is dealt with by Peter is intriguing.

A first point to note is the absence of any utterance from Mike during Extract 4. Elaine's "stage whisper" (Line 657) can be assumed to be directed at Mike, but is immediately and vociferously denied by Peter, the four-repeat of "no" scripting denial as an extreme case formulation, as undeniable. Moreover, Peter's interruption of Elaine in Line 661 renders her about-to-be-asked question as irrelevant, which has the effect of working to sideline the rest of her turns in this extract (minimal continuers in Lines 665 and 670; corroborating echo in Line 667) as equally unnecessary to the business of Peter at this point.

What is interesting about this interaction is the contrast between Peter's utterances in Lines 661–664 and his conjuring of "gravity" in Line 671. In the former part, Peter first scripts "I was think..." and "I was thinking...": according to Jackie Abell and her coworker (2001), such phrases can serve to signal that what follows may not necessarily be fact. Robin Wooffitt (2005), on the other hand, proposes that "'I think' formulations of knowledge claims are rooted in social activities" (117): he convincingly argues that such cognitive phrases are designed to do delicate interactional work, orientating to social norms, and face-saving. In contrast, Paul Chilton (2004) suggests such phrases work as explicit opinion markers indicating further expansion to come. The expanded opinion slot that follows scripts a contingency ("... if you're ... [then] I would say ..."). These two resources working together here suggest a delicate avoidance of a face-threatening act. According to Brown and Levison's theory of politeness (1987; as cited in Benwell and Stokoe, 2012), speakers attempt to preserve their self and others' esteem or "face" (see also Myers' 1989 study of scientists use of positive and negative politeness to redress face-threatening acts). In other words, Peter is orienting to, and quietly brushing to one side, the previous discourse acts by Mike and Elaine, which are now shown to have been uninformed. All are off the hook, while Peter formulates his requirement for the Acme Jobs logo to be the same size (or close to it) of the company's logo as a *suggestion*.

This interpretation of Peter's delicate orienting to face-saving can be seen in the light of his subsequent account in Lines 668–671. This account serves as a warrant for the foregoing "suggestion": putting the Acme Jobs logo into a prominent position on the stand will be a good thing because it is so recognizable to visitors. Then, he concretizes this with his account of how visitors will "gravitate" to the stand. Here, "gravitate" serves as scientific discourse with an evaluative inference (Hepburn and Wiggins, 2005) calling on scientific, and in the case of gravity, inevitable fact. According to Justin Charlebois (2010), scientific arguments are rhetorically strong because they refer to things that are unchangeable. In Derek Edwards and his coworker's (1992) terms, this utterance would be classed as empiricist accounting, which, they argue, bolsters accounts as factual.

As such, this phraseology is arguably a far more powerful account of future events than calling on indirectly reported *thoughts* of imaginary visitors.

Finally, note the use of the future tense modal "will" (Line 671), shown to be stronger than a standard (e.g., "should") modal (Sneijder and te Molder, 2005). Peter delicately deals with a potential threat to face, both Mike's and the client's, and then formulates a strong warrant for adopting his suggested actions. Further, it is claimed that this strategy works because of his already established credentials as "seasoned exhibitionist" and that these actions invoke reputation in their mitigation work in respect of both contractor and client.

14.5 PRELIMINARY REFLECTIONS

A few speculative observations can now be made about how positioning actions are shown to influence the course of knowledge sharing and how identity works relationally with trust, reputation, and authenticity. During the first part of the meeting, Mike drives both the agenda and its direction accomplished through conjuring epistemic superiority and experience, a discourse of persuasion, and invocation of trust, reputation, and authenticity. Risk is shown to be invoked by Mike, but, arguably, only as a rhetorical device to bolster his persuasion actions. But, in thus driving the agenda, the delivery of the brief—the actual requirements of the client—becomes somewhat lost, and it transpires that a significant requirement has been omitted. Mike's stance, and its reflexive construction of Elaine as an amateur, has influenced how she has shared her knowledge of the brief.

However, this interpretation only has substance if Elaine was in fact in possession of the information about "Acme Jobs" in the first place: this is not made explicit in the discourse. Yet, it is claimed here that during the second meeting part, in orienting to the potential face-threatening act and in scripting Elaine's turns as irrelevant (Extract 4), Peter orients to his understanding that she *did* possess this knowledge but failed to impart it. He effectively "wallpapers" over the issue and thus indexes concerns with reputation and authenticity. An alternative and potentially valid analysis suggests that Elaine may simply have been displaying reluctance—in not mentioning the "Acme Jobs" logo—to issue knowledge of a fifth logo in response to Mike's persuasive rhetoric against such "clutter."

During the course of the second part of the meeting, Peter and Mike collaboratively conjure the context and category of "seasoned exhibitionist" with mutual membership. This has the effect of recontextualizing Peter's subsequent turns in the sequence. There is an irony here in that Peter, while claiming the rights and responsibilities of the category of seasoned exhibitionist, is a senior manager of the client firm and it is this same firm that Mike had earlier implied was responsible for a previous stand's problem of having too many people. There is also the question of why Peter waited until some way into the meeting before making this explicit claim to knowledge. It is speculated that this is connected to lack of familiarity between contractor and client representatives, in that people do not tend to lay out credentials until it becomes necessary.

In issuing the "bombshell," Peter takes full control over the direction of the knowledge sharing: he displays his power to manage the potentially face-threatening act consequential to the client–contractor etiquette breach. Then, he accounts for the change of plan, initially introduced as a suggestion, as a mandatory requirement. While, according to

Mike's arguments, this may add further risk in the potential for confusing and complicating messages, the particularly strong warrant that Peter issues for its adoption works to mediate this. In fact, if one follows Peter's logic, it would not matter how many logos and so forth are on display because visitors' eyes will "glide over" them in favor of the Acme Jobs one. While this is a formulation of opinion sharing, as *his* version of what will transpire, it is conjured as fact, common sense, and the product of what is tacitly known to happen at such events. Add to this Peter's earlier positioning work, and this version of affairs is hard to deny. As Margaret Wetherell (2001) remarks, people speak from positions, which come loaded with inference and are consequential to rhetorical accomplishment.

Identity is shown to be relationally bound to matters of trust and risk, with a reprise of context such as authenticity and reputation seen in the previous analyses of trust and risk work.

Building positions of authority, expertise and trust are equally central to the business of sharing knowledge in the context of online discussion forums, and it is to this context that the investigations now turn in the following chapter.

FURTHER READING

Antaki, C., Ardevol, E., Nunez, F. and Vayreda, A. (2006). "For she knows who she is:" managing accountability in online forum messages. *Journal of Computer-Mediated Communication*, 11, 114–132.

Benwell, B. and Stokoe, E. (2012). *Discourse and Identity.* Edinburgh: Edinburgh University Press.

Davies, B. and Harre, R. (1990). Positioning: the discursive production of selves. *Journal for the theory of social behaviour*, 20, (1): 43–63.

Myers, G. (1989). The pragmatics of politeness in scientific articles. *Applied Linguistics*, 10, (1): 1–35.

Silverman, D. (2007). *A Very Short, Fairly Interesting and Reasonably Cheap Book About Qualitative Research.* London: Sage.

15

BUILDING IDENTITIES AS EXPERT IN AN ONLINE FORUM*

15.1 INTRODUCTION

The analysis again focuses on positioning and identity work, this time making a more technical and granular investigation of how forum contributors, in this instance, position themselves as knowledgeable experts with entitlement to be heard. That is, the investigation concerns how participants construct positions as expert whose voluntarily shared knowledge is worth having, thus orienting to what David Silverman refers to as category entitlements. This is shown to be a delicate, intricate, and even problematic action in the context of discussion forums (see Chapter 6 for a discussion of discourse analysis and computer-mediated communications). So, whereas the meeting analysis in the previous chapters takes a more holistic, interactionalist approach (because it is a live interaction), forum data affords the opportunity to study what might be called "the nuts and bolts" of positioning and knowledge sharing from the perspective of discursive psychology.

15.2 DATA

In November 2010, a member of a LinkedIn "Knowledge Managers" discussion forum posed some "basic questions" around KM. LinkedIn is an online social networking service for professionals, facilitating virtual networks of contacts ("connections") and special interest discussion forums. Over a seven-day period, 14 individuals (all male) made

*Elements of this Chapter have been previously published as a research paper in the Journal of Knowledge Management, 2012, 16, (3): 448–460.

contributions to the forum: one contributor was subsequently excluded from the analysis because of confusing irregularities in written English. Otherwise, the data was downloaded in its entirety from the forum. No changes of any nature were made to its contents, and note that I took no part in the forum myself. For these reasons, the data can be said to be naturally occurring, which in Silverman's book "… can serve as a wonderful basis for theorizing about things we could never imagine" (2007: 59). As this is written text, there is no need for any notation protocols, so the text is shown as is. To protect individual identities, all names have been changed to letters of the alphabet, reflecting the order in which they appear in the discussion.

15.3   THE TRIGGER: MORE THAN A REQUEST FOR ADVICE

The trigger for the discussion is a set of questions posted by A to start a new discussion:

EXTRACT 1

1. A: I have some basic question in knowledge management. What
2. are the objectives of knowledge management? What is the main
3. role of knowledge manager? How can encourage technician and users to use it?
4. B: Great question, I'm interested in the answer of this also.

Superficially, A scripts himself as simply seeking advice, where the framing of questions as "basic" (Line 1) works to mitigate any potential criticism (Abell and Stokoe, 2001), which would suggest that the contributor holds the questions to be problematic in some way. However, according to Gricean maxims, the first sentence can be seen as superfluous to the business of asking questions (Wood and Kroger, 2000): so what is it doing there? A tone of frustration can be heard in Line 1, suggesting that a return to basics is needed in the face of difficulties or complexities and insufficiencies elsewhere: it is not just doing a request for advice. B's turn orients to this problem, scripting a warrant (Willig, 2003) for the questions (Line 4). This effects a form of collaborative recognition in which, according to professor of sociology Anssi Peräkylä (2005), two people work together to create a status for each other: thus, A is not the only one who needs a return to basics.

Gricean Maxims
Herbert Paul Grice was a British philosopher of language whose work in pragmatics has influenced many academic disciplines. Pragmatics is the study of language from the perspective of the language user. Originally published in the mid-1970s, Grice's most well-known contribution is the notion of a universal set of principles—or maxims—that guide language use (Benwell and Stokoe, 2012). Thomas Suddendorf (2013) neatly summarizes these:

- *We should say what we believe is true.*
- *We should provide the appropriate level of information required by the situation.*
- *Contributions should be relevant to the goals of the conversation.*
- *Contributions should be clear and avoid obfuscations and unnecessary jargon.*

A breach of "Gricean maxims" in everyday conversation constitutes, then, an unusual occurrence and worthy of analysis for "what is going on."

A's questions create a gift of an opportunity: they serve as an open invitation to KM practitioners/managers to "shopwindow" and share their knowledge and expertise. One would expect each participant to engage in the business of displaying their wares—in this case, expertise—with little discussion interaction between them. According to Greg Myers' (2010) study of how blog writers orient to self-presentation and positioning, individual stance-taking has precedence over discussion in online forum contexts. At top level, this is indeed what the forum looks like, with only one overt instance of direct between-participant engagement over several turns. However, analysis of the forum shows that the actions and business being performed are—for the most part—complex and highly relational: positions of expertise and knowledge by one contributor are dependent on orienting to others. Further, it is shown how constructing expertise is linked to competitive rivalry. Two primary actions are revealed: group work, performed in social interaction between contributors, and claims to privileged knowledge ("epistemic primacy"; Clifton, 2012b), which do not necessarily rely on discursive interaction between contributors. Beginning with the theme of group work, this is shown to constitute a multilayered rhetorical practice, which can be grouped into four subthemes: construction, positioning, rivalry, and consensus patterns. Each of these is investigated in turn.

15.4 CONSTRUCTING "IN-GROUPS" AS MARKERS OF EXPERT STATUS

A conversation analytic study by Rasmussen (2010) of teenage boys' assessments of social experience posits that members of social groups assume that other members have the same view of the world as they do. The implication of this is that group members have group empathy, a socially shared perspective (Gergen, 1991). Various studies have explored how people use their discourse to construct "in-groups" and "out-groups" as an essential strategy for managing position and accomplishing some desired outcome (e.g., Hobbs, 2003; Ainsworth and Hardy, 2004). In their study of the category of "older workers," Susan Ainsworth and her coresearcher suggest that "...discourse constructs identities by defining groups, their interests, their position within society and their relationship to other groups" (2004: 240). Thus, the conjuring of groups and group membership is a performative resource strategically and relationally used to construct and manage position. Extract 2 is the first "group construction" action in the forum and has important consequences for what follows:

EXTRACT 2

82. C: Remember a strategy without tactics is like a head without legs.
83. It is the what without the how. The strategy and tactics will be
84. different for each organisation, as each organisation is unique.
85. While we cannot describe the exact route we can advise on the
86. road rules to guide you there.

This is the second contribution from C, in response to A's reformulation of his questions, implying that C and D, the first responders to the original questions, had not understood them. In Line 82, C uses an imperative with a call to action, to "remember," scripting the importance of tactics to strategy through the use of a metaphor, thus accounting (Silverman, 2007) for his previous "tactically loaded" turn. In Elisabeth Gülich's (2003) study of doctor–patient consultations, her analysis suggests that metaphorical language is often used to conceptualize knowledge, experience, and feelings, particularly where there is a perceived gap between the speaker's and recipient's understanding of a particular state of affairs. Here, C formulates a "strategy without tactics" as being extraordinary, further compounded by matter-of-factly constructing this as deficient and illogical—the "what without the how" (Line 83).

In-Groups and Out-Groups
The study of how people create groups, warrant and dispute membership, draw compar-
isons with other groups and so forth, from a psychological perspective, has a lengthy and
fascinating record. From the discursive perspective, analysts are interested in how
speakers bring such groups into being and what they do with them. The phrase "in-groups
and out-groups" refers, simply, to the idea that when a person talks a group into being
(e.g., membership of a sports team), the reflexive effect may be to consign the listener to
the "out group," as not being a member of the speaker's group, and this may have
psychological consequences for both speaker and listener. Besides the example here—the
"elite" group—another can be seen in Extract 1 of Chapter 16, where two speakers work
to construct a group of shared understanding to the exclusion of the third participant.

Note how he announces his account with a call to "remember": rather than orienting to memories that readers may already have, the analysis here suggests that C is issuing a command for A (and A in particular) to "pay attention" and commit what follows to memory with the metaphor working to script this as both memorable and as addressing an implied "gap" in A's understanding of these affairs. This can be heard as an admonishment to A, thus scripting A's reformulated questions, and their emphasis on strategic over tactical, as being ridiculous. The admonishment starts the business of constructing an expert elite group (Lines 85/86), to which C scripts his membership.

The reference to advising and road rules, combined with the use of the inclusive pronoun "we", shown to construct consensus (Thompson, 2004), establishes this group as expert, reflexively scripting A as being in the out-group, as the one needing to be guided. This can be conceptualized as invoking themes of trust, authenticity, and even, perhaps, reputation. C accounts for the scope and boundaries of the group (Lines 83–85), which accomplishes a second function of positioning himself as a leading in-group member in the claim to rights to set such boundaries. At the same time, he neatly orients to and manages the expectations of the "out-group." This is reminiscent of Petra Sneijder and Hedwig te Molder's (2005) finding that trustworthiness is bolstered when online contributors say no more than they can be sure of. What this utterance does is fascinating in that, on the one hand, C warrants for the group's inability to offer concrete direction ("…each organisation is unique," Line 84), but he nonetheless scripts the potential advice of the group as worth having albeit the advice can only go so far.

15.5 POSITIONING AND GROUP MEMBERSHIP

Extract 2 shows how C constructs a group and then takes a position or stance within it as a direction-determining member. Almost all subsequent forum contributions—while not making explicit reference to group membership—formulate relational positions to it, which they do using one of two actions. In this way, C's actions are shown to have consequences not just for the limits and boundaries of the group, but for how successive contributors display their recognition and membership of this. The first of these is a warrant for membership through displays of credentials:

EXTRACT 3

82. G: I am working in knowledge intensive sectors for more than
83. 15 year now and I switched on purpose between areas with a

---

In Extract 3, which comes immediately after Extract 2, G indexes his membership to the expert group with a display of credentials as a warrant (Silverman, 2007) for membership. The claimed experiential longevity allied with a claim to purposefulness is used explicitly as a passport for group admission. The second type of membership scripting is more subtle and involves relational stance-taking or positioning.

According to Bronwyn Davies and her coworker (1990), people position themselves through their language practices in relational interaction with others. Myers (2010), in his study of public discussion blogs, argues that stance-taking uses opinion as a tool to align or misalign with some other. In this sense, stance-taking is relational and reflexive. There are similarities between Myers' bloggers and the participants in the present forum: both display themselves as *entitled* to an opinion (Myers), which is both functional and consequential.

In Extract 4, E uses a verb of cognition, "I think" (Line 46), to position himself in relation to C and the elite group. Here, opinion has the function of warranting group membership:

EXTRACT 4

46. E: I think C accurately "touched on" the second
47. part of your concerns, "…encouraging technicians/users"—this
48. requires incentives that satisfy the "what's in it for me" requirement
49. people have, in order to gain their investment of time/energy/support.

As we have already seen in previous analyses, the fragment "I think" has been shown to work as a doubt marker (Wooffitt and Allistone, 2008), as a condition on what follows (Abell and Stokoe, 2001), and as rooted in social action with an indexing characteristic to "face" (Wooffitt, 2005). Here, it works both to signal and strengthen an expanded opinion turn to come (Chilton, 2004), yet to soften any potential face-threatening actions (Wooffitt). The use of a container ("touched on," Line 46) reflexively marks what follows as an elaboration on C's earlier contribution and simultaneously serves to undermine C, scripting C's account, and therefore C, with the category of credibility problem (Silverman, 2007). The "touched on" nature of C's earlier contribution can be heard as marking it insufficient, too light, limited in its substance, with the use of parentheses serving to draw attention to this deficiency. So E's initial complementary note about the accuracy of C's contribution is effectively downgraded (Potter and Edwards, 2003). This is compounded by the elaboration work in Lines 48/49, again signaling the insufficiency of C's earlier contribution. In short, this can be heard as "I know more than he does!," with an associated appeal to authenticity.

Container
"Container" is the term given to any textual device or symbol used to wrap and segregate one part of a text from another. The term "container" is used to distinguish between this and "parentheses," for instance, which are specific elaborative or explanatory or expansion remarks added to a given text, which would otherwise still be complete without it. A container can thus denote a parenthesis, or not. In the example here, the container is used, it is argued, to direct the comment directly to one participant and not to others.

Category of Credibility Problem
"People categories" are the basic building blocks of discursive interaction, I would argue. Categories are used routinely in everyday talk and text: employee, boss, manager, father, teacher, team player, student, vacationer, wise man, person of doubtful credibility, and so on. The important thing about categories is that they come loaded with shared meaning. That is, within any given group of people, they will have a shared meaning of a commonly used category such as "housewife" or "doctor." Consequently, when a category is applied to a person or a person conjures a category for themselves, the key point is that what is known about that category is also known about that person. Moreover, categories come with entitlements—thus, the category of "doctor" consigns certain rights, knowledge, abilities, experiences, and thus entitlements to an individual who carries that category. Importantly, as David Silverman points out, categories can change over time and have different meanings in different cultures. Similarly, a speaker invokes a category of credibility problem when their discursive actions cast a doubt or question over a category that another speaker has scripted for themselves, or another speaker.

What is interesting about this formulation is the work that it achieves in terms of groups and membership. On the one hand, it is shown that E effectively downgrades C's contribution as insufficient, but on the other, he actively works to warrant membership of the elite in-group of KM experts. Is he constructing a new, rival group? It is suggested that what E is doing here is establishing what will become an in-group pattern in subsequent contributions: rivalry. In this instance, E conjures rivalry through ascribing a note of insufficiency to a previous contribution. Another way to construct the category of rivalry is through disagreement.

15.6 IN-GROUP RIVALRY

The next extract marks a display of some very complex actions with consequences serving as an example of the competitive rivalry that marks the in-group:

EXTRACT 5

155. K: You can get people to use the system, by ensuring that they
156. find knowledge that helps them
157. (and J, I am going to disagree with you I am afraid. It
158. should be more about knowledge seeking and re-use than about
159. knowledge sharing. No point in sharing if nobody is seeking, no
160. point in sharing if nobody re-uses)
161. J: I'd agree about the seeking but I've always thought of re-use as
162. part of sharing.
163. That said, the number of organisations that collect knowledge
164. but make no effort to encourage is re-use is legion!!

This extract is one of the few occurrences where participants directly address one another in a form of debate. The first part of K's claim (Lines 155/156) is clearly addressed to the forum in general, with the use of the second-person pronoun scripting what "you" can and (by default) cannot do, which works up this version as factual. Then, K formulates the entirety of his disagreement with J in a container of brackets, invoking the orality of an aside (Lines 157–160), framing it as being something that he prefers not to do (Line 157), thus scripting the category of politeness. As an aside, it is directed to J and only J, despite its environment of a public forum. Myers (1989) argues that such politeness devices are used to mitigate against face-threatening acts and that speakers generally attempt to avoid threats to their own face and that of others. By placing his disagreement in a container, he confines the face-saving work to only himself and J, thus minimizing it and avoiding the complexity of attempting to orient to the "face" of every single contributor. Other examples of managing potential face-threatening acts are shown in the exhibition stand meeting analysis in the previous chapter and in the analysis focusing on risk (Chapter 13). Here, the politeness device works to construct K's desire to agree with J, but in the event, he cannot. He then formulates a warrant for his disagreement stance with an elaboration of a set of affairs (Lines 158–160).

Face-Threatening Acts
A face-threatening act is an action that undermines, criticizes, bullies, or otherwise threatens the status, identity, stance, or position of one or more others. Or has the potential to do so. Greg Myers of the UK's University of Bradford studies the "pragmatics of politeness" in the context of scientific writing, noting how writers use both negative and positive politeness to mitigate against face-threatening acts. Actions of stake management and stake inoculation, for instance, are routinely used to ward off potential face-threatening acts from other speakers.

In doing this, K constructs a version (Willig, 2003) of KM that is at variance to that constructed earlier by J. In this case, the elaboration turn does not function as an insufficiency note but rather as an alternative formulation presented as practical, pragmatic, and beyond doubt: "should be …. No point ….no point." In particular, the invocation of "no point" (Lines 159/160) conjures J's contribution as having a potential credibility problem (Silverman, 2007), reflexively casting K himself as having more experience and expertise, with stronger entitlement to in-group membership—that is, positioning self as more trustworthy. Such "jockeying for influence" (Clifton, 2012b) is a frequent occurrence in the meeting analyses.

As a further point, all of these actions and devices not only script the speakers' positions but also, importantly, serve to display their tacit knowledge of the forum's social norms of politeness and respect for each other's positions. One can only speculate on what might have happened if one of these contributors had posted a comment *without* the delicate maneuvers such as those employed by K (for instance, "I am going to disagree with you I am afraid").

J initially indexes agreement with K but then conjures a disclaimer framed with an extreme case formulation (Abell and Stokoe, 2001): "... but I've always thought ..." (Line 161). This works to reposition the stance claimed in the first part of the talk with a contrasting new stance. Jonathan Potter and his coauthor (1987) speculate that such contrast structures can make speech messages more convincing, invoking trust and authenticity. The invocation of credibility problems comes in Lines 163/164 where J makes a claim to privileged knowledge (Willig, 2003), framed with a disclaimer, "That said ...," indexing his first stance in Line 161. J contrasts the practice of "seeking" (Line 163) with another extreme case formulation, "legion!!," marked with two exclamations to increase the "volume" of his rhetoric. This latter also underlines the validity status (authenticity) of his claims in his personal access to real data, which emphasizes the failure of "the number of organizations" to reuse knowledge, in direct contradiction to J's argument. Thus, the interaction between these two contributors is marked by claim and counterclaim, attending to the forum's social norms of politeness, but nonetheless choreographing a membership ranking rising from rivalry.

15.7 CONSENSUS PATTERNS

This is a commonplace pattern of accounting in the text (Charlebois, 2010): a participant indexes consensus agreement to the previous turn and then performs an elaboration, which serves both as an account for warranting in-group membership and conjures the insufficiency of previous contributions. In the understood sense of a "discussion" forum, this pattern is the nearest the participants get to in terms of achieving a discussion. This consensus pattern is well displayed in Extract 6:

EXTRACT 6

192. M: I also want to support K on the topic of incentives—people
193. should "do" good KM things because it makes sense in the
194. pursuit of a business objective, not because they are offered a
195. carrot or beaten with a stick.
196. As K said, that leads simply to gaming behavior.
197. The rewards should be mostly intrinsic, rather than extrinsic.

This is the last participant in the forum data. M scripts his support for K (Line 192) and then constructs an elaboration that warrants this support (Lines 193–195). But why does M display the need to provide justification for his support? An alternative analysis suggests that the elaboration component can be heard as scripting K's earlier contribution as being insufficient in that it requires more elaborate detail from M. M frames further consensus agreement with K in Line 196, accomplishing a confirmatory note. He then reflexively accomplishes two actions again in Line 197: he both scripts an elaboration of what "K said" and performs a warrant for his consensus agreement with K. But, again, one could interpret this as a note of insufficiency inherent in K's earlier contribution.

By scripting previous turns as less than adequate in the business of explicating KM, contributors position themselves as competitive to others—as "knowing more." In this way, participants are shown to employ stance-taking (Myers, 2010) or subject positions (Charlebois, 2010), which are wholly reliant on and contingent to the invocation of others' credibility problems (Silverman, 2007) in the endeavor of casting self as trusted expert and as the possessor of authentic knowledge. In other words, the stances scripted by many of the contributors are shown to be accomplished relationally to others, and by extension, knowledge is the outcome of such relational interactions. It stands to reason that one can only become authoritative and knowledgeable in the company of others, or, as Kenneth Gergen succinctly claims, "(O)one cannot be authentic alone" (2009: 41).

The importance of in-group construction linked to competitive rivalry has some synergies with group creative abrasion theory proposed by Dorothy Leonard and her colleague (2002). Abrasion theory proposes that innovation relies on groups comprising individuals with different skills, experiences, and knowledge creating a melting pot in which innovation can ignite. Through their group work, participants work collaboratively to provide a solution to A's questions while at the same time working up position credentials as expert with entitlement to be heard as such through the deployment of competitive rivalry devices—creative abrasion in action. Forum participants may not be in the business of generating innovation, but in the business of displaying expertise, interactional abrasion is shown as essential.

15.8 CLAIMS TO PRIVILEGED KNOWLEDGE

One of the most commonly displayed repertoires in the forum is the scripting of claims to privileged knowledge or, to use Jonathan Clifton's (2012b) term, "epistemic primacy." This is accomplished through various devices: listing, references to information "out there," use of metaphors, display of experience, use of parentheses, alignment with authority/leadership, and use of abbreviations for domain specific terminology. Arguably, these devices index more directly to the call to basics in their explicit and straightforward presentation. Two of these are explored here.

Repertoires
The notion of repertoires stems from the theory of social representations, in which it is theorized that people use "agreed codes for communication" where the extent to which these are shared between people will determine the level of mutual understanding. Consequently, people who share a repertoire are also likely to share the same group membership, for instance. Jonathan Potter and his coworker are, however, critical of this formulation in its suggestion of talk as a channel to people's inner mental thoughts. Instead, they propose

"interpretive repertoires," defined as "... recurrently used systems of terms used for characterizing and evaluating actions, events and other phenomena" (1987: 149).

15.8.1   Listing

Several contributors "do listing": this is a widely studied discursive strategy shown to bolster and/or display factuality (Edwards and Potter, 1992) and hence knowledgeableness: Extract 7 serves as an example. This is the third response to the questions posted by A, and its organization explicitly indexes the questions in its organization as "Objectives, Role, and Reach" (the first part of which is included here). The rhetorical pattern created by this structure of response *attempts* to script D as knowledgeable expert who can offer answers to such questions:

EXTRACT 7

11. D: Objectives: The main aim of KM is to simplify and improve the
12. process of creating, capturing, sharing, and distributing of knowledge
13. in a company. Implementing KM solutions helps making better
14. informed decisions, fewer errors, less reinventing of wheels
15. increased innovation, and responsiveness, improved products
16. services and profitability.

The listing evident in Lines 12, 14, 15, and 16 refers to process as well as outcomes. Rasmussen (2010) shows how listing, performed in this way, provides a warrant to be heard as more knowledgeable than others—that is, invoking claims to epistemic primacy (Clifton, 2012b) with its reflexive accomplishment of trust work. Here, listing functions as a display of practiced knowledge: it is constructive and ordered, serving as a "calling card." Listing is also a feature noted in the analysis of the meeting in Chapter 14 and in fact is seen in most of the other analytics chapters. Listing is particularly connected to scripting a position of authenticity with detail—or vivid accounting (Edwards and Potter, 1992)—bolstering the authenticity of claims. Additionally, the positive emphasis invoked by D ("... simplify and improve ..." and "better informed ... fewer .... Less ... increased ... improved ...") scripts KM as a beneficial practice, something worth doing, reflexively scripting D as an expert worth knowing, with connotations of reputation. What is missing from this text is any suggestion of interaction with others. The scripting intent, then, is clear, but is it as effective at constructing expert identity as the insufficiency–elaboration strategy? In this instance, one can only venture an opinion as the analyst, in the unfortunate absence of any direct or otherwise interaction with or from others. Perhaps this absence can be speculated to be the consequence of other contributors' assessing this particular posting as not worthy of response.

15.8.2   Metaphors

Metaphors are complex devices that depend on social discursive interaction for meaning and consequence: rooted in history and culture, they play a crucial role in discourse (Wee, 2005). In Extract 8, the use of metaphors arguably works to construct the category of expert through displaying the ability to draw analogies between a KM practice and something completely different, with overtones of sympathy toward A's difficulties. Extract 8 is the first actual response to A's questions. It is quite short and indicative of a response made at speed, perhaps in a bid to be seen as the first to formulate an answer:

EXTRACT 8

5. C: KM objective is to utilse [sic] distributed implicit and explicit knowledge
6. of people. The main role of the K manager is to employ methods to use
7. this knowledge. User adoption builds when benefits are visible and tangible.
8. Yes it is like herding cats or starting a mobile phone network, you
9. start small & build participants who see the benefits of adoption.

The two metaphors (Line 8) contain categories, which are particularly inference rich (Abell and Stokoe, 2001). The "yes" at the start of Line 8 functions as a both a receipt and a disclaimer for the difficulty of "doing" KM, with the advice given in Line 9 conjuring the mitigating circumstances. It indexes directly to A's frustration tone in invoking the difficulties of doing KM. The first metaphor (Line 8) constructs KM as requiring extreme skill and experience, functioning as an extreme case formulation (Abell and Stokoe). The indicated tone of orality (Montero et al., 2007) also serves to invoke sympathy with A's difficulties. The second metaphor is interesting in its variance from the first and its potential to be seen as a constructed source (Wee, 2005), but one that, on its own, would probably not function as metaphors are intended in its apparent obscurity. However, in the absence of any further explication by C, the first metaphor works to shine meaning on the second, implying that "starting a mobile phone network" is as hard as "herding cats." The consequence of this construction of KM scripts C as a KM expert, but one who is sympathetic to A's issues and who has the expertise to provide guidance. Note how this claim to privileged knowledge works interactionally with others (in this case, A) through its orality, unlike the listing in Extract 8. It also acknowledges the difficulties of KM, which is at variance to the issue-softening effect of discursive devices such as listing.

Orality
Specific to written text, "orality" is an interesting phenomenon in which people include in their texts words and phrases that would more generally be expected to be included in spoken discourse. That is, people use written text to "simulate" the spoken word. Bethan Benwell and her coworker propose that computer-mediated communication is influenced by such discursive devices. A study by Montero, Watts, and Garcia-Carbonell finds that orality is implicit in discussion forums. The question for the analyst is, then, why: what is the action of orality accomplishing that would not otherwise be accomplished if the writer adhered to accepted standards for written text?

15.9 PRELIMINARY REFLECTIONS

The analysis investigates how KM practitioners construct and manage position as expert in a public online forum as an enabler of knowledge sharing. Two principal strategies are revealed, the simpler of which is that of making claims to privileged knowledge—epistemic superiority. This strategy does not depend on interaction with others, and it is not necessarily relational, arguably limiting in its power to persuade, for instance. The more effective strategy involves group work around the four themes of in-group construction, positioning and membership, in-group rivalry, and consensus-elaboration. We also saw how, even within the group itself, participants script a form of hierarchy. What these strategic themes demonstrate is the fundamental variance in talk interaction. On the one hand, participants work collaboratively to invoke consensus with others (with only one instance of "polite" disagreement). But, on the other, this is invariably followed by an elaboration turn that effectively casts a question over the completeness and sufficiency of previous turns, while reflexively billposting the turn-maker as more knowledgeable. Expertise is shown to be consequential to rivalry, which has some consistency with Dorothy Leonard and her colleague's (2002) creative abrasion theory.

Similarly to the findings of the analyses in previous chapters, the forum actors are seen here to tacitly invoke categories of trust and trustworthiness and of authenticity and reputation connected to identity, all of which phenomena are shown to be worked up relationally. It can also be speculated that the *context* of the discussion forum as a public arena in which contributors are explicitly unknown to each other, with all of the attendant risks of engaging in discourse concerning what for many can be surmised to be their profession, is an influencing factor in the sequential organization. If Gülich (2003) is followed, identity is inevitably bound to context, and the meaning of a discourse depends on the context of its use (Wetherell, 2001). What is arguably shown is a clear relationship between thematic categories of identity and trust—perhaps in this instance, less so with risk—as contexts made live by speakers themselves.

Based on all of the preceding analytic chapters, including this one, it would seem logical to suggest that an analytical focus purely on what contexts speakers make live in their knowledge sharing discourse, with no particular thematic category in mind, would discover identity, trust, and risk work. It is to context that we turn to next.

FURTHER READING

Gülich, E. (2003). Conversational techniques in transferring knowledge between medical experts and non-experts. *Discourse Studies*, 5, (2): 235–263.

Leonard, D. and Sensiper, S. (2002). The role of tacit knowledge in group innovation. In Choo, C. and Bontis, N. (Eds). *The Strategic Management of Intellectual Capital and Organisational Knowledge*. Oxford: Oxford University Press.

Myers, G. (2010). Stance-taking and public discussion in blogs. *Critical discourse studies*, 7, (4): 263–275.

Otterbacher, J. (2011). Being heard in review communities: communication tactics and review prominence. *Journal of Computer-Mediated Communication*, 16, (3): 424–444.

Silverman, D. (2007). *A Very Short, Fairly Interesting and Reasonably Cheap Book About Qualitative Research*. London: Sage.

Stommel, W. and Koole, T. (2010). The online support group as a community: a micro-analysis of the interaction with a new member. *Discourse Studies*, 12, (3): 357–378.

16

ON MATTERS OF CONTEXT

16.1 THE IMPORTANCE OF CONTEXTUAL PARTICULARS

"Contextual particulars such as setting or behavioural environment are important because they are *perceived, experienced, attended to, understood*, and so on."

(Jonathan Potter, 1998b: 32: italics in original)

There is one feature of the notion of context that needs to be reiterated and made clear from the outset of this chapter. This has already been amply demonstrated in the previous discussions around trust, risk, and identity: that people invoke—script, construct, conjure, materialize, bring into being, whatever—contexts as live concerns in everyday talk and text in social interaction. So from this perspective while trust, risk, and identity can be explicitly expressed in descriptions and accounts for instance, they can also be displayed discursively as implicitly understood and constructed contexts. Recall the idea from Chapter 7 that tacit knowing is context driven with context understood as the actor's interpretation and understanding of their environment and its contents as a consequence of unconscious and automatic abstraction of information from that environment. It is not the environment and its contents that is, in all cases, that which influences the actors' actions but rather their interpretation of it— their sense-making. In the quotation from Jonathan Potter cited previously, he locates "setting or behavioral environment" *as a subset of* contextual particulars, with those particulars described as the product of perception, experience, attention, understanding, and so forth. That is, participants in any given environment act upon that environment, influenced by their often tacit understanding of contextual particulars. It is, in its simplest sense, a very circular affective action. Contextual particulars are the way in which individuals make sense of the world, and know how to act.

Knowledge and Discourse Matters: Relocating Knowledge Management's Sphere of Interest onto Language, First Edition. Lesley Crane.

Similar ideas can be seen in the following brief review of some of the perspectives on context that have already been encountered (see in particular Chapter 7), which provides some further useful background to the present analysis and discussions.

In the knowledge management (KM) field, Mark Thompson and his coworker describe context as comprising the shared meanings and experiences of an organization's members, as integral to knowledge. According to Haridimos Tsoukas, context is bound to knowing, which suggests that a strategy of removing context (which is the understood intention of some theoretical approaches to KM reviewed in Chapter 4) results in a meaningless state of affairs because context cannot be extracted. From Max Evans' perspective, context is embedded in shared language: "(S)since knowledge is highly contextual and circumstantial, it is always developed in a specific context and rarely interpreted by the receiver in exactly the same way as was intended by the transmitter" (2013: 1350038-5). This is also reminiscent of the ideas proposed by Dorothy Leonard, for instance. Paul Duguid, again with correspondence to these ideas, claims that human action is the product of both "knowing how" (tacit knowing) and "knowing that": "knowing how" is formulated as background context and facilitates and mediates "knowing that." In this version, the actor's "knowing how," as the tacitly known understanding and interpretation of the environment and its contents, influences action. This is equally reminiscent of Max Boisot's notion of knowledge sharing being dependent on degrees of resonance achieved between the repertoires of actors. Thus, shared understanding—sense-making—is essential to the sharing of knowledge.

From the discourse analysis perspective (while noting that "context" is the topic of some debate across the various different approaches, as touched on in Section 8.5), one proposal claims that context is integral to accounts of identity and stance-taking. Jonathan Potter proposes that context and cognition should be treated by the analyst in the same way—as phenomena formulated, worked up, constituted, and oriented to by speakers in interaction. From this perspective, cognition is context, which actually has correspondence with those ideas of context drawn from the KM field noted earlier. Moreover, all these perspectives can be interpreted as approaching context as the individual's interpretation of the world. Specifically, from the viewpoint of discursive psychology, it is the speaker's interpretation of the world and its contents which influences action, not the other way around.

In the previous chapters, we have investigated organizational discourse with a concern for the thematic categories of knowledge sharing. Trust, risk, and identity are shown to function corelationally in discourse as concerns made live by the speakers themselves. We have also claimed that these thematic constructs particularly influence the directions and scope of knowledge sharing actions. If, as claimed at the beginning of these discussions, these thematic constructs can be understood as contexts or contextual particulars constructed in discourse, then it follows that turning the analytic focus onto the question of what *contexts* speakers make live in their discourse in knowledge sharing meetings will bring those same themes to the fore. However, analysis should not second-guess findings so the question that the present chapter addresses is this: what *contexts* are invoked and how, in organizational meeting discourse, and with what effect on the trajectory of that discourse and knowledge sharing actions in particular?

Several meetings from both of the participating organizations are analyzed with findings organized into three principle categories: shared understanding, stance-taking, and historicity. The analysis reveals some intriguing insights and some surprising findings, which lend support to the findings in the previous analytic chapters.

16.2 DATA

Data are drawn from four meetings, three from Company A. The fourth, with Company B, is a meeting involving three participants, two males and one female; it is short (under 15 minutes) and concerned with developing proposals in response to a client's brief. Of the Company A meetings, one involves seven participants in a conference call (not all participants speak so the gender ratio is unknown), which is a regular weekly meeting of the company's project management team. The other two involve a different group of participants (unknown number) in two consecutive weekly, face-to-face senior management team meetings. In all four instances, participants are clearly familiar with one another, and all meetings can be categorized as "knowledge sharing" activities. Five extracts are included here.

16.3 SHARED UNDERSTANDING

In her analysis of the famous Princess Diana television interview for the BBC's Panorama show, Margaret Wetherell (2001) shows how, in discourse, all meaning is relational. An utterance comes into meaning in the light of others' understanding, which makes meaning-making a joint production. Recall how Paul Duguid makes a very similar point in his discussion of the importance of "knowing how": "(A)a tacit understanding of the ground rules for interpretation thus plays a role in grounding a particular interpretation of a text—a facet of interpretation that originates outside the text to be interpreted" (2005: 112). When a speaker makes an utterance (or a writer produces a text), it is the receiver (or reader) who displays and brings into being a version of its meaning, and thus, meaning does not solely exist in the utterance or text. Meaning is relational and accomplished in social interaction.

Recall also Max Boisot's (2002) notion of the action of knowledge sharing as contingent to degrees of resonance accomplished between the repertoires of speakers. Looking beyond the veneer of the contents of discourse, it is the constructed-in-talk context that drives that meaning. A good example of the functional accomplishment of invoked context can be seen in the University of California's Pamela Hobb's (2003) study of a defense lawyer's courtroom talk, showing how she uses an American vernacular to invoke group membership and shared identity with the jury members. It is not *what* the lawyer said, but *how* she said it that works to conjure shared context—shared understanding. Although there is a caveat to add to this: in reality, one can only conjecture a sense of shared context between lawyer and jury members, as there is no corroborating account from the jury members themselves.

Drawing on two of the meeting recordings, the analysis shows how members use different discursive resources to invoke shared understanding or "common context" (e.g., Boisot's shared repertoires). Two are considered here in detail: the "collaborative continuer" and "gisting and elaboration."

The simplest and probably most commonly used resource is the "collaborative continuer" in which one speaker finishes the sentence of another, which is described as displaying knowledge of what is on another's mind (Clifton, 2012b). We have all commonly experienced this: someone says something, and you know, or think you do in a kind of automatic and tacitly accomplished assessment, what is coming next. It is irrelevant to our purposes here whether the action of scripting a collaborative continuer is influenced by some sort of assessment before the fact. The point is that speakers display shared context and collaborative engagement (Drew, 2003b) through explicit displays of knowing what is on another's mind—that is, what another is about to say. Extract 1 comes some 10 minutes into the meeting. Throughout, Andy and Peter (the same Peter as in Chapter 14) have worked up collaborative continuers as a frequently recurring pattern of their talk, which has the effect of limiting contributions from the third member.

Collaborative Continuer
This is the phrase used by Jonathan Clifton to describe the action by one speaker stepping in to complete a turn initiated but not yet completed by another. It is used in cases where the second speaker not only completes the other's turn, but also scripts a compatible or consistent completion phrase. In this way, speakers are said to display knowledge on what is on each others' minds.

16.3.1   Displaying Knowing What's on Others' Minds

EXTRACT 1   130320_004 COMPANY B (A = ANDY, P = PETER, C = CINDY)

200. A:... certainly in the central government an' an'
201. an' the police space and I hope the justice
202. space whereas (.) <u>it ↑works</u>] it's delivering what they need to ↓do=
203. P: [hmm]
204. C:=yep
205. A: let's let's plan on it] and make sure it ↑works=
206. C: [()]
207. P: = [*noise of agreement*]
208. A: um we're seeing it from the [*Government Agency*], we're seeing it from
209. the [*Government Department*], [*names*] did it through their (.)
210. managed service before someone's gonna bite on it an' ↑°we can
211. make it work°
212. P: Yeah. An' have the experience to ↑do it.
213. (2)
214. C: [*name*] wants to meet with you next Wednesday.
215. (3)
216. P: Are you paying attention to our meeting (.) [*name*]?
217. C: I can multitask I'm female.
218. P: .hhh so no

The imperative to work collaboratively and consensually can be seen in Line 205 with the repeat of the inclusion pronoun "let's" (Abell and Stokoe, 2001) followed by a call to action ("make sure it works"), which scripts group responsibility. Cindy (the "Chair" in Chapter 13) and Peter both issue affirmative tokens invoking agreement (Clifton, 2012; Edwards and Potter, 1992).

An interesting variation of the standard collaborative continuer can be seen in Line 212. Peter's turn does not explicitly work to complete Andy's sentence, rather it completes the listing work that Andy has begun. The pattern for this action is established in Lines 208–210 in which Andy produces his first three-part list. As we have seen in previous analyses, this is a device that has been shown to be a particularly effective rhetorical device in doing persuasion (Chilton, 2004; Edwards and Potter, 1992)—which is probably why politicians use it a lot. So, here, we have (1) "we're seeing it from the [*government agency*]," (2) "we're seeing it from the [*Government Department*]," and (3) "[*names*] did it through their managed service." This is followed immediately by the start of what looks like another three-part list started in Line 210: (1) "someone's gonna bite"; (2) "we can make it work." It is to this that Peter adds the continuer (Line 212: "An' have the experience"), in a direct display of knowing where his colleague is going, with its suggestion of a frequently produced "mantra." Peter's utterance is a variation on the standard collaborative continuer in that it does not just continue what Andy has started, but also serves to complete it, with the further suggestion of this being the final element in the "mantra" with its appeal to reputation. It almost serves as a *topic* completer.

In this way, Andy and Peter work collaboratively to build a case framed in a context of persuasion, thus displaying "being a team" (Clifton, 2012b). (As shown in Chapter 12, persuasion is connected to "trust.") This raises a question: who is the persuasion aimed at? Clearly, not at each other and clearly, not at the third meeting participant (as will be shown momentarily). There is a suggestion of a "rehearsal" of a case that will be given elsewhere, and this could be seen as a characteristic of "proposal talk." What happens next is intriguing.

The silence, coming just after Peter's "mantra" completer, in Line 213 suggests that the two men's business is done. In their study of workplace meetings, Cecilia Ford and her coworker (2012) demonstrate how transition from one speaker to another is a highly collaborative interaction, which is closely monitored and managed. Here, Cindy displays her understanding of the silence (and possibly the "mantra completer") as being topic closure in claiming rights to issue a new topic (Line 214). The subsequent three-second silence conjures a problem in the making. Paul Drew (2003b), for instance, suggests that even a one-second delay in responding to a speaker indicates "troubles in interaction."

Peter's eventual utterance could be interpreted in one of two ways: either he indexes the previous business as *incomplete*, or he orients to Cindy's choice of next topic as inappropriate to the here and now and/or her not possessing rights to issue a new topic. Both interpretations mark Cindy's position as located outside the work of the "shared context" group. Thus, she is side-lined from the group. Arguably, this is the interpretation that Cindy orients to in invoking a warrant in Line 217 ("I can multitask I'm female"), with the latter part of the construction reflexively indexing the inability of "males" to multitask. In other words, Cindy works up her own membership of the group "female," which has abilities that are beyond that of the group "male" to which the other two members belong. It would be a simple matter to interpret these exchanges as being concerned with gender— it is, after all, Cindy who explicitly introduces the category "female." However, in contrast, the analysis here suggests that this is more concerned with group membership, with one group (females who can multitask) being scripted as better than the other (males who cannot), which effectively works up a display of lack of interest—or perhaps not lack of interest, more lack of being impressed, by the work of the "shared context" group.

Peter's turn works up a "skeptical rejoinder" (Hutchby, 2011), scripting rejection of Cindy's claims. So, in this case, while Andy and Peter are shown to display mutual teamwork and collaborative engagement in a shared understanding of context, with Cindy effectively excluded, Cindy displays her understanding of this version of affairs through the conjuring of a competing group. Shared context, then, can be a contested enterprise raising issues of stake and interest. Note also how the collaborative continuer and "doing being team" work by Peter and Andy have effectively exiled Cindy from the knowledge-sharing actions.

16.3.2 Gisting and Elaboration

The second extract comes from Company A's project manager meeting which is managed by the Chair (Stuart) and who has an agenda. The extract comes some three-fourth of the way into the meeting (unnecessary elaborative lines are excluded here for brevity). The extract concerns a complaint made by another team in the business (Team Z) and which has been brought to his attention.

Just prior to this extract, Stuart has introduced the complaint topic to the meeting which he does with a display of considerable discomfort: project managers are requesting Team Z's help in using a computer software package which is interfering with their busy schedule. After much hedging, he finally spells out his request: "Has anybody been

---

EXTRACT 2   130521_003 COMPANY A

215. Stuart: … is that why you've been asking those kinds of questions?
216. Dorothy: ↑Um well it was trying to get um ( ) ↓and so trying to work out
217. the process of how you do that and who you go to cos it just seemed
218. like Team Z are jus- kind of like playing me around back and forth to
219. each other but (.) now it makes sense who who to go to
220. Mark: I mean I I can back that up as well um because (.) from my point of view
221. I've got to build a new <u>theme</u> not me personally, but I I need t::o em build
222. a new theme into [*software package*]…

… [*approx. 10 lines omitted—all Mark*]

231. Mark: …so ↑I had this question ↑<u>previously</u> um, a::nd I didn't quite get
232. the clear answers from Team Z; it was like we::ll it's a bit more complicated
233. and s-so on and so forth…

… [*approx. 5 lines omitted—all Mark*]

238. Mark: …but ↑<u>internally</u> we need
239. to know what the what the ( ) is what is at stake when you say uh we need to
240. change the particular <u>theme</u> for uh for a client (.) as in <u>my</u> case
241. Stuart: OK that that's helped a lot actually e::m so yes thank you thank
242. you, Dorothy, thank you, Mark, that's um that's helped me understand where
243. you're coming from, and I can <u>see</u> and I I can ↑answer the ( ) that
244. that <u>pain</u> of being (.) passed from one desk to another and then slightly feeling
245. apologetic about going an' knocking on somebody's door and and asking
246. the question and them them saying oh no that's not me an' you know I've
247. been there too s::o I I I can I can totally see um what you're saying but
248. that's great thank you.

building any apps in [*software package*]"? As a mark for the discomfort which Stuart displays over this matter, note how he does not ask who has been making requests to Team Z, but rather who has been using the software. So, at the outset, Stuart invokes a context of discomfort, unease, and difficulty—but who is this targeted at, his meeting members or Team Z? In response to his question, Dorothy metaphorically raises her hand. Stuart presses her with several questions, trying to get to the bottom of the matter, before resorting to a more targeted question (Line 215).

In contrast to his earlier question, Stuart now overtly indexes to the reported problem— the asking of questions. Dorothy orients to this as constituting an "accusatory why question," which is loaded (Rautajoki, 2012): that is, she displays her understanding of the question being loaded with consequence depending on what answer she gives, which can be seen in the hesitation in her response and repeated account of "trying to" (Line 216). Her display of understanding of the invocation of discomfort, as well as the loaded nature of the question, can also be seen in how she serves a warrant for her actions with mitigating circumstances (Abell and Stokoe, 2001). In this way she displays her knowledge of her stake being at risk of potentially negative consequences which renders it accountable (Silverman, 2007) and subject to blame. What this is all concerned with then is where blame should be attributed. Difficulties are further worked up in Lines 217–219 in scripting Team Z as "…kind of like playing me around…," attributing Team Z with the characteristic of time-wasting and as the candidate target for blame.

Accusatory-why Question
This is a type of question which places a speaker in the position of being compelled to answer a specific question which is "loaded." In other words, it is the sort of question which demands a warrant or explanation, making this conditional.

While Dorothy concludes her account on a positive note, in now knowing who to go to, it is her *prior* account of difficulties that Mark indexes with his affiliating (Clifton, 2014) evidence ("I mean I I can back that up as well": Line 220). He launches an elaborate description of his experiences with Team Z, working up a position as eyewitness (Hutchby, 2001). Ian Hutchby's analysis of radio talk shows reliably demonstrates how first-hand knowledge, such as eyewitness accounts, work up authenticity of experience with entitlement to formulate opinion as a legitimate raconteur. The upshot is given in Lines 231–233: he was also not given clear answers. The two eyewitness accounts are thus heard as working up consensus and corroboration that mutually attest to the factuality of versions (Edwards and Potter, 1992). So, here, Mark's elaboration account serves to inoculate mutual stake and interest from potential criticism and bias, for instance. This constitutes his turn as also orienting to the "loaded nature" of Stuart's question.

Mark concludes his lengthy account with a warrant for his actions, reflexively constructing Team Z as unforthcoming with knowledge (Lines 238–140). A shared context of dissatisfaction with between team support is thus invoked, with procedural consequentiality (Potter, 1998b). That is, the invoked "contextual particulars," to use Potter's terms, have effects on the progress, structure, direction, and so forth of subsequent talk. Accordingly, the mutually invoked context by Mark and Dorothy is designed to have a particular effect on subsequent discursive directions.

The relief displayed by Stuart is clearly evident. For instance, in receipting the two accounts given, he simultaneously scripts evaluation ("… helped a lot": Line 241) which starts the business of working up exoneration from any wrongdoing. It can also be speculated that what he is displaying here is the source of his earlier discomfort: that is, his being placed in the position of potentially having to attribute blame to his team members as a consequence of the actions of another team. He follows this with a "gist account" summing up the talk so far (Clifton, 2006, 2014). Gist accounting is shown to *fix the meaning* of prior talk, inoculating it from any other version, and which is a particular formulation of leadership. He prefaces this with affiliation ("... helped me understand...": Line 242) with the previous speakers (Clifton, 2014) conjuring consensus with a warrant for truth (Edwards and Potter, 1992). This has the effect of issuing instructions concerning how his subsequent gist account is to be understood: as an authentic and incontestable account of affairs.

Gist Accounting
Gist accounting provides a summary of the sense of prior talk (as contrasted with an "upshot" which scripts the consequences of previous talk). In his essay on The case of leadership, *Jonathan Clifton describes this as a "formulation of leadership" in that gist accounting can be used to "fix the meaning" of the talk so far, thus preventing the potential for other perspectives or meanings to emerge. Consequently, gist accounting can be viewed as a positive resource for speakers in summarising "the case so far" which might mediate the onward progression of discussions, or it can be seen as a rhetorical stumbling block to the emergence of further ideas and perspectives.*

The gisting work in Lines 244–247 upgrades the prior reports (Rasmussen, 2010) made by the other two speakers in his scripting of experiences as "painful." He expands the context of "dissatisfaction" by introducing the emotional response, "slightly apologetic" (Lines 244/245). The final flourish is his invocation of himself as a witness ("... I've been there too": Lines 246/247) with first-hand knowledge and therefore authenticity of experience. This can be heard in marked contrast to Stuart's earlier difficulties and hesitancies in raising Team Z's complaint. Consequently, Stuart is doing more than summing up prior talk: he is adding to its authenticity with his own first-hand knowledge, and thus its truth is made impeccable and trustworthy. As shown in Chapter 12, matters of authenticity and truth are bound to trust.

In the follow-on talk, both Dorothy and Mark volunteer turns in which they spin *positive accounts* of Team Z, indexing a sense of fair balance. It is suggested that this volunteered additional information, which turns out to be important to the team, is "released" by Stuart's actions in exonerating all blame from his team members. In Chapter 12 on Trust, we see an almost identical set of affairs (Extract 6) in which the meeting leader's removal of blame from another speaker results in the latter becoming more willing to share knowledge than in previous extracts from the Company B meeting. What has also been displayed is strong between team rivalry, combined with equally strong intrateam loyalty—within the same business—which is likely to have considerable impact on knowledge sharing within the organization as a whole.

In these extracts, working up shared understanding of context has resulted in important knowledge being shared, with participants shown to work collaboratively to accomplish consensus. It would also be a reasonable assessment to propose that contextual particulars of trust, risk and identity are implicit to these actions. In the following discussion, participants are shown to engage in a very different kind of contextual talk.

16.4   STANCE-TAKING

In the next extracts, matters of stake and interest are brought to the fore in a constructed context of competing claims. What emerges is a highly complex mesh of connected psychological phenomena at work conjuring a live context of attribution of blame and a discourse of "them and us" as a form of identity work. The analysis further connects these themes to frustration and disagreement, reputation and risk.

16.4.1   Invoking the Context of Courtroom

Extract 3 comes from the first of the two senior management meetings (Company A). John (the same as in Chapter 13) has just arrived late to the meeting (around 30 minutes into a 90 minute meeting). The extract is drawn from an extended argument between John

---

EXTRACT 3   VN550143 COMPANY A

1. Roger: … ↑OK well in summary without me me trying to keep very calm
2. at this point .hhh we had that [*name*] job that was sold yest]erday
3. John: [mmm]
4. Roger: which was great you know [*contract value*] new project <u>new</u> client in
5. [*name*] .hhh the ummm I'll try not to exaggerate but the <u>proposal</u> went out
6. the presentation was done without <u>anybody</u> seeing the budget (.) schedule (.)
7. design (.) technology
8. John: OK is that entirely true?
9. (1)
10. John: <u>Is</u> that entirely ↓true=
11. Roger: =Well]nobody saw the budget
12. John: [(   )]yeah
13. Roger: Nobody <u>saw</u> the [*reading*] technical solution (.) certainly nobody
14. saw the schedule
15. (1)
16. Roger: unless you know /you think otherwise] (   )
17. John: [No I I I'd just seen a couple of
18. emails passed between Tom and Jim where ah
19. (1)
20. John: Jim outlined how he'd got to the point where he'd got he did say he'd
21. not passed the budget through up here but he said that he'd worked
22. through the budget with [*name—said slowly as if reading the name*]
23. Roger: Well it was using a (.) spreadsheet that was is isn't (.) umm <u>released</u>
24. I understand the [*project type*] one was done two months ago (.) but=
25. John: =OK we'll talk about this specifically () we all know there is a big issue
26. where [*project type*] is concerned and I <u>think</u> Jim went through what he
27. <u>thought</u> was (   )]
28. Roger: [Be↑cause we all know there was a big issue where [*project type*]
29. was concerned the <u>dangers</u> of saying we can do something for [*contract value*]
30. (.) in two months making assumptions like that are ( )=.

and Roger (also note that the "Jim" referred to is the "Chair" from Extract 1, Chapter 13), which is initiated by an accusation brought by Roger. Just prior to this, Roger has raised an issue, which he intends to talk to John about "probably outside of this meeting," as it is "very specific." John reformulates this, activating it as a valid topic for the present meeting discussion: "Is it specific to the people that you see?" Does he want an audience, or does he want witnesses? Arguably, he knows what is coming.

The dispute centers on a project proposal/presentation given to a new client by a member of John's team (Jim), which the client has accepted. The sequential unfolding is patterned by claim and counterclaim, with reputation as a contextual undercurrent allied to matters of stake and interest (Edwards and Potter, 2005). The key claim made by Roger is that nobody saw any part of the proposal/presentation (Lines 5–7) before being given to the client. This is forcibly repeated in Lines 11 and 13, working up an extreme case formulation ("nobody"), a device which is characteristic of argumentative discourse (Hutchby, 2011). The upshot is that Jim's actions are formulated as wrong and contrary to the organization's interests, with implications of risk to reputation. John's counter-claim is that Jim *did* show the budget to someone, thus rendering Roger's claim to be false. The extract can be heard as conjuring a context of courtroom drama where members adopt stances of prosecutor (Roger) and defense (John). Both speakers orient to "the truth of what really happened" (Edwards and Potter, 1992) but, unlike courtroom cross-examination, their concerns are less with "memory" of events and more with the truth of where the blame lies. The stakes are high with Roger making explicit reference to "dangers" (Line 29). How does this play out?

Roger prefaces his account of the problem by scripting its seriousness: he is trying to "keep very calm" (Line 1), reflexively displaying possession of rights to the exact opposite—explosion and panic—and to avoid exaggeration (Line 5), which scripts matters as alarming enough without being embellished. Sandwiched in the middle, he sets out a context ("that job that was sold": Line 3), which he positively evaluates ("great," "new project new client": Line 4). So, he invokes an emotional cognitive state followed by an objective evaluation, which can serve to "do persuasion" (Wiggins and Potter, 2003), and then he upgrades the ante (Schegloff, 1997) in invoking rights to be alarmed. These actions frame his claim as "loaded." This is high drama invoking the displayed contexts of attribution of blame, with prospective consequences for reputation. Thus, an explanation is made conditional (Clifton, 2012b), with the suggestion that Roger himself may be called to answer the case to others further up the hierarchical ladder.

Epistemic Doubt Marker
Utterances such as "I think" and "I don't know," in the sense of referencing what one knows, can be understood as scripting uncertainty, as a device to manage stake and interest, and as a means of deflecting potential criticism. However, phrases such as "I dunno" can also be analyzed as a display of concern for the feelings and beliefs of others, for instance, and not necessarily cognitive uncertainty. Hence, the importance of attending to the context invoked by the speaker, and in particular the context oriented to by other speakers. In other words, in determining how such phrase fragments can be understood by the analyst, and consequently what actions speakers are engaged in, the question to ask is: how and what meaning do speakers share?

John's repeat turns (Lines 8 and 10) index Roger's prior turn as attributing blame, which makes them the subject of defense. This initiates the business of claim and counterclaim, invoking courtroom rhetoric. He explicitly calls for an account of truth working up an epistemic doubt marker (Wooffitt and Allistone, 2008) calling trust and authenticity into question, and reflexively indexing to possession of mitigating facts. His questioning of what is "entirely true" scripts matters as needing to be *entirely* true or not true at all. Thus, Roger's subsequent turn is also made conditionally relevant (Clifton, 2012b), prompting him to repeat his claim. Similarly to Lines 5–7, Roger does listing— this time as a clear three-part list—working up the factuality of his claim (Lines 11–14). In their analysis, Derek Edwards and his coworker (1992) show how three-part listing is rhetorically important in environments such as courtrooms, which adds to the sense of a courtroom drama unfolding. This can also be seen as an unmitigated display of rights to knowledge—these are the facts, and they are "out there" for anyone to see (Clifton), working up their status as undeniably authentic and trustworthy. Thus, Roger invokes epistemic primacy (Clifton), indexing John's concern with the entire truth. Truth and blame are thus made live within the context of "courtroom."

Up to this point (Line 15), both speakers display their knowledge of the facts "as out there," which are put in motion to warrant the direction of blame attribution. That is, they attempt to use their respective knowledge of the facts of the matter as the evidence of what actually happened, and consequently whether this or that person should be blamed. This is precisely what Robin Wooffitt (2005) advises cannot work as a strategy for dispute resolution: in such disputes, it is precisely the facts that are called into question, and consequently an appeal to facts as a means of resolving the dispute or persuading the other to one's point of view will be ineffectual. Or at least, ineffectual where both speakers (in this case) are equal within the given social group in which the dispute occurs. Roger apparently orients to this understanding of the context as it is developing.

The pause between Roger's repeated claim and his take up of a next turn suggests that he expects a response from John at this point, which the latter declines to give. In his subsequent turn, Roger's repair from what John "knows" to what he "thinks" (Line 16) opens the possibilities not just to what John knows but also to what he *thinks* he knows, casting doubt over John's possession of objective facts: thus, John is scripted as having personal stake and interest in these accounts (Edwards and Potter, 1992). So, while his previous turns served the accusation, here, Roger issues a call for witness account but which is already painted as subjective. The dispute is thus made more personal.

John interrupts his colleague to construct his version of events. The pause in Line 19 suggests reading from papers he has to hand (perhaps the emails referred to in Line 18) implying that his evidence is drawn, not from memory recall, but rather from written material which scripts concerns with authenticity and objective factual accounting. This is further implied in how John states the name of the person who has "worked through the budget" with Jim—slowly and carefully as if reading from documented evidence. So, while John makes a concession that Jim did not pass the budget "through up here" (presumably to head office), the "but" marks the end of the concessionary material signaling that what follows is in opposition to this (Wood and Kroger, 2000): Jim did show it to *someone*, and consequently Roger's claim that "nobody" saw the budget is false. This is the kind of logical accounting that one would expect in a courtroom (see, for instance, Abigail Locke and Derek Edwards', 2003, discursive study of (then) President Clinton's Grand Jury Testimony). Both orient to evidence and witnesses.

In formulating his defense, John ignores reference to the other elements of the proposal made explicit by Roger: the "schedule, design, and technology" as not being seen by anybody. He has moved the argument's focus solely onto the topic of "budget." This is an effective rhetorical strategy: in limiting the scope of the argument, it is more easily pulled apart. In response to Roger's "factual accounting of accusation," John adopts a stance, which manages stake and interest by doing objective accounting, building an alternative version of accounts, which works simultaneously to undermine Roger's (Edwards and Potter, 2005).

Roger orients to his accusatory claim having been undermined by introducing new evidence—"spreadsheet" (Line 23)—prefaced by "well": Linda Wood and her colleague (2000) suggest that this conversation particle scripts previous accounts as insufficient, while Derek Edwards and his coworker (1992) suggest that it signals a "dispreferred response" on the way. With his initial claim undermined, it is proposed that here this particle scripts what comes next is a "weak argument," with the slight pause and "umm" (Line 23) conjuring a metaphorical "scrapping of barrels." Like any effective defense lawyer, John pounces on this weakness: "OK we'll talk about this specifically ..." (Line 25), displaying the same argument-limiting tactic used earlier. He then invokes witnesses ("we all know"): "... a major way of warranting the factuality of a version is to depict it as agreed across witnesses ..." (Edwards and Potter: 163). Thus, John works up consensus and corroboration. The interruptive response by Roger transforms this witness call into a warrant for concerns with "dangers" (Lines 28/29).

The to and fro of argumentative rhetoric continues for several more minutes, with other members joining in, and increasingly includes detailed displays of "what actually happened" and mitigation. The upshot comes in Extract 4.

Conversation Particle
Conversation particles come in many shapes and sizes, but are generally of a monosyllabic structure, and serve some purpose in the on-going conversation sequences. For instance, "oh" can denote a change of the speaker's current state of knowledge.

Dispreferred Response
This refers to a response that one speaker is not expecting nor wanting to hear from another. The conversation scrap "well" is often used by a speaker to signal their knowledge that what they are about to utter will be received by the listener as being dispreferred. Similarly, a "dispreferred structure" refers to a rhetorical structure such as "yes ... but ...."

16.4.2 Doing "them and us"

EXTRACT 4   VN550143 COMPANY A

150. John: I'll tell you what is inflaming=
151. Roger: =yeah=
152. John: =and this has come from Tom this morning (.) how ↑utterly
153. pissed off he is (.) that (.) <u>no-one</u> nobody in this organization is
154. remotely happy (.) that we've won a new piece of ↑work=
155. Roger: =↓We're very very hap]py
156. John: [well they need to communicate that

157. a little bit=
158. Roger: =Well we will sit y'know this is gre↓at and then I've got two
159. days to find a whole team pull everyone off everything else to
160. to do it! Of course, I think it's brilliant but I said similarly (.) John
161. (.)
162. Roger: Where did the budget come from he's the one who had
163. to (.) be under 50 so (.) it's 48

In this extract, coming toward the end of the argument, John effectively reverses the earlier prosecutor–defense stances, by issuing a claim to epistemic primacy (Clifton, 2012b: Line 150), which prefaces a new accusatory claim, simultaneously reversing the direction of attribution. This claim is even more "inflaming" than the previously conjured risks and dangers for the business. His secondary preface conjures a witness report—Tom's phone call this morning—as reported speech, shown to work up the factuality and authenticity of versions (Wood and Kroger, 2000), and is also a classic stake management/inoculation tactic (Edwards and Potter, 2005). Thus, John is able to use "inflammatory" language ("utterly pissed off": Lines 152/153) without fear of criticism: he is simply reporting another's words. The accusation that nobody is happy "that we've won a new piece of work" (Line 154) sets in motion a new context of them and us. Winning contracts is precisely what he and his team are employed to do. Thus, "this organization" is scripted as irrational and flawed in not welcoming success. It is further speculated that John has pressed for the client/proposal meeting topic (discussed at the outset of this analysis) precisely in order to raise this "inflaming" state of affairs. It also raises the question of why the firm should be troubled with newly won contracts, which reappears in Extract 5.

The context of "them and us" emerges interactionally across Lines 154–160. Indexing to John's reflexive scripting of organizational unhappiness with its connotations of irrationality, Roger formulates the opposite ("we're very very happy"), marking this as extreme. Jonathan Clifton (2006) notes that extreme case formulations can leave a speaker open to disagreement in that all that is required is one exception to the case. Arguably, this is what John indexes with his overlapping interruption of preferred organizational action: "what *they* need to communicate" (Line 156). In referring to "they," John makes explicit his stance apart from the organization: on one side of the line, he and his team, successful at winning contracts, with intact reputation; on the other, the organization, irrational, which cannot communicate, and is thus conjured as having "the problem."

Roger orients to this serious turn of context with what can be heard as a conciliatory message ("well we will sit...,": Line 158). This is quickly discarded and replaced with the formulation "y'know." Elsewhere, this is shown to work up collaborative consensus, but here it works with "gre↓at" (Line 158) to script a skeptical rejoinder (Hutchby, 2011). The subsequent "spelled out" consequence of winning the new contract is invoked as extreme ("whole team... everyone off everything else": Line 159) and coated in irony ("Of course, I think it's brilliant": Line 160). Because of the actions of John's team, extreme measures will need to be taken by others, with his own earlier avowal of organizational "happiness" rendered as ironic. The organization cannot be both happy and having to take extreme measures. The teams *he* refers to will be extremely disrupted because of the actions of John's team: "them and us" is consequently capitalized.

While it is argued that both speakers arrive at a point of mutually shared context of "unhappiness" and "organizational schism," they clearly do so from conflicting perspectives—thus, this context is contested. Frustration is brought to the fore through disagreement. Having made this point, Roger returns the rhetorical trajectory back to the matter at hand (the troubling budget, Lines 162/163), thus "doing" authority (Clifton, 2006). This can be nicely contrasted with Stuart's hesitancy over delivering the precise nature of the problem complaint to his team meeting in Extract 2: Jonathan Potter and his coworker's (2010) study of governance rules in an institutional meeting suggests that such hesitancy and informality scripts, in their case, the governance rules as *not* to be heard as authoritarian and impersonal. Here, Roger is unproblematically setting the agenda and scripting himself as not yet being satisfied with the answers he has been given.

What has started out as an issue over a proposal/presentation with concerns for truth and blame has transformed into conflicting contexts of organization, and a clear demarcation between them and us: recall Pamela Hobb's (2003) study of courtroom rhetoric with a focus on conjuring opposing groups—them and us. Two further points: (1) no-one questions the consequential link between proposals/presentations unseen by others and risks/dangers to the organization, and (2) no-one questions or requests clarification on the nature of those risks. It can therefore be construed that such knowledge is already tacitly understood and known by meeting members.

In the final extract, further and related debate unfolds, but in a very different way.

16.5 DOING HISTORICITY

Extract 5 is drawn from the following week's senior management team meeting. As background, the previous week's meeting makes an explicit reference to a "big message" concerning resources and capacity, which needs to be conveyed to the organization's board of directors.

EXTRACT 5   VN550144 COMPANY A

1. Roger: The I ↑think I don't know this but I think there are several reasons
2. ↓wh::y we might slow something down (.) historically one would be the
3. technology isn't quite ready (.) something like [*client name*] we weren't
4. we-we slowed that down because we wanted to use [*software package*] and
5. it wasn't ready and so on and so on (.) make decisions
6. John: [*sniff*]Could have used something else
7. (.)
8. Roger: Could've.
9. (1)
10. Alan: I don't know that that's the ↑actual reason why we °slowed that down°
11. (1)
12. Roger: We held off for a while yeah uh I dunno ummm another one
13. might be that .hhh we <u>are</u> trying to use our (.) our own resources and not
14. get new people in so push out (.) tha- earlier in the year °definitely

---

15. don't know°

... [16 lines excluded]

33. Alan: ... So (.) It begins with (.) PMs=
34. Ted:=mm]mm
35. Alan: [being fast to react=
36. Roger: =yeah=
37. Alan: =and then us having the (.) necessary people in but ↑if we <u>DO</u> that
38. the benefit t::o our ↑numbers is the ↑revenue comes in faster=
39. Roger: =mm]m
40. Vicky: [It's that is <u>all</u> theoretically I kno::w I can remember when you first tried
41. to ramp up the freelancers and looked at it=
42. Ted: =mmmm=
43. Vicky: = that four clients were delayed=
44. Ted: =Yup=
45. Vicky: =so we ↑can't control that....

The issue under discussion is why start-up on new contracts is sometimes "slowed down." The organization employs a full-time staff of developers/designers, supplemented by hiring "freelancers." The primary shared context invoked here is "history," with recollection of what has happened in the past in the search for reasons. But, arguably, there is a further tacitly understood context made live by the speakers, and which relates to frustration–disagreement and power. The hint of these can be seen in the first three rhetorical transactions.

Across Lines 1–5, Roger speculates a reason for the deliberate actions of slowing "something" down invoking historically located knowledge of technology not "quite ready." The invocation of historical events has the effect of limiting potential contributions from speakers to those who have direct knowledge of the events: it thus works as a "tacit form of addressing" (Svennevig, 2012b). There are two features about his utterance which are relevant: first, he works to mitigate against criticism or disagreement with stake inoculation work ("I think," "I don't know": Edwards and Potter, 1992), orienting to the potentially contentious or problematic nature of his speculation, but he then invokes historical "fact" ("something like [*client name*] we weren't we slowed...": Lines 3/4) as a warrant for his stance. Second, he neatly attributes blame for "slowing down" to the technology, which reflexively deflects attribution from the team. Note also the scripting of "and so on and so on" (Line 5), which attempts to establish shared knowledge (Potter, 1998a), with its assumption that recipients will "fill in the blanks," marking his account as authentic. His disconnected reference to "make decisions" is curious: he does not use the past tense, inferring that the decisions that affected the client's project (Line 3) are still being made.

John indexes these "decisions" (Line 6), effectively reformulating (Chilton, 2004) Roger's historical version and reflexively scripting self as eyewitness with consequential claims to knowledge. In doing so, he tacitly displays his knowledge as being relevant and appropriate and actioned within the boundaries of Roger's earlier "tacit addressing." He redistributes blame to "the decision-maker" by activating an alternative strategy— choosing a different technology—implying that knowingly opting for a technology that was not ready was/is misguided.

Roger, after a brief silence, corroborates his colleague's version with a matching phrase ("could've": Line 8). There is a sense of an "uncomfortable truth" lurking here. No one asks why such a decision was made, knowing that technology was not ready, and no one refers to who took that decision. Alan's utterance in Line 10 arguably works to close down this nebulous, "between the lines" talk by scripting doubt over Roger's version, implying a directional change is needed with the quietly spoken "slowed that down" marking the current trajectory as problematic.

Roger self-selects with a following turn in which he accounts for other reasons. The key points to notice are the hesitancy, repeat of doubt markers (Wooffitt, 2007, "I dunno": Line 12, and "definitely don't know": Lines 14–15), and repair in Line 14. This is in considerable contrast to this speaker's measured speech patterns in the earlier meeting talk (Extract 3). Roger can be heard as orienting to concerns with authenticity and stake and the problematic nature of the context of "misguided decisions" that has been made live. Further, he relocates his accounts into the present.

The excluded lines see the debate continuing, placing increasing importance on the need to "ramp up" staff numbers to cope with workload. Thus, the direction of the discussion has shifted from the troubling matter of misguided decisions about technology, to staff numbers. Vicky comments that ramping up is contingent to "profitability," scripting herself as a "financial" person in which matters the other participants appear to accept her judgment. The "denouement" comes in Lines 33–45. In this part, Alan carefully builds a case, affiliated to (Clifton, 2014) by other members. Note how across Lines 33–37 Alan is three-part listing: (1) "it begins with PMs," (2) "fast to react," and (3) "having the necessary people." This works up persuasion rhetoric (Edwards and Potter, 1992), with its associated claims to factuality. In contrast to historical accounting, Alan is projecting future actions (Clifton, 2012). This can be seen in his display of a conditional structure (Sneijder and te Molder, 2005): "↑if we DO that (then) the benefit …," scripting him as knowledgeable of cause and effect on future outcomes (Chilton, 2004).

Conditional Structure
Conditional structures are particular formulations which can be used to describe events as having particular consequences. It follows that those events which can be constructed as having predictable patterns and consequences (e.g., "as long as you do this … then this will work … "), with those consequences knowable in advance, are events which are constructed linguistically as factually robust. This effectively negates the need for any further elaboration of the predicted case in terms of proof or evidence.

Vicky serves the rhetorical "bombshell" across Lines 40–45, reinvoking historicity, effectively undermining Alan's projection of future outcomes with a call to historical events, which evidence his version as unworkable. She orients to Roger's confirmation token (Rautajoki, 2012) in Line 39 with "you first tried," targeting her turn directly to him. She scripts knowledge and memory ("I kno::w I can remember …": Line 41), with the stretched vowel conjuring a concern with authenticity, allied to the importance of learning lessons from the past: Roger has already "looked" at ramping up freelancers, but "four clients were delayed." The implication is that, in these circumstances, a ramp up would have been risky: ramping up would have meant staff members sitting with nothing to do because new projects are delayed in starting up by the clients who, it is implied, cannot be controlled. Thus, the speaker scripts an evaluation of Alan's built-up case, with the upshot that as they have no control over what the clients do, ramping up is a poor choice of action. Thus, the context of history is called upon to provide facts to warn against future actions which works in contrast to Roger's earlier historical accounting as a *route to reasons*.

Finally, returning to the notion of "frustration–disagreement and power" raised earlier, it is suggested that while this senior management team display claims to rights and powers to discuss such sensitive and important matters, and in possessing the knowledge to do so, what they do not display having are rights and power to make decisions. In the first part of the extract, we saw how the decision to use unready technology is cast as misguided, but no one asks why such a decision was made, with the author of the decision unnamed. It is inferred that this author is not present in the meeting—if they had been they would almost certainly have defended their past actions. It is further suggested that this decision-maker is located higher up the organization's hierarchy. This being the case, the senior mangers' meeting is reduced to a "talking shop," which can be seen in the frustration–disagreement, which marks both meetings.

16.6 PRELIMINARY REFLECTIONS

Findings suggest that context in the sense of speakers' interpretation and understanding of their environment and its contents is a catalytic dimension of knowledge sharing, which both influences the discursive trajectory and is consequential to these activities. In analyzing the contexts that speakers invoke as live concerns, we can also see that, in many cases, these can be categorized as contexts of identity (reputation, for instance), trust (e.g., authenticity and claims to epistemic primacy), and risk (the consequences of one team's actions on another and the implication of decision-making beyond the control of the senior management team, for instance).

In the analysis here, findings display two ways in which speakers conjure shared understanding of context: first, through displaying knowledge of what's on another's mind and, second, in gisting and elaboration work. Displays of others' cognition are an efficient way to "short hand" a meeting, for instance, where speakers share a common purpose and similar experiences and are familiar with and trust each others' abilities. But there is a suggestion that repeated enactment leads to a potential barrier to other contributors taking up turns, with implied consequences for the sharing of knowledge in equitable measures.

With gisting and elaboration, displays are shown to work up consensus and affiliation—group membership with a shared emotional experience ("pain" and embarrassment leading to an apologetic state) conjuring mutually shared and understood context. This constructed affiliation inevitably leads to mutual exoneration: the meeting host (Extract 2) for raising the troubling issue in the first place and the two others for any wrong-doing in their actions. The important upshot is that the latter two speakers are both prompted to volunteer further knowledge of the incidents resulting in the sharing of important and useful knowledge with all meeting participants.

The construction of a context of "them and us" emerges in the analysis of stance-taking in the first of the senior management meetings (Extract 4). The extended discourse of argument initiates with the invocation of a courtroom drama (Extract 3) in speakers' extreme concerns for truth and objectivity, claim and counterclaim, claims to knowledge superiority, and blame attribution. There is a marked pursuit of detail against an undercurrent of reputational risk made explicit in the warnings of risks and dangers to the business. When the stances become reversed, and a claim of wrong-doing at the organizational level is introduced, this quickly coalesces into a context of them and us. Arguably this emerges from the context of courtroom rhetoric. In a courtroom, the prosecution and defense are expected to "take sides," to promote alternate versions of events, and to question claims to knowledge. This clearly has an effect on the directions of knowledge sharing.

Perhaps the most contentious interpretation is made of the final extract in which the invoking of history in the search for reasons for a particular issue raises the ghost of a contextual difficulty—the existence of a decision-maker who makes flawed decisions, which, it is implied, is the reason for the "slowing down" of contract work. The silences and absence of discussion on this matter suggests an anomaly. Analysis suggests that while meeting members have a right to discuss such issues, they have no rights to make decisions leading to the further conjecture that the disagreement–frustration, which marks both meetings, emanates from this status. Taken as a whole, Extracts 2–5, drawn from the same company but representing different tiers within the hierarchy of the business, script an organization with some profound and deep-seated organizational problems.

The final chapter brings together all of the findings from this and previous chapters in a discussion largely centered around the research questions shown at the start of Part Two. Findings are also considered from the perspective of how they can be related to those key issues and debates found to be so challenging for the field of knowledge management in the first part of this book.

POSTSCRIPT

Within a year of making these meeting recordings, Company A had been taken over by a rival with, today, the only vestige of its lengthy track record and existence maintained in the name of a legacy product.

FURTHER READING

Hobbs, P. (2003). "Is that what we're here about?": a lawyer's use of impression management in a closing argument at trial. *Discourse & Society*, 14, (3): 273–290.

Hutchby, I. (2001). "Witnessing": the use of first-hand knowledge in legitimating lay opinions on talk radio. *Discourse Studies*, 3, (4): 481–497.

Locke, A. and Edwards, D. (2003). Bill and Monica: memory, emotion and normativity in Clinton's Grand Jury Testimony. *British Journal of Social Psychology*, 42: 239–256.

Potter, J. (1998). Cognition as context (whose cognition?) *Research on Language and Social Interaction*, 31, (1): 29–44.

Svennevig, J. (2012). The agenda as resource for topic introduction in workplace meetings. *Discourse Studies*, 14, (1): 53–66.

17

FINDING MEANING, IMPLICATIONS, AND FUTURE DIRECTIONS

17.1 A MANAGEMENT PRACTICE IN SEARCH OF AN OBJECT

> Using an approach drawing on discursive psychology, discourse in organizational settings is analysed for how the thematic categories of trust, identity, risk and context are made live, and with what, if any, influence and effect on what are understood as knowledge sharing meeting/forum contexts. In particular, will such an analysis inform an understanding of these thematic categories as tacitly invoked phenomena, and can these themes be shown to be co-relational?
>
> (Summary of indicative research questions, Chapter 11)

This project started out with a view of knowledge management (KM) as a problematic field characterized by its range and scope of debates and issues (see Chapters 1–4). One might even go so far as to describe it as a management practice in search of an object, in more ways than one. In spite of the broad often competing perspective and theory, there is a persistent theme of knowledge as embedded in or as constituting social interaction within which the "knowing how–knowing that" formulation is considered to be the most important. This led to the speculation that relocating the sphere of interest onto everyday organizational discourse would create the opportunity for studying knowledge work in action. With a particular interest in organizational knowledge sharing (KS), a critical review and analysis of KM research and theory identified a number of factors considered to be influential, in one direction or another, on those types of activities. These were subsequently mapped to the thematic categories of trust, risk, identity, and context. Recall that the latter of these is positioned as the corroborating phenomenon for the relationship between trust, risk, and identity in KS practices, as discussed in Section 8.6.

Knowledge and Discourse Matters: Relocating Knowledge Management's Sphere of Interest onto Language, First Edition. Lesley Crane.
© 2016 John Wiley & Sons, Inc. Published 2016 by John Wiley & Sons, Inc.

Taking these themes as the subject, the research reported in the previous five chapters draws on discursive psychology (DP) for both a theory and a methodology for the investigation of KS actions in organizational meeting and online discussion forum discourse. As outlined toward the end of Part One, the research also acknowledges an understanding of tacit knowing as the cognitive "input" resulting from the unconscious, automatic abstraction of information from the environment, which has been shown in studies of implicit learning to be influential on action (the "output"). Lines of connection are drawn between this and the formulation of "knowing how–knowing that" promoted by, for instance, Paul Duguid among others in the KM field. Central to this formulation is the idea that knowing how makes knowing that actionable, with the former representing the "uncodifiable substrate" that informs the use of codified knowledge (the "code") to borrow Duguid's terms once again. Tying these points together, it is suggested that the (extended) discursive psychology methodology reveals tacit knowing (knowing how) as an accomplishment in discourse in social interaction—the output mentioned earlier.

Reprising a caveat included in the Introduction, and laid out in more detail in Chapter 9, it is important to differentiate between the concept of knowledge adhered to here and the dualist version of knowledge seen so prominently in the KM field. In referring to "tacit knowing" and "knowing how," a distinction is not being drawn nor acknowledged between these and explicit knowledge. Knowledge is approached here as a holistic concept comprising both tacit (know how) and explicit (know that) fragments, with the sum of both constituting knowledge. One does not exist without the other.

The principle claim is that the research findings show how these thematic categories are invoked by speakers in meetings where the aim is to share knowledge, that they are corelationally and locally situated. More to the point, they are shown to influence the direction and scope of KS actions. The substance on which these claims are based can be seen in the findings of the focus on context as a generic theme, in which trust, risk, and identity are shown to be invoked by speakers in KS action.

Before establishing the aims, objectives, and directions of this chapter, it is worth a brief pause to reflect back on the KS factors (see Table 1) that underlie the thematic categories.

What is immediately clear is that not all of these (19 in all) could be said to be present in the data. Some are obvious in their absence: "values placed on mentoring," for instance, and the "time–costs" implication. Interestingly, the analysis that shows up the greatest number of KS factors is "context" (12: as one might expect), with that showing the least being "risk." Trust has the next highest number present (9). This assessment is not in the least scientifically done, but, as a "gist" picture, one interpretation might be as follows: trust, risk, and identity are pervasive concerns of speakers engaged in KS actions, with trust shown to be the most significant, and risk, the least.

This picture can, fortunately, be easily dismantled. There is sufficient evidence to support the thesis of trust as corelational with risk (see, for instance, Section 8.4 and Chapter 13). There is also sufficient evidence to support the notion of constructed identity as pretty much foundational and fundamental to the accomplishment of discourse in social interaction (see Sections 6.4 and 8.2, and Chapters 14 and 15). Even, for instance, in the attempt to write scientifically and objectively, the subjective creeps in. Recall Margaret Wetherell's simple but effective insight that to speak (to utter, to write) is to speak from a position of personal beliefs, agendas, values, experiences, preferences, knowledge, and so on. Discourse is a subjective accomplishment.

What, then, can be concluded from this brief retrovisit to the source KS factors? Arguably, the only conclusion that can be drawn is that the KS factors, as sourced from research and theory in the KM field, are for the most part far too specific to the context in which they are originally situated. Moreover, factors such as people's natural tendency to store and hoard their knowledge and the inhibiting effects of an absence of incentives to share simply do not figure (with the exception of the speculative discussion in Section 13.5) in the present analyses. Collectively what the KS factors did do, though, was prompt an interest in trust, risk, and identity.

The aim of this chapter is to discuss the research findings relevant to the detailed indicative research questions (first stated in Section 11.5.1), which are used as a framework to guide the discussions. Drawing from this, the next section explores the potential implications of these findings in relation to the key issues and debates in KM (see Chapters 1–4) leading to some future directions for the development of these ideas, and for further research. (The reader is referred to Section 11.5.1 for a reminder of the validation procedures that the present research has employed and Section 11.6 on its potential limitations.)

17.2   FINDING MEANING

17.2.1   Constructing Live Issues and Concerns

In the environment of organizational KS, how are matters of identity, trust and risk constructed as live issues and concerns of speakers?

Taken as a whole, the findings represent a rich and intricate, even bewildering range of discursive devices and strategies which speakers routinely use in their everyday discourse. In the present case, the invoking of trust, risk, and identity as accomplishments in social interaction are shown to work as displays of knowledge of mutually shared understanding of the context and meeting precepts in which those discursive actions take place. A further feature to draw attention to is the implicit nature of these actions: these discursive accomplishments are not the outcome of conscious goal-directed linguistic behavior. That would suggest a distinction between thought and discursive action and inner minds as the "driver behind the wheel" of language. Even the most measured and careful utterance (and there are several examples of this in the data) is a complex mesh of probing the context, sense-making informed by tacit knowing, and a sophisticated orientation to shared understanding.

What is also clear is that while there is a certain amount of consistency in the display of discursive devices and strategies between the different analyses, there is also a great deal of diversity. Bearing in mind the claim that shared understanding is essential to sharing knowledge (see Chapter 16), it is even more bewildering to think that speakers possess an innate understanding of, and ability with, such an extensive communicative "tool set."

A key finding is that in instances of social interaction where the objective and purpose is to share knowledge, speakers ("speakers/participants" collectively refer to speakers in meetings and forum contributors) are shown to invoke identity, trust, and risk as live concerns. That is, KS is shown to be contingent to these three contexts and more than likely, vice versa. As a caveat, this is not to suggest that these are the only KS influencing discursive contexts—a wider research focus might well reveal others. As a first observation, though, it is quite clear that at the outset of all of the interactions analyzed here few of the speakers explicitly refer to these contexts (one exception being Chapter 16, Extract 3). So how do they emerge in the action? The first research question is concerned with how speakers go about the business of constructing these particular thematic categories: what discursive tools (devices and strategies) are mobilized, and how can such tools be shown to have the effect of constructing trust, risk, and identity as speakers' live concerns? A consideration of some of the more prominent and commonly deployed of these serves to clarify the findings in respect of these enquiries.

Authenticity
Constructing accounts and reports as authentic is perhaps one of the most common discursive actions in the data, seen in virtually all of the interactions analyzed here, which immediately suggests a fundamental role in KS. What is interesting is the length to which speakers go to formulate their utterances as factual, objective, honest, and beyond dispute: in other words as trustworthy and immune from risk, which in turn are relational with identity. Derek Edwards and his colleague, in their account of *Discursive Psychology*, list nine different discursive devices that their research shows are used by speakers to construct accounts as factual—in our terms, authentic. Of these, the analyses have found examples of *category entitlements* (e.g., Section 14.4: the construction of "seasoned exhibitionists"), *vivid description* (Section 13.4: "uber authenticity" through vivid accounting and Section 16.3.2: doing "gisting and elaboration"), *narrative* (Section 13.3.3: structuring an account in the form of a narrative), *empiricist accounting* (Section 14.4.2: orienting to scientific facts), *rhetoric of argument* (Section 16.4.1: invoking the context of courtroom), *extreme case formulations* (Section 16.4.1: as a marker of argumentative discourse), *consensus and corroboration* (Sections 16.3.2 and 16.5: eyewitness accounts have the effect of scripting mutual consensus and corroboration), and *lists and contrasts* (Sections 15.8.1 and 16.4.1: using three-part lists to construct accounts as factual and complete, also associated with persuasion talk).

It is self-evident that the action of constructing accounts as authentic has direct connotations with trust through orienting to the trustworthiness of accounts, as noted earlier. It is also evident that trust works reflexively in the sense that when a speaker scripts their account as authentic, worthy of trust, they are simultaneously scripting their self as trustworthy. Thus, in invoking trust, one is also invoking identity. Moreover, trust is also reflexive in the sense that speakers and their utterances cannot exist as trustworthy independently of others: claims and identities come into existence in the light of others' displays of shared consensus. For an account or report to be understood as authentic and trustworthy, it requires cospeakers to index to this understanding. But what of the relation between risk and authenticity?

Discursive actions, which challenge the authenticity of another's version of affairs, are found to be connected to the context of risk. Recall, for instance, the sequence (Section 13.3, Extract 3) in which one speaker (John) gives an account of financial status: his account is shown to be hedged with caution and an attention to accuracy, reflexively invoking the risks associated with noncompliance with such concerns, it is claimed that John's response to his colleague's (Brian) "token of agreement" interprets this as a challenge to the authenticity of his (John's) account. Both are then shown to be mutually concerned with giving an accurate version of affairs, albeit both giving slightly different versions, and which is interpreted as the two working collaboratively to script an authentic set of events. These actions, it is claimed, effectively set a "benchmark" for what follows in scripting live concerns with truth and accuracy in a high-stakes (risk) context.

An explicit scripting of high stakes and risk can be seen in Chapter 16 (Extract 3). The extract concerns a project proposal given to a client allegedly without anyone on Roger's team having seen it (which constructs Roger and his team as possessing power over the others and what they do), with Roger overtly referring to the "dangers" of "saying we can do something" and "making assumptions." This state of affairs is interpreted as risky to the company's interests, and to its reputation, which again can be seen working reflexively as an account of Roger and his team as the guardians of organizational reputation and well-being. Both speakers are shown to take their concerns with "what really happened" to extremes: trust and authenticity are questioned, and assignation of blame made a live issue. In this extract, a range of discursive devices are displayed, including three-part listing, unmitigated displays of rights to knowledge, facts "out there" as authentic and trustworthy, the extreme attention to accuracy of account (something is either "entirely true" or not true at all), and calling on witnesses. It is these and other features of the extract that result in the sense of "courtroom drama" unfolding. In this one sequence alone, it is claimed that trust, risk, and identity are invoked through shared concerns with authenticity.

Competency Challenge
Another discursive tool that is seen in the data and which is connected to trust, risk, and identity is challenge to competency. Variations on this action can be seen in speakers' invoking of a context of lack of trust (in another) and blame attribution (Chapter 12), challenge to authenticity (Chapter 13), conjuring potential credibility problems (Chapter 14), the consensus-elaboration (insufficiency) constructs seen in Chapter 15, and the actions around invoking competitive rivalry, the construction of rival groups (Sections 16.3 and 16.4), and the scripting of skeptical rejoinders (Sections 12.5, 12.7, 13.3, 16.3, and 16.4).

Competency challenges are shown to be fundamental to argumentative rhetoric with skeptical rejoinders particularly associated with stance-taking actions—that is, constructing identity from this or that position. What the findings demonstrate is that when speakers are shown to script competency challenges, in one form or another, they are both issuing a challenge to the competency of another while simultaneously working to bolster their own competency. Actions of this type, it is claimed, work up contexts of risk (by implicating the lack of competency of others), trust (in framing one's own version as the preferred version), and identity (as accomplishing a stance on a particular issue).

A good example of this phenomenon is seen in the construction of two competing versions of the same witness accounts in the discussions around trust (Section 12.5.2). The topic at issue is whether what clients say is relevant as sound evidence of a risk to the project ("four months that's a long time") if particular actions are not taken as priority by the project team or whether what clients say is irrelevant and not worthy of notice. The second version of affairs is shown to work to undermine the first and, in so doing, calls into question the first speaker's (Steve) competence in using such "evidence" when it is in fact groundless according to the second speaker (Damien). The risk that Steve conjures is not only deleted by Damien in his preferred description of what clients say, but this also works reflexively to script Steve's account as risky in its faulty perspective.

Clearly, Damien can only make such a claim if he himself occupies a position of knowledge of what clients say. This exchange on its own does not however produce an effective *challenge* to competency: this comes to the fore in Damien's immediately following account of needing "a bigger discussion" on the subject. This implies lack of sufficient discussion to date with the potential for flawed decisions being made, and that this is the real issue, not what clients say. Thus, risk, trust, and identity are displayed as socially constructed, indexical, and locally situated concerns.

Attributing Blame

Displays of knowledge are connected to blame attribution in the context of trust work (Chapter 12) and identity (Chapter 16). Attribution theory is a particularly substantial topic of study in social psychology, and it would be inappropriate to turn the present discussions in those directions in any detail (see Edwards and Potter, 1992, for a succinct summary). From the perspective of DP, attributions are approached as social acts accomplished in discourse rather than the verbal expression of inner mental attitudes about social acts, for instance. The claims made here are that in the context of producing social acts which are interpreted as attributing blame in some direction, speakers are simultaneously shown to work up concerns with trust and identity as tacitly understood contexts. In both of the following examples, blame attribution emerges as the upshot of a complex set of interactional moves by speakers.

In the scenario from Chapter 16, the attribution of blame is shown to be a significant contributing factor to the construction of "them and us," which is initiated with the invoked context of "courtroom drama." The attribution of blame is made live by Roger, warranted by the potential risk to reputation posed by the actions of members of John's team, and his invocation of rights to be alarmed. With blame conjured and attributed in John's direction, a trajectory of claim and counterclaim ensues implicating the high stakes of the argumentative actions and with no speaker willing to give way. Actions of authenticity and trustworthiness are deployed in bolstering competing accounts: for example, Roger's three-part listing works as a display of self as the possessor of superior knowledge. What is at stake is the direction of blame attribution. John is shown to deflect blame back in the direction of Roger through issuing a new accusatory claim, which is scripted as even more "inflaming" than Roger's original accusation. This, it is shown, leads directly to the problematic formulation of "them and us" with all of its connotations of taking sides, blame and fault, and so forth. In this scenario, speakers accomplish matters of trust, identity, and risk as the underpinning constructs to attributing blame, using a range of discursive tools to bolster their mutually competing perspectives.

The scenario from Chapter 12 concerning "something missing" from a software product similarly displays a pattern of blame being made live and attributed, which leads to competing versions of states of affairs. The difference here is that the inaugurator of the blame (Steve) is the agent of its eventual redirection away from his initial target (Damien). The fine-grained analysis of the discourse interprets Steve as "pointing the finger" of blame directly at his colleague. Damien's interpretation of Steve's actions as constituting blame are shown in his attempts to reflect blame back by reformulating the source of the problem: the "something missing" could be resolved by spending more money, which is within the governance of the project leader, Steve, and it is his implied failure to do so that results in the "problem." Eventually, Steve is shown to explicitly reattribute blame away from his colleague (and himself) and onto the software product itself. This scenario particularly displays the consequences for matters of trust, identity, and risk.

Both this and the scenario from Chapter 16 demonstrate how speakers bring matters of trust, risk, and identity into action as locally situated concerns, and this, as the next discussion addresses, has consequences for the actions of KS.

17.2.2   Influencing Knowledge Sharing

It is suggested that such matters or themes are influencing in the context of KS—how and with what effect for speakers and their business?

This is an interesting question, and if shown to be substantiated, it would have particular ramifications for organizational practices of KS and the "knowing how–knowing that" formulation. It is claimed that the analyses and their findings suggest four ways in which KS is influenced by the speakers' invoked contexts of trust, risk, and/or identity. The first concerns blame attribution, the second implicates actions of consensus, the third concerns the scenarios of financial accounting in Chapter 13, and the fourth centers on the role reversal actions in Chapter 14. The following discussions unpick each of these in turn.

The Attribution of Blame

In two different meetings, one each from Company A and B, blame previously attributed to members present in the meetings is explicitly removed and reattributed to an expressly stated target beyond the meeting participants themselves. This, it is claimed, results in the subsequent voluntary sharing of knowledge appropriate to the goals of the business at hand, and which had not been forthcoming up to that point. Why does it require members to be effectively and explicitly exonerated from blame in order for them to reengage in KS? One suggestion is that the business of sharing knowledge is, in these cases, diverted or prevented by the speakers giving priority to managing attributed blame. That is, they orient to the present threat to their reputation, for instance, over the business of the meeting, which is to share knowledge.

The more acrimonious of the two instances concerns the argument between Steve and Damien (Section 12.7) over the "something missing" from the software, noted in the earlier discussion on attributing blame from the perspective of discursive tools and strategies. The scenario quite quickly develops into questions over Damien's competence (in, e.g., Steve's suggestion that his colleague should seek advice from someone else on how to "trick" the software) followed by Steve's change of strategy toward persuasion and the suggestion that Damien possesses, but is simply not sharing, relevant knowledge and this, it is claimed, implicates an erosion of trust. Changing direction again, Steve suddenly reattributes blame onto the software product itself. It is this action that triggers both a reinstatement of mutual trust and a more detailed sharing of knowledge by Damien.

In the other instance (Section 16.3.2), the action of blame is more subtly accomplished, with its attribution immediately becoming the topic of concern in the three-way dialog between Stuart (meeting leader) and two of his project managers, Dorothy and Mark. The entire gist of the piece is concerned with actors working collaboratively and consensually, first Mark with Dorothy, and then Stuart with both, to arrive at a reasoned and agreed outcome which attributes blame clearly to Team Z. In this scenario, unlike the first, KS actions are not shown to be specifically impeded: they are instead more compromised.

That is, their KS actions at this point in the scenario are more concerned with attending to the potential attribution of blame than with sharing the knowledge they have gained as a result of their respective encounters with Team Z. This can also be seen in the two project managers' volunteered subsequent accounts concerning Team Z *after* Stuart has exercised rights of full exoneration for the team.

Consensus as a Component in Sharing Knowledge

Consensus has been shown to be displayed in the data in some very different ways and with variable effects for both speakers and hearers. Two of these are considered here: the first is seen in the scenario in Chapter 16, in which two meeting participants are shown to display what is on the other's mind, with the second drawn from Chapter 15's discussions of identity construction in an online forum, in particular the "consensus-elaboration" action.

In the meeting example, analysis shows how, of the three meeting participants, the two males display "doing being a team" and mutually shared understanding by repeated use of "collaborative continuers"—that is, one speaker completes the utterance that another has started. On the one hand, this demonstrates active team work and close collaboration, mutual trust and understanding, commonly shared knowledge of context, and so forth. On the other, these actions effectively block the third participant (female) from participating in the KS dialog. A further interpretation drawn is that the two men are conjuring what could be seen as a frequently expressed "mantra." Or alternatively, rather than seeing the contents of their turns as being "well rehearsed," it is the deployment of collaborative continuers that is the frequently used discursive strategy. In other words, when these two speakers are together, and the goal is the preparation of some kind of business proposal, they do this a lot.

It is suggested that it is toward this latter understanding that the female participant leans in her counterformulation of "group of females who can multitask," to which she (obviously) belongs and others do not. The implied order of their "not belonging" is their inability to multitask *because* they are not female. The upshot is that any potential knowledge contribution from one of three meeting participants is effectively blocked. In this case, then, consensus has a blocking effect, with identity and trust foregrounded.

In the discussion forum, a rather different accomplishment is ascribed to the action of consensus. Here, KS is shown to be mediated by the "consensus-elaboration" strategy in which contributors first orient to preceding contributors/contributions in the discussion, displaying consensus often through explicit opinion markers, and then they elaborate on these same prior turns. They effectively set about adding to the knowledge by sharing more of their own while simultaneously scripting the prior turn (which they are orienting to) as being insufficient. This, it is claimed, is one of the principle actions used by forum contributors in scripting identity as expert with entitlement to be heard as such. An extension to this analysis might even speculate that the "consensus" part of consensus-elaboration turns is very similar to a collaborative continuer in the displays of shared understanding between two contributors. But unlike the meeting example, this display of shared understanding is largely one way and paves the way for competitive claims to more knowledge than previous contributors.

In both of these examples, identity in particular is shown to be implicated in the actions of doing consensus, but with very different consequences for the directions and scope of KS.

The final two cases—financial accounting and role reversal—show singular and perhaps surprising findings rising from events that could be considered to be fairly common in regular organizational meetings. Both display the influencing effects that speakers' interpretation of context, in this case risk and identity positioning, have on how and what KS unfolds.

Financial Accounting

The risk case is interesting because we have a direct comparison between sales and marketing meetings from the two different participating organizations. In both cases, the account of financial position, given by the meeting chair (Section 13.3), headlines the meeting. This, it is claimed, sets in motion a context of high stakes and risk with a mandate for truth-telling, accuracy, authenticity, and so on, in the giving of reports. Participants' reports are conjured as accountable and consequential to the financial health of their respective organizations. In other words, the stakes are too high to accommodate for exaggerated, overly embellished, inaccurate, or even misleading accounts. That is where the similarity between the two meetings ends. What is shown is that the way in which the chairs produce the financial reports influences subsequent KS actions.

In the case of Company A, the report is constructed as something to which all meeting participants contribute, as a collaborative accomplishment. With the other meeting, the financial accounting is from the perspective of individual team members or "mini-teams": individual achievements are compared, judged, and attributed, thus invoking competition and rivalry. Between team member competition and rivalry may be seen as a way of motivating actors to achieve more, surpass their colleagues, or receive publicly attributed award. In theory, members are thus motivated by comparative success and reward. The analysis shows an alternative understanding. In terms of the team's individual sales performance that may well be the case but, here, the interest lies in the jointly accomplished knowledge sharing activities, and these, it is argued, are shown to be potentially compromised by the financial accounting.

In short, the comparison between the two meetings reveals how the construction of rivalry at the outset of the Company B meeting has the effect of limiting subsequent speakers' accounts of activities. These accounts, it is claimed, are constructed to give no more than the basics and, in all cases, are not freely volunteered. For instance, when the Chair is shown to invite further elaboration on a particular account (Section 13.3.3), the speaker displays hesitation and circumspection, even reluctance. A direct comparison of a representative example of discourse from each of the meetings (Section 13.5) highlights the considerable difference in levels of detail contained in each.

A further variation between the two meetings can be seen in how the respective chairs call for members' accounts: Company A's chair either issues a call to the floor for participants to self-select to initiate the delivery of their account, or he issues a question with a candidate answer to a particular participant. In contrast, Company B's chair issues calls to report to each participant individually, more often than not with an open-ended question (e.g., "what's happenin' in your world"). It is suggested here that the construction of the context of team member rivalry, combined with the way in which participants are called to report, with its display of an absence of knowledge on the part of the chair concerning what is likely to be reported, has the effect of limiting accounts to the bare "facts."

In contrast, Company A's meeting accounts are shown to be often vivid and considered. The deviant case (Section 13.4) is an instance from Company A's meeting in which the participant, it is claimed, uses vivid accounting, quantitative rhetoric, and extreme attention to authenticity to paper over the somewhat vague and insubstantial account of his meeting with prospective clients. In other words, this participant orients to the tacitly understood norms for accuracy, authenticity, trustworthiness, cautious evaluation, and so on, as constructed in social interaction by other participants. While he takes these actions to the extreme, *he does not exaggerate* and even goes to considerable lengths to formulate his account as highly accurate.

Role Reversal

The last example comes from Chapter 14 in which the analysis focuses on the positioning actions of three participants in a client-contractor meeting. In the first part of the analysis, it is claimed that the strategically accomplished role reversal actions by the contractor (Mike) have the effect of positioning him as the possessor of "what the client wants and needs," which is worked up as a preferred substitute for any brief that the client (Elaine) may actually have. The upshot of these complex, collaborative actions—for instance, scripting persuasion, trust, corroboration, objective and factual accounting, and potential creditability problems—is that the contractor talks his version of the client's brief into existence as "what she wants and needs." He cements this in his scripting of what Elaine should say at a forthcoming meeting with the client's partners and in their jointly accomplished summary of the "agreed" brief toward the end of their meeting. If it had not been for the arrival of a third participant, that would have been the conclusion of the meeting. However, as we saw in the analysis, the contractor's version of the brief is in fact misguided, the result of vital information not being shared by Elaine herself.

This is a good example of how the positions that people create for themselves and others through their discursive actions can have a direct effect on KS outcomes. Here, it is not a case of KS being limited, as in the sales and marketing meeting from Company B, but rather its being misdirected.

The variation in effect on KS actions in three of these thematic examples is really quite revealing. The attribution of blame can be both an inhibitor and a trigger: the pattern in both of the scenarios here is "blame made live and attributed directly to an actor or made live with the threat of attribution in the direction of meeting actors" followed by "explicit blame exoneration with blame redirected in an entirely different direction," which leads to explicit increases in KS. This suggests that if blame is introduced in a meeting context, without its being attributed to any specific actor present in the meeting and subsequently redirected, then it may not have the same effect on KS actions.

The interesting feature about the consensus actions is the suggestion that displays of sharing what is on another's mind, where other actors are present and who are not included in the "mind sharing" actions, could result in a sense of competitive rivalry ("them and us")—in this case, seen in the construction of a rival group of "females who multitask." From the financial accounting scenarios, there is the hint that, if constructing between team member competitive rivalry is seen as a motivating factor in energizing greater accomplishment, this can also be seen to have practical consequences for team KS, with further implications for leading to a fragmented collective team effort. Is motivation in this scenario misguided?

17.2.3   The Corelational Nature of Invoked Concerns

It is also suggested that these themes work corelationally—how is this displayed in discourse in social interaction and with what effect?

There are so many instances where the analyses show the corelational way in which the contexts of trust, risk, and identity are worked up in discourse that they seem to be mutually dependent: that one context cannot "be" without the others. This has a couple of implications, the most significant of which is that these are contexts which the speakers themselves construct as corelational. That is, if trust is invoked—implicitly or explicitly— by one speaker, it is shown to be common knowledge and understanding that risk, for instance, is also implicated. This might, in fact explain how speakers go to such lengths to formulate their accounts as authentic and trustworthy, as we touched on earlier. They are effectively engaging in risk management. This raises a further question: if trust, as an example, is invoked by a speaker without any corelational context of risk and identity, then will it still be orientated to as "trust" by cospeakers?

Paradoxically, however, as the analysis is concerned with the interpretations and sense-making actions of speakers—what they display as shared understood contexts in interaction—this would be difficult if not impossible to substantiate as it would rely on the researcher interpreting a particular construct as being present in the discourse and then showing how cospeakers *do not* orient to this construct. While analysis is concerned with what is not present in any given set of data, to rely on the interpretation of one speaker, which is not shown to be comparatively shared as understood by other speakers, would result in a potentially invalid analysis. It could also be argued that the fundamental corelational nature of these contexts is such that it would be hard to even imagine a situation in which speakers might collaboratively "do trust" without simultaneously invoking risk and identity as concerns.

Arguably, the most that we can do is accumulate enough cases of corelation to warrant the claim. There is no particular pattern in the data for how speakers display these contexts as corelated. However, a few instances from the data serve as good examples.

In the first, participants in the discussion forum are shown to invoke their identity as expert with appropriate rights to be "heard" as such and as trustworthy (Chapter 15). At the same time, they are shown to display previous contributors as giving insufficient accounts, thus working up a warrant for the necessity of additional explanation. Those additional explanations are explicitly conjured as emanating from the speaker's experience and knowledge. So, in this case, identity and trust are constructed corelationally, designed to achieve a particular effect: the "I'm the expert because I know more than he does" strategy. The risk element—which in the analysis is related to the public, online nature of the forum—can be seen particularly in how two contributors delicately call one another's accounts into question while at the same time attending to matters of politeness and face-saving (e.g., Section 15.6). Recall the way that one contributor quite delicately and explicitly scripts his disagreement with a previous contributor (see Section 15.6, Extract 5) in a container of parentheses, conjuring the sense of an "aside" directed only to that contributor. This is an interesting case, which shows how people are willing to debate topics publicly but are nonetheless reluctant to do outright disagreement and argument in such public arenas.

As a further and more complex example of this type of action, recall how Roger, in the actions prior to Extract 3 (Section 16.4), raises a topic of concern with his colleague, John, in the first of the two senior management meetings. He then proposes that it is something that can be dealt with "probably outside of this meeting," a move that John explicitly resists. It can thus be inferred that while Roger seeks to avoid public disagreement, John works to keep it firmly in the public eye of the other meeting members. It is subsequently speculated that John may have deliberately worked to ensure Roger's topic stays on the meeting's agenda, as he is shown to use this as the springboard to launch into an even more "inflaming" topic. In these displays, all three contexts are shown to work relationally and, in fact, quite forcefully, with the result that KS becomes highly contested.

Continuing with this particular meeting analysis, which takes on the characteristics of a courtroom drama scenario (Section 16.4.1), this contains one of the few examples of explicit identity construction in the data: Roger displays himself as alarmed by the events brought about by the actions of John's team. Consequently, blame is displayed as a live concern for both participants, which in fact becomes the rhetorical object of subsequent interactions. Throughout, speakers are shown to use several rhetorical devices to script themselves and their accounts as more trustworthy than the other (epistemic primacy, for instance).

It has earlier been claimed that trust, risk, and identity are shown to have an influencing effect on KS actions. The corelational nature of these contexts has an effect, which is perhaps even more obvious. Trust, risk, and identity, as contexts mutually invoked by speakers, do more than influence: they mediate KS, either positively or negatively. All of these interactions, including those in the discussion forum, are concerned with the sharing of knowledge, with trust, risk, and identity interpreted as discursive thematic actions that are integral to this accomplishment. This explains the effects of influence discussed earlier.

The final question considers whether these accomplishments can be understood as tacitly done.

17.2.4 A Tacit Accomplishment

It is proposed that these matters are accomplished tacitly as psychological phenomena, with the implication that speakers orient to them as live matters consequent to their understanding of what is going on in the environment (analogous to the automatic, unconscious abstraction of structures and patterns in the environment): how is this displayed and oriented to in discourse?

An important aim of the research is to use the analysis of discourse to show how the various discursive actions, in particular the invocation of trust, risk, and identity, are accomplished tacitly by speakers—both in their scripting and displayed understanding of other speaker's utterances. Drawing from the study of Implicit Learning, tacit knowing is understood as the product of the unconscious and automatic abstraction of information from the environment and its contents. This is deployed equally automatically and unconsciously in mediating the individual's sense-making of their context of action, which is shown to influence their own action. Reprising the "knowing how–knowing that" formulation, knowing how, which can be thought of as the "tacit fraction," is the unspecifiable foundation that makes knowing that actionable and meaningful. Added to this, language is approached as action orientated and consequential for speakers and recipients. The interest in the tacit fragment stems from the field of KM's attention to the concept of tacit knowledge as a phenomenon of value and as integral to the actions of KS and creating, among others.

A first observation, touched on earlier, is the near absence, with only one or two exceptions, of speakers making explicit reference to contexts of trust, risk, and identity. The interpretation of the discursive action, and the displayed invocation of these contexts, is entirely made through bringing to the fore those contexts which speakers themselves collaboratively and implicitly construct as live concerns. For example, in the two sales and marketing meetings, neither of the two chairs explicitly states the high-stakes nature of the interaction nor mandates that the delivery of participants' accounts must attend to accuracy, truth, trustworthiness, and authenticity in order to be acceptable. These features, it is claimed, are constructed as integral to their reports and as an unstated requirement on those subsequently made by other meeting participants. In this way, the actors display a shared understanding of a context of high stakes and the necessity of staying within the parameters of acceptability— the shared and displayed understanding of the meetings' precepts.

A second observation is that these displays of the tacit fragment—shared understanding of context—could not be shown through conventional research methods. It is only through the application of the methodology (and similar methodologies) used here that discourse can be shown to be action orientated, with function and consequence—the majority of which is arguably performed by the actors on what might be termed an unconscious level. Recall Max Boisot's theory that KS is the consequence of resonance being achieved between the repertoires of different speakers. In his study of KS, M Max Evans also finds shared vision (and trust) to be important influencing factors. If shared vision and resonant repertoires are determinants of KS, it is highly unlikely that conventional methods of investigation would demonstrate this. However, the discourse analysis method adopted in the present study is particularly geared toward how such psychological phenomena, at once both hidden from sight but in plain view, are done as collaborative accomplishments. Even when speakers are shown to be engaged in some serious arguing, they are, despite this, shown to be working collaboratively: it takes two to argue.

It is worth bringing in a particular point concerning the data from Company A. The sales and marketing meeting actions can be seen as a role model for KS as effectively and efficiently done. However, the same company's project management meeting actions bring to the fore a particular problem concerning dealings with another department within the same firm. This is particularly compounded by the displays of intrateam member support and loyalty, an example being the "gisting and elaboration work" displayed by the project leader. In other words, a kind of "them and us" is implicated, with connotations of between departmental (horizontal) KS issues.

In the same organization, the first of the two senior management meetings brings a sense of "them and us" more bluntly to the fore, with the organization ("them") scripted as acting irrationally. Then, in second meeting, there is the "ghost" of a contextual difficulty: the decision to use a particular technology on a project, knowing that the technology was not ready to use. It is not stated explicitly that this refers to another person who is not present in the meeting nor is the decision to use this technology explicitly described as being wrong. Instead, it is constructed by Roger as the excuse to "slow down" the project start-up. John's suggestion that another technology could have been used, the weak acknowledgement of this given by Roger, and the denial by a third speaker that the choice of this particular technology was in fact the reason for "slowing down" the project, combined with Roger's moves to change the topic, suggest an "uncomfortable truth." Decisions are perhaps not within the governance of the meeting members. This leads to the speculation that the members of the senior management team lack the power to make important decisions: all they are entitled to do is to make recommendations to a higher level of the business (could this be the level at which the decision to use technology known to be not ready was taken?). This is displayed by at least one member as problematic and can also be seen as a further kind of "them and us." This has implications for bottom-up (vertical) KS problems.

The following section discusses the research findings in relation to debates and issues in KM summarized and synthesized in Chapter 9, drawing some implications for KM in general.

17.3   RELATING THE FINDINGS TO DEBATES AND ISSUES IN KNOWLEDGE MANAGEMENT

On a practical note, as the focus of the present research has been exclusively on organizational meeting and online discussion forum discourse, the findings can only realistically be seen from those perspectives. Other types of organizational discourse that could be used in future similar projects include KS practices in the context of mentoring and learning and employee exit interviews, for instance, even the contents of "knowledge repositories" such as "expert biographies," project reports, and consumer surveys. Those, and many other instances, would represent valid, relevant, and potentially advantageous lines of future research. For now, however, the discussions reprise some of KM's principle concerns in the light of the present findings.

17.3.1   The Central Concern of Knowledge Management with "How" and "What"

Central to KM's concerns are the questions around "how" to manage knowledge and "what" should be the focus of KM actions. "How" and "what" questions are precisely the concerns of DP—and indeed most other discourse analysis methods. Consequently, the findings demonstrate how speakers (in these instances included here) perform KS actions; how these are constructed as contingent to trust, risk, and identity; and how these thematic categories influence the scope and directions of KS actions. It has also been shown how these themes are invoked by speakers as corelational constructs with a suggestion of covariance. These discursive actions and their consequences for both speakers and hearers are, it is claimed, the outcome of actors' unconscious and automatic appraisal of the environment and its contents, as displayed in discourse.

As an emic approach to the study of organizational action, the present research methods have revealed phenomena which conventional methods could not because our principle concern is with the contexts and other accomplishments actors themselves display as shared understanding and concerns in discourse. This is contrasted with the etic approach adopted in mainstream research which gives precedence to the researcher's understanding, interpretation, categorization and so forth over that of participants in the data. It is suggested that such an approach risks irrelevance in foregrounding concerns and understandings that are not necessarily those of the actors.

To address KM's "what" question—what should our actions and practice focus on—a constructionist view approaches knowledge as constructed in everyday discourse in social interaction, which can be studied directly using discourse analysis methodologies. This moves the focus of interest onto the social relationships integral to discourse. Lawrence Prusak and his colleague, in their review of failure factors in KM, note that a lack of focus on the social aspects of relationships, including trust, is one of the major reasons for high KM failure rates. The empirical research reported here would certainly lend support to this perspective.

Similarly, in relation to KM's "how" question—how do we manage knowledge—it seems clear from the findings that speakers routinely manage their knowledge in socially enacted discourse. This gives rise to suggestions of some specific cases for how such actions could be mediated, even improved. For instance, the scripting of financial accounting is shown to invoke very particular concerns with high stakes, authenticity, the need for trustworthiness, and so on. How such accounts are made, how they are formulated in relation to the members of a meeting, and at what point in the meeting these are included, have effect on speakers and their actions. There is also the case of "attributing blame": blame made live and attributed, even theoretically, to group members needs to be firmly removed elsewhere in order to restore normative KS practices. A further point that one could derive from the findings is support for the idea that people routinely and ubiquitously shared knowledge all of the time: it is a normative function of social discourse. But, like the inevitable variance in people's command of their own language, just because a practice is occasioned in normal everyday action, it does not epiphenomenally follow that they are "good" at it.

This type of study adds to the debates over what KM is, what it should or can be concerned with, by extending the directions already indicated by many researchers and theorists in the KM field. This touches on a couple of issues connected to the previous discussions concerning DP's relevance to KM, which are considered next.

17.3.2   The "Relevance" Issue Concerning Discursive Psychology

Is it being suggested that KM practitioners should, as a matter of routine, record and analyze their organization's meetings, trawl through endless documentation, and subject them to the kind of forensic analysis of discourse undertaken here? Well, no, at the very least, that would be impractical. What is suggested is that this particular approach can be seen as an additional and potentially valuable tool in working toward and accomplishing specific goals or in aiding the resolution of specific problems. An example would be where there is a need for a fresh strategy for the management of an organization's knowledge. Rather than an individual, or a group of people, working in isolation to develop such a strategy (akin to Gergen's description of the decision-maker making decisions behind closed doors as fraught with problems, in his account of *Relational Being*), might it not be a better approach to uncover how an organization's members define and understand "knowledge," what it means to their work, and what they hold to be the most valuable type of knowledge to the business? That is, in taking an emic approach, as opposed to an etic one, one can tap into the group's shared common understandings, rather than imposing understanding—which might be alien—from a distance.

This latter point is, I believe, important. Recall some of the ideas in Chapter 1 around what meaning "means." Both Michael Polanyi and Kenneth Gergen claim that the meaning of a concept takes its form through repeated use, as conventions of language expressed by certain groups at certain times, given certain circumstances. Meaning is, accordingly, the outcome of shared consensus. This suggests that to impose an understanding or definition of any given category is, frankly, unnatural.

A second point, related to the "relevance" issue, concerns DP's terminology. In short, this is difficult and does not sit well with natural talk (ironically enough). One of the reasons behind this type of terminology is that DP draws on conversation analysis for its methodology. This latter, in its purest form, is very specifically focused on discovering and specifying the "architecture of the structure of verbal interaction" to borrow Robin Wooffitt's description (see Section 6.3.2). It has developed, of necessity, a complex, precise and very technical vocabulary for accomplishing this. To the layperson, conversation analysis reports might seem like a foreign language, but then analysts are for the most part not addressing the layperson. At the end of Chapter 6, it was speculated that the "sense-making" paradigm promoted by Christian Madsbjerg and his colleague, for instance, could potentially constitute a vocabulary more suited to the organization and its concerns. This has not been explored, but is one potential avenue for future research and development.

17.3.3 A Theory of Language

The KM field, it is concluded, is largely lacking a theory of language (with a noted exception being Nonaka's reference to Speech Act Theory in his *A Dynamic Theory of Organizational Knowledge Creation*), despite many theories in KM emphasizing the importance of social interaction as the location of knowledge work. Frank Blackler, for instance, explicitly underlines the key role of communication in his view of organizations as systems of activity. It is argued in Chapter 9 that if one approaches knowledge from such perspectives, and which most in the KM field do in one respect or another, then it makes sense to draw upon a theory of language to inform an understanding and explanation of how knowledge emerges in language. It is hoped that the present research is seen as an example of the potential benefits and progress that could be achieved by doing just this. In the present case, the approach to a theory of language draws on DP and social constructionist theory.

17.3.4 A Different Conceptualization of Knowledge Sharing

In short, the findings from the research project reported here provide support to those theories that specifically locate knowledge work in social interaction and in particular for the formulation of "knowing how–knowing that" (see Section 4.5, Chapter 9, and Section 17.1 for explanations) specific to KS practices. In scoping the research of KS discourse, it was noted that while research and theories in KM identify factors that influence KS, they have little to say on how they influence these practices in action. There are of course some exceptions that offer empirical support for what influences KS—Max Evans' recent study of trust in organizational KS for instance. It could be argued that the findings here have some coherence with Evans' findings. The present findings can thus be approached as attempting to at least start to answer the question of how factors influence KS actions, and with what consequences, at a much deeper level. One further point to add is the suggestion that the findings also lend support to those who are critical of an approach to KM which is wholly or mostly focused on IT. The reasons for this should be obvious.

Does this research add up to a different conceptualization of KS? That would be quite a substantial claim to make, and would require considerably more research to warrant. What can be cautiously stated is that the findings open up the potential for an alternative conceptualization of KS. That is, alternative in terms of the conventional approach to KM, but which can be seen in the insights given by, for example Max Boisot, Paul Duguid, and Haridimos Tsoukas. KS, to be effective, relies on speakers' shared understanding of context, as displayed in interactional discourse, which is influenced by the individual's personal stocks of "knowing how." It relies on speakers' attention to the potential effects of discursive actions such as blamings, high stakes, normative roles and their entitlements, rivalry, and consensus work on KS outcomes. That would suggest that members of organizations might well benefit from training in how to be effective communicators from a discourse-savvy perspective.

17.3.5 A Different Approach to Core Issues in Knowledge Management

Similarly to the previous question, a consideration of some of the other principle concerns in KM from the perspectives of the present findings suggests the potential for an alternative approach. Previous discussions suggested that a strategy drawing on the DP approach renders such matters as the commodification–reification issue, and measuring KM outcomes as irrelevant (see, e.g., Section 9.3). That is essentially justified from the viewpoint of DP as a research methodology. Drawing on this, the commodification–reification formulation of knowledge is effectively dismantled. A strategy, which reifies knowledge as an object or commodity, is dealing with what would be more accurately described as information. It may have intrinsic market value, it may be vital to the organization's operations and growth, and so forth, but it is information. Knowledge is that which is coconstructed in social interaction between persons. Knowledge exists in the action of reading another's written words, or interpreting visual displays. Without risking becoming caught in the seemingly endless philosophical arguments over the nature of knowledge, the argument concerning commodification–reification can be rested with the simple claim that what has been displayed in the analyses of the previous chapters is not an objectified knowledge being distributed.

The issue of measuring KM success or failure, from a conventional understanding, is also rendered somewhat meaningless. But, in this case, some alternative questions can be offered in its stead. For instance, on a case by case basis—project teams, Communities of Practice, management teams, and so on—what inhibits and what promotes knowledge work from a discursive perspective? The analyses show considerable variance in outcome from the use of certain discursive strategies—the case of consensus, for instance—and between the different groups of speakers. This suggests that a blanket strategy is unlikely to work. But, again, further research in this particular area may lead to the development of approaches which may, in combining the DP approach with other methods of organizational analysis, realize a method of comparing knowledge work outcomes between groups, for instance, or over time.

Relating the findings to issues around culture, and criticism of the "one size fits all" (see Chapter 3 for discussions), raises an interesting point. The criticism of "one size fits all," referring to concrete rules and procedures, strategies, and policies (the infamous "checkbox approach"), argues quite reasonably that what suits one organization or team in a particular environment and set of circumstances is unlikely to have pan-generic attributes. In contrast, what the findings suggest is that trust, risk, and identity are universally enacted contexts and concerns in KS discursive action. But care should be taken with the use of "universal" here. What can be claimed is that the data used in the present study, drawn from various sources, shows participants' commonly displayed shared understandings of these contexts as live concerns. It is an unfortunate limitation of the present study that effects of disparate national cultures, for instance, are not a factor. However, this does suggest a particular line for future research.

The point that is speculated is this: one size fits all in the manifestation of rules, processes, and so forth may well not be adequate to the task of mediating the goals and objectives of the organization, but we all communicate using language, we do things with our words, and the uncodifable substrate, it is conjectured, is essential to accomplishing shared understanding.

This raises one final question: why the apparent persistence in adopting the term "tacit knowledge" with its popularly accepted characteristics of difficult to articulate, tricky to share, yet representing the most valuable type of knowledge, when there is a far more practical, pragmatic, and rational formulation—"knowing how–knowing that?" This is perhaps no more than a matter of terminology—"tacit knowledge" sounds more real and tangible and requires less explanation. It is an interesting question. The important point to draw, however, is that the contents of this book are considered to provide empirical support for the knowing how–knowing that formulation of knowledge in the organizational context.

17.4 FUTURE DIRECTIONS

If there is one simple truism that could be drawn, it is this: knowledge work (however you choose to describe and understand it) is an accomplishment of the social interaction between persons, their environment, and its contents, which axiomatically positions discourse—talk and text—in the top chair. Add to this the indexicality of language in the sense that meaning is contingent to the context in which it is embedded and that this context is the fabrication of the speaker, which emerges from and is influenced by their tacit knowing or practical knowledge or knowing how. (Tautology, as should be clear by now, is rife in the field of KM.) What is also true is that discourse, as the source and site of knowledge work, has been somewhat neglected. So, when it was stated that this project has the aim of shifting the focus of interest onto the site of language, what was being proposed in reality was a recognition of the values and advantages to be gained by moving the sphere of interest and action to a much deeper level of organizational action, to the level at which everything transpires.

So what for future directions? There are a couple of directions for further research which we will come to in a moment. In general, it is hoped that the ideas and research findings laid out in these pages will inspire a greater interest in discourse as an organizational resource in KM. Language is, to paraphrase Benjamin Whorf's proposition, "the best show that man puts on." It is also hoped that the practice of KM can be steered away from an insistence on process and technology and back in the direction on which it was originally set back in the 1990s by (no irony intended) Ikujiro Nonaka when he argued that the focus of analysis should be on how an organization interacts with its environment and the ways in which it creates and disseminates "information and knowledge." And all that involves people and discourse. There is a lot to be done.

To complete these discussions, a few specific suggestions for lines of future research. It was suggested at the end of Chapter 6 that the "sense-making" paradigm promoted by Christian Madsbjerg and his colleague, for instance, could potentially offer a vocabulary more suited to the study of the organization and its concerns, which might be adapted for use in DP projects with a focus in these directions. While this has not been explored here, research and development may lead to a more useable terminology and would address the issues raised earlier (Section 17.3.2).

In the earlier discussions around criticism of the "one-size-fits-all" approach, a potential paradox is indicated. From any direction, differences in culture, organization, team, and individual would suggest that such an approach will simply not be effective. But the present research findings suggest that there are commonalities in discourse constructed and shared in interaction. This is not a reference to a commonly shared technical vocabulary within a given team, for instance, but refers to discursive action accomplished at the tacit level. The present research is limited to a small number of organizations and an online discussion forum: a larger scale study would focus on teams in a variety of cultures, multinational organizations, for instance, and multinational teams who come together to solve particular problems, or to take part in particular joint exercises. Such a project would build on the present findings, and those from the (much) broader discourse analysis field, to develop a closer understanding of how and whether discursive action at the tacit level—and the kinds of shared displays of the contexts of trust and identity, for example—is accomplished from a cross-cultural perspective.

Finally, a third potentially fruitful topic for research would be a project aimed at developing a methodology to enable a robust and valid comparative analysis of knowledge outcomes as an accomplishment of discourse in interaction. Directions likely to produce some interesting results could be research comparing outcomes between different teams, and comparing those from the same team over a period of time, perhaps starting with the initial setup of the team. Of course, the key to this particular project's success lies in the definition of "knowledge outcome"—that is perhaps not so difficult because, in reality, a knowledge outcome is determined by the individual case by case. What is problematic— and something that perhaps should be now consigned to the archive of historic but no longer needed management practices—is the idea of attempting to measure knowledge outcomes and the success or failure of KM as a whole.

APPENDIX

TABLE 4 Summary of Data Extracts

No	Extract Filename	Subject/Speakers	Location (Section)
1	130319_005	Company B: weekly project team meeting, with participants including Steve, Bob, Ade, Damien, and Manoj. Extract concerns the agenda	12.3
2	130319_005	Company B: weekly project team meeting, with participants including Steve, Bob, and Ade. Extract concerns challenge, epistemic superiority, and authenticity	12.4.1
3	130319_005	Company B: weekly project team meeting, with participants including Steve, Bob, Ade, and Damien. Extract concerns risk and reputation	12.5.1
4	130319_005	Company B: weekly project team meeting, with participants including Steve, Bob, and Damien. Extract concerns trust breakdown	12.6.1
5	130319_005	Company B: weekly project team meeting, with participants including Steve and Damien. Extract concerns trust and blame	12.7.1
6	130319_005	Company B: weekly project team meeting, with participants including Steve, Bob, Ade, Damien, and Manoj. Extract concerns competence and knowledge sharing	12.7.3

(Continued)

Knowledge and Discourse Matters: Relocating Knowledge Management's Sphere of Interest onto Language,
First Edition. Lesley Crane.
© 2016 John Wiley & Sons, Inc. Published 2016 by John Wiley & Sons, Inc.

TABLE 4   (*Continued*)

No	Extract Filename	Subject/Speakers	Location (Section)
1	130520_003	Company A: weekly sales and marketing meeting with participants including the chair, Sam, and John. Extract concerns reputational face saving and accuracy in mitigating against risk	13.2
2	130319_003	Company B: weekly sales and marketing meeting with one participant, the chair. Extract concerns financial discourse	13.3.1
3	130520_003	Company A: weekly sales and marketing meeting with participants John and Brian. Extract concerns financial discourse	13.3.2
4	130319_003	Company B: weekly sales and marketing meeting, with participants Ann and the chair. Extract is concerned with narrative accounting and consensus corroboration	13.3.3
5	130520_003	Company A: weekly sales and marketing meeting, with participants including the chair and Mark. Extract concerns vivid and narrative accounting.	13.3.3
6	13050_003	Company A: weekly sales and marketing meeting, with participants including Mark, John, male, and female. Extract is concerned with "uber authenticity": a potential deviant case	13.4
7	130520_003	Company A: weekly sales and marketing meeting, with participants including John and Tom. Extract is compared with Extract 8 in terms of patterns and elaboration in accounting	13.5
8	130319_003	Company B: weekly sales and marketing meeting, with participants including the chair and Jane. Extract is compared with Extract 7 in terms of patterns and elaboration in accounting	13.5
1	130320_02	Company B: client–contractor meeting to discuss a brief for an exhibitin stand. Extract concerns the need to include more partners in the stand's branding than solely that of the client. Involves "M" and "E"	14.3
2	130320_02	Company B: client–contractor meeting to discuss a brief for an exhibition stand. Extract concerns how visitors will "see" the stand. Involves "M" and "E"	14.3.3
3	130320_02	Company B: client–contractor meeting to discuss a brief for an exhibition stand. Extract concerns a third participant claiming to have experience of exhibition stands. Involves "M," "E," and "P"	14.4.1

TABLE 4   (*Continued*)

No	Extract Filename	Subject/Speakers	Location (Section)
4	130320_02	Company B: client–contractor meeting to discuss a brief for an exhibition stand. Extract concerns P adding what appears to be a fundamental change in the brief so far discussed. Involves "P" and "E."	14.4.2
1	Lines 1–4	Online discussion forum: the question is asked which starts off the forum discussion	15.3
2	Lines 82–86	Online discussion forum: contributor "C" constructs an "in group"	15.4
3	Lines 87–88	Online discussion forum: contributor "G" claims lengthy experience	15.5
4	Lines 46–49	Online discussion forum: contributor "E" constructs relational stance-taking	15.5
5	Lines 155–164	Online discussion forum: disagreement sequence between contributors "K" and "J"	15.6
6	Lines 192–197	Online discussion forum: consensus pattern followed by elaboration	15.7
7	Lines 11–16	Online discussion forum: example of a three-part listing as a strategy for displaying knowledge	15.8.1
8	Lines 5–9	Online discussion forum: using metaphor to display knowledge	15.8.2
1	130320_004	Company B: meeting to discuss proposal for a client. Extract concerns participants displaying what is on each other's minds. Includes Andy, Peter, and Cindy	16.3.1
2	130521_003	Company A: project manager's regular meeting. Extract concerns participants working up shared understanding of context through gisting and elaboration. Includes Stuart, Dorothy, and Mark.	16.3.2
3	VN550143	Company A: the first of two senior management meetings. Extract concerns a dispute over a proposal recently given to a prospective client. Includes Roger and John	16.4.1
4	VN550143	Company A: the first of two senior management meetings. Extract concerns continuing unfolding disagreement from Extract 3 and conflicting contexts of the organization. Includes John and Roger	16.4.2
5	VN550144	Company A: the second of two senior management meetings. Extract concerns displays of frustration, disagreement, and power. Includes Roger, John, Alan, Ted, and Vicky	16.5

TABLE 5   Transcription Conventions

Alndfnkn [jkdsafjhd] hksd [hfdkjhfkjd]	**Square brackets** used between lines, or bracketing two lines of talk, indicate the onset and end of overlapping talk
Jllklklkl= =jlkjlkjlkljk	The use of the **equals sign** at the end of one utterance and the onset of the next indicates no interval between utterances
(.)	**Round brackets encasing a period** indicate an untimed (i.e., just hearable) pause
(number)	**Round brackets encasing a number** indicate a pause of x seconds
Lklkklnlk-	A **dash** indicates a sharp cut off to speech
<u>Ldflasmdlf</u>	**Underlining** indicates emphasis
LMLFGMSDFLGM	The use of **capitals** indicates markedly louder talk
°kdfkldsf°	**Degree signs** indicate talk is markedly softer than surrounding talk
Kjlkjkjk::kjhlkhj	**Inserted colons** indicate word stretching
↑↓	**Upward/downward pointing arrows** indicate increase or decrease in intonation
.hh	**Audible breath**
Heh or hah	**Indicates laughter**
( )	**Use of round brackets** denotes unclear speech
[kjandfkdnfkjdn]	**Square brackets** are used to denote contextual or explanatory information
…	**Repeated periods** indicate talk omitted from the extract

The transcript notations used in the excerpts presented here adopt a "lite" version of the Jefferson standard, originally developed by Gail Jefferson and widely used throughout discourse analytic research (Wood and Kroger, 2000).

INDEX TO GLOSSARY TERMS

The following is a list of the technical terms used in discourse analysis. These terms are used in the analytics content of Part Two. Where these terms are used for the first time in the text (Chapters 12–16), they are given a short explanatory description in the form of an "insert". This is by no means an exhaustive list of such terms used in discourse analysis

Knowledge and Discourse Matters: Relocating Knowledge Management's Sphere of Interest onto Language,
First Edition. Lesley Crane.
© 2016 John Wiley & Sons, Inc. Published 2016 by John Wiley & Sons, Inc.

BIBLIOGRAPHY

Abell, J. and Stokoe, E. (2001). Broadcasting the royal role: constructing culturally situated identities in the Princess Diana Panorama interview. *British Journal of Social Psychology*, 40: 417–435.

Abrams, M. and Reber, A. (1988). Implicit learning: robustness in the face of psychiatric disorders. *Journal of Psycholinguistic Research*, 17, (5): 425–439.

Ainsworth, S. and Hardy, C. (2004). Critical discourse analysis and identity: why bother? *Critical Discourse Studies*, 1, (2): 225–259.

Akhavan, P., Jafari, M. and Fathian, M. (2005). Exploring failure-factors of implementing knowledge management systems in organisations. *Journal of Knowledge Management Practice*, 6, (May): 1–8.

Akhavan, P. and Pezeshkan, A. (2013). Knowledge management critical failure factors: a multi-case study. *VINE*, 44, (1): 22–41.

Alguezaui, S. and Filieri, R. (2010). Investigating the role of social capital in innovation: sparse versus dense networks. *Journal of Knowledge Management*, 14, (6): 891–909.

Alvesson, M. (1998). Gender relations and identity at work: a case of masculinities and femininities in an advertising agency. *Human Relations*, 51, (8): 969.

Anderson, J.R. (1996). ACT: a simple theory of complex cognition. *American Psychologist*, 51, (4): 355–365.

Andreeva, T. and Kainto, A. (2011). Knowledge processes, knowledge-intensity and innovation: a moderated mediation analysis. *Journal of Knowledge Management*, 15, (6): 1016–1034.

Antaki, C. (2000). Simulation versus the thing itself: commentary on Markman and Tetlock. *British Journal of Social Psychology*, 39: 327–331.

Antaki, C. (2012). What actions mean, to whom, and when. *Discourse Studies*, 14, (4): 492–498.

Knowledge and Discourse Matters: Relocating Knowledge Management's Sphere of Interest onto Language, First Edition. Lesley Crane.
© 2016 John Wiley & Sons, Inc. Published 2016 by John Wiley & Sons, Inc.

Antaki, C., Ardevol, E., Nunez, F. and Vayreda, A. (2006). For she knows who she is: managing accountability in online forum messages. *Journal of Computer-Mediated Communication*, 11: 114–132.

Antaki, C., Billig, M., Edwards, D. and Potter, J. (2002). Discourse analysis means doing analysis: a critique of six analytical shortcomings, *Discourse Analysis Online*. [Online]. http://extra.shu.ac.uk/daol/articles/v1/n1/a1/antaki2002002-paper.html. Accessed October 31, 2012.

Argyris, C. (1977). Double loop learning in organizations. *Harvard Business Review*, September–October: 115–125.

Argyris, C. (2009). Skilled Incompetence. *Harvard Business Review*, May: 74–79.

Austin, J. (1962). *How to Do Things with Words*. Urmson, J. and Sbisa, M. (Eds). 2nd Edn. Cambridge: Harvard University Press.

Baddeley, A. (1999). *Essentials of Human Memory*. Hove: Psychology Press.

Barabba, V., Pourdehnad, J. and Ackoff, R. (2002). Above and beyond knowledge management. In Choo, C. and Bontis, N. (Eds). *The Strategic Management of Intellectual Capital and Organizational Knowledge*. Oxford: Oxford University Press.

Bargh, J. and Chartrand, T. (1999). The unbearable automaticity of being. *American Psychologist*, 54, (7): 462–479.

Benwell, B. and Stokoe, E. (2012). *Discourse and Identity*. Edinburgh: Edinburgh University Press.

Berry, D. and Broadbent, D. (1988). Interactive tasks and the implicit-explicit distinction. *British Journal of Psychology*, 79: 251–272.

Bhatt, G. (2001). Knowledge management in organizations: examining the interactions between technologies, techniques and people. *Journal of Knowledge Management*, 5, (1): 68–75.

Billig, M. (2001). Discursive, rhetorical and ideological messages. In Wetherell, M., Taylor, S. and Yates, S. (Eds). *Discourse Theory and Practice: A Reader*. London: Sage.

Bjorkeng, K., Clegg, S. and Pitsis, T. (2009). Becoming (a) practice. *Management Learning*, 40, (2): 145–159.

Blackler, F. (1993). Knowledge and the theory of organizations: organizations as activity systems and the reframing of management. *Journal of Management Studies*, 30, (6): 863–884.

Blackler, F. (1995). Knowledge, knowledge work and organisations: an overview and interpretation. *Organization Studies*, 16, (6): 1021–1046.

Bock, G., Zmud, R., Kim, Y. and Lee, J. (2005). Behavioural intention formation in knowledge sharing: examining the roles of extrinsic motivators, social-psychological forces, and organisational climate. *MIS Quarterly*, 29 (1): 87–111.

Boisot, M. (2002). The creation and sharing of knowledge. In Choo, C. and Bontis, N. (Eds). *The Strategic Management of Intellectual Capital and Organizational Knowledge*. Oxford: Oxford University Press.

Boje, D., Oswick, C. and Ford, J. (2004). Language and organization: the doing of discourse. *Academy of Management Review*, 29, (4): 571–577.

Bontis, N. (2002). Managing organizational knowledge by diagnosing intellectual capital: framing and advancing the state of the field. In Choo, C.W. and Bontis, N. (Eds). *The Strategic Management of Intellectual Capital and Organizational Knowledge*. Oxford: Oxford University Press.

Bouthillier, F. and Shearer, K. (2002). Understanding knowledge management and information management: the need for an empirical perspective. *Information Research*, 8, (1). [Online]. http://www.informationr.net/ir/8-1/paper141.html. Accessed June 16, 2015.

Braganza, A. and Mollenkramer, G. (2002). Anatomy of a failed knowledge management initiative: lessons from PharmaCorp's experiences. *Knowledge and Process Management*, 9, (1): 23–33.

Brown, A. and Phua, F. (2011). Subjectively construed identities and discourse: towards a research agenda for construction management. *Construction Management and Economics*, 29: 83–95.

Brown, J. and Duguid, P. (1999). Organizing knowledge. *Reflections*, 1, (2): 28–44.

Buchel, B. (2007). Knowledge creation and transfer. In Ichijo, K. and Nonaka, I. (Eds). *Knowledge Creation and Management: New Challenges for Managers*. Oxford: Oxford University Press.

Bucholtz, M. and Hall, K. (2005). Identity and interaction: a sociocultural linguistic approach. *Discourse Studies*, 7, (4–5): 585–614.

Burford, S., Kennedy, M., Ferguson, S. and Blackman, D. (2011). Discordant theories of strategic management and emergent practice in knowledge-intensive organisations. *Journal of Knowledge Management Practice*, 12, (3).

Chalmers, A. (1999). *What Is This Thing Called Science?* 3rd Edn. Maidenhead: Open University Press.

Charlebois, J. (2010). The discursive construction of femininities in the accounts of Japanese women. *Discourse Studies*, 12, (6): 699–714.

Chilton, P. (2004). *Analysing Political Discourse: Theory and Practice*. London: Routledge.

Chirrey, D. (2011). Formulating dispositions in coming out advice. *Discourse Studies*, 13, (3): 283–298.

Choo, C. (2002). Sensemaking, knowledge creation, and decision making: organizational knowing as emergent strategy. In Choo, C. and Bontis, N. (Eds). *The Strategic Management of Intellectual Capital and Organizational Knowledge*. Oxford: Oxford University Press.

Chourides, P., Longbottom, D. and Murphy, W. (2003). Excellence in knowledge management: an empirical study to identify critical factors and performance measures. *Measuring Business Excellence*, 7, (20): 29–45.

Clifton, J. (2006). A conversation analytical approach to business communication: the case of leadership. *Journal of Business Communications*, 43, (3): 206–219.

Clifton, J. (2012a). "Doing" trust in workplace interaction. In Mada, S. and Saftoiu, R. (Eds). *Professional Communications across Languages and Cultures*. Amsterdam: John Benjamins Publishing Co.

Clifton, J. (2012b). A discursive approach to leadership: assessments and managing organizational meanings. *Journal of Business Communication*, 49, (2): 148–168.

Clifton, J. (2014). Being in the know: socio-epistemics and the communicative constitution of a management team. *Organization Management Journal*, 11: 4–14.

Collins, H. (1993). The structure of knowledge. *Social Research*, 60, (1): 95–116.

Condor, S. (2000). Pride and prejudice: identity management in English people's talk about "this country". *Discourse & Society*, 11, (2): 175–205.

Cook, S. and Brown, J. (1999). Bridging epistemologies: the generative dance between organizational knowledge and organizational knowing. *Organization Science*, 10, (4): 381–400.

Cooper, P. and Branthwaite, A. (1977). Qualitative technology: new perspectives on measurement and meaning through qualitative research. In *Proceedings of the Annual Conference of the Market Research Society*. Brighton: MRS Conference, 79–92.

Côté, J. (2006). Identity studies: how close are we to developing a social science of identity?—An appraisal of the field. *Identity: An International Journal of Theory and Research*, 6, (1): 3–25.

Crane, L. (2011). What do knowledge managers manage? Practitioners' discourse in an online forum compared and contrasted with the literature. *Journal of Knowledge Management Practice*, 12, (4).

Crane, L. (2012). Trust me, I'm an expert: identity construction and knowledge sharing. *Journal of Knowledge Management*, 16, (3): 448–460.

Crane, L. (2013). A new taxonomy of knowledge management theory and the turn to knowledge as constituted in social action. *Journal of Knowledge Management Practice*, 14, (1).

Crane, L. and Bontis, N. (2014). Trouble with tacit: developing a new perspective and approach. *Journal of Knowledge Management*, 18, (6): 1127–1140.

Crane, L., Longbottom, D. and Self, R. (2012). Discourse and knowledge matters: can knowledge management be saved? In Uden, L., Herrera, F., Perez, J. and Rodriguez, J. (Eds). *Proceedings 7th International Conference on Knowledge Management in Organizations: Service and Cloud Computing*. London: Springer.

Crane, L. and Self, R. (2014). Big data analytics: a threat or an opportunity for knowledge management. In *Proceedings 9th International Conference on Knowledge Management in Organizations*, Santiago, Chile. London: Springer.

Cromdal, J., Landqvist, H., Persoon-Thunqvist, D. and Osvaldsson, K. (2012). Finding out what's happened: two procedures for opening emergency calls. *Discourse Studies*, 14, (4): 371–397.

Darlaston-Jones, D. (2007). Making connections: the relationship between epistemology and research methods. *The Australian Community Psychologist*, 19, (1): 19–27.

Darroch, J. (2003). Developing a measure of knowledge management behaviours and practices. *Journal of Knowledge Management*, 7, (5): 41–54.

Davenport, T. (2007). Information technologies for knowledge management. In Ichijo, K. and Nonaka, I. (Eds). *Knowledge Creation and Management: New Challenges for Managers*. Oxford: Oxford University Press.

Davies, B. and Harré, R. (1990). Positioning: the discursive production of selves. *Journal for the Theory of Social Behaviour*, 20, (1): 43–63.

De Long, D. and Fahey, L. (2000). Diagnosing cultural barriers to knowledge management. *Academy of Management Perspectives*, 14, (4): 113–127.

Deeds, D.L. (2003). Alternative strategies for acquiring knowledge. In Jackson, S., Hitt, M. and DeNisi, A. (Eds). *Managing Knowledge for Sustained Competitive Advantage*. San Francisco: Jossey-Bass.

Dennen, V. (2009). Constructing academic alter-egos: identity issues in a blog-based community. *Identity Journal*, 2: 23–38.

Denning, S. (2012). Ten things you need to know about managing knowledge. Forbes. [Online]. http://www.forbes.com/sites/stevedenning/2012/05/31/ten-things-you-need-to-know-about-managing-knowledge/. Accessed September 29, 2014.

Despres, C. and Chauvel, D. (2002). Knowledge, context, and the management of variation. In Choo, C. and Bontis, N. (Eds). *The Strategic Management of Intellectual Capital and Organizational Knowledge*. Oxford: Oxford University Press.

Dienes, Z., Broadbent, S. and Berry, D. (1991). Implicit and explicit knowledge bases in artificial grammar learning. *Journal of Experimental Psychology*, 17, (5): 875–887.

Donate, M. and Guadamillas, F. (2011). Organizational factors to support knowledge management and innovation. *Journal of Knowledge Management*, 15, (6): 890–914.

Drew, P. (2003a). Conversation analysis. In Smith, J. (Ed). *Qualitative Psychology: A Practical Guide to Research Methods*. London: Sage.

Drew, P. (2003b). Precision and exaggeration in interaction. *American Sociological Review*, 68: 917–938.

Drew, P. and Holt, E. (1988). Complainable matters: the use of idiomatic expressions in making complaints. *Social Problems*, 35, (4): 398–417.

Drucker, P. (1998a). The coming of the new organization. In *Harvard Business Review on Knowledge Management*. Harvard: Harvard Business Press.

Drucker, P. (1998b). The discipline of innovation. *Harvard Business Review* (November–December): 149–157.

Duguid, P. (2005). The art of knowing: social and tacit dimensions of knowledge and the limits of the Community of Practice. *The Information Society*, 21: 109–118.

Dulany, D., Carlson, R. and Dewey, G. (1984). A case of syntactical learning and judgment: how conscious and how abstract? *Journal of Experimental Psychology*, 113, (4): 541–555.

Earl, M. (2001). Knowledge management strategies: toward a taxonomy. *Journal of Management Information Systems*, 18, (1): 215–233.

Edwards, D. and Potter, J. (1992). *Discursive Psychology*. London: Sage.

Edwards, D. and Potter, J. (2005). Discursive psychology, mental states and descriptions. In te Molder, H. and Potter, J. (Eds). *Conversation and Cognition*. Cambridge: Cambridge University Press.

Ehin, C. (2008). Un-managing knowledge workers. *Journal of Intellectual Capital*, 9, (8): 337–349.

Elliott, R., Fischer, C. and Rennie, D. (1999). Evolving guidelines for publication of qualitative research studies in psychology and related fields. *British Journal of Clinical Psychology*, 38: 215–229.

Evans, M. (2013). Is trust the most important human factor influencing knowledge sharing in organizations? *Journal of Information & Knowledge Management*, 12 (4): 1350038 (17 pages).

Eysenck, M. and Keane, T. (2000). *Cognitive Psychology: A Student's Handbook*. 4th End. Hove: Psychology Press.

Fairclough, N. (2001). The discourse of New Labour: critical discourse analysis. In Yates, S., Taylor, S. and Wetherell, M. (Eds). *Discourse as Data: A Guide for Analysis*. London: Sage.

Fairclough, N. and Wodak, R. (1997). Critical discourse analysis. In Van Dijk, T. (Ed). *Discourses as Social Interaction*, Volume 2. London: Sage.

Fayard, A. and DeSanctis, G. (2005). Evolution of an online forum for knowledge management professionals: a language game analysis. *Journal of Computer-Mediated Communication*, 10, (4). [Online]. http://onlinelibrary.wiley.com/doi/10.1111/jcmc.2005.10.issue-4/issuetoc. Accessed June 16, 2015.

Ferres, N., Connell, J. and Travaglione, A. (2004). Co-worker trust as a social catalyst for constructive employee attitudes. *Journal of Managerial Psychology*, 19, (6): 608–622.

Feyerabend, P. (2010). *Against Method*. 4th Edn. London: Verso.

Ford, C. and Stickle, T. (2012). Securing recipiency in workplace meetings: multimodal practices. *Discourse Studies*, 14, (1): 11–30.

Gaines, B. (1989). Social and cognitive processes in knowledge acquisition. *Knowledge Acquisition*, 1: 39–58.

Garcia-Perez, A. and Ayres, R. (2010). Wikifailure: the limitations of technology for knowledge sharing. *Electronic Journal of Knowledge Management*, 8, (1): 43–52.

Garfinkel, H. (2002). *Ethnomethodology's Program: Working Out Durkeim's Aphorism*. Oxford: Rowman and Littlefield.

Garvin, D. (1998). Building a learning organisation. In *Harvard Business Review on Knowledge Management*. Harvard: Harvard Business Press.

Gergen, K. (1973). Social psychology as history. *Journal of Personality and Social Psychology*, 26, (2): 309–320.

Gergen, K. (1991). *The Saturated Self: Dilemmas of Identity in Contemporary Life*. New York: Basic Books.

Gergen, K. (2009). *Relational Being: Beyond Self and Community*. Oxford: Oxford University Press.

Giles, D. (2006). Constructing identities in cyberspace: the case of eating disorders. *British Journal of Social Psychology*, 45: 463–477.

Godden, D. and Baddeley, A. (1975). Context-dependent memory in two natural environments: on land and underwater. *British Journal of Psychology*, 66, (3): 325–331.

Gourlay, S. (2006). Conceptualizing knowledge creation: a critique of Nonaka's theory. *Journal of Management Studies*, 43, (7): 1415–1436.

Grant, K. (2007). Tacit knowledge revisited—we can still learn from Polanyi. *The Electronic Journal of Knowledge Management*, 5, (2): 173–180.

Grant, K. and Qureshi, U. (2006). Knowledge management systems—why so many failures? *Innovations in Information Technology*, November: 1–5.

Grant, R. (1996). Toward a knowledge-based theory of the firm. *Strategic Management Journal*, 17: 109–122.

Grant, R. (2002). The knowledge-based view of the firm. In Choo, C. and Bontis, N. (Eds). *The Strategic Management of Intellectual Capital and Organizational Knowledge*. Oxford: Oxford University Press.

Greatbatch, D. (2009). Conversation analysis in organization research. In Buchanan, D. and Bryman, A. (Eds). *The Sage Handbook of Organizational Research Methods*. London: Sage.

Greatbatch, D. and Clark, T. (2002). Laughing with the Gurus. *Business Strategy Review*, 13, (3): 10–18.

Greenwood, D. and Levin, M. (2005). Reform of the social sciences and of universities through action research. In Denzin, N. and Lincoln, Y. (Eds). *The Sage Book of Qualitative Research*. 3rd Edn. London: Sage.

Greer, C. and Lei, D. (2012). Collaborative innovation with customers: a review of the literature and suggestions for future research. *International Journal of Management Reviews*, 14: 63–84.

Grover, V. and Davenport, T. (2001). General perspectives on knowledge management: fostering a research agenda. *Journal of Management Information Systems*, 18, (1): 5–21.

Guba, E. and Lincoln, Y. (2005). Paradigmatic controversies, contradictions, and emerging confluences. In Denzin, N. and Lincoln, Y. (Eds). *The Sage Handbook of Qualitative Research*. 3rd Edn. London: Sage.

Gulich, E. (2003). Conversational techniques in transferring knowledge between medical experts and non-experts. *Discourse Studies*, 5, (2): 235–263.

Guzman, G. (2009). What is practical knowledge? *Journal of Knowledge Management*, 13, (4): 86–98.

Hardy, C. (2001). Researching organizational discourse. *International Studies of Management and Organization*, 31, (3): 25–47.

Heisig, P. (2009). Harmonisation of knowledge management—comparing 160 KM frameworks around the globe. *Journal of Knowledge Management*, 13, (4): 4–31.

Hepburn, A. and Wiggins, S. (2005). Developments in discursive psychology. *Discourse & Society*, 16, (5): 595–601.

Hislop, D. (2010). Knowledge management as an ephemeral management fashion? *Journal of Knowledge Management*, 14 (6): 779–790.

Hobbs, P. (2003). Is that what we're here about? A lawyer's use of impression management in a closing argument at trial. *Discourse & Society*, 14, (3): 273–290.

Hogg, M. and Vaughan, G. (2005). *Social Psychology*. 4th Edn. London: Pearson Prentice Hall.

Holden, M. and Lynch, P., (2004). Choosing the appropriate methodology: understanding research philosophy. *The Marketing Review*, 4: 397–409.

Holmes, J. (2005). Story-telling at work: a complex discursive resource for integrating personal, professional and social identities. *Discourse Studies*, 7, (6): 671–700.

Horton-Salway, M., Montague, J., Wiggins, S. and Seymour-Smith, S. (2008). Mapping the components of the telephone conference: an analysis of tutorial talk at a distance learning institution. *Discourse Studies*, 10, (6): 737–758.

Housley, W. and Smith, R. (2011). Telling the CAQDAS code: membership categorization and the accomplishment of "coding rules" in research team talk. *Discourse Studies*, 13, (4): 417–434.

Howard, D. and Howard, J. (1992). Adult age differences in the rate of learning serial patterns: evidence from direct and indirect tests. *Psychology and Aging*, 7, (2): 232–241.

Hutchby, I. (2001). "Witnessing": the use of first-hand knowledge in legitimating lay opinions on talk radio. *Discourse Studies*, 3, (4): 481–497.

Hutchby, I. (2011). Non-neutrality and argument in the hybrid political interview. *Discourse Studies*, 13, (3): 349–365.

Ichijo, K. (2007). Enabling knowledge-based competence of a corporation. In Ichijo, K. and Nonaka, I. (Eds). *Knowledge Creation and Management: New Challenges for Managers.* Oxford: Oxford University Press.

Jakubik, M. (2011). Becoming to know. Shifting the knowledge creation paradigm. *Journal of Knowledge Management*, 15, (3): 374–402.

Jimes, C. and Lucardie, L. (2003). Reconsidering the tacit-explicit distinction—a move towards functional (tacit) knowledge management. *Electronic Journal of Knowledge Management*, 1, (1): 23–32.

Jordan, M., Schallert, D., Park, Y., Lee, S., Chiang, Y. and Cheng, A. (2012). Expressing uncertainty in computer-mediated discourse: language as a marker of intellectual work. *Discourse Processes*, 49: 660–692.

Kahneman, D. (2011). *Thinking, Fast and Slow*. London: Penguin.

Kleiner, A. and Roth, G. (1998). How to make experience your company's best teacher. In *Harvard Business Review on Knowledge Management*. Harvard: Harvard Business Press.

Korobov, N. (2011). Gendering desire in speed-dating interactions. *Discourse Studies*, 13, (4): 461–485.

Krathwohl, D. (2002). A revision of Bloom's Taxonomy: an overview. *Theory Into Practice*, 41, (4): 212 -218.

Kuhn, T. (1996). *The Structure of Scientific Revolutions*. 3rd Edn. London: University of Chicago Press.

Lambe, P. (2011). The unacknowledged parentage of knowledge management. *Journal of Knowledge Management*, 15, (2): 175–197.

Lee, M. and Lan, Y. (2007). From Web 2.0 to conversational knowledge management: towards collaborative intelligence. *Journal of Entrepreneurship Research*, 2, (2): 47–62.

Lee, S., Kim, B.G. and Kim, H. (2012). An integrated view of knowledge management for performance. *Journal of Knowledge Management*, 16, (20): 183–203.

Leonard, D. (2007). Knowledge transfer within organisations. In Ichijo, K. and Nonaka, I. (Eds). *Knowledge Creation and Management: New Challenges for Managers*. Oxford: Oxford University Press.

Leonard, D. and Sensiper, S. (2002). The role of tacit knowledge in group innovation. In Choo, C. and Bontis, N. (Eds). *The Strategic Management of Intellectual Capital and Organisational Knowledge*. Oxford: Oxford University Press.

Leonard, D. and Straus, S. (1997). Putting your whole company's brain to work. In *Harvard Business Review on Knowledge Management*. Harvard: Harvard Business Press.

Lester, J. and Paulus, T. (2011). Accountability and public displays of knowing in an undergraduate computer-mediated communication context. *Discourse Studies*, 13, (6): 671–686.

Levy, M. (2009). Web 2.0 implications on knowledge management. *Journal of Knowledge Management*, 13, (1): 120–134.

Lewicki, P., Czyzewska, M. and Hill, T. (1997). Cognitive mechanisms for acquiring "experience": the dissociation between conscious and nonconscious cognition. In Cohen, J. and Schooler, J. (Eds). *Scientific Approaches to Consciousness*. London: Psychology Press.

Lin, T. and Huang, C. (2010). Withholding effort in knowledge contribution: the role of social exchange and social cognitive on project teams. *Information & Management*, 47: 188–196.

Lindvall, M., Rus, I. and Sinha, S. (2003). Software systems support for knowledge management. *Journal of Knowledge Management*, 7, (5): 137–150.

Locke, A. and Edwards, D. (2003). Bill and Monica: memory, emotion and normativity in Clinton's Grand Jury Testimony. *British Journal of Social Psychology*, 42: 239–256.

Loftus, E. (2002). Memory faults and fixes. *Issues in Science and Technology*, Summer 2002: 41–50.

Lytras, M. and Pouloudi, A. (2006). Towards the development of a novel taxonomy of knowledge management systems from a learning perspective: an integrated approach to learning and knowledge infrastructures. *Journal of Knowledge Management*, 10, (6): 64–80.

Madsbjerg, C. and Rasmussen, M. (2014). An anthropologist walks into a bar.... *Harvard Business Review*, March: 80–88.

Markham, A. (2005). The methods, politics, and ethics of representation in online ethnography. In Denzin, N. and Lincoln, Y. (Eds). *The Sage Book of Qualitative Research*. 3rd Edn. London: Sage.

Markram, H. and Markram, K. (2011). Frontiers research: seek, share & create. In Cockell, M., Billotte, J. Darbellay, F. and Waldvogel, F. (Eds). *Common Knowledge: The Challenge of Transdisciplinarity*. Boca Raton: CRC Press.

Markus, M. (2001). Toward a theory of knowledge reuse: types of knowledge reuse situations and factors in reuse success. *Journal of Management Information Systems*, 18, (1): 57–93.

Marra, R., Moore, J. and Klimczak, A. (2004). Content analysis of online discussion forums: a comparative analysis of protocols. *ETR&D*, 52, (2): 23–40.

Marshall, H. (1994). Discourse analysis in an occupational context. In Cassell, C. and Symon, G. (Eds). *Qualitative Methods in Organizational Research*. London: Sage.

Mathews, R., Buss, R., Stanley, W., Blanchard-Fields, F., Cho, J. and Druhan, B. (1989). Role of implicit and explicit processes in learning from examples: a synergistic effect. *Journal of Experimental Psychology: Learning, Memory and Cognition*, 15, (6): 1083–1100.

Mayer-Schonberger, V. and Cukier, K. (2013). *Big Data: A Revolution That Will Transform How We Live, Work and Think*. London: John Murray.

McFarlane, D. (2011). Personal knowledge management (PKM): are we really ready? *Journal of Knowledge Management Practice*, 12, (3).

McKenzie, W. and Murphy, D. (2000). I hope this goes somewhere: evaluation of an online discussion forum. *Australian Journal of Educational Technology*, 16, (3): 239–257.

Mieroop, D. (2005). An integrated approach of quantitative and qualitative analysis in the study of identity in speeches. *Discourse & Society*, 16, (1): 107–130.

Montero, B., Watts, F. and Garcia-Carbonell, A. (2007). Discussion forum interactions: text and context. *System*, 35: 566–582.

Mulkay, M. and Gilbert, G. (1982). Accounting for error: how scientists construct their social world when they account for correct and incorrect belief. *Sociology*, 16: 164–183.

Myers, G. (1989). The pragmatics of politeness in scientific articles. *Applied Linguistics*, 10, (1): 1–35.

Myers, G. (2010). Stance-taking and public discussion in blogs. *Critical Discourse Studies*, 7, (4): 263–275.

Nielsen, M. (2012). Using artifacts in brainstorming sessions to secure participation and decouple sequentiality. *Discourse Studies*, 14, (1): 87–109.

Nilsen, M. and Makitalo, A. (2010). Towards a conversational culture? How participants establish strategies for co-ordinating chat postings in the context of in-service training. *Discourse Studies*, 12, (1): 90–105.

Nissen, M., Willingham, D. and Hartman, M. (1989). Explicit and implicit remembering: when is learning preserved in amnesia? *Neuropsychologia*, 27, (3): 341–352.

Nonaka, I. (1991). The knowledge-creating company. *Harvard Business Review*, November–December: 96–104.

Nonaka, I. (1994). A dynamic theory of organisational knowledge creation. *Organization Science*, 5, (1): 14–37.

Nonaka, I., Byosiere, P., Borucki, C. and Konno, N. (1994). Organizational knowledge creation theory: a first comprehensive test. *International Business Review*, 3, (4): 337–351.

Nonaka, I. and Konno, N. (1998). The concept of Ba: building a foundation for knowledge creation. *California Management Review*, 40, (3), Spring: 40–54.

Nonaka, I. and Takeuchi, H. (1995). *The Knowledge-Creating Company*. New York: Oxford University Press.

Nonaka, I. and Toyama, R. (2007). Why do firms differ: the theory of the knowledge-creating firm. In Ichijo, K. and Nonaka, I. (Eds). *Knowledge Creation and Management: New Challenges for Managers*. Oxford: Oxford University Press.

Nonaka, I., Umemoto, K. and Senoo, D. (1996). From Information processing to knowledge creation: a paradigm shift in business management. *Technology in Society*, 18, (2): 203–218.

Oguz, F. and Sengun, A. (2011). Mystery of the unknown: revisiting tacit knowledge in the organizational literature. *Journal of Knowledge Management*, 15, (3): 445–461.

Otterbacher, J. (2011). Being heard in review communities: communication tactics and review prominence. *Journal of Computer-Mediated Communication*, 16, (3): 424–444.

Panahi, S., Watson, J. and Partridge, H. (2013). Towards tacit knowledge sharing over social web tools. *Journal of Knowledge Management*, 17, (3): 379–397.

Paulus, T. (2007). CMC modes for learning tasks at a distance. *Journal of Computer-Mediated Communication*, 12: 1322–1345.

Peräkylä, A. (2005). Analyzing talk and text. In Denzin, N. and Lincoln, Y. (Eds). *The Sage Handbook of Qualitative Research*. 3rd Edn. London: Sage.

Pervin, L. (2003). *The Science of Personality*. 2nd Ed. Oxford: Oxford University Press.

Phillips, N. and Di Domenico, M. (2009). Discourse analysis in organizational research: methods and debates. In Buchanan, D. and Bryman, A. (Eds). *The Sage Handbook of Organizational Research Methods*. London: Sage.

Phillips, N., Lawrence, T. and Hardy, C. (2004). Discourse and institutions. *Academy of Management Review*, 29, (4): 635–652.

Phillips, N. and Oswick, C. (2012). Organizational discourse: domains, debates and directions. *The Academy of Management Annals*, 6, (1): 435–481.

Polanyi, M. (1962). *Personal Knowledge: Towards a Post-critical Philosophy*. Chicago: The University of Chicago Press.

Popper, K. (1959). *The Logic of Scientific Discovery*. London: Routledge Classics.

Pothos, E. (2007). Theories of artificial grammar learning. *Psychological Bulletin*, 133, (2): 227–244.

Potter, J. (1998a). Discursive social psychology: from attitudes to evaluative practices. In Stroebe, W. and Hewstone, M. (Eds). *European Review of Social Psychology*. London: John Wiley & Sons.

Potter, J. (1998b). Cognition as context (whose cognition?) *Research on Language and Social Interaction*, 31, (1): 29–44.

Potter, J. (2001). Wittgenstein and Austin. In Wetherell, M., Taylor, S. and Yates, S. (Eds). *Discourse Theory and Practice: A Reader*. London: Sage.

Potter, J. (2005). Making psychology relevant. *Discourse & Society*, 16, (5): 739–747.

Potter, J. (2006). Cognition and conversation. *Discourse Studies*, 8, (1): 131–140.

Potter, J. and Edwards, D. (2003). Sociolinguistics, cognitivism and discursive psychology. *International Journal of English Studies*, 3, (1): 93–109.

Potter, J. and Edwards, D. (2012). Conversation analysis and psychology. In Sidnell, J. and Stivers, T. (Eds). *The Handbook of Conversation Analysis*. London: Blackwell Publishing.

Potter, J. and Hepburn, A. (2010). A kind of governance: rules, time and psychology in institutional organization. In Hindmarsh, J. and Llewellyn, N. (Eds). *Organization, Interaction and Practice* (pp. 49–73). Cambridge: Cambridge University Press.

Potter, J. and te Molder, H. (2005). Talking cognition: mapping and making the terrain. In te Molder, H. and Potter, J. (Eds). *Conversation and Cognition*. Cambridge: Cambridge University Press.

Potter, J. and Wetherell, M. (1987). *Discourse and Social Psychology: Beyond Attitudes and Behaviour*. London: Sage.

Potter, J., Wetherell, M. and Chitty, A. (1991). Quantification rhetoric—cancer on television. *Discourse & Society*, 2, (3): 333–365.

Potter, J., Wetherell, M., Gill, R. and Edwards, D. (1990). Discourse: noun, verb or social practice? *Philosophical Psychology*, 3, (2): 205–217.

Prusak, L. (2001). Where did knowledge management come from? *IBM Systems Journal*, 40, (4): 1002–1007.

Prusak, L. and Weiss, L. (2007). Knowledge in organizational settings: how organizations generate, disseminate, and use knowledge for their competitive advantage. In Ichijo, K. and Nonaka, I. (Eds). *Knowledge Creation and Management: New Challenges for Managers*. Oxford: Oxford University Press.

Puusa, A. and Eerikainen, M. (2010). Is tacit knowledge really tacit? *Electronic Journal of Knowledge Management*, 8, (3): 307–318.

Quinn, J., Anderson, P. and Finkelstein, S. (1996). Managing professional intellect. In *Harvard Business Review on Knowledge Management*. Harvard: Harvard Business Press.

Quintane, E., Casselman, R., Reiche, S. and Nylund, P. (2011). Innovation as a knowledge based outcome. *Journal of Knowledge Management*, 15, (6): 928–947.

Ragab, M. and Arisha, A. (2013). Knowledge management and measurement: a critical review. *Journal of Knowledge Management*, 17, (6): 873–901.

Rai, R. (2011). Knowledge management and organizational culture: a theoretical integrative framework. *Journal of Knowledge Management*, 15, (5): 779–801.

Rajaram, S. and Roediger, H. (1997). Remembering and knowing as states of consciousness during retrieval. In Cohen, J. and Schooler, J. (Eds). *Scientific Approaches to Consciousness*. New Jersey: Lawrence Erlbaum Associates Inc.

Rasmussen, G. (2010). "Going mental": the risks of assessment activities (in teenage talk). *Discourse Studies*, 12 (6): 739–761.

Rautajoki, H. (2012). Membership categorization as a tool for moral casting in TV discussion: the dramaturgical consequentiality of guest introductions. *Discourse Studies*, 14, (2): 243–260.

Reber, A. (1989). Implicit learning and tacit knowledge. *Journal of Experimental Psychology – General*, 118, (3): 219–235.

Reber, A. (1993). *Implicit Learning and Tacit Knowledge: An Essay on Cognitive Unconsciousness*. Oxford: Oxford University Press.

Reber, A. (1997). How to differentiate implicit and explicit modes. In Cohen, J. and Schooler, J. (Eds). *Scientific Approaches to Consciousness*. New Jersey: Lawrence Erlbaum Associates Inc.

Reber, A., Allen, R. and Regan, S. (1985). Syntactical learning and judgment, still unconscious and still abstract: comment on Dulany, Carlson and Dewey. *Journal of Experimental Psychology*, 114, (1): 17–24.

Reber, A., Kassin, S., Lewis, S. and Cantor, G. (1980). On the relationship between implicit and explicit modes in learning of a complex rule structure. *Journal of Experimental Psychology*, 6, (5): 492–502.

Reber, A. and Lewis, S. (1977). Implicit learning: an analysis of the form and structure of a body of tacit knowledge. *Cognition*, 5: 333–361.

Reber, A., Walkenfeld, F. and Hernstadt, R. (1991). Implicit and explicit learning: individual differences and IQ. *Journal of Experimental Psychology: Learning, Memory and Cognition*, 17, (5): 888–896.

Rechberg, I. and Syed, J. (2013). Ethical issues in knowledge management: conflict of knowledge ownership. *Journal of Knowledge Management*, 17, (6): 828–847.

Rhodes, C. and Pullen, A. (2009). Narrative and stories in organizational research: an exploration of gendered politics in research methodology. In Buchanan, D. and Bryman, A. (Eds). *The Sage Handbook of Organizational Research Methods*. London: Sage.

Ringel-Bickelmaier, C. and Ringel, M. (2010). Knowledge management in international organisations. *Journal of Knowledge Management*, 14, (4): 524–539.

Ryle, G. (1949). *The Concept of Mind*. London: Hutchison's University Library.

Schacter, D., Delaney, S. and Cooper, L. (1990). Implicit memory for unfamiliar objects depends on access to structural descriptions. *Journal of Experimental Psychology*, 119, (1): 5–24.

Schegloff, E. (1997). Whose text? Whose context? *Discourse and Society*, 8, (2): 165–187.

Schooler, J. and Fiore, S. (1997).Consciousness and the limits of language: you can't always say what you think or think what you say. In Cohen, J. and Schooler, J. (Eds). *Scientific Approaches to Consciousness*. New Jersey: Lawrence Erlbaum Associates Inc.

Schoorman, F., Mayer, R. and Davis, J. (2007). An integrative model of organizational trust: past, present, and future. *Academy of Management Review*, 32, (20): 344–354.

Schrire, A. (2006). Knowledge building in asynchronous discussion groups: going beyond quantitative analysis. *Computers & Education*, 46: 49–70.

Schultz, D. and Schultz, S. (2004). *A History of Modern Psychology*. 8th Edn. London: Thomson Wadsworth.

Schultze, U. and Stabell, C. (2004). Knowing what you don't know? Discourses and contradictions in knowledge management research. *Journal of Management Studies*, 41, (4): 549–573.

Searle, J. (1969). *Speech Acts: An Essay in the Philosophy of Language*. Cambridge: Cambridge University Press.

Seger, C. (1994). Implicit learning. *Psychological Bulletin*, 115, (2): 163–196.

Selznick, P. (1948). Foundations of the theory of organization. *American Sociological Review*, 13, (1): 25–35.

Shadbolt, N. and Milton, N. (1999). From knowledge engineering to knowledge management. *British Journal of Management*, 10: 309–322.

Shiffrin, R. (1997). Attention, automatism and consciousness. In Cohen, J. and Schooler, J. (Eds). *Scientific Approaches to Consciousness*. London: Psychology Press.

Silverman, D. (2007). *A Very Short, Fairly Interesting and Reasonably Cheap Book about Qualitative Research*. London: Sage.

Smith, D. (1978). "K is mentally ill" the anatomy of a factual account. *Sociology*, 12, (23): 23–53.

Smith, J. (2003). Validity and qualitative psychology. In Smith, J. (Ed). *Qualitative Psychology: A Practical Guide to Research Methods*. London: Sage.

Smith, L. (2005). On tricky ground: researching the native in the age of uncertainty. In Denzin, N. & Lincoln, Y. (Eds). *The Sage Book of Qualitative Research*. 3rd Edn. London: Sage.

Smithson, J., Sharkey, S., Hewis, E., Jones, R., Emmens, T., Ford, T. and Owens, C. (2011). Problem presentation and responses on an online forum for young people who self-harm. *Discourse Studies*, 13, (4): 487–501.

Sneijder, P. and te Molder, H. (2005). Moral logic and logical morality: attributions of responsibility and blame in online discourse on veganism. *Discourse & Society*, 16, (5): 675–696.

Snowden, D. (2002). Complex acts of knowing: paradox and descriptive self-awareness. *Journal of Knowledge Management*, 6, (2): 100–111.

Spender, J. (1996). Making knowledge the basis of a dynamic theory of the firm. *Strategic Management Journal*, 17 (Winter): 45–62.

Spender, J. (2002). Knowledge management, uncertainty, and an emergent theory of the firm. In Choo, C. and Bontis, N. (Eds). *The Strategic Management of Intellectual Capital and Organizational Knowledge*. Oxford: Oxford University Press.

Spender, J.C. and Grant, R. (1996). Knowledge and the firm: overview. *Strategic Management Journal*, 17 (winter): 5–9.

Stainton-Rogers, W. (2003). *Social Psychology: Experimental and Critical Approaches*. Maidenhead: Open University Press.

Starbuck, W. (2002). Keeping a butterfly and an elephant in a house of cards. In Choo, C. and Bontis, N. (Eds). *The Strategic Management of Intellectual Capital and Organizational Knowledge*. Oxford: Oxford University Press.

Stokoe, E. (2004). Gender and discourse, gender and categorization: current developments in language and gender research. *Qualitative Research in Psychology*, 1: 107–129.

Stokoe, E. (2012). Moving forward with membership categorization analysis: methods for systematic analysis. *Discourse Studies*, 14, (3): 277–303.

Stommel, W. and Koole, T. (2010). The online support group as a community: a micro-analysis of the interaction with a new member. *Discourse Studies*, 12, (3): 357–378.

Stubbe, M., Lane, C., Hilder, J., Vine, E., Vine, B., Marra, M., Holmes, J. and Weatherall, A. (2003). Multiple discourse analyses of a workplace interaction. *Discourse Studies*, 5, (3): 351–388.

Suddendorf, T. (2013). *The Gap: The Science of What Separates Us from Other Animals*. New York: Basic Books.

Sveningsson, S. and Alvesson, M. (2003). Managing managerial identities: organizational fragmentation, discourse and identity struggle. *Human Relations*, 56, (10): 1163–1193.

Svennevig, J. (2012a). Interaction in workplace meetings. *Discourse Studies*, 14 (1): 3–10.

Svennevig, J. (2012b). The agenda as resource for topic introduction in workplace meetings. *Discourse Studies*, 14, (1): 53–66.

Thompson, M. (2004). Discourse, "development" & the "digital divide": ICT & the World Bank. *Review of African Political Economy*, 99: 103–123.

Thompson, M. and Walsham, G. (2004). Placing knowledge management in context. *Journal of Management Studies*, 41, (5): 725–747.

Tong, J. and Mitra, A. (2009). Chinese cultural influences on knowledge management practice. *Journal of Knowledge Management*, 13, (2): 49–62.

Tsoukas, H. (1997). The Tyranny of light: the temptations and the paradoxes of the information society. *Futures*, 29, (9): 827–843.

Tsoukas, H. and Vladimirou, E. (2001). What is organizational knowledge? *Journal of Management Studies*, 38, (7): 973–993.

Tsoukas, H. (2011). How should we understand tacit knowledge? A phenomenological view. In Easterby-Smith, M. and Lyles, M. (Eds). *Handbook of Organizational Learning and Knowledge Management*. 2nd Edn. Chichester: Wiley.

Tulving, E. (1987). Multiple memory systems and consciousness. *Human Neurobiology*, 6: 67–80.

Umemoto, K. (2002). Managing existing knowledge is not enough: knowledge management theory and practice in Japan. In Choo, C. and Bontis, N. (Eds). *The Strategic Management of Intellectual Capital and Organizational Knowledge*. Oxford: Oxford University Press.

Van Dijk, T. (2001). Principles of critical discourse analysis. In Wetherell, M., Taylor, S. and Yates, S. (Eds). *Discourse Theory and Practice: A Reader*. London: Sage.

Van Dijk, T. (2006). Discourse, context and cognition. *Discourse Studies*, 8, (1): 159–177.

Van Dijk, T. (2013). The field of epistemic discourse analysis. *Discourse Studies*, 15, (5): 497–499.

Van Doren, C. (1991). *A History of Knowledge: Past, Present and Future*. New York: Ballantine Books.

Veerman, A. and Veldhuis-Diermanse, E. (2001). Collaborative learning through computer-mediated communication in academic education. [Online] www.eculturenet.org. Accessed November 27, 2012.

Venkitachalam, K. and Busch, P. (2012). Tacit knowledge: review and possible research directions. *Journal of Knowledge Management*, 16, (2): 356–371.

Virtanen, I. (2011). Externalization of tacit knowledge implies a simplified theory of cognition. *Journal of Knowledge Management Practice*, 12, (3).

Wagner, R. and Sternberg, R. (1985). Practical intelligence in real-world pursuits: the role of tacit knowledge. *Journal of Personality and Social Psychology*, 49, (2): 436–458.

Waring, H., Creider, S., Tarpey, T. and Black, R. (2012). A search for specificity in understanding CA and context. *Discourse Studies*, 14, (4): 477–492.

Wasson, C. (2004). The paradoxical language of enterprise. *Critical Discourse Studies*, 1, (2): 175–199.

Weber, R. (2007). Addressing failure factors in knowledge management. *The Electronic Journal of Knowledge Management*, 5, (3): 333–346.

Wee, L. (2005). Constructing the source: metaphor as a discourse strategy. *Discourse Studies*, 7, (3): 363–384.

Wenger, E. (2000). Communities of practice and social learning systems. *Organization*, 7, (2): 225–246.

Wetherell, M. (2001). Themes in discourse research: the case of Diana. In Wetherell, M., Taylor, S. and Yates, S. (Eds). *Discourse Theory and Practice: A Reader*. London: Sage.

Whittle, A. (2005). Preaching and practising "flexibility": implications for theories of subjectivity at work. *Human Relations*, 58, (10): 1301–1322.

Whittle, A. and Mueller, F. (2011). The language of interests: the contribution of discursive psychology. *Human Relations*, 64, (3): 415–435.

Whorf, B. (1942). Language, mind and reality. *The Theosophist*, (January and April): 167–188.

Widdicombe, S. and Wooffitt, R. (1990). "Being" versus "doing" punk: on achieving authenticity as a member. *Journal of Language and Social Psychology*, 9, (4): 257–277.

Wiggins, S. and Potter, J. (2003). Attitudes and evaluative practices: category vs item and subjective vs objective constructions in everyday food assessments. *British Journal of Social Psychology*, 42: 513–531.

Wiig, K. (1997). Knowledge management: where did it come from and where will it go? *Expert Systems with Applications*, 13, (10): 1–14.

Willig, C. (2001). *Introducing Qualitative Research in Psychology: Adventures in Theory and Method*. Maidenhead: Open University Press.

Willig, C. (2003). Discourse analysis. In Smith, J. (Ed). *Qualitative Psychology: A Practical Guide to Research Methods*. London: Sage.

Wittgenstein, L. (1986). *Philosophical Investigations*. 3rd Edn. Oxford: Basil Blackwell.

Wood, L. and Kroger, R. (2000). *Doing Discourse Analysis: Methods for Studying Action in Talk and Text*. London: Sage.

Wooffitt, R. (2001). Raising the dead: reported speech in medium-sitter interaction. *Discourse Studies*, 3, (3): 351–374.

Wooffitt, R. (2005). *Conversation Analysis and Discourse Analysis: A Comparative and Critical Introduction*. London: Sage.

Wooffitt, R. (2007). Communication and laboratory performance in parapsychological experiments: demand characteristics and the social organization of interaction. *British Journal of Social Psychology*, 46: 477–498.

Wooffitt, R. and Allistone, S. (2005). Towards a discursive parapsychology: language and the laboratory study of anomalous communication. *Theory Psychology*, 15, (3): 325–355.

Wooffitt, R. and Allistone, S. (2008). Participation, procedure and accountability: "you said" speech markers in negotiating reports of ambiguous phenomena. *Discourse Studies*, 10, (3): 407–427.

Yanow, D. and Ybema, S. (2009). Interpretivism in organizational research: on elephants and blind researchers. In Buchanan, D. and Bryman, A. (Eds). *The Sage Handbook of Organizational Research Methods*. London: Sage.

Yardley, L. (2000). Dilemmas in qualitative health research. *Psychology and Health*, 15: 215–228.

Yoo, Y. and Torrey, B. (2002). National culture and knowledge management in a global learning organization. In Choo, C. and Bontis, N. (Eds). *The Strategic Management of Intellectual Capital and Organizational Knowledge*. Oxford: Oxford University Press.

Zack, M. (2002). Developing a knowledge strategy. In Choo, C. and Bontis, N. (Eds). *The Strategic Management of Intellectual Capital and Organizational Knowledge*. Oxford: Oxford University Press.

Zajacova, A. (2002). The background of discourse analysis: a new paradigm in social psychology. *Journal of Social Distress and the Homeless*, 11, (1): 25–40.

SUBJECT INDEX

accounting, forms of in discourse *see also*
  glossary
  competing, 177–185, 240–242, 255–260,
    269–270
  factual, 174, 180–181, 186–188, 193,
    213–214, 257–258, 274
  indexical, 174, 224, 282
  issuing news headlines, 196, 202,
    209–211
  narrative, 206–212
  normative, 178, 182, 221, 230–231
  objective, 14–15, 258
  preferred versions, 179–180, 185, 214, 258,
    269–270
  quantification rhetoric, 188, 209, 213, 224
  reported speech, 183–184, 228, 231, 259
  vivid, 200, 209–214, 227–229, 244
  witness, 182–185, 253–254, 257–259, 269
ages of knowledge management, three, 12
architecture of cognition, 70, 72
  declarative and procedural memory, 72–73
assumptions in discursive psychology
  core assumptions, 91–94
  core questions, 160–161
  observational science, 161

Ba, 21, 70 *see also* context
blame, attribution of, 256, 261, 270–272, 279
Bloom's Taxonomy, 44–45

cognition and discourse, 92, 109, 116–117,
    130–131, 248
cognitive psychology
  consciousness, 113, 116, 121, 123–124
  memory, 20–21, 44, 99
commodification and reification of
    knowledge
  commodification-reification of knowledge
    issue, 38–39, 48, 63–64, 147, 281
  commodity view, 13–14, 62
communities of practice, 40–41, 65, 67–68,
    73, 147
computer mediated communications (CMCs)
    and discourse *see also* identity and
    discourse
  advice-giving sites, 106–107
  ethical concerns, 169–170
  membership, 101, 106, 237–240, 246
  role of the researcher, 104–105
  strategies in, 101, 105–107
  technologies, 103–104

Knowledge and Discourse Matters: Relocating Knowledge Management's Sphere of Interest onto Language,
First Edition. Lesley Crane.
© 2016 John Wiley & Sons, Inc. Published 2016 by John Wiley & Sons, Inc.